Stephen Lazoritz, MD
Vincent J. Palusci, MD
Editors

The Shaken Baby WITHDRAWN
Syndrome:
A Multidisciplinary Approach

The Shaken Baby Syndrome: A Multidisciplinary Approach has been co-published simultaneously as *Journal of Aggression, Maltreatment & Trauma,* Volume 5, Number 1(#9) 2001.

Pre-publication
REVIEWS,
COMMENTARIES,
EVALUATIONS . . .

"Should be required reading for all physicians and mental health professionals who come in contact with children, as well as all child protective service workers, criminal investigators, and prosecuters throughout the United States. This is the first book to bring together in one place a wealth of medical information, investigative strategies, prosecution know-how, and social welfare aspects of this prevalent form of child abuse."

Rob Parrish, JD
Deputy Director
National Center on Shaken Baby
Syndrome
Ogden, Utah

HMTP
The Haworth Maltreatment & Trauma Press
An Imprint of The Haworth Press, Inc.

The Shaken Baby Syndrome: A Multidisciplinary Approach

The Shaken Baby Syndrome: A Multidisciplinary Approach has been co-published simultaneously as *Journal of Aggression, Maltreatment & Trauma*, Volume 5, Number 1(#9) 2001.

The *Journal of Aggression, Maltreatment & Trauma* Monographic "Separates"

Below is a list of "separates," which in serials librarianship means a special issue simultaneously published as a special journal issue or double-issue *and* as a "separate" hardbound monograph. (This is a format which we also call a "DocuSerial.")

"Separates" are published because specialized libraries or professionals may wish to purchase a specific thematic issue by itself in a format which can be separately cataloged and shelved, as opposed to purchasing the journal on an on-going basis. Faculty members may also more easily consider a "separate" for classroom adoption.

"Separates" are carefully classified separately with the major book jobbers so that the journal tie-in can be noted on new book order slips to avoid duplicate purchasing.

You may wish to visit Haworth's Website at . . .

http://www.HaworthPress.com

. . . to search our online catalog for complete tables of contents of these separates and related publications.

You may also call 1-800-HAWORTH (outside US/Canada: 607-722-5857), or Fax 1-800-895-0582 (outside US/Canada: 607-771-0012), or e-mail at:

getinfo@haworthpressinc.com

The Shaken Baby Syndrome: A Multidisciplinary Approach, edited by Stephen Lazoritz, MD, and Vincent J. Palusci, MD (Vol. 5, No. 1 [#9] 2001). *The first book to cover the full spectrum of Shaken Baby Syndrome (SBS). Offers expert information and advice on every aspect of prevention, diagnosis, treatment, and follow-up.*

Trauma and Cognitive Science: A Meeting of Minds, Science, and Human Experience, edited by Jennifer J. Freyd, PhD, and Anne P. DePrince, MS (Vol. 4, No. 2 [#8] 2001). *"A FINE COLLECTION OF SCHOLARLY WORKS that address key questions about memory for childhood and adult traumas from a variety of disciplines and empirical approaches. A MUST-READ VOLUME FOR ANYONE WISHING TO UNDERSTAND TRAUMATIC MEMORY." (Kathryn Quina, PhD, Professor of Psychology & Women's Studies, University of Rhode Island)*

Program Evaluation and Family Violence Research, edited by Sally K. Ward, PhD, and David Finkelhor, PhD (Vol. 4, No. 1 [#7], 2000). *"OFFERS WISE ADVICE to evaluators and others interested in understanding the impact of their work. I learned a lot from reading this book." (Jeffrey L. Edleson, PhD, Professor, University of Minnesota, St. Paul)*

Sexual Abuse Litigation: A Practical Resource for Attorneys, Clinicians, and Advocates, edited by Rebecca Rix, MALS (Vol. 3, No. 2 [#6], 2000). *"An INTERESTING AND WELL DEVELOPED treatment of the complex subject of child sexual abuse trauma. The merger of the legal, psychological, scientific and historical expertise of the authors provides a unique, in-depth analysis of delayed discovery in CSA litigation. This book, including the EXTREMELY USEFUL APPENDICES, is a must for the attorney or expert witness who is involved in the representation of survivors of sexual abuse." (Leonard Karp, JD, and Cheryl L. Karp, PhD, co-authors, Domestic Torts: Family Violence, Conflict and Sexual Abuse)*

Children Exposed to Domestic Violence: Current Issues in Research, Intervention, Prevention, and Policy Development, edited by Robert A. Geffner, PhD, Peter G. Jaffe, PhD, and Marlies Sudermann, PhD (Vol. 3, No. 1 [#5], 2000). *"A WELCOME ADDITION to the resource library of every professional whose career encompasses issues of children's mental health, well-being, and best interest . . . I STRONGLY RECOMMEND THIS HELPFUL AND STIMULATING TEXT." (The Honorable Justice Grant A. Campbell, Justice of the Ontario Superior Court of Justice, Family Court, London, Canada)*

Maltreatment in Early Childhood: Tools for Research-Based Intervention, edited by Kathleen Coulborn Faller, PhD (Vol. 2, No. 2 [#4], 1999). *"This important book takes an international and cross-cultural look at child abuse and maltreatment. Discussing the history of abuse in the United States, exploring psychological trauma, and containing interviews with sexual abuse vic-*

tims, Maltreatment in Early Childhood provides counselors and mental health practitioners with research that may help prevent child abuse or reveal the mistreatment some children endure."

Multiple Victimization of Children: Conceptual, Developmental, Research, and Treatment Issues, edited by B. B. Robbie Rossman, PhD, and Mindy S. Rosenberg, PhD (Vol. 2, No. 1 [#3], 1998). *"This book takes on a large challenge and meets it with stunning success. It fills a glaring gap in the literature . . . " (Edward P. Mulvey, PhD, Associate Professor of Child Psychiatry, Western Psychiatric Institute and Clinic, University of Pittsburgh School of Medicine)*

Violence Issues for Health Care Educators and Providers, edited by L. Kevin Hamberger, PhD, Sandra K. Burge, PhD, Antonnette V. Graham, PhD, and Anthony J. Costa, MD (Vol. 1, No. 2 [#2], 1997). *"A superb book that contains invaluable hands-on advice for medical educators and health care professionals alike . . . " (Richard L. Holloways, PhD, Professor and Vice Chair, Department of Family and Community Medicine, and Associate Dean for Student Affairs, Medical College of Wisconsin)*

Violence and Sexual Abuse at Home: Current Issues in Spousal Battering and Child Maltreatment, edited by Robert Geffner, PhD, Susan B. Sorenson, PhD, and Paula K. Lundberg-Love, PhD (Vol. 1, No. 1 [#1], 1997). *"The Editors have distilled the important questions at the cutting edge of the field of violence studies, and have brought rigor, balance and moral fortitude to the search for answers." (Virginia Goldner, PhD, Co-Director, Gender and Violence Project, Senior Faculty, Ackerman Institute for Family Therapy)*

The Shaken Baby Syndrome: A Multidisciplinary Approach

Stephen Lazoritz, MD
Vincent J. Palusci, MD
Editors

The Shaken Baby Syndrome: A Multidisciplinary Approach has been co-published simultaneously as *Journal of Aggression, Maltreatment & Trauma*, Volume 5, Number 1(#9) 2001.

HMTP

The Haworth Maltreatment & Trauma Press
An Imprint of
The Haworth Press, Inc.
New York • London • Oxford

Published by

The Haworth Maltreatment & Trauma Press®, 10 Alice Street, Binghamton, NY 13904-1580 USA

The Haworth Maltreatment & Trauma Press® is an imprint of The Haworth Press, Inc., 10 Alice Street, Binghamton, NY 13904-1580 USA.

The Shaken Baby Syndrome: A Multidisciplinary Approach has been co-published simultaneously as *Journal of Aggression, Maltreatment & Trauma*, Volume 5, Number, 1(#9) 2001.

Cover design by Thomas J. Mayshock Jr.

Library of Congress Cataloging-in-Publication Data

The shaken baby syndrome: a multidisciplinary approach / Stephen Lazoritz, Vincent J. Palusci editors.
    p. cm.
    "Has been co-published simultaneously as 'Journal of aggression, maltreatment & trauma' volume 5, number 1 (#9) 2001."
    Includes bibliographical references (p.) and index.
    ISBN 0-7890-1351-7 (alk. paper)–ISBN 0-7890-1352-5 (pbk: alk. paper)
    1. Battered child syndrome. 2. Battered child syndrome–Social aspects. 3. Battered child syndrome–Law and legislation. 4. Child abuse. I. Lazoritz, Stephen. II. Palusci, Vincent J. III. Journal of aggression, maltreatment & trauma.
RJ375 .S437 2001
618.92'858223–dc21
                                       2001051555

Indexing, Abstracting & Website/Internet Coverage

This section provides you with a list of major indexing & abstracting services. That is to say, each service began covering this periodical during the year noted in the right column. Most Websites which are listed below have indicated that they will either post, disseminate, compile, archive, cite or alert their own Website users with research-based content from this work. (This list is as current as the copyright date of this publication.)

(continued)

Special Bibliographic Notes related to special journal issues (separates) and indexing/abstracting:

- indexing/abstracting services in this list will also cover material in any "separate" that is co-published simultaneously with Haworth's special thematic journal issue or DocuSerial. Indexing/abstracting usually covers material at the article/chapter level.
- monographic co-editions are intended for either non-subscribers or libraries which intend to purchase a second copy for their circulating collections.
- monographic co-editions are reported to all jobbers/wholesalers/approval plans. The source journal is listed as the "series" to assist the prevention of duplicate purchasing in the same manner utilized for books-in-series.
- to facilitate user/access services all indexing/abstracting services are encouraged to utilize the co-indexing entry note indicated at the bottom of the first page of each article/chapter/contribution.
- this is intended to assist a library user of any reference tool (whether print, electronic, online, or CD-ROM) to locate the monographic version if the library has purchased this version but not a subscription to the source journal.
- individual articles/chapters in any Haworth publication are also available through the Haworth Document Delivery Service (HDDS).

This book is dedicated to the memory of Stephen A. Chartrand, MD, Professor and Chairman of Pediatrics at Creighton University School of Medicine. He was truly a man of science and a man of God. His lifelong advocacy for the well-being of children serves as an inspiration for us to be passionate in all that we do for their benefit.

The Shaken Baby Syndrome: A Multidisciplinary Approach

CONTENTS

ABOUT THE EDITORS

Stephen Lazoritz, MD, is Vice President of Medical Affairs at Children's Hospital, Omaha, Nebraska. He also serves as Clinical Professor in the Department of Pediatrics, Creighton University School of Medicine, and Adjunct Professor in the Department of Pediatrics of the University of Nebraska Medical Center. Dr. Lazoritz was formerly medical director of the Child Protection Center of the Children's Hospital of Wisconsin. In that capacity, he was a member of a team that evaluates allegations of child abuse and neglect and was responsible for consultation with medical staff regarding the medical diagnosis of child abuse, training of professionals, and assisting law enforcement and child protection professionals in their investigations. Dr. Lazoritz has been active in the child abuse field for 15 years as a pediatrician who had dedicated an increasing percentage of his practice to the evaluation of child abuse.

Vincent J. Palusci, MD, is Assistant Professor of Pediatrics and Human Development at Michigan State University College of Human Medicine. He is Director of the DeVos Children's Hospital Child Protection Team. His research interests include traumatic brain injury, child sexual abuse and prevention of child maltreatment and he is a TRECOS Fellow of Epidemiology at Michigan State University.

ABOUT THE CONTRIBUTORS

Angela Bier is a medical student at the Medical College of Wisconsin.

William Brooks, MD, is an emergency department pediatrician and child abuse consultant, Tampa, Florida.

Hobart Davies, PhD, is Assistant Professor of Psychology at University of Wisconsin-Milwaukee and an affiliated investigator at the Child Protection Center of Children's Hospital of Wisconsin. He received his PhD in Clinical Psychology from Michigan State University.

Ranier Gedeit, MD, is Assistant Professor of Pediatrics at the Medical College of Wisconsin and specializes in pediatric critical care medicine at Children's Hospital of Wisconsin in Milwaukee.

Molly Murphy Garwood, PhD, is Associate Lecturer in Psychology at the University of Wisconsin-Milwaukee and formerly a clinical psychologist in the Child Psychiatry Center at Children's Hospital of Wisconsin. She received her PhD in Counseling/Developmental Psychology from the University of Notre Dame.

Halim Hennes, MD, MS, is Associate Professor of Pediatrics and Emergency Medicine in the Department of Pediatrics at the Medical College of Wisconsin.

Brian K. Holmgren, JD, is Assistant District Attorney General in the Davidson County District Attorney Generals Office in Nashville, Tennessee. He previously served as Assistant District Attorney in Kenosha, Wisconsin where he directed their sensitive crimes unit. He later became Senior Attorney with the American Prosecutors Research Institute's National Center for the Prosecution of Child Abuse. Mr. Holmgren is a member of the Board of Directors of the American Professional Society on the Abuse of Children and serves on the National Advisory Panel on Shaken Baby Syndrome. He has authored numerous articles and book chapters regarding child maltreatment.

Jean M. Hudlett, MSW, is a social worker in the Department of Psychology at the Children's Hospital of Wisconsin in Milwaukee.

Jeffrey M. Jentzen, MD, is Chief Medical Examiner, Milwaukee County, Wisconsin.

Narendra Kini, MD, is Vice President for Clinical Support Services, Children's Hospital of Wisconsin and Clinical Associate Professor of Pediatrics in the Department of Pediatrics at the Medical College of Wisconsin.

Jane Kivlin, MD, is Professor of Opthalmology, Medical College of Wisconsin, and Pediatric Opthalmologist, Children's Hospital of Wisconsin.

Steven R. Leuthner, MD, MA, is Assistant Professor of Pediatrics and Bioethics at the Medical College of Wisconsin.

Brian Lundeen, MD, is a Pediatric Radiologist at Children's Hospital of Wisconsin.

Henry J. Plum, JD, is an attorney in private practice in Milwaukee, Wisconsin.

Robert M. Reece, MD, is Clinical Professor of Pediatrics at Tufts University School of Medicine and Director of the Institute for Professional Education at the Massachusetts Society for the Prevention of Cruelty to Children in Boston, MA. He is the editor of the books *Child Abuse: Medical Diagnosis and Treatment* (1994, Williams & Wilkins, Baltimore, MD) and *The Treatment of Child Abuse: Common Ground for Medical, Mental Health and Legal Professionals* (2000, Johns Hopkins University Press, Baltimore, MD) and the Executive Editor of *The Quarterly Child Abuse Medical Update*, a publication seeking to keep the multidisciplinary professional community informed or recent medical literature relevant to child abuse. He was honored by the American Professional Society on the Abuse of Children in 1997 as "Outstanding Professional in the Field of Child Abuse" and is named in all editions of the peer-reviewed book *Best Doctors in America.*

Kenneth W. Reichert, MD, is pediatric neurosurgeon in Waukesha, Wisconsin.

Meic H. Schmidt, MD, is Chief Resident of Neurological Surgery at the Medical College of Wisconsin.

Jacy Showers, EdD, is Director SBS Prevention Plus in Florence, Colorado.

Betty S. Spivack, MD, is a graduate of the State University of New York at Buffalo School of Medicine. She is Board Certified in Pediatrics and Pediatric Critical Care Medicine. Since 1984, she has dedicated her practice to the diagnosis and treatment of abused children with particular interest in the mechanism of abusive injury.

Mark Splaingard, MD, is an Associate Professor of Pediatrics, Medical College of Wisconsin.

Michael Vendola, is a Special Agent for the State of Wisconsin Deptartment of Justice.

Laura Weathers, MD, is Assistant Professor of Pediatrics, University of South Florida.

Preface

Shaken Baby Syndrome (SBS) has become a leading issue for those who are involved with the evaluation of and response to child maltreatment. There is a great deal of interest nationwide among physicians, nurses, social workers, child welfare workers, law enforcement personnel, prosecutors, attorneys and others who deal with this issue at work and among members of the community at large. In 1996, the First National Shaken Baby Conference attracted over 800 participants; in 1998, the Second National Shaken Baby Conference attracted over 1000. Shaken Baby Syndrome has come to the forefront in legal and medical circles for a variety of reasons which include the significant numbers and notoriety of cases nationwide, the controversies and disagreements it has highlighted among professionals and the important issues of parenting, family and care of our children which it touches.

More than 1000 children die each year in the United States as a result of child maltreatment (McClain, Sacks, Froehlke, & Ewigman, 1993; Sedlak & Broadhurst, 1996; Wang & Daro, 1998). Of these, at least 250 are victims of the Shaken Baby Syndrome. Given inaccuracies in death certificate information and inability to properly label child abuse fatalities, we can have no idea of exactly how many children have suffered from abusive head trauma (AHT) and shaking injuries. Even less is known about the estimated 18,000 children per year who suffer serious injuries associated with non-fatal child maltreatment, SBS and AHT (Sedlak & Broadhurst, 1996). Children's hospitals such as Children's Hospital of Wisconsin and DeVos Children's Hospital see several dozen cases of serious head trauma per year, most of which is related to SBS. Many more infants are shaken who do not come to immediate medical attention. We can speculate that many victims may only come to light after non-fatal injuries such as cognitive and educational needs are identified at some time after the abuse. While we know that abusive head trauma and child maltreatment fatalities are often missed (Ewigman, Kivlahan, & Land, 1993; Herman-Giddens et al., 1999; Jenny, Hymel, Ritzen, Reinert, & Hay, 1999;

[Haworth co-indexing entry note]: "Preface." Lazoritz, Stephen, and Vincent J. Palusci. Co-published simultaneously in *Journal of Aggression, Maltreatment & Trauma* (The Haworth Maltreatment & Trauma Press, an imprint of The Haworth Press, Inc.) Vol. 5, No. 1(#9), 2001, pp. xix-xxii; and: *The Shaken Baby Syndrome: A Multidisciplinary Approach* (ed: Stephen Lazoritz, and Vincent J. Palusci) The Haworth Maltreatment & Trauma Press, an imprint of The Haworth Press, Inc., 2001, pp. xix-xxii. Single or multiple copies of this article are available for a fee from The Haworth Document Delivery Service [1-800-342-9678, 9:00 a.m. - 5:00 p.m. (EST). E-mail address: getinfo@ haworthpressinc.com].

Spivak, 1998), we also suspect that Shaken Baby Syndrome is presently underdiagnosed both on death certificates, in clinical settings and among child abuse reports.

Part of the difficulty in ascertaining the incidence of Shaken Baby Syndrome stems from our difficulty in defining the syndrome. While Caffey's original description of "whiplash shaking" in 1972 has come to be known as SBS, others have suggested "Shaken Impact Syndrome," "Shaken Infant Syndrome" (Duhaime, Christian, Rorke, & Zimmerman, 1998; Duhaime et al., 1987; Lazoritz, Baldwin, & Kini, 1997). We do know that SBS reflects a subset of injuries caused by abusive head trauma and that AHT is part of Kempe Silverman, Steele, Droegemueller, and Silver's (1962) "Battered Child Syndrome." As our knowledge evolves about the mechanisms of injury in SBS and AHT, diagnostic schema (such as the International Classification of Disease, 10th Revision; DHHS, 1998) will need to be adopted to accurately reflect SBS and AHT in medical, injury and death certificate records. In this book, we have chosen to label the pattern of abusive head trauma caused by shaking as SBS, with or without the presence of impact; this is done for the benefit of the reader and does not imply that impact is not a part of SBS. Rather, we hope to present information regarding the multidisciplinary evaluation of SBS regardless of whether impact is present to increase the reader's understanding of the overall pattern of abusive head trauma associated with shaking. The reader is encouraged to integrate the role of impact into their understanding and professional practice.

It is precisely this multi-factorial nature and lack of precise diagnostic categories and incidence data, which compounds the medical evaluation of SBS as a form of child abuse. While much is known about other forms of child maltreatment, SBS has young victims who cannot reveal what happened and perpetrators who rarely completely disclose their actions. In addition to the medical aspects of the Shaken Baby Syndrome, there are tremendous implications for law enforcement, social service, and legal professionals. Each is faced with critical decisions regarding cases of SBS for which they may not be professionally or personally prepared. By sharing their individual knowledge and expertise, the variety of professionals called to respond to cases of SBS are able to bridge the limits of their individual professions and collaborate for the benefit of children and families in cases which often require extraordinary professional effort and experience. The Shaken Baby Syndrome is a problem that is best approached in a multidisciplinary manner, thus the title and the approach of this book.

The goal of *The Shaken Baby Syndrome: A Multidisciplinary Approach* is to make available, in one place, the entire constellation of current information regarding Shaken Baby Syndrome. It is important to note that each professional who deals with this syndrome would benefit from the knowledge of all of the information in the book. A social worker or police investigator has a great need to understand the medical issues involved. The physician would benefit from knowledge of the legal implications. Each chapter is of vital importance for all potential readers, and the sum of all the chapters presents a picture of a community response, which transcends professional boundaries.

As with all medical texts, however, knowledge in the fields of child development, brain injury, biomechanics and cellular metabolism is rapidly changing. SBS has only recently been well described in the medical literature, and new information is expected as research efforts and clinical experience grow. We can only encourage the reader to understand what is known currently about SBS and to critically review areas of disagreement to reach their own opinion. This is particularly true when faced with a particular case; the reader is explicitly warned to use best professional clinical judgment and to not rely solely on *The Shaken Baby Syndrome: A Multidisciplinary Approach* when evaluating SBS given the rapidly changing knowledge in the field and the inadvisability of using any medical text to solely dictate clinical care. One must continually review new research findings and participate in periodic training to keep abreast of new developments in the field. It is not unexpected that some of the material presented in *The Shaken Baby Syndrome: A Multidisciplinary Approach* is changing even as it goes to press; such is the rapid pace of clinical advancement in modern medicine. Yet we hope to provide the reader with a basic understanding of SBS from a variety of professional viewpoints, which will serve as a framework for the application of new knowledge as it develops.

The reader must also develop a healthy scientific skepticism in reviewing new (and old) medical literature to effectively separate opinion from science as it applies to SBS. This applies as well to the evaluation of "controversies"; the reader must be able to evaluate the theoretical basis underlying any divergence of scientific opinion to understand the underpinning of any true scientific differences in the interpretation of scientific data. While *The Shaken Baby Syndrome: A Multidisciplinary Approach* cannot replace rigorous training in this scientific method, we hope that the Chapters and their authors' viewpoints can be a starting point for those professionals who seek a more in-depth understanding of SBS. And while we believe that the Chapters in *The Shaken Baby Syndrome: A Multidisciplinary Approach* reflect a consensus of professional opinion regarding SBS, they also represent the opinions of their author(s) which may reflect honest disagreements with some aspects of the its current diagnosis and management.

We hope that *The Shaken Baby Syndrome: A Multidisciplinary Approach* will become a resource for those professionals who deal with, or may potentially deal with, cases of Shaken Baby Syndrome (i.e., nurses, family practitioners, emergency room physicians and nurses, pediatricians, including pediatric subspecialists, child protective workers, social workers, law enforcement officers, lawyers, prosecutors, and guardians ad litem). Every county in the United States has a child protective services unit, a District Attorney's Office, Coroner/Medical Examiner, Sheriff's Department and other child welfare agencies. This book will hopefully serve as a single source covering the complex entity we call SBS, becoming required reading for CPS, social work, medical and law students and for law enforcement officers and other professionals who deal with abused children and for the lay public. It is only with this multidisciplinary response involving a variety of professionals and society as a whole that we can begin to address the medical, social and developmental needs of the shaken baby.

Stephen Lazoritz, MD
Vincent J. Palusci, MD

REFERENCES

Caffey, J. (1972). On the theory and practice of shaking infants: Its potential residual effects of permanent brain damage and mental retardation. *American Journal of Diseases of Children, 124,* 161-169.

Duhaime, A.C., Christian, C.W., Rorke, L.B., & Zimmerman, R.A. (1998). Non-accidental head injury in infants: The "shaken baby syndrome." *New England Journal of Medicine, 338,* 1822-1829.

Duhaime, A.C., Gennarelli, T.A., Thibault, L.E., Bruce, D.A., Marguiles, S.S., & Wiser, R. (1987). The shaken baby syndrome: A clinical, pathological and biomechanical study. *Journal of Neurosurgery, 66,* 409-415.

Ewigman, B., Kivlahan, C., & Land, G. (1993). The Missouri child fatality study: Underreporting of maltreatment fatalities among children younger than 5 years of age, 1983 through 1986. *Pediatrics, 91,* 330-337.

Herman-Giddens, M.E., Brown, G., Verbiest, S., Carlson, P.J., Hooten, E.G., Howell, E., & Butts, J.D. (1999). Underascertainment of child abuse mortality in the United States. *Journal of the American Medical Association, 282,* 463-467.

Jenny, C., Hymel, K., Ritzen, A., Reinert, S., & Hay, S. (1999). Analysis of missed cases of abusive head trauma. *Journal of the American Medical Association, 281,* 621-626.

Kempe, C.H., Silverman, F.N., Steele, B.F., Droegemueller, W., & Silver, H.K. (1962). The battered child syndrome. *Journal of the American Medical Association, 181,* 17-24.

Lazoritz, S., Baldwin, S., & Kini, N. (1997). The whiplash shaken infant syndrome: Has Caffey's syndrome changed or have we changed the syndrome? *Child Abuse & Neglect, 21,* 1009-1014.

McClain, P.W., Sacks, J.J., Froehlke, R.G., & Ewigman, B.G. (1993). Estimates of fatal child abuse and neglect, United States, 1979 through 1988. *Pediatrics, 91,* 338-343.

Sedlak, A.J., & Broadhurst, D.D. (1996). *The Third National Incidence Study of Child Abuse and Neglect (NIS-3).* Washington, DC: US Dept of Health and Human Services.

Spivak, B.S. (1998). Statistics and death certificates (letter). *Pediatrics, 102,* 1000-1001.

US Dept of Health and Human Services, Centers for Disease Control and Prevention, National Center for Health Statistics. (1998). *ICD-10: International Statistical Classification of Diseases and Related Health Problems, Tenth Revision,* Vol. 1.

Wang, C.T., & Daro, D. (1998). Current trends in child abuse reporting and fatalities: The results of the 1997 annual fifty-state survey. Washington, DC: National Committee to prevent child abuse.

Acknowledgments

The editors would like to thank the following individuals: Nigel Paneth, MD, MPH, Associate Dean and Chairman of Epidemiology in the College of Human Medicine at Michigan State University for his review of the epidemiology chapter and support in our efforts to improve the science of SBS; Margaret McHugh, MD, MPH for her mentorship and support of our work for many years; Members of the Ray E. Helfer Society and all professionals who dedicate their careers and lives to helping vulnerable children and victims of SBS; and our wives, children and families who support us in this important work and make it possible to continue this important work.

Chapter One

Overview of Shaken Baby Syndrome

William Brooks
Laura Weathers

SUMMARY. An overview of the problem of the Shaken Infant Syndrome and the impact it has on society, as well as the great importance of the use of a multidisciplinary approach to the problem, and a general overview of what, exactly, Shaken Infant Syndrome is. This chapter will be of general interest to all readers. *[Article copies available for a fee from The Haworth Document Delivery Service: 1-800-342-9678. E-mail address: <getinfo@haworthpressinc.com> Website: <http://www.HaworthPress.com> © 2001 by The Haworth Press, Inc. All rights reserved.]*

KEYWORDS. Shaken Baby Syndrome, diagnosis, prognosis, prevention

INTRODUCTION

The most common cause of traumatic death in infants under one year of age is head injury (American Academy of Pediatrics, 1993; Coody, Brown, Montgomery, Flynn, & Yetman, 1994). Since Caffey (1974) first described "whiplash shaken infant syndrome," injuries from severe shaking have gained attention as a cause of significant morbidity and mortality. Shaken

---

[Haworth co-indexing entry note]: "Overview of Shaken Baby Syndrome." Brooks, William, and Laura Weathers. Co-published simultaneously in *Journal of Aggression, Maltreatment & Trauma* (The Haworth Maltreatment & Trauma Press, an imprint of The Haworth Press, Inc.) Vol. 5, No. 1(#9), 2001, pp. 1-7; and: *The Shaken Baby Syndrome: A Multidisciplinary Approach* (ed: Stephen Lazoritz, and Vincent J. Palusci) The Haworth Maltreatment & Trauma Press, an imprint of The Haworth Press, Inc., 2001, pp. 1-7. Single or multiple copies of this article are available for a fee from The Haworth Document Delivery Service [1-800-342-9678, 9:00 a.m. - 5:00 p.m. (EST). E-mail address: getinfo@haworthpressinc.com].

1

Baby Syndrome (SBS) is now a widely recognized diagnosis in the medical literature.

The medical components of Shaken Baby Syndrome include retinal hemorrhage, subdural or subarachnoid hemorrhage and associated fractures with a paucity of external physical findings. It is this absence of external signs of abuse, which makes the early diagnosis of SBS so difficult. In this chapter, we will provide an overview of SBS and discuss the importance of recognition and prevention of the syndrome.

INCIDENCE

The incidence of SBS is difficult to ascertain. Because the perpetrator is reluctant to provide an accurate history, most children with the constellation of injuries seen in SBS and without obvious external trauma are initially "presumed" to have been shaken (Hadley, Sonntag, Rekate, & Murphy, 1989; Ludwig & Warman, 1984; Spaide, 1987). Some infants with less serious forms of shaking may not have significant immediate sequelae from the shaking event, and the diagnosis can be missed (Caffey, 1974; Jenny, 1999).

Most victims of SBS are less than six months of age (AAP, 1993; Chiocca, 1995; Riffenburgh & Sathyavagiswaran, 1991; Swenson & Levitt, 1997). Some studies show more male than female victims (Riffenburgh & Sathyavagiswaran, 1991; Starling, Holden, & Jenny, 1995). While there appears to be a predominance of Caucasian and African-American children with fewer Latino and Asian infants injured, SBS has been shown to affect all racial, ethnic and socio-economic groups (Riffenburgh & Sathyavagiswaran, 1991).

RISK FACTORS

There are several risk factors that are important to recognize as potential crisis situations in which SBS may occur. Parents who are likely to abuse their children are often described as having reversed nurturing needs. They are looking to be nurtured by their infants, and when this does not happen, abuse can occur (AAP, 1993; Coody et al., 1994; Chiocca, 1995; Spaide, Swengel, Scharre, & Mein, 1990; Swenson & Levitt, 1997). Environmental stressors such as emotional or financial problems, illness, or lack of support at home can increase the likelihood of abuse (AAP, 1993; Coody et al., 1994; Chiocca, 1995).

Some children may possess factors, which contribute to their own abuse. Children with colic can cry most of the day, increasing stress and frustration and leading to abuse. Children born prematurely or with handicaps may cause frustration because they do not reach developmental milestones as quickly as their parents think they should, and may require more care (AAP, 1993; Coody et al., 1994).

People who have admitted to shaking a child usually state that they were not trying to harm the infant but wanted to "make the baby stop crying" (Swenson & Levitt, 1997). Others admit to shaking the infant during "vigorous play" which is later found to be inconsistent with the severity of injury. Starling et al. (1995) found that fathers and boyfriends were the most common abusers, accounting for over half the cases reviewed. Baby-sitters were involved in over 20% of cases.

MECHANISMS OF INJURY

Infants are thought to be more susceptible to whiplash shaking injuries that older children and adults because of several factors. Their relatively large head supported by weak neck muscles increases their head movement during shaking. Their unmyelinated brain, soft sutures, open fontanelles, and relatively increased cerebrospinal fluid result in a brain that is more vulnerable to injury (Alexander, Crabbe, Sato, Smith, & Bennett, 1990; Caffey, 1974; Chiocca, 1995; Hadley et al., 1989; Ludwig & Warman, 1984; Nashelsky & Dix, 1995; Spaide et al., 1987;). The cerebral bridging veins are more easily stretched or lacerated with excessive acceleration, deceleration and rotation of the brain. This tearing of the bridging veins can lead to subdural hemorrhage (AAP, 1993; Coody et al., 1994; Spaide et al., 1990).

Various types of ocular injury have been recognized in SBS, including retinal and vitreal hemorrhages and retinal folds and retinoschesis. Several mechanisms have been suggested for these injuries, including consequences of increased intracranial pressure, increased ocular pressure, rapid brain acceleration/deceleration and direct trauma to the retina from being struck by vitreous moving within the eye during shaking or retraction upon the retina by the vitreous pulling away from the retina during shaking (Coody et al., 1994; Lambert, Johnson, & Hoyt, 1986; Ludwig & Warman, 1984; Ober, 1980; Spaide, 1987; Matthews & Das, 1996).

There has been vast disagreement regarding whether the mechanism of vigorously shaking an infant alone, as Caffey described, produces sufficient force to result in the significant intracranial injuries found in SBS. Duhaime et al. (1987) used laboratory and animal models and found that some form of impact was necessary in at least the most severe cases of SBS, stating: "Although shaking may, in fact, be part of the process, it is more likely that infants suffer blunt impact" (p. 414). Alexander et al. (1990) suggest, "shaking, in and of itself, is sufficient to cause serious intracranial injury or death" (p. 726). Irrespective of the presence of impact, SBS injuries occur because of severe acceleration/deceleration and remain a significant cause of morbidity and mortality.

CLINICAL PRESENTATION

The clinical presentation of the infant of SBS can be very non-specific, hindering a timely diagnosis. The paucity of external signs of trauma can be misleading. Because of the head injuries present, the child may present in a coma, with a bulging fontanelle or with more subtle signs such as vomiting, irritability, seizures, poor feeding or failure to thrive. Children may be misdiagnosed as having meningitis, and a lumbar puncture is performed. Bloody spinal fluid can mistakenly be thought to be related to a spinal tap rather than a sign of subarahnoid bleeding because of a "normal" head CT; lumbar puncture is more sensitive than CT in identifying small SDH/SAH (Coody et al., 1994; Ludwig & Warman, 1984; Spaide et al., 1990).

The classic finding of retinal hemorrhage may be missed if the diagnosis is not made early. Small flame-shaped retinal hemorrhages resolve in only a few days and may no longer be present by the time the suspicion of abuse is raised. Some would argue that retinal hemorrhages were pre-existing as the result of birth trauma. In fact, 14-40% of newborns sustain retinal hemorrhages at birth (Budenz, Farber, Mirchandani, Park, & Rorke, 1994; Caffey, 1974), but these are usually resolved in several days and certainly within two weeks. After the initial neonatal period, any finding of retinal hemorrhage should suggest abusive head trauma unless another obvious traumatic or anatomic reason is apparent.

The victim of SBS may have bruising over the upper extremities, neck or the chest where the child was held and shaken (Coody et al., 1994). However, bruising is more the exception than the rule. Traction lesions of the periostium or old or new fractures of the large bones may also be present (AAP, 1993; Caffey, 1974).

The amount of time from injury to the onset of symptoms is also not completely understood. The absence of an accurate history from the caretakers complicates the clinical picture. It appears that some patients become significantly symptomatic immediately with severe injury, whereas others with less severe injury are less symptomatic (Nashelsky & Dix, 1995). It is theorized that these more insidious cases may have sustained mild initial shaking with subsequent severe shaking causing more visible symptoms to develop. This remains a point of controversy and topic for further research.

DIAGNOSIS

The diagnosis of brain injury in SBS has become easier to make with the wide availability of the computed tomography (CT) scan. CT has become the method of choice for initial imaging of patients with suspected brain injury because it readily identifies lesions requiring operative intervention (AAP, 1993). Sometimes, several CT scans are necessary to show the full evolution of brain injury, particularly if the patient deteriorates.

Magnetic Resonance Imaging (MRI) has shown to detect 50% more subdural hemorrhages than CT scan and detect smaller injuries missed by CT (Spaide, 1987). However, the cost and availability of MRI makes it more useful as a second study in the diagnosis and evolution of brain injury.

An ophthalmologist or other physician trained in detecting retinal hemorrhages should examine the eyes as early as possible after the diagnosis of SBS is suspected. RH has been found in 75-90% of cases of SBS when searched for early in its course (AAP, 1993).

While external signs may be minimal, that is one of the hallmarks of SBS. When bruises are present, they should be carefully documented. A bulging fontanelle was shown to be present in 55% of infants with subdural hematoma when reviewed by Ludwig and Warman (1984). The physician must closely review the non-specific signs and symptoms, which may be present and the risk factors in the caretakers in addition to the history provided to make the diagnosis.

PROGNOSIS

The victims of SBS suffer significant morbidity and mortality. Ludwig and Warman (1984) showed a 15% mortality rate and a 50% morbidity rate in their review of 20 cases. Permanent brain damage, hydrocephalus, developmental delay, blindness, deafness, paralysis and mental retardation have been noted in SBS victims (AAP, 1993; Coody et al., 1994; Spaide et al., 1990). Brown and Minns (1993) noted 10 deaths and 10 cases of mental retardation in 30 SBS victims. Caffey (1974) suggested that milder forms of SBS might present with mental retardation and developmental delay upon reaching school age.

RECOGNITION AND PREVENTION

The recognition of child abuse in our society is often difficult; this is especially true with victims of SBS. The diagnosis of shaken baby syndrome requires a high index of suspicion. The clinical manifestations are non-specific, external signs are sometimes lacking, and the history is often inconsistent or non-existent. A missed diagnosis could be life threatening for the child. Early recognition is paramount to institute treatment in a timely manner in order to decrease the high mortality and morbidity. Although the medical literature is becoming abundant with information about SBS, many pediatricians and health professionals lack the knowledge, willingness or ability to make the diagnosis.

Even more concerning is the lack of SBS knowledge by the general public. Recent high profile cases such as the "nanny" case in Massachusetts document this lack of information, sometimes by judges, juries and even the medical profession. Despite campaigns to educate the public about the dangers of shaking a child, awareness remains low, with many teenagers and adults still unaware about SBS. With poor neurologic outcomes in many cases, it is obvious that prevention is key. Many confessed perpetrators believed that shaking an infant for discipline or during vigorous play could not harm the child in such a devastating way. Continued work in public and professional education will be necessary to help combat these false assumptions.

REFERENCES

Alexander, R., Crabbe, L., Sato, Y., Smith, W., & Bennett, T. (1990). Incidence of impact trauma with cranial injuries ascribed to shaking. *American Journal of Diseases in Children, 144*, 724-726.

American Academy of Pediatrics (AAP). (1993). Committee on child abuse and neglect. Shaken baby syndrome: Inflicted cerebral trauma. *Pediatrics, 92*, 872-875.

Brown, J.K., & Minns, R.A. (1993). Nonaccidental head injury, with particular reference to whiplash shaking injury and medico-legal aspects. *Developmental Medicine and Child Neurology, 35*, 849-869.

Budenz, D.L., Farber, M.G., Mirchandani, H.G., Park, H., Rorke, L.B. (1994). Ocular and optic nerve hemorrhages in abused infants with intracranial injuries. *Ophthalmology, 101*, 559-565.

Caffey, J. (1974). The Whiplash Shaken Baby Syndrome: A manual shaking by the extremities with whiplash-induced intracranial and intraocular bleeding, linked with residual permanent brain damage and mental retardation. Pediatrics, 54, 396-403.

Chiocca, E.M. (1995). Shaken Baby Syndrome: A nursing perspective. *Pediatric Nursing, 21*, 33-38.

Coody, D., Brown, M., Montgomery, D., Flynn, A., Yetman, R. (1994). Shaken Baby Syndrome: Identification and prevention for nurse practitioners. *Journal of Pediatric Health Care, 24*, 536-540.

Duhaime, A.C., Gennarelli, T.A., Thibault, L.E., Bruce, D.A., Marguiles, S.S., & Wiser, R. (1987). The Shaken Baby Syndrome: A clinical, pathological and biochemical study. *Journal of Neurosurgery, 66*, 409-415.

Hadley, M.N., Sonntag, V.K., Rekate, H.L., & Murphy, A. (1989). The infant whip-lash-shaken injury syndrome: A clinical and pathological study. *Neurosurgery, 24,* 536-540.

Lambert, S.R., Johnson, T.E., & Hoyt, C.S. (1986). Optic nerve sheath and retinal hemorrhages associated with the shaken baby syndrome. *Archives of Ophthalmology, 104,* 1509-1512.

Ludwig, S., & Warman, M. (1984). Shaken Baby Syndrome: A review of 20 cases. *Annals of Emergency Medicine, 13,* 104-107.

Matthews, G.P., & Das, A. (1996). Dense vitreous hemorrhages predict poor visual and neurological prognosis in infants with shaken baby syndrome. *Journal of Pediatric Ophthalmology and Strabismus, 33,* 260-265.

Nashelsky, M.B., & Dix, J.D. (1995). The time interval between lethal infant shaking and onset of symptoms: A review of the shaken baby syndrome literature. *The American Journal of Forensic Medicine and Pathology, 16,* 154-157.

Ober, R.R. (1980). Hemorrhagic retinopathy in infancy: A clinicopathologic report. *Journal of Pediatric Ophthalmology and Stabismus, 17,* 17-20.

Riffenburgh, R.S., & Sathyavagiswaran, L. (1991). Ocular findings at autopsy of child abuse victims. *Ophthalmology, 98,* 1519-1524.

Spaide, R.F. (1987). Shaken Baby Syndrome: Ocular and computed tomographic findings. *Journal of Clinical Neuro-Opththalmology, 7,* 108-111.

Spaide, R.F., Swengel, R.M., Scharre, D.W., Mein, C.E. (1990). Shaken Baby Syndrome. *American Family Physician, 41,* 1145-1152.

Starling, S.P., Holden, J.R., & Jenny, C. (1995). Abusive head trauma: The relationship of perpetrators to their victims. *Pediatrics, 95,* 259-262.

Swenson, J., & Levitt, C. (1997). Shaken Baby Syndrome: Diagnosis and prevention. *Minnesota Medicine, 80,* 41-44.

Chapter Two

Historical Perspectives

Stephen Lazoritz
Angela Bier

SUMMARY. Although the Shaken Baby Syndrome was not formally described by John Caffey until 1972, it can be traced back at least 500 years. Beginning with a prophecy made by Nostradamus in 1555, many have described subdural hematoma and its relationship to trauma and abuse. This chapter explores aspects leading up to Caffey's work, from early attempts to understand this in children through our present understanding of abusive head trauma. *[Article copies available for a fee from The Haworth Document Delivery Service: 1-800-342-9678. E-mail address: <getinfo@haworthpressinc.com> Website: <http://www.HaworthPress.com> © 2001 by The Haworth Press, Inc. All rights reserved.]*

KEYWORDS. Historical aspects, pachymeningitis interna hemorrhagica, subdural hematoma, John Caffey, whiplash shaken infant syndrome

In recent years the Shaken Baby Syndrome has become increasingly recognized not only by child abuse professionals but also increasingly by the lay public. History has taught us, however, that timely topics are frequently timeless as well. The Shaken Baby Syndrome is an excellent example of how a cur-

---

[Haworth co-indexing entry note]: "Historical Perspectives." Lazoritz, Stephen, and Angela Bier. Co-published simultaneously in *Journal of Aggression, Maltreatment & Trauma* (The Haworth Maltreatment & Trauma Press, an imprint of The Haworth Press, Inc.) Vol. 5, No. 1(#9), 2001, pp. 9-18; and: *The Shaken Baby Syndrome: A Multidisciplinary Approach* (ed: Stephen Lazoritz, and Vincent J. Palusci) The Haworth Maltreatment & Trauma Press, an imprint of The Haworth Press, Inc., 2001, pp. 9-18. Single or multiple copies of this article are available for a fee from The Haworth Document Delivery Service [1-800-342-9678, 9:00 a.m. - 5:00 p.m. (EST). E-mail address: getinfo@haworthpressinc.com].

rent medical syndrome possesses deep historic roots, which can be traced back to the prophesy of a French physician in 1555 and followed to the pages of today's medical journals.

In 1559, times were good for Henri II of France. He had just signed a peace treaty with Spain at Chateau Cambresis, and his two daughters, Elizabeth and Margaret, were to be married. To mark the occasion, a large celebration was planned including, among other things, a jousting tournament. Although he usually chose to forego such tournaments Henri II made the fateful decision to participate. On June 29, 1559, Henri jousted the Compte de Montgomery, captain of the Scottish guards, receiving a blow from the Montgomery's lance. Despite every effort, including accident reconstruction using the heads of recently beheaded criminals, the king died 11 days later. Here we can read a description of the event:

> The muscular skin of the forehead, over the bone, was torn across to the inner angle of the left eye, and there were many little fragments or splinters of the broken shaft lodged in the eye; but no fracture of the bone. Yet because of such commotion or shaking of the brain, he died on the eleventh day after he was struck. (Packard, 1926)

King Henri's personal surgeon, Ambroise Paré, wrote this description. Paré was born in 1510 in Burg-Hersent France. He studied as a barber-surgeon at a time when the Church forbid physicians from shedding blood. Paré served in the French army from 1536-1545. He advanced the treatment of war wounds and developed new methods of amputation, impressing Henri II. Paré also wrote on the treatment of firearm wounds, plague, smallpox, measles and leprosy.

It was Paré's vast knowledge of anatomy, however, that earned him his place as one of the fathers of modern surgery. This knowledge allowed him to make the following observations during the autopsy of Henri II: "After his death a quantity of blood was found collected between the dura and the pia mater, in the area opposite the blow near the suture of the occipital bone" (Packard, 1926). He received a blow on one side of the head, and the blood collected on the other side. Not only is this a classic description of a contra-coup injury, but also it is the first description of what we now know as a subdural hematoma. Thus, Paré's description clearly laid the foundation for the subdural hematoma to be considered as traumatic injury. Interestingly, the first mention of a subdural hematoma came not in Paré's *description* of Henri II's death, but rather in its *prediction*.

Michael de Nostre-dame was born on December 13, 1503, at St. Remi, France. He studied philosophy at Avignon and received a medical degree from

Monpellier in 1529. During the plague of 1545, Nostre-dame became well known for his care of victims at Aix and Lyon, although he was unable to save those closest to him. After the death of his family from the plague, Nostre-dame turned increasingly to the study of astrology, the field with which he is popularly associated today. His name was latinized to Nostradamus, and in 1555 he published a collection of prophecies in rhymed quatrains, which were grouped in hundreds and called Centuries. One of these quatrains is of particular interest:

> The young lion shall overcome the old
> In a warlike field in single combat,
> He will pierce his eyes in a cage of gold
> One of two breakings, then he shall die a cruel death.
> –(Nostradamus, 1982)

The old lion was Henri II, the young lion his son, Francois II, who suc-ceeded him, the cage of gold his lancing helmet, and the breaking was his le-thal subdural hematoma. So impressive was Nostradamus' forecast of Henri II's death that his widow, Catherine de Medici, dismissed Paré as court physi-cian in favor of the astrologer. Despite Catherine's decision, Paré's association of subdural hematoma with impact trauma remained popularly accepted for many years.

Although Paré's discovery shed light on the subject, it took further observa-tions to link subdural hematoma in children with their abuse. One of the first to realize this association was James Parkinson. Although most well known for describing the "shaking palsy" which now bears his name, Parkinson was also an avid pacifist and social reformer in his time. Parkinson was born in 1755 in Shoreditch, a suburb of London, where he received his medical training as an apothecary and surgeon. Between his medical practice and his involvement as a leader in his church, Parkinson saw firsthand the social injustices that plagued London. Rather than becoming immune to the plight of the poor, Par-kinson became an advocate for change, writing on such varied topics as war, the military, poverty and industry, the rights of the laborer, civil disobedience, revolution, and the sad state of "modern" medical education. So inflammatory were his opinions that Parkinson was forced to write under the pseudonym "Old Hubert" and was actually accused of treason.

In 1799, Parkinson shifted his focus back to clinical medicine. However, he continued to promote his agenda of social reform. In 1800, Parkinson pub-lished a book meant specifically for the lay public; The *Villager's Friend and Physician,* gave practical advice on the treatment of a wide range of maladies and promoted healthful practices. In this work, Parkinson became one of the first physicians to publicly condemn child abuse, addressing the issue of head trauma and its implications directly:

> DROPSY OF THE BRAIN, or WATERY HEAD, may be suspected when a child appears uncommonly heavy and dull, complains of pain the head, has it's [sic] sleep disturbed with alarming dreams, reluctantly moves it's [sic] head from the pillow, or attends to surrounding objects; and is affected with frequent sickness and slight fever . . . This complaint is frequently occasioned by the falls on the head . . . Guard their heads, therefore, at this time, with the old-fashioned head-dress for children, a quilted stuffed cap, or pudding. I am sorry to be obliged to add another cause of this malady, severe blows on the head, inflicted in the corrections of children. Parents too often forget the weight of their hands and the delicate structure of a child . . . Duties are required of parents as well as of children; and though an undutiful child may be termed a monster, know that the worst of monsters is an *undutiful parent.* (Parkinson, 1800)

Although unaware of the etiology of "dropsy of the brain" or the exact nature of subdural hematoma, Parkinson was well aware of the existence of child abuse and the ramifications of traumatic head injury in children.

Although Paré's earlier description had laid the foundation for subdural hematoma to be considered a traumatic injury, the work of a famous pathologist cast doubt on this etiology 300 years later. Rudolf Carl Virchow was born in Schivelbein, Germany, on October 15, 1821 and was educated at the University of Berlin. Virchow, like Parkinson, did not see his medical career as being separate from his social one, writing that, "if medicine is to fulfill her great task, then she must enter the political and social life" (Ackerknecht, 1953). While he was best known for his advancement of cell theory, he also engaged in extensive research in archaeology and anthropology. Early in his career, Virchow began to advocate an abandonment of the humoral theory, suggesting instead that future research be based squarely on clinical observation, animal experimentation, and necropsy.

To Virchow, life was a series of phenomena subject to the control of ordinary physical and chemical laws. Perhaps it was it this mechanistic view that allowed him to imagine a cause for subdural hematoma other than traumatic injury. In 1856, he described the subdural hematoma and maintained that its cause was infection. He referred to this disorder as "pachymeningitis interna," a term which remained in use for almost 100 years. It is interesting to note that Virchow also rejected Pasteur's germ theory of disease and Darwin's theory of evolution.

A French physician doing pioneering work of his own, Ambroise Auguste Tardieu had been born in Paris in 1818, received his doctorate in 1843, and began to practice general medicine. He entered the field of legal medicine in 1856 at the University of Paris, where he eventually became professor of legal medicine. In his work as an expert witness, he was frequently called upon to investigate unexplained deaths, including those of children. In 1860, Tardieu published a report detailing the abuse and maltreatment of children. In it he described 32 children, 24 of whom were abused by their parents and 18 of whom died. His descriptions included most of the forms of physical abuse seen today, including mention of fractures without the benefit of x-ray. Of particular interest was Tardieu's description of "thickening of blood on the surface of the brain" (Silverman, 1972). He associated this condition to trauma. Thus, it was Ambroise Tardieu who presented the first description of a subdural hematoma in a child caused by traumatic head injury in the form of abusive treatment. Tardieu's work was not widely known and did little to challenge Virchow's popularly-accepted theory.

Although Virchow's pachymeningitis interna remained largely embraced by the scientific community for some time, several little-known English physicians continued to attribute subdural hematoma to traumatic head injury. One, Dr. Thomas Scattergood, lived in Leeds between 1826-1900. Officially, Scattergood was a general practitioner, lecturer in chemistry, and Dean of the Faculty of Medicine at Yorkshire College. Unofficially, however, Scattergood was something of an amateur sleuth, performing necroscopies, analyzing crime scenes and investigating murder weapons. Between 1856 and 1897 he kept a journal of medico-legal cases. Under the heading of "Battered Babies & Cot Deaths" he describes the death of a three-year-old child in 1875:

> This was the body of a male child, said to be 3 years old, but looking very small. It was in a miserable cellar, dirty, cold, with broken windows and doors, and nothing that could be called furniture . . . much emaciation . . . blood pale and watery . . . pale firm clot in the lateral sinus and a firm coagulation beneath the dura mater in the occipital fossa. (Green, 1973)

Scattergood attributed the child's death to the subdural hematoma; the coroner's jury accepted the mother's story of a fall.

A second Englishman who more directly attacked Virchow's theory was the delightfully named J. Wiglesworth. In 1892 he presented a paper titled "Remarks on the Pathology of So-Called Pachymeningities Interna Haemorrhagica." Wiglesworth argued quite sarcastically against an inflammatory etiology of subdural hematoma. Instead, he suggested that the inflammation, which Virchow described, was in fact *secondary* to the effusion of blood into the subdural space through shearing of the bridging vessels. However, he then went on to argue that this condition occurred in children only as a result of previous weakening of the vessels due to paralysis and general wasting of the brain. Thus, while Wiglesworth was correct in citing trauma as the cause of subdural hematoma, he incorrectly identified the conditions, which led to the condition.

As time passed, various contributions to the area of child abuse in the medical literature went largely unnoticed. In 1891, the German pathologist, Dohle, published a study of autopsies in children and found subdural hematoma to be a common finding. In 395 autopsies of children less that one-year of age, 14% were found to have subdural hemorrhage. In children over one year of age, the incidence was 8%.

In 1914, Kovitz extended Dohle's work and performed one of the largest autopsy studies of children to date. He examined nearly 6,000 children less than 2 years of age. He found subdural hemorrhage in 14% of infants 1-3 months old, in 10% of infants 3-12 months old, and in 9% of children 1 to 2 years old. These two German studies showed that subdural hemorrhage was not a rare occurrence in young infants or children. Neither study, however, addressed causality and did not challenge Virchow or the existence of abusive head trauma in children.

While Kovitz and Dohle described the pathology of subdural hematoma with little attention to its cause, a physician across the Atlantic addressed its causality with little knowledge of the exact pathological outcome. In 1907 in Massachusetts, William Preyer published his text, *Mental Development of the Child.* in which he described several potentially harmful practices, including "too vigorous" rocking of the cradle. He wrote, "the inexcusable violent rocking in the cradle which puts the baby into a dazed condition in order that he may not trouble those that have care of him is extremely injurious" (Preyer, 1907). Preyer did not, however, describe what these injuries might be.

A landmark investigation of subdural hematoma came in 1930 with David Sherwood's publication of a classic review of subdural hematoma in children. In addition to an extensive review of all previous descriptions, Sherwood reported nine new cases of subdural hematoma in children. Of these, many had retinal hemorrhages and five came from "dubious home conditions" (Sherwood, 1930); none had reported histories of trauma. Unlike his predecessors, Sherwood did not attribute these cases either to infection leading to inflammation or to traumatic birth. Instead, he concluded that the fact that these infants came from "dubious" environments made the histories provided by the parents less valuable, and therefore raised the question of possible head trauma with no accompanying admission of guilt. Sherwood began to connect all the dots, proposing that children were being injured and presenting with subdural hematoma, with no admission of any traumatic event. Despite his insight, Sherwood did not take the final step and suggest the possibility of abuse. Instead, he merely pointed to a "dubious" environment as presenting increased risk for head trauma in children.

Several of Sherwood's contemporaries drew similar connections between the occurrence of subdural hematoma in children and a less than ideal home environment. Holt's *Diseases of Infants and Children* was a popular pediatric textbook in the 1930s and 1940s. In it, Holt stated that the etiology of "hemorrhagic pachymeningitis" was unknown. Despite this, he still made certain observations which were quite astute: (1) "The frequency with which the condition is encountered in foundlings, illegitimate children and those in institutions have often been commented on," and (2) "Breast-fed infants are notoriously immune from this disorder" (Holt, 1940). Like Sherwood, Holt realized that the infant's home environment was, in some way, related to the condition.

In 1939, Ingraham and Heyl presented 11 cases of subdural hematoma in children. One case is particularly noteworthy; Case #4 was an 8-month-old boy presenting with seizures. The child had multiple bruises on the extremities, bruises on the face, bilateral retinal hemorrhages, and fractures of both forearms–now recognized as a classic case of child abuse. The authors make two major points in this study: (1) the frequency of subdural hematoma in children was more or less proportional to the intensity with which it is sought, and (2) the etiology of subdural hematoma was traumatic in most cases, putting to rest Virchow's theory of inflammation.

For a time, the correlation between subdural hematoma in children and a poor home environment led to the incorrect conclusion that scurvy predisposed these children to the condition. In a 1936 review, Ingalls observed that poor hygiene and nutrition were common to both subdural hematoma patients and those with Vitamin C deficiency. The weakening of tissues associated with scurvy was thought to disrupt healing in the veins bridging the dura, thus leading to chronic subdural hematoma. This theory did not persist for very long, however, as other researchers were quick to point out the possibility that both a poor diet and traumatic head injury could occur as independent results of parental mistreatment.

The greatest advances in the identification of the Shaken Baby Syndrome came with the emergence of radiology as a medical specialty. Foremost among the many monumental studies in the 1940s and 1950s, was the work done by the pediatric radiologist, John Caffey. Like so many of his predecessors in the history of Shaken Baby Syndrome, Caffey joined his medical and social interests with great success. His humanitarian career included work with the Red Cross in Serbia and Poland, as well as efforts in the Russian Unit of the American Relief Administration at the end of WWI.

Caffey's contemporaries remembered him best for his inquisitive attitude. An attending physician at the time of his internships recounted that, "he was skeptical at the explanations given for many clinical events . . . and asked many embarrassing questions" (Silverman, 1994). Indeed, Caffey earned his position as chief of radiology at Babies' Hospital of New York only after complaining of the time wasted by incompetent radiologists–within earshot of the chair of the department of pediatrics. Perhaps it was this dissatisfaction with conventional wisdom that enabled him to make the discoveries that he did.

In 1946, Caffey published the landmark article "Multiple fractures in the long bones of infants suffering from chronic subdural hematoma" (Caffey, 1946). In this report, he described the cases of six children with subdural hematoma, among which there were 23 long bone fractures and a uniform absence of a history of trauma. Caffey noted that, although the traumatic theory of the causation of subdural hematoma had been almost universally accepted, it was possible that no history of trauma would be reported. This seemed acceptable, due to the possible delay between an accident and the onset of symptoms. Caffey went on to point out that the same could *not* be said of long bone fractures. The clinical signs of long bone fractures usually appeared immediately, and the causal relationship between traumatic force and damage to the bone was clear. While he noted this fact with suspicion, Caffey stopped short of attributing the cause of this trauma to parental abuse. Caffey concluded, that in children who have subdural hematomas, we should look for fractures, and conversely, when we see children with fractures, we should look for subdural hematomas. The medical evaluation of abusive trauma was born.

In 1968, the neurosurgeon Ommaya set the stage for what would be Caffey's next historic revelation four years later. He showed that subdural hemorrhage could be caused by rotational displacement alone. Using rhesus monkeys, Ommaya was able to produce subdural hematoma by whiplash injury *without* impact. This set the stage for John Caffey's 1972 article, "On the theory and practice of shaking infants" (Caffey, 1972). In this report, he described 27 examples of children with subdural hematoma who had received whiplash shaking; there was no history of trauma in any of these children. Caffey was characterized his "Whiplash Shaken Infant Syndrome" as "The whiplash shakings of infants and younger children (which) are precarious, pervasive, prevalent, and pernicious practices which can be observed whenever parents, parent substitutes, infants, and small children congregate" (Caffey, 1972).

Of Caffey's 27 cases, 15 were found to be attributed to a nurse, Virginia Jaspers, who was employed to care for these infants. Her story was told in *Newsweek Magazine* in 1956, explaining that, "[t] he brutal and tragic career of nurse Virginia Jaspers is tied to her massive physical traits. She is an ungainly six feet, weights 220 pounds, and has a 52-inch waist. Police conclude that she probably had no idea of the strength of her cruelly big arms and hands." And how did she injure these children? The story is eerily familiar: "That evening Abby Kaspinov, 11 days old, didn't want to take her formula. Exasperated, the nurse picked her up and gave her a good shaking. ('It was all uncontrollable . . . I don't know why I did it')" (*Newsweek*, 1956).

Based largely on the tale of Virginia Jaspers, Caffey delineated the Whiplash Shaken Infant Syndrome. Since 1972, we have broadened Caffey's Syndrome to include other forms of abusive head trauma in addition to shaking. Today's Shaken Baby Syndrome has seen a shift in the demographics of the perpetrators, with changes in the pattern of child care and the family unit that have allowed the baby's father and the mother's boyfriend to emerge as significant perpetrators, and the father as the principal perpetrator. Yet Caffey's warning still rings true:

Hear ye good parents to my words true and plain
when you are shaking your baby, you could be bruising his brain,
so save the limbs, the brain and even the life of your tot
by shaking him never, never and not. (1972)

REFERENCES

Caffey, J. (1946). Multiple fractures in the long bones of infants suffering from chronic subdural hematoma. *American Journal of Roentgenology, 56*, 163-173.

Caffey, J. (1972). On the theory and practice of shaking infants. *American Journal of Diseases of Children, 124*, 161-169.

Currier, R. D., & Currier, M. M. (1991). James Parkinson: On child abuse and other things. *Archives of Neurology, 48*, 95-97.

Green, M. A. (1973). Dr. Scattergood's casebooks. *The Practitioner, 211*, 679-684.

Holt, L. (1933). *Holt's diseases of infancy and childhood* (10th ed.). New York: Appleton-Century Crofts.

Ingalls, T. H. (1936). The role of scurvy in the etiology of chronic subdural hematoma. *New England Journal of Medicine, 215*, 1279-1281.

Ingraham, F., & Heyl, H. (1939). Subdural hematoma in infancy and childhood. *Journal of the American Medical Association, 113*, 198-204.

Newsweek (1956). *48*, 90.

Nostradamus (1982). *The complete works of Nostradamus*. Oyster Bay, New York: Nostradamus, Inc.

Ommaya, A. K. (1968). Whiplash injury and brain damage. *Journal of the American Medical Association, 204*, 285-289.

Packard, F. (1926). *Life and time of Ambroise Pare*. 2nd ed. New York: Paul N. Hoeber.

Paré, A. (1960). *Case reports and autopsy records of Ambroise Paré*. Springfield, IL: Thomas.

Parkinson, J. (1800). *The villager's friend & physician*. London: H. D. Symonds.

Preyer, W. (1907). *Mental development in the child*. New York: D. Appleton and Co.

Silverman, F. (1972). Unrecognized trauma in infants, the battered child syndrome, and the syndrome of Ambroise Tardieu. *Radiology, 104*, 347-353.

Sherwood, D. (1930). Chronic subdural hematoma in infants. *American Journal of Diseases of Children, 39*, 980.

Simpson, D. (1997). Pare as a neurosurgeon. *Australian & New Zealand Journal of Surgery, 67*, 540-6.

Wiglesworth, J. (1892). Remarks on the pathology of so-called pachymeningitis interna haemorrhagica. *Brain, 15*, 431-436.

Yahr, M. D. (1978). A physician for all seasons. *Archives of Neurology, 35*, 185-188.

Chapter Three

The Epidemiology, Clinical Characteristics and Public Health Implications of Shaken Baby Syndrome

Halim Hennes
Narendra Kini
Vincent J. Palusci

SUMMARY. The sociodemographic characteristics of the Shaken Baby are discussed, as well as common risk factors found among infants, families and perpetrators. The initial history and physical examination findings in SBS are reviewed and the need for early dentification and treatment is highlighted. We then discuss the epidemiology of Shaken Baby Syndrome (SBS), including a review of its definitions, governmental reporting systems and public health implications. Little is known regarding specific incidence and prevalence of SBS because it has only recently been identified in vital statistics, health, law enforcement and social welfare data systems in the US. The public health implications of SBS are reviewed based on long-term health consequences of SBS and societal costs associated with traumatic brain injury in children. Future epidemiologic research should be directed at improved recording of SBS fatality, monitoring of SBS non-fatalities and evaluating primary and secondary prevention activities. *[Article copies available for a fee from The Haworth Document Delivery Service:*

[Haworth co-indexing entry note]: "The Epidemiology, Clinical Characteristics and Public Health Implications of Shaken Baby Syndrome." Hennes, Halim, Narendra Kini, and Vincent J. Palusci. Co-published simultaneously in *Journal of Aggression, Maltreatment & Trauma* (The Haworth Maltreatment & Trauma Press, an imprint of The Haworth Press, Inc.) Vol. 5, No. 1(#9), 2001, pp. 19-40; and: *The Shaken Baby Syndrome: A Multidisciplinary Approach* (ed: Stephen Lazoritz, and Vincent J. Palusci) The Haworth Maltreatment & Trauma Press, an imprint of The Haworth Press, Inc., 2001, pp. 19-40. Single or multiple copies of this article are available for a fee from The Haworth Document Delivery Service [1-800-342-9678, 9:00 a.m. - 5:00 p.m. (EST). E-mail address: getinfo@haworthpressinc.com].

19

1-800-342-9678. E-mail address: <getinfo@haworthpressinc.com> Website: <http://www.HaworthPress.com> © 2001 by The Haworth Press, Inc. All rights reserved.]

KEYWORDS. Abuse, head trauma, subdural hemorrhage, skull fracture, victim, family, perpetrator, prevalence, public health

INTRODUCTION

Child abuse has been known and well documented for centuries; unfortunately it only gained public attention about a century ago. The first organized society addressing child abuse was established in New York in 1874. The Society for the Prevention of Cruelty to Children was created to protect children from abusive acts (Lazoritz, 1990). By the mid 1960s, all states passed laws requiring reporting of child abuse and established various programs to help victims and families. Almost 10 years later in 1974, the Child Abuse Prevention and Treatment Act (CAPTA) was passed. The act required mandatory reporting of abuse in every state by designated personnel, including health care providers, educators, social workers, and law enforcement personnel. CAPTA (Public Law 104-235, section 111; 42USC5106G) defines child abuse and neglect as any recent act or failure to act: Resulting in imminent risk or serious harm, death, serious physical or emotional harm, sexual abuse or exploitation of a child under the age of 18 by a parent or caretaker.

Caffey made the first reference to the shaken baby syndrome in 1946. He described a group of children with chronic subdural hematomas and associated fractures in various stages of healing (Caffey, 1946). In 1974 he published the first landmark report describing the association between shaking the child and the development of intracranial and ocular hemorrhage (Caffey, 1974). Numerous reports examining various epidemiologic, clinical, and diagnostic aspects of shaken baby syndrome have been published since Caffey's first report (Alexander, Sato, Smith, & Bennett, 1990; Baron & Zanga, 1996; Baum & Bulpitt, 1970; Benzel & Hadden, 1989; Bergman, Larson, & Muller, 1986; Billmire & Myers, 1985; Budenz, Farber, Mirchandani, Park, & Rorke, 1994; Duhaime et al., 1987; Duhaime, Christian, Rorke, & Zimmerman, 1998; Jason, 1983; Jenny, Hymel, Ritzen, Reinert, & Hay, 1999; Kaplun & Reich, 1976; Lazoritz, Baldwin, & Kini, 1997; Ludwig & Warman, 1984; Sills, Thomas, & Rosenbloom, 1977; Starling, Holden, & Jenny, 1995; Wang & Daro, 1998). Several of these reports examined the biomechanics of injury in shaken baby syndrome and provided insight into differentiating accidental from non-accidental head trauma (Duhaime et al., 1987; Duhaime et al., 1992; Duhaime et al., 1998; Goldstein, Kelly, Bruton, & Cox, 1993; Hahn, Raimondi, McLore, & Yamanouchi, 1983). With this wealth of knowledge one would think that we are able to readily identify these children when they first present to a health care facility. However, Jenny et al. (1999) recently identified that nearly 30% of the children with shaken baby syndrome were misdiagnosed when their caretaker sought medical care for the first time. The authors concluded that early identification of these infants and toddlers could reduce morbidity and mortality. Other investigators also reported similar results (Benzel & Hadden, 1989; Conway, 1998). Therefore, it appears that the diagnosis of non-accidental head injury in infants and toddlers can be difficult. It is suggested that an inaccurate history by the caretaker and non-specific presenting symptoms play a major role in the delayed diagnosis of victims of shaken baby syndrome (Duhaime et al., 1987; Goldstein et al., 1993; Jenny et al., 1999; Lazoritz et al., 1997). In this review we will discuss the epidemiologic characteristics, clinical characteristics and public health implications of the shaken baby syndrome.

EPIDEMIOLOGY

In 1997, over 3 million reports of child maltreatment were made to child protective agencies across the United States. This figure represents an increase of 1.7% over the number reported in 1996. Between 1988 and 1997, child abuse reporting levels have increased nearly 41% (US DHHS, 1999). This increase in reporting is attributed to greater public awareness of child maltreatment and changes in report collection practice by authorities. At the present time the incidence of child maltreatment is estimated to be 47 per 1000 children. Fatalities among maltreated children have increased 34% since 1988, and it is currently estimated that three or more children die each day as a result (US DHHS, 1999). Although data on the death rate from child maltreatment is available, questions have been raised regarding its accuracy, and specific data on the incidence of shaken baby syndrome is not known (Ewigman, 1993; Herman-Giddens et al., 1999; Spivak, 1998). ICD-10 as proposed recommends expanded codes for "shaking" and inflicted head trauma (US DHHS, 1998).

Most clinical studies of child maltreatment and Shaken Baby Syndrome attempt to address the factors associated with the victim, perpetrator and the family (Table 1). Some have also looked at geographic differences and at timing and triggers as a cause for shaking.

TABLE 1. Common risk factors for Shaken Baby Syndrome

Perpetrator

    Males (60-70%)
    Mother boyfriend (34%)
    Baby sitter (4-30%)
    Mother (6.5%)

Family

    Single parent
    Maternal age (less than 18 years)
    Maternal education (did not complete high school)
    Poor socioeconomic status (welfare recipients)
    Known to social service

Victim

    Age (less than one year)
    Male infants
    Prematurity / Low birth weight
    No prenatal care

THE PERPETRATOR

The relationship of the perpetrator to the child is frequently unavailable from the death certificate or hospital medical records. A limited number of studies linking death certificate, social service reports, and police records have been published over the past three decades. Early studies suggested that women are the perpetrators in more than 50% of fatal child abuse cases (Klein & Stern, 1971; Ludwig & Warman, 1984). Bergman et al. (1986) found that the father, stepfather, and mothers' boyfriends were the most common perpetrators in cases of severe or fatal child abuse. More recent studies confirmed this finding (Kunz & Bahr, 1996; Starling et al., 1995). Margolin (1992) in a landmark study on the role of mothers' boyfriend in child abuse reported that the boyfriend was the perpetrator in 64% of the cases. Starling et al. (1995) noted that men are 2.2 times more likely the perpetrators in cases of abusive head trauma. Lazoritz et al. (1997) reported that in 71 cases of shaken baby syndrome the father was the perpetrator in 33% and the mothers' boyfriend in 20% of the cases. The authors noted that the mother was the perpetrator in 6.5% of the cases. Schlosser, Pierpont, and Poertner (1992) noted that stepfathers and boyfriends were more likely to fatally abuse their children, causing over 70% of child fatalities in Kansas during 1983 to 1988. Among child fatalities measured by child death review teams in Michigan, 23 of 40 perpetrators of child beatings were noted to be male, including 10 biologic fathers and 10 maternal boyfriends. Among these child beatings and shakings, two were less than one month of age, 12 were one month to one year of age, and 14 were one to four years (MPHI, 1999).

Recent attention has been focused on baby-sitters as possible perpetrators in cases of fatal child abuse. With more than 60% of the mothers working outside the home, childcare is often provided by unrelated babysitters. Three studies reported that baby-sitters were the perpetrators in 4-30% of child abuse cases (Kunz & Bahr, 1996; Margolin, 1992; Starling et al., 1995). In 1997, child maltreatment in daycare centers, foster homes and other institutional care settings represented only 3% of all confirmed cases of child maltreatment (US DHHS, 1999; Wang & Daro, 1998). The relationship of the perpetrator appears to change with the child's age; mothers are the most likely perpetrator during the first week of life and often the father or stepfather after the first week of life (Duhaime et al., 1998; Jason, 1983; Kaplun & Reich, 1976; Overpeck, Brenner, Trumple, Trifiletti, & Berendes, 1998; Starling et al., 1995).

THE FAMILY

According to the U.S. Department of Human Health Services statistics, in 1996 nearly 77% of the perpetrators were the parents and 11% were relatives (US DHHS, 1999). Parental involvement in child abuse is a frightening notion for clinicians, yet several familial risk factors strongly associated with infant homicide. Single parent families have a well-documented positive association with child abuse (NCPCA, 1998). Maternal age and education are also strong risk factors in infant homicide. Goldstein et al. (1993) compared the family characteristics of infants with inflicted and accidental head trauma admitted to a pediatric intensive unit over a two-year period. The authors found a higher frequency of inflicted head trauma among single parents younger than 18 years of age, did not complete high school, receiving welfare and known to social services and child protection agencies. Overpeck et al. (1998) noted that the highest risk was associated with maternal education of less than 12 years (relative risk 6.8) followed by maternal age less than 15 years (relative risk 6.8). Among single mothers the boyfriend is the most frequently implicated perpetrator (Starling et al., 1995). Margolin (1992) explored the role of the boyfriend as a perpetrator in a cohort of 982 mothers from a single county. Although the mother's boyfriends, in this cohort, performed 1.75% of the total childcare hours, they were responsible for 64% of the abuse cases. Alcohol and drug abuse, past history of child abuse, and partner or spouse abuse are also well-documented risk factors (Conway, 1998; Dykes, 1986).

Family characteristics were also reviewed in NIS-3. Physical abuse was significantly higher among children in the lowest income levels (< $15,000 per year), which was nearly 2.25 times that for children in the middle-income group and almost 16 times the incidence rate for children in the highest income group (> $30,000 per year). Families with less than $15,000 per year income were 60 times more likely to die from maltreatment and over 22 times more likely to die from neglect under the Harm Standard. Given uncertainty as to variation of reporting from mandated professionals (Saulsbury & Campbell, 1985), this may reflect ascertainment bias in reporting or diagnosis which results in more children from poor families being found to suffer from fatal child abuse or SBS than among children from more affluent families (Brenner, Fischer, & Mann-Gray, 1989).

Family structure differences were noted for physical abuse under the NIS-3 Harms Standard with a disproportionate incidence of physical abuse among children in father-only households with a > 2.6 higher incidence than children living with both their parents (Table 2). Children in mother-only families were not abused at a rate different from those in two-parent households. Among families with four or more children, there was a 25% increase in physical abuse resulting in harm (Sedlak & Broadhurst, 1996). In a study of risk factors associated with multiple types of abuse in New York, Brown, Cohen, Johnson, and Salzinger (1998) noted that physical child abuse was significantly related to demographic risk factors such as low maternal education (odds ratio 2.6), low religious attendance (OR 2.2), maternal youth (OR 3.5), single parenting (OR 2.2), and receiving welfare (OR 3.7). Familial risk factors such as early separation from mother (OR 4.1), maternal dissatisfaction (OR 2.4), serious maternal illness (OR 2.6), and maternal sociopathy (OR 4.9) were also identified.

TABLE 2. Estimates of risks (odds ratio) for family charateristics

Study	Year(s)	Study Population	Income	Household	Fam Size
DHHS, 1999	1997	CPS fatality reports	NA	Mothers only, OR 1.8	NA
Brown, 1998	1975-1992	New York families in 2 counties, physical abuse	"Welfare" OR 3.7	Single parent OR 2.2	3+ children OR 3.21
Sedlak, 1996	1993	U.S. estimate, 42 counties	<$15,000 OR 22.0	Fathers only, OR 2.7	4+ children
Jason, 1982	1975-9	Georgia physical abuse reports	"Poor" OR 4.0	NA	NA

OR = odds ratio; NA = not available

THE VICTIM

In 1997, over 1 million children were confirmed by child protective services as victims of child maltreatment (US DHHS, 1999). In general, young children are at high risk for loss of life from child maltreatment. From 1995 to 1997, nearly 78% of the victims were under five years of age and 38% were under one year (Wang & Daro, 1998). The NIS-3 reported that significant gender differences were present for child maltreatment under the "Harm Standard" in 1993 (Table 3). The relative risk for males compared to females was 4.0 for fatality. Significant age differences also emerged in the incidence of overall maltreatment, abuse and neglect under the Harm Standard. Physical abuse was found to be significantly higher among 12-14 year olds than among children ages zero to two years (relative risk 2.5) while most fatal abuse occurred under age five. No differences were noted among racial categories (Sedlak & Broadhurst, 1996).

Differences based on victim age and gender, have been noted, particularly with the gender of the victim (male) and offender (male among infant victims, female among neonates) in FBI Uniform Crime Reports. Homicide rates for

TABLE 3. Estimates of relative risks for child characteristics associated with child maltreatment

Study	Year(s)	Study Population	Gender	Age	Race/Other
DHHS, 1999	1997	U.S. CPS reports	Males OR 1.33	0-3 years, OR 3.1 compared to all children	"African-American" RR 20 compared to "white"
Sedlak, 1996	1993	U.S. estimate, 42 counties, fatalities	Males OR 4.0	12-14 yrs compared to 0-2 years OR 2.5	"numbers too small to reliably estimate"
Starling, 1995	1982-1994	Colorado children's hospital, AHT	Males OR 1.2	NA	NA
Schloesser, 1992	1983-8	Kansas fatalities	Female OR 1.7	<2 yrs OR 5.0	LBW (<5.5 lbs) OR 2.0
Fingerhut, 1989	1900-85	U.S. Death certificates, homicides, ages 1-4	Males> females	NA	Excess Black deaths, 12-16% compared to W
Jason, 1983	1976-9	FBI UCR child homicide reports	Male OR 1.3	NA	NA

NA = not applicable / not available   NS = no significant findings neonates (1.3/100,000) and infants (4.3/100,000) per year were reported. Males outnumbered females in reports of physical abuse (25,269 to 23,495) in the US in 1997 (ACYF-DHHS, 1999). Most child fatalities from child maltreatment occurred in the zero to three age group (244 out of 317 total fatalities). Males outnumbered females by 138 to 106.

Victims of shaken baby syndrome are usually young children under one year of age with a mean age between five and six months, and children of poorly educated parents younger than 18 years of age, poor socioeconomic background, minority ethnic groups in particular African Americans and American Indians are at higher risk for maltreatment (Dykes, 1986; NCPCA, 1998; Simons, Downs, Hurster, & Archer, 1996). Males, children born prematurely, higher birth order, and those born to mothers who had no prenatal care also appear to be at a higher risk (Simons et al., 1996).

In reviewing triggers for physical abuse or shaking, Michigan death review teams noted that 15 children were "crying," two were disobedient, three had feeding difficulty, and seven had other issues including toilet training (MPHI, 1999). No studies report increased incidence in particular seasons or times of the year, although anecdotal reports suggest holidays, snowstorms and the end of the school year are changes in reports to Child Protective Services (Kim Mendels, personal communication) or vital statistics data (Herman-Giddens et al., 1999). Brewster et al. (1998) noted that among infant maltreatment deaths, infant victim crying was noted in 58% and the child was alone with the caretaker or perpetrator in 86%, on the weekend 47%, or at around noon in the home (71%) among the sample of families in the United States Air Force.

No significant differences were noted among families in urban, rural or suburban areas regarding most forms of child maltreatment, including physical abuse resulting in serious harm in NIS-3. Homicides among older children have been noted to occur more frequently in urban areas based on FBI UCR statistics. Trends have been noted regarding neglect in that more neglect has been identified in rural and urban centers compared to suburban areas. U.S. death certificates identify areas of increased child homicide among 1-4 year-olds in the southwest U.S. with rates greater than 26 per 100,000 compared to NY and Illinois with rates < 17.2 per 100,000 (Fingerhut, 1989). Any geographic or race/ethnicity factors associated with child maltreatment disappear when adjusted for family income (Sedlak & Broadhurst, 1996). Secondary analysis of NIS-2 data suggests that professional response to SBS is related to local and regional practice standards in child welfare (Ards & Harrell, 1993). Local trends of race/ethnicity associated with SBS have also been reported in Michigan (Brenner et al., 1989).

CLINICAL CHARACTERISTICS

The characteristic physical findings in shaken baby syndrome include retinal hemorrhage, subdural and or subarachnoid hemorrhages in the absence of external trauma. These injuries may result when the infant is held by the chest, shoulder, or extremity and vigorously shaken (Caffey, 1974; Duhaime et al., 1987). The generated acceleration and deceleration forces can shear the intracranial bridging veins and incompletely myelinated cortical nerves. Another contributing factor may be slamming the infant against a soft surface like a bed or sofa. The sudden deceleration of the head generates a tremendous force on delicate intracranial structure without external damage (Duhaime et al., 1987). As a result of these significant injuries shaken baby syndrome has a very high morbidity and mortality rates especially in young infants less than six months of age (Billmire & Myers, 1985).

THE PRESENTING SYMPTOMS

The initial presentation of children with shaken baby syndrome is frequently non-specific, with irritability, poor feeding, and vomiting (Table 4). These symptoms may mimic other common diseases seen in young children with viral infection, colic, or feeding intolerance (Conway, 1998). In a review of shaken baby syndrome cases at our institution, the initial presenting symptoms were vomiting or irritability in 23% of the cases. Jenny et al. (1999) also noted that several factors were significantly missed in cases of abusive head trauma. These were age (younger than 180 days), race (more often in white children), family composition (where both parents lived with the child) and severity of symptoms at the initial visit. Therefore, identifying these children at the first encounter can be difficult or delayed. It is important that clinicians maintain a high index of suspicion when evaluating a young infant with

TABLE 4. Common presenting symptoms in children with Shaken Baby Syndrome

Upper respiratory infection
Vomiting
Diarrhea
Poor feeding
Irritability
Lethargy
Apnea
Seizure
History of minor trauma

non-specific symptoms especially when the history seems to be at odds with the physical findings.

THE HISTORY

The history is an important component in the evaluation of suspected child abuse. The use of a structured approach can simplify the process and make it more complete. Baron and Zanga (1996) suggested that using a standardized form would enhance the quality and quantity of the collected information. History should be obtained in a non-accusatory manner from all those accompanying the child and those who were in contact with the child when the event occurred. Each individual should be interviewed separately and caretakers at the scene should also be contacted. Obtaining the history from all individuals would allow for evaluating the consistency and timing of events. Activities immediately preceding the event such as colic, crying, feeding difficulties or toilet accidents must be recorded, as these kinds of activity may have been the precipitating event for abuse. Several investigators have reported that history not consistent with physical findings and even denial of abusive acts is common (Goldstein et al., 1993; Lazoritz et al., 1997). Lazoritz and colleagues noted that approximately 34% of caretakers denied any history of trauma and only 13% admitted to shaking the child. Parents reported a minor accidental injury more than 50% of the time.

As a result of advances in understanding the biomechanics of injuries, it is possible to correlate a pattern of trauma with the associated history and make a reasonable judgment as to whether the injury was accidental or not (Duhaime et al., 1992). Because the history given when children present for evaluation can be vague or misleading, knowledge of forces in witnessed accidental trauma and experimental models is very helpful. Any force that results in a rotation of the brain about its center will cause diffuse injury. Falls or other accidental head injuries usually result in low velocity, translational injury that is less damaging to the brain (Duhaime et al., 1998).

Recording when the event allegedly occurred and documenting any delay in seeking medical attention will allow for further evaluation by law enforcement and social services agencies in determining consistency of the history. A complete record of the past medical history, family and social history as well as developmental assessment is necessary as there is evidence in the literature that risk factors for abuse include low socioeconomic status, prematurity, large family size, young parents (less than age 19) and disability (Klein & Stern, 1971; Sills et al., 1977). Finally, evidence of previous social services evaluation should be sought, as there may be documentation of any of the above-mentioned risk factors and other circumstances that may not be available when the history is being obtained.

THE PHYSICAL EXAMINATION

The physical examination should be thorough and comprehensive. All findings should be clearly documented using detailed diagrams or photographs. Any lesions should be measured and their color described; photography can be useful (Ricci, 1991). Special attention should be directed toward vital signs because hypothermia, bradycardia and irregular respiration are associated with the intracranial injury seen in this syndrome. A meticulous search for external bruises and tenderness all over the body should be carried out, as there may have been previous trauma prior to the presenting event. The absence of external trauma to the head and neck is common with this form of abuse. Hemotypanum, cerebrospinal fluid rhinorrhea, otorrhea and Battle's sign are further clues to intracranial injury Kapklein & Mahadeo, 1997). Other general physical findings can be a pattern of skin marks or burns. It is possible that soft tissue injury including scalp hematomas will be evident only at autopsy (Alexander, Crabbe, Sato, Smith, & Bennett, 1990). Ocular findings are often present and may include orbital and lid ecchymoses, subconjunctival hemorrhage, anisocoria and dysconjugate eye movements. Retinal hemorrhages are found in up to 95% of patients. These are best visualized with mydriatic agents and may require the skills of a pediatric ophthalmologist to differentiate them from nonabusive or birth-related injury (Harcourt & Hopkins, 1971). In addition, retinal folds and traumatic retinoschisis have been described in the shaken baby syndrome (Massicotte, Folberg, Torczynski, Gilliland, & Luckenback, 1971). Retinal hemorrhages are not diagnostic of the shaken baby syndrome and cannot be dated accurately. They have been associated with papilledema, cardiopulmonary resuscitation and accidental trauma (Luerssen, 1991). They are commonly associated with vaginal delivery and usually resolve by the first month of life (Baum & Bulpitt, 1970). Other causes include sepsis, galactosemia, and subarachnoid hemorrhage.

THE LABORATORY AND IMAGING

The shaken infant may present with clotting dysfunction, which is reflective of a disseminated intravascular coagulopathy secondary to intracranial trauma (Hymel, Abshire, Luckey, & Jenny, 1997). There may be mild or moderate anemia as a result of bleeding into the cranial cavity. It should be noted that a lumbar tap done to evaluate for sepsis in these infants will yield bloody or xanthochromic fluid reflecting past intracranial injury (Ludwig & Warman, 1984). If there is a suspicion of raised intracranial pressure, a computed tomographic scan of the head should be obtained prior to the lumbar tap.

Long bone fractures should be suspected in the presence of extremity tenderness or swelling. Skeletal findings on x-ray may include metaphyseal fractures of the distal femur. Similarly, chest radiographs obtained to evaluate respiratory symptoms may reveal an old healing rib fractures that will further support the diagnosis of this syndrome. Skeletal survey and bone scan are both acceptable techniques for detecting subtle injury to the bony skeleton, the reliability of which depend on the age of the infant and skill of the radiographer. The presence of skull fractures is uncommon because the mechanism of intracranial trauma is tearing of veins or arteries as a result of the shaking force. When present, linear or diastatic fractures are more common than depressed skull fractures. It is common for a presumed mechanism of fall or impact to be offered as an explanation for this clinical or radiologic finding. The most consistent finding in this syndrome is the presence of a subdural hematoma on head computed tomography scan. Various series place the incidence of this finding between 38% and 100% of all cases. Additional findings are epidural hematoma, interhemispheric and subarachnoid hemorrhage, and cerebral contusions. Magnetic resonance imaging is useful in characterizing smaller extra-axial bleeds and defining cerebral contusions.

DIFFERENTIAL DIAGNOSIS

Several pathologic conditions such as coagulopathy, Osteogenesis Imperfecta and Glutaric Aciduria type 1 (GA-1) should be considered in the differential diagnosis of these infants. Familial or acquired coagulation disorders generally present with variable bruises, petechia and mucosal bleeding in addition to intracranial bleeding. In the case of Osteogenesis Imperfecta, other manifestations such as blue sclerae, joint hypermobility, hearing deficits, inadequate mineralization and dental defects provide clues to the diagnosis. GA-1 is characterized by developmental delay, disorders of tone and movement as well as evidence of cerebral atrophy. The integration of clinical findings with past medical and family history generally leads to an appropriate nonabusive diagnosis.

PUBLIC HEALTH IMPLICATIONS

Given the difficulties in estimating the true incidence of Shaken Baby Syndrome mortality and the true burden of non-fatal Shaken Baby Syndrome cases, it is difficult to estimate the real public health implications of this serious form of child physical abuse. While the burden of child homicide has been noted to be increasing with other external causes of child fatality, the specific contribution of Shaken Baby Syndrome has yet to be calculated (Christoffel, 1984). Once estimates of Shaken Baby Syndrome can be made, calculations of societal burden can be more precisely evaluated. Current burden in individual cases can be inferred from longitudinal case studies of victims, but reports to date have not addressed the specific financial burden of SBS to families, the medical system and society.

LONG-TERM MEDICAL BURDEN

Shaken baby syndrome is associated with a high incidence of mortality and neurologic morbidity in survivors. Published reports estimate that shaken baby syndrome accounted for 10% to 12% of all child maltreatment-related deaths. Approximately 25% of all shaken baby syndrome victims will die as a result of their injury (Jason, Guilliland, & Tyler, 1983). In those who survive, neurologic complications could affect as many as 57% (Goldstein et al., 1993). However, the presence and extent of injuries correlate poorly with the final outcome. These children may suffer severe motor deficits, seizures, developmental delay, and blindness. A NIH consensus panel concluded that identifying children at risk and recognizing the subtle historical and clinical findings that are noted in victims of this syndrome might help reduce morbidity and mortality. Brain injury is a serious public health problem affecting 100 per 100,000 persons and resulting in 52,000 annual deaths in the U.S. and resulting in lifelong impairment of 2.5 to 6.5 million individuals. While the majority of individuals affected were over five years of age, there was a "striking peak" in incidence in children age five years or younger. The Panel concluded that "Shaken Baby Syndrome results specifically in TBI and spinal cord injury and 10% of traumatic brain injury are the result of violence. Mild TBI is significantly underdiagnosed and the likely societal burden is therefore even greater" (p. 978). The Panel recommended cognitive and behavioral rehabilitation strategies for TBI victims, but prevention was thought to be of paramount importance (NIH, 1999).

Several case studies on the long-term outcome in infants with Shaken Baby Syndrome detail the devastating nature of the traumatic brain injury. Charts were reviewed from 25 shaken baby victims admitted to Children's Hospital of Michigan between 1979 and 1985. Four children died during hospitalization yielding a case fatality rate of 16%. Ten years after discharge, 10 of the 25 patients could be located, and among those survivors, two were noted to have cerebral palsy, three were noted to have epilepsy, one was in a persistent vegetative state, one required a VP shunt but had normal mentation, and three were described as "normal" (Fischer & Allasio, 1994). Of note, six of the 21 survivors had been sent back to the homes of abuse and four were reinjured. The authors concluded, "It appeared that most children's brains do not recover from the injuries of Shaken Baby Syndrome and only one of three babies discharged was normal on follow-up" (p. 698).

Bonnier, Nassogne, and Evrard (1995) reported on the 13 victims of Shaken Baby Syndrome, one of whom died after discharge from the hospital. Blindness (2), visual impairment (2), impaired head growth (4), epilepsy (4), hemiparesis (2), psychomotor retardation (9), psychiatric problems (6), mental retardation (11), and other learning disabilities (11) were noted among the 12 survivors. Six children with who apparently recovered "fully" after the shaking had physical manifestations 12 to 24 months after hospitalization.

In a case control study of 40 children ages zero to six years hospitalized for traumatic brain injury (TBI), 20 children with inflicted injuries were compared to 20 TBI children with non-inflicted injuries. Forty-five percent of the inflicted injury children were noted to have signs of pre-existing brain injury, including cerebral atrophy, subdural hygroma, and ex-vacuo ventriculomegaly. Subdural hematomas and seizures occurred significantly more often in children with inflicted TBI. Retinal hemorrhages were only identified in the inflicted TBI group. Glasgow Outcome Scales Scores indicated a significantly less favorable outcome after inflicted than non-inflicted traumatic brain injury and mental deficiency was present in 45% of the inflicted and only 5% of the non-inflicted TBI groups (Ewing-Cobbs et al., 1998). Early neurobehavioral mental outcomes were measured using children's orientation and amnesia test scores and Bailey Scales of Mental and Motor Scores on average 1.3 months after traumatic brain injury. Scores were corrected for prematurity, and Stanford Benet Intelligence Scale and McCarthy Scales of Children's Abilities Motor Scales were administered for older children. This suggests that among the approximately 12% of confirmed cases of physical child abuse in which traumatic brain injury occur have a more likely incidence of mental deficiency and prior injury than do the children with non-inflicted TBI.

In a survey of 100 children receiving early intervention services at a regional referral center in Grand Rapids, three children were noted to have child maltreatment as a cause for severe multiple impairment and four children were noted to have maltreatment as a cause for less severe impairment (Wolfe, Hwang, & Palusci, 1999). Premature birth and congenital malformations produced 16 and 75 cases respectively of disability among this early intervention population less than five years of age. It was suggested that, although child maltreatment causes some long-term impairment, the majority of severe or lesser impairment is not known to be the result of child abuse and neglect.

In a series of 84 infants ages two years of age and younger with the "Shaking Impact Syndrome" who were consecutively admitted to a single hospital between 1978 and 1988, 12 children died during hospitalization. Among the 14 surviving children who could be located on average nine years after injury, seven were severely disabled or vegetative, two were moderately disabled, and five had a good outcome. The authors concluded "the majority of children surviving the Shaking Impact Syndrome suffer major permanent morbidity and that acute factors predicting long-term outcome may help guide aggressiveness of care" (Duhaime, Christian, Moss, & Seidl, 1996, p. 296).

THE COST OF SBS

Although direct costs of medical services for SBS are not known, estimates of the societal cost of child abuse in the state of Michigan approximate $92 million (Caldwell, 1994). Caldwell states "the costs are hardest to calculate in the case of preventable infant mortality and death due to child abuse" (p. 28) and attempts to measure "the worth of human life" by using per capita income in the state of Michigan ($17,745 in 1990) and average lifetime participation in the labor force (33 years). This results in a calculation that "each fatality during the year will result in a person not earning over half a million in 1992 dollars" (p. 39) over their lifetime which results in a loss of tax revenue to the state of Michigan of approximately $30,000 per person. For the 16 child maltreatment deaths in 1990, the cost to the state of Michigan was "$430,000 in lost tax revenue." Costs associated with medical treatment of injuries are calculated assuming 3.2% of abused children require hospitalization for these injuries. This leads to approximately $4.64 million annually used for hospitalization and $350,000 used for outpatient treatment in Michigan alone. Special education costs were calculated for approximately 30% of abused children who have some type of language or cognitive impairment and the 50% of abused children who have difficulty in school including poor attendance and misconduct and the approximately 22% of abused children who have a learning disorder. This resulted in approximately $6.5 million for special education delivered to child maltreatment victims in 1992. Additional costs were incurred for the juvenile justice system, child protective system and foster care placement. Psychological care adds an additional $16 million annually. It is unclear what percentage of these costs is related specifically to Shaken Baby Syndrome. Based on a conservative estimate that SBS comprises 10% of all serious physical abuse, SBS-related services cost society a minimum $5-10 million annually, given that most SBS victims require hospitalization, mental health, developmental and other long-term services. This calculation does not include lost earnings or tax revenues.

PREVENTION

Several prevention activities have been undertaken to begin to address child maltreatment and SBS. Public and private prevention efforts have only begun to address public information regarding shaking and its devastating impact on infants. Given the factors identified in Shaken Baby Syndrome and maltreatment fatalities, several approaches may be possible as primary or secondary prevention activities. While materials such as "Don't Shake the Baby" have been made commercially available, their effectiveness has only begun to be evaluated (Showers, 1998). Kotch, Browne, Dufort, Winsor, and Catellier (1999) stressed the need to address predisposing risk factors soon after birth such as maternal depression, lack of education, substance abuse, and need for financial assistance but did not address the outcomes of such programs. Home visitation programs based on the Hawaii model of professional visitors have been studied in several areas and have shown dramatic reductions in overall child abuse, but their application to SBS and serious physical abuse in fatality has not been addressed (Olds, 1992).

Yet families want to participate in preventing child abuse. Daro (1999) performed a telephone survey of 1250 randomly selected adults across the country regarding parenting practice and their attitudes toward parenting behaviors in 1998. Seventy-three percent of all parents surveyed reported feeling they could do a lot to prevent child abuse. Nine percent of all parents with children under age 18 living at home surveyed reported that they received home visitation services at the time one or more of their children were born, and 75% of these parents were satisfied regarding this assistance. Additionally, 27% of parents requested out-of-home nursery or daycare services for their infant, and 14% sought support groups for new mothers. No specific comments were addressed to Shaken Baby Syndrome prevention.

FUTURE RESEARCH NEEDS

While significant strides have been made in the identification, diagnosis, reporting and treatment of child maltreatment and Shaken Baby Syndrome, Finkelhor (1999) suggests that "the compilation and monitoring of good epidemiologic data on the problem and real experimental studies to test the efficacy of remedies and practices" (p. 973) are needed. Significant impact from technology in the identification, treatment and prevention of Shaken Baby Syndrome is anticipated and improvements can also be made in the treatment of violence itself. "Scientific evaluation is an important criterion for guiding policy" and "child advocacy practice needs to accept a scientific paradigm in the establishment and operation of data systems, record keeping systems, internal feedback systems, and following of long-term outcomes" (Finkelhor, 1999, p. 974). Improved use of administrative data systems offer promise for child maltreatment research in large populations (Drake & Jonson-Reid, 1999), and mixed designs may be needed to analyze multi-factorial problems such as child maltreatment (Bertolli, Morgenstern, & Sorenson, 1995).

We need to accurately identify and properly report Shaken Baby Syndrome as a unique form of abusive head trauma. We need to specifically monitor fatal SBS cases to ascertain mortality and case-fatality rates. Death review teams can add significant information about children who die in a community, yet near-fatality and morbidity of SBS also need to be determined before the public health burden can be quantitatively estimated. Statewide projects such as those in Michigan funded by the Children's Trust Fund have the potential to collect data beyond death certificate information and child abuse reports (Teri Covington, personal communication). Longitudinal studies in child abuse and neglect such as the LONGSCAN study currently underway in several communities can prospectively identify the incidence and burden of Shaken Baby Syndrome in large populations. Until such estimation can be made, the value of primary and secondary prevention programs remains unknown.

CONCLUSIONS

Based on the information available regarding Shaken Baby Syndrome, there are several conclusions that can be reached regarding the epidemiology of this devastating condition:

1. Significant controversy exists regarding definition of Shaken Baby Syndrome, with particular emphasis on the necessity for impact. Current ICD-9 and E-codes are often not used for coding of Shaken Baby Syndrome on death certificates or hospital records. ICD-10 offers specific shaken baby coding with more delineation of specific abusive injuries.
2. A minimum of 1000 serious SBS cases occur annually in the US, based on estimates of child abuse and traumatic brain injury. The incidence of non-fatal SBS as a cause for illness and disability cannot be estimated. SBS contributes significant societal burden through lost income, utilization of special education services, medical and mental health services,

and results in a prevalence of approximately 2,500 to 5,000 cases of brain injured children in the United States.

3. Little is known regarding the benefit of primary prevention efforts addressing Shaken Baby Syndrome. Home visitation has been shown to be helpful in prevention of child abuse and neglect, but prevention of fatality and SBS has not been demonstrated to be successful in primary prevention despite availability of commercial prevention products. Families have expressed interest in home visiting programs and support groups.

4. It is unclear whether secondary prevention activities addressing risk factors associated with SBS can be successful. Family income, child and perpetrator gender and caretaker relationship in family settings are not easily amenable to prevention. Financial assistance or daycare services could lessen putative triggers. Excluding unrelated adults caregivers would affect only a fraction of cases.

5. Physicians and other health care providers should maintain a high index of suspicion when evaluating a young infant with subtle clinical findings. In these situations, detailed information of the family structure, care taker, and parental stress should be obtained. Early identification of children at risk may improve their outcome by minimizing the delay in diagnosis and optimizing the institution of appropriate therapy.

REFERENCES

Administration for Children, Youth and Families, US Dept Health and Human Services. (1992). *Child abuse and neglect: A shared community concern.* Washington DC: DHHS Publication (ACF) 92-30531.

Alexander, R., Crabbe, L., Sato, Y., Smith, W., & Bennett, T. (1990). Serial abuse in children who are shaken. *American Journal of Diseases in Children, 144,* 58-60.

Alexander, R., Sato, Y., Smith, W., & Bennett, T. (1990). Incidence of impact trauma with cranial injuries ascribed to shaking. *American Journal of Diseases in Children, 144,* 724-726.

Ards, S., & Harrell, A. (1993). Reporting of child maltreatment: A secondary analysis of the national incidence surveys. *Child Abuse & Neglect, 17,* 337-344.

Baron, M.E., & Zanga, J.R. (1996). Child abuse: A model for the use of structured clinical forms. *Pediatrics, 98,* 429-433.

Baum, J.D., & Bulpitt, C.J. (1970). Retinal and conjunctival haemorrhage in the newborn. *Archives of Diseases in Childhood, 45*(241), 344-349.

Benzel, E.C., & Hadden, T.A. (1989). Neurologic manifestations of child abuse. *Southern Medical Journal, 82,* 1347-1351.

Bergman, A., Larson, R., & Muller, B. (1986). Changing spectrum of serious child abuse. *Pediatrics, 77,* 113-116.

Bertolli, J., Morgenstern, H., & Sorenson, S.B. (1995). Estimating the occurrence of child maltreatment and risk factor effects: Benefits of a mixed-design strategy in epidemiologic research. *Child Abuse & Neglect, 19,* 1007-1016.

Billmire, M.G., & Myers, P.A. (1985). Serious head injury in infants: Accidents or abuse? *Pediatrics, 75*, 340-342.

Bonnier, C., Nassogne, M.C., & Evrard, P. (1995). Outcome and prognosis of whiplash shaken infant syndrome: Late consequences after a symptom-free survival. *Developmental Medicine and Child Neurology, 37*, 943-956.

Brenner, S.L., Fischer, H., & Mann-Gray, H. (1989). Race and the shaken baby syndrome. *Journal of the National Medical Association, 81*, 183-184.

Brewster, A.L., Nelson, J.P., Hymel, K.P., Colby, D.R., Lucas, D.R., McCanne, T.R., & Milner, J.S. (1998). Victim, perpetrator, family and incident characteristics of 32 infant maltreatment deaths in the United States Air Force. *Child Abuse & Neglect, 22*, 91-101.

Brown, J., Cohen, P., Johnson, J.G., & Salzinger, S. (1998). A longitudinal analysis of risk factors for child maltreatment: Findings of a 17-year prospective study of officially recorded and self-reported child abuse and neglect. *Child Abuse & Neglect, 22*, 1065-1078.

Budenz, D.L., Farber, M.G., Mirchandani, H.G., Park, H., & Rorke, L.B. (1994). Ocular and optic nerve hemorrhages in abused infants with intracranial injuries. *Ophthalmology, 101*(3), 559-565.

Caffey, J. (1946). Multiple fractures of the long bones of infants suffering from chronic subdural hematoma. *American Journal of Roentgenology, 56*, 163-173.

Caffey, J. (1974). The whiplash shaken infant syndrome: Manual shaking by the extremities with whiplash-induced intracranial and intraocular bleeding, linked with residual permanent brain damage and mental retardation. *Pediatrics, 54*, 369-403.

Caldwell, R. (1994). *The 1992 cost of child abuse in Michigan.* East Lansing: MSU.

Christoffel, K.K. (1984). Homicide in childhood: A public health problem in need of attention. *American Journal of Public Health, 74*, 68-70.

Conway, E. (1998). Nonaccidental head injury in infants: The shaken baby syndrome revisited. *Pediatric Annals, 27*, 677-690.

Daro, D. (1999). Public Opinion and behaviors regarding child abuse prevention: 1998 Survey. Prevent Child Abuse America.

Drake, B., & Jonson-Reid, M. (1999). Some thoughts on the increasing use of administrative data in child maltreatment research. *Child Maltreatment, 4*, 308-315.

Duhaime, A.C., Allario, A.J., Lewander, W.J., Schut, L., Sutton, L.N., Seidl, T.S., Nudelman, S., Budenz, D., Hertle, R., & Tsiaras, W. (1992). The shaken baby syndrome. Head injury in very young children: Mechanisms, injury types, and ophthalmologic findings in 100 hospitalized patients younger than 2 years of age. *Pediatrics, 90*, 179-185.

Duhaime, A.C., Christian, C., Moss, E., & Seidl, T. (1996). Long-term outcome in infants with the shaking impact syndrome. *Pediatric Neurosurgery, 24*, 292-298.

Duhaime, A.C., Christian, C.W., Rorke, L.B., & Zimmerman, R.A. (1998). Nonaccidental head injury in infants. The 'Shaken-Baby Syndrome.' *New England Journal of Medicine, 338*, 1822-1829

Duhaime, A.C., Gennarelli, T.A., Thibault, L.E., Bruce, D.A., Margulies, S.S., & Wiser, R. (1987). The shaken baby syndrome. A clinical, pathological, and biomechanical study. *Journal of Neurosurgery, 66*(3), 409-415.

Dykes, L.J. (1986). The whiplash shaken infant syndrome: What has been learned? *Child Abuse and Neglect, 10,* 211-221.

Ewigman, B., Kivlahan, C., & Land, G. (1993). The Missouri child fatality study: Underreporting of maltreatment fatalities among children younger than 5 years of age, 1983 through 1986. *Pediatrics, 91,* 330-337.

Ewing-Cobbs, L., Kramer, L., Prasad, M., Canales, D.N., Louis, P.T., Fletcher, J.M., Vollero, H., Landry, S.H., & Cheung, K. (1998). Neuroimaging, physical and developmental findings after inflicted and non-inflicted brain injury in young children. *Pediatrics, 102,* 300-307.

Fingerhut, L.A. (1989). *Trends and current status in childhood mortality, U.S. 1900-1985.* Washington, DC: Dept of Health and Human Services (PHS) 89-1410.

Finkelhor, D. (1999). The science: Working toward the elimination of child maltreatment. *Child Abuse & Neglect, 23*(10), 969-974.

Fischer, H., & Allasio, D. (1994). Permanently damaged: Long-term followup of shaken babies. *Clinical Pediatrics, 33,* 696-698.

Goldstein, B., Kelly, M.M., Bruton, D., & Cox, C. (1993). Inflicted versus accidental head injury in children. *Critical Care Medicine, 21,* 1328-1332.

Hahn, Y.S., Raimondi, A.J., McLore, D.G., & Yamanouchi, Y. (1983). Traumatic mechanisms of head injury in child abuse. *Child's Brain, 10,* 229-241.

Harcourt, B., & Hopkins, D. (1971). Opthalmic manifestations of the battered baby syndrome. *British Medical Journal, f3,* 398-401.

Herman-Giddens, M.E., Brown, G., Verbiest, S., Carlson, P.J., Hooten, E.G., Howell, E., & Butts, J.D. (1999). Underascertainment of child abuse mortality in the United States. *Journal of the American Medical Association, 282,* 463-467.

Hymel, K.P., Abshire, T.L., Luckey, D.W., & Jenny, C. (1997). Coagulopathy in pediatric abusive head trauma. *Pediatrics, 99,* 371-375.

Jason, J. (1983). Fatal child abuse in Georgia: The epidemiology of severe physical child abuse. *Child Abuse & Neglect, 7,* 1-9.

Jason, J., Guilliland, J.C., & Tyler, C.W. Jr. (1983). Homicide as a cause of pediatric mortality in the United States. *Pediatrics, 72,* 191-197.

Jenny, C., Hymel, K., Ritzen, A., Reinert, S., & Hay, S. (1999). Analysis of missed cases of abusive head trauma. *Journal of the American Medical Association, 281,* 621-626.

Kapklein, M.J., & Mahadeo, R. (1997). Pediatric trauma. *Mt Sinai Journal of Medicine, 64,* 302-310.

Kaplun, D., & Reich, R. (1976). The murdered child and his killers. *American Journal of Psychiatry, 133,* 809-813.

Klein, M., & Stern, L. (1971). Low birth weight and the battered child syndrome. *American Journal of Diseases in Children, 122,* 15-18.

Kotch, J.B., Browne, C.B., Dufort, V., Winsor, J., & Catellier, D. (1999). Predicting child maltreatment in the first four years of life from characteristics assessed in the neonatal period. *Child Abuse & Neglect, 23,* 22-32.

Kunz, J., Bahr, S. (1996). A profile of parental homicide against children. *Journal of Family Violence, 11,* 347-362.

Lazoritz, S. (1990). Whatever happened to Mary Ellen? *Child Abuse & Neglect, 14,* 143-150.

Lazoritz, S., Baldwin, S., & Kini, N. (1997). The whiplash shaken baby syndrome: Has Caffey's syndrome changed or have we changed his syndrome? *Child Abuse & Neglect, 21,* 1009-1014.

Ludwig, S., & Warman, M. (1984). Shaken baby syndrome: A review of 20 cases. *Annals of Emergency Medicine, 13,* 104-107.

Luerssen, T.G. (1991). Retinal hemorrhages, seizures, and intracranial hemorrhages: Relationships and outcomes in children suffering traumatic brain injury. In A.E. Marlin (Ed.), *Concepts in pediatric neurosurgery* (pp. 1124-1127). Basel, Switzerland: Karger.

Margolin, L. (1992). Child abuse by mothers' boyfriends: Why the overrepresentation? *Child Abuse & Neglect, 16,* 541-551.

Massicotte, S.J., Folberg, R., Torczynski, E., Gilliland, M.G., Luckenbach, M.W. (1991). Vitreoretinal traction and perimacular retinal folds in the eyes of deliberately traumatized children. *Opthamology, 98,* 1124-1127.

Michigan Public Health Institute (MPHI). (1999). *Child deaths in Michigan: Michigan child death state advisory team first annual report.* Okemos, MI.

National Committee to Prevent Child Abuse. (1998). *Child abuse and neglect statistics.* Chicago, IL.

NIH Consensus Development Panel on Rehabilitation of Persons with Traumatic Brain Injury. (1999). Rehabilitation of persons with traumatic brain injury. *Journal of the American Medical Association, 282,* 974-983.

Olds, D.L. (1992). Home visitation for pregnant women and parents of young children. *American Journal of Diseases in Children, 146,* 704-708.

Overpeck, M., Brenner, R., Trumple, A., Trifiletti, L., & Berendes, H. (1998). Risk factors for infant homicide in the United States. *New England Journal of Medicine, 339,* 1211-1216.

Ricci, L.R. (1991). Photographing the physically abused child: Principles and practice. *American Journal of Diseases in Children, 145*(3), 275-281.

Saulsbury, F.T., & Campbell, R.E. (1985). Evaluation of child abuse reporting by physicians. *American Journal of Diseases in Children, 139,* 393-395.

Schlosser, P., Pierpont, J., & Poertner, J. (1992). Active surveillance of child abuse fatalities. *Child Abuse & Neglect, 16,* 3-10.

Sedlak, A.J., & Broadhurst, D.D. (1996). *The third national incidence study of child abuse and neglect (NIS-3).* Washington, DC: US Dept of Health and Human Services.

Showers, J. (1996). Executive Summary, "Don't Shake The Baby: Replication of a Successful Model." Final report to the National Center on Child Abuse and Neglect (NCCAN Grant #90-CA-1523).

Sills, J.A., Thomas, L.J., & Rosenbloom, L. (1977). Non accidental injury: A two year study in central Liverpool. *Developmental Medicine and Child Neurology, 19,* 26-33.

Simons, B., Downs, E.F., Hurster, M.M., & Archer, M. (1996). An epidemiologic study of medically reported cases of child abuse. *New York State Medical Journal, 66,* 2783-2788.

Spivak, B.S. (1998). Statistics and death certificates (letter). *Pediatrics, 102,* 1000-1001.

Starling, S.P., Holden, J.R., & Jenny, C. (1995). Abusive head trauma: The relationship of perpetrators to their victims. *Pediatrics, 95,* 259-262.

US Dept of Health and Human Services, Centers for Disease Control and Prevention, National Center for Health Statistics. (1998). *ICD-10: International statistical classification of diseases and related health problems. Tenth revision,* Vol. 1.

US Dept of Health and Human Services, Children's Bureau. (1999). *Child maltreatment 1997: Reports from the states to the national child abuse and neglect data system.* Washington, DC: US Government Printing Office.

Wang, C.T., & Daro, D. (1998). *Current trends in child abuse reporting and fatalities: The results of the 1997 annual fifty states survey.* Chicago IL: National Committee to Prevent Child Abuse.

Wolfe, A.E., Hwang, M., & Palusci, V.J. (1999). *Child maltreatment in developmentally delayed children.* Abstract presented at GRAMEC Research Day. Grand Rapids, MI.

Chapter Four

Who Are the Perpetrators and Why Do They Do It?

W. Hobart Davies
Molly Murphy Garwood

SUMMARY. This chapter will explain the data regarding who the perpetrators of Shaken Baby Syndrome (SBS) are and what triggers their behavior. Specific epidemiologic risk factors will be discussed, as well as the approach to the psychopathology of the parents and perpetrators, adult-child interactions, psychosocial isolation, child factors and situational dynamics contributing to SBS. Key factors in understanding developoment, temperament, behavior and parental expectations will also be discussed. *[Article copies available for a fee from The Haworth Document Delivery Service: 1-800-342-9678. E-mail address: <getinfo@haworthpressinc.com> Website: <http://www.HaworthPress.com> © 2001 by The Haworth Press, Inc. All rights reserved.]*

KEYWORDS. Shaken Baby Syndrome, risk factors, protective factors, child abuse, isolation, psychopathology, child factors, temperament, crying

[Haworth co-indexing entry note]: "Who Are the Perpetrators and Why Do They Do It?" Davies, W. Hobart, and Molly Murphy Garwood. Co-published simultaneously in *Journal of Aggression, Maltreatment & Trauma* (The Haworth Maltreatment & Trauma Press, an imprint of The Haworth Press, Inc.) Vol. 5, No. 1(#9), 2001, pp. 41-54; and: *The Shaken Baby Syndrome: A Multidisciplinary Approach* (ed: Stephen Lazoritz, and Vincent J. Palusci) The Haworth Maltreatment & Trauma Press, an imprint of The Haworth Press, Inc., 2001, pp. 41-54. Single or multiple copies of this article are available for a fee from The Haworth Document Delivery Service [1-800-342-9678, 9:00 a.m. - 5:00 p.m. (EST). E-mail address: getinfo@haworthpressinc.com].

. . . frustrated because she couldn't stop the baby's tears and fearing it meant that her daughter "did not want her" . . . Shirley said to herself: "I'm your mother. Why am I not good enough for you? Why won't you accept me?" (McBride, 1998, p. 3B)

There is a tremendous need to understand the characteristics of caregivers at risk for shaking their infants, and to understand the situational and enduring factors that increase or decrease the risk of this behavior. Prevention efforts must be directed towards populations at risk, and the information necessary to usefully guide such an effort is only beginning to emerge. A central question that must be addressed is whether Shaken Baby Syndrome is a "typical" form of child physical abuse (with regard to risk and protective factors) or whether this represents unique phenomena for which at-risk populations and environments must be separately defined.

The Social-Situational model of child abuse (Parke & Collmer, 1975; Watkins & Bradbard, 1982) provides a useful heuristic for categorizing what we know about risk and protective factors for parents who may shake an infant and the environmental factors that contribute to risk or protection. The Social-Situational model views an abusive incident as the outcome of a combination of child and parent characteristics, patterns of parent-child interaction, and environmental factors. It is important to remember that there will be factors that buffer against a shaking incident, and that these are important elements of the model (Cicchetti & Rizley, 1981). We will consider, in order, the available knowledge of perpetrator characteristics, characteristics of the caregiver-child relationship (ranging from overt child behavior to attributions that the caregiver creates about the child's behavior), and situational factors that increase the risk of a shaking incident. We propose a model of risk cumulation that fits the limited existing data and provides a starting point for defining a research agenda. Finally, implications for prevention are discussed.

GENERAL CHARACTERISTICS OF PERPETRATORS OF SHAKEN INFANT SYNDROME

Most cases of shaken infant syndrome are perpetrated by parents or caregivers such as a mother's boyfriend who are placed in a "near-parent" role (Lazoritz, Baldwin, & Kini, 1997). For convenience, we will refer to "caregivers" in discussing risk and protective factors in this review. Discovered perpetrators have been both male and female, although male perpetrators have generally been in the majority (Lazoritz et al., 1997). There is a clinical consensus that the intent of those who shake infants is generally not to injure them, but rather to attempt to control their behavior, to make them submissive or sub-servient (Spaide, Swengel, Scharre, & Mein, 1990) or to provide discipline (Caffey, 1974). In this regard, it is not unlike many other cases of child physi-cal abuse in which a frustrated parent shows poor judgment in confronting a trying interaction with a child. It has been suggested that parents unaware of the dangers of shaking may view it as a gentler and more appropriate response than striking a child (Coody, Brown, Montgomery, Flynn, & Yetman, 1994; Thomas, 1994).

As we might expect, most perpetrators do not admit to a shaking incident at the time of presentation for medical care (Spaide et al., 1990). In many cases, even the existence of a traumatic injury is denied, while in other cases a story is told of some other sort of trauma (e.g., a fall; Lazoritz et al., 1997; Thomas, 1994).

In different surveys, shaken infants have been found to be either predomi-nately Caucasian (Brenner, Fischer, & Mann-Gray, 1989) or non-Caucasian (Howard, Bell, & Uttley, 1993 in the United Kingdom and Munger, Peiffer, Bouldin, Kylstra, & Thompson, 1993 in the United States). More complete in-formation is necessary, especially since the suggestion of racial differences in risk leads to speculation about cultural factors that may make shaking more or less likely (Brenner et al., 1989). As we begin to construct models of risk to guide prevention efforts, it is important that they are grounded in accurate in-formation. Caution must also be taken in assuming that the ethnicity of the vic-tim sample is the same as the ethnicity of the perpetrators.

We found no information on risk status as a function of birth order, although one's experience as a caregiver could be assumed to play an important role in coping with the task. Parents of first-borns have consistently been found to be more responsive to infant signals than parents of later-borns (Donate-Bartfield & Passman, 1985; Jacobs & Moss, 1976). Similarly, there is no information on risks associated with child gender or interaction of child and caregiver gender. For physical abuse in general, it has been reported that male/male and fe-male/female are most common (Muller, 1995).

At this time, little information exists regarding the psychological and bio-logical backgrounds of perpetrators. We need to understand the connections to their abuse histories (Coody et al., 1994), experience with taking care of infants, and other factors that they may bring with them to a potentially high-risk environment. As has been done with sexual abuse (e.g., Kaufman, Hilliker, & Daleiden, 1996), we need to begin utilizing interviews and other assessments with convicted or confessed perpetrators to learn about typical patterns.

PERPETRATOR CHARACTERISTICS

Milner and Dopke (1997) provided a review of perpetrator characteristics associated with child physical abuse, and their chapter provides a useful framework for considering the special case of shaken infants in the context of other forms of physical abuse.

PSYCHOPHYSIOLOGICAL FACTORS

As Milner and Dopke (1997) determine, "investigators have uniformly concluded that child physical abusers are more physiologically reactive to child related stimuli" (p. 29) than are non-abusing parents (see also McCanne & Milner, 1991). Mothers who had been physically abusive have been shown to be more physiologically reactive (increases in heart rate, diastolic blood pressure, and skin conductance) to videotapes of a crying infant compared to demographically matched controls (Frodi & Lamb, 1980). Friedrich, Tyler, and Clark (1985) found similar differences on skin resistance measures for mothers using audiotapes of a crying child.

Mothers who have been physically abusive also show greater reactivity to viewing scenes involving parent-child conflict (Disbrow, Doerr, & Caulfield, 1977; Wolfe, Fairbank, Kelly, & Bradlyn, 1983). Nonparents who score highly on measures of risk for abuse show these same types of physiological responses (Crowe & Zeskind, 1992; Pruitt & Erickson, 1985). It is important to note, however, that these studies provide no consensus about which particular psychophysiological measures show increased reactivity. Unfortunately, no data are currently available on these variables with regard to physically abusive fathers, and there are none on caregivers who are known to have abused by shaking. Lamb (1978) found that non-clinical samples of mothers and fathers showed no group differences in their patterns of responding to different infant cries. However, mothers have been found to be more responsive than fathers when the infant on a taped cry is their own infant (Wiesenfeld, Malatesta, & DeLoach, 1981). The physiological reactivity hypothesis is largely consistent with clinical reports of shaken infant cases (Carty & Ratcliffe, 1995), but direct evidence is not available. We also do not know whether screening for a caregiver's physiological risk predisposition would be dependent on the characteristics of a specific infant's cry.

Psychopathology

Psychiatric disorders in the caregiver will directly increase the risk for shaking as it impacts a caregiver's ability to tolerate stress and manage the myriad demands of caring for an infant. There are also indirect effects as psychopathology impacts the relationship between caregiver and child, and as it contributes to misperceptions or misattributions regarding the child's behavior. Little direct evidence is available regarding the relative increase in risk associated with particular diagnoses. It is certainly not typical to see infants shaken during a period of florid psychosis, although the misattributions of some caregivers may approach criteria for a delusional disorder.

Caregiver depression is a likely risk factor given its interference with the parent-child relationship and the likelihood of reduced stress tolerance and impaired problem solving (Downey & Coyne, 1990). Cohn and Tronick (1983) stated that if mothers are not responsive or emotionally available (often consequences of a depressed state), infants are likely to experience frustration and may exhibit less positive and more negative affective responses during interaction with their mothers. A history of such negative interaction may increase the risk of shaking. Whereas caregiver psychopathology is likely to be an important contributor to the overall picture of shaken infants, it appears unlikely that it will be seen as directly causative in many cases.

Substance abuse has been identified as a risk factor for shaking infants (Chiocca, 1995; Coody et al., 1994). As with connections between substance abuse and other forms of interpersonal violence (Zucker, Fitzgerald, & Moses, 1995), there are likely to be both immediate situational impacts (e.g., reduced impulse control while intoxicated) and broader systemic effects, including those effects that are associated with but not specific to substance abuse (e.g., reduced economic stability, increased family and marital conflict). A particular association has been proposed between shaken infants and "cocaine rage" (Chiocca, 1995).

Isolation and Social Support

Social isolation and lack of social support have been identified as increasing the risk for infant shaking (Coody et al., 1994). This parallels findings for physical abuse in general, where abusers have been found to have fewer social contacts, perceive less social support, and feel more isolated than comparison parents (Milner & Dopke, 1997). It also appears that abusive parents may actively seek isolation from others, while perceiving a lack of support. Social isolation will likely interact with a number of other risk factors for shaking, compounding tension and frustration and limiting access to sources of more appropriate information on child development and infant behavior.

The Caregiver-Child Relationship

There are a number of areas to consider that we place broadly under the rubric of the caregiver-child relationship. This includes behavior on the part of the child that may overtly increase their risk of being shaken. However, it is more important to consider the child in the context of the relationship with the perpetrating caregiver and other caregivers, and the perceptions, understanding, and attributions that the caregiver develops regarding the child's behavior. Crittenden (1985) provided evidence of a bidirectional effect between mother and infant in which mothers initiated the maltreatment but abused infants behaved in ways that appeared to maintain the mother's maltreating behavior (e.g., abused children tended to be more difficult and openly angry). While it seems clinically obvious that an adult shaking an infant would see themselves as reacting to the child, it is currently an unanswerable question whether they are reacting primarily to overtly identifiable behavior or misperceptions and misattributions that result from intrapsychic processes (or some combination). The shaking incident must also be placed in developmental and chronological contexts; that is, these caregiver-child and relationship processes interact over time to produce a negative outcome. It is the developing process that creates the opportunity for identification and intervention. While research directly testing infant and parent-infant interaction as precursors to shaking are limited (e.g., Frodi & Lamb, 1980), investigations examining the role of infant difficult temperament and caregiver sensitivity in child development offer some insight into these important factors in the risk matrix.

Child Behavior

Crying is the only child-specific variable consistently identified as important in the cycle of escalation to shaking (Carty & Ratcliffe, 1995), although it seems possible that any other behaviors (e.g., refusal to eat) that parents find frustrating could set off the abusive cycle. As noted, we have little information about whether there are particular characteristics of an infant's cry that may place them at higher risk, either across the board or in relation to the idiosyncrasies of a particular caregiver. However, developmentalists have investigated some aspects of infant crying behavior and its relationship to caregiver response. Hubbard and van Ijzendoorn (1991) described the development of frequency and duration of infant crying during the first year and the role of caretaker responsiveness. They found that infant crying peaks during the first three months of life. These authors suggested that a parent's lack of response to the infant's cries during the first three months may increase crying frequency in the later months and that greater crying could increase caregiver unresponsiveness later. Another study indicated that 4-month-old infants who express more negative affect during a stressful situation were found to be less able to self-regulate and thus, soothe themselves in the absence of parental involvement (Braungart-Rieker, Garwood, Powers, & Notaro, 1998). Applying these studies to our discussion of shaken infant syndrome, we suggest that caregiver ineffectiveness or unresponsiveness during an infant's first months of life may increase the expression of infant distress, which in turn may increase the caregiver's frustration, rendering the caregiver at-risk for shaking the infant.

Infant Temperament and Caregiver Sensitivity

Temperament and caregiver sensitivity are important processes in the development of attachment between infants and caregivers, and can be considered directly with respect to the developing risk for shaking. Infant temperament and behavior occur within the context of the child-caregiver relationship and it has been suggested that temperament should be recast as a social perception rather than as a within-child characteristic (Thomas, Chess, & Korn, 1982). Thomas, Chess, and Birch (1986) first addressed the role of child characteristics in the caregiver-child relationship, stressing the "goodness-of-fit" between the child (e.g., temperament, gender) and the caregiver (e.g., sensitivity) and the active role the infant played in eliciting responses from the caregiver. Infants who are fussy, demanding, and difficult to soothe may elicit anxiety, feelings of incompetence and anger in their caregivers (Campbell, 1990). These caregivers likely become less responsive over time (Crockenberg, 1981), and this lack of responsiveness may lead to increased infant demandingness (Bates & Bayles, 1988). Bates and Bayles further suggested that difficult temperament paired with decreased sensitive caregiving may fuel a coercive cycle of interaction. To this caregiver the "difficult" child may become an aversive stimulus, rendering the child's cries more unpleasant and arousing. Inconsolable crying could then elicit an abnormal emotional response from the "ineffective" caregiver that is likely to be aggressive (Frodi & Lamb, 1980). In fact, early work suggests that caregiver disapproval or rejection of the child is consequent rather than antecedent to the child's difficult temperament (Thomas et al., 1982). Thus, for some caregivers a coercive cycle of interacting develops early and with great intensity, and when coupled with environmental stressors, may produce risk for shaking.

To date, no research has looked specifically at the role of caregiver sensitivity toward infant signals as a predictor of Shaken Baby Syndrome. However, developmental researchers (Belsky & Isabella, 1988; Sroufe & Waters, 1979) suggest that the responsivity of the caregiver to the infant's emotional signals is an important factor in the developing caregiver-child relationship. Caregivers who misread or misinterpret their child's signals are not likely to respond in a sensitive manner. We may extrapolate that caregiving responses based on misinterpretation (e.g., trying to feed a child in pain) are likely to be ineffective and will not soothe the distressed infant. The repetition of interaction in which both the caregiver's and child's needs are not being met, may lead to increased aggression on the part of the caregiver (e.g., shaking; Kropp & Haynes, 1987). Further, caregivers may feel responsible for their child's behavior and thus, highly frustrated when unable to modulate the infant's distress. Thomas et al. (1986) suggest that theories of child development inadvertently propose:

> . . . a loving and accepting mother should have a happy and contented child, from which it follows that an unconscious maternal attitude of rejection could be the only explanation for a difficult screaming child. As a result of reliance on these theories, it was not unusual for the mother of a difficult infant who screamed frequently and who make all routines a crisis, to develop self-doubts and feelings of guilt, anxiety, and helplessness. (p. 79)

Caregivers under great environmental stress may not be able to modulate additional stressors due to difficult child behavior. It appears that children with a high frequency and duration of crying in early infancy may be at risk for ineffective or insensitive parenting, which may increase the risk of aggressive caretaker responses to inconsolable crying.

Expectations, Perceptions, and Attributions Regarding Child Behavior

The quote at the beginning of this chapter (McBride, 1998) is from a 22-year-old man accused of smothering his infant daughter by holding her tightly against his chest. The incident as described has many of the characteristics of shaking incidents, and his quote clearly demonstrates a lack of basic understanding of child development and inappropriate expectations for the parent-child relationship. Holding unrealistic expectations of infant behavior is commonly identified as an important precursor to shaking (Carty & Ratcliffe, 1995; Coody et al., 1994; Schmidt, 1980). More specifically, many shakers identify a wish that the infant had been doing a better job of meeting the caregiver's own emotional needs (Coody et al., 1994; Spaide et al., 1990). This wish for role-reversal requires the additional faulty understanding that the infant is capable of intentionality in directing his/her behaviors (Milner & Dopke, 1997). Thus, a fussy or uncooperative infant is seen by the caregiver as being directly rejecting, and perhaps even attempting to annoy the adult. For example, Thomas et al. (1982) describe two parents who greatly differed in reaction to their own child. The father accepted his infant's behavior as "normal," while the mother reported her impression that the child's behavior was a "pathological response to her presumed inadequacy as a mother" (p. 12).

There is evidence that physically abusive caregivers in general view their children's behavior as more problematic and more negative in typical daily situations and when their children engage in minor transgressions (Milner & Dopke, 1997). There is no direct evidence yet on whether perpetrators of shaken infant syndrome show systematic inaccuracies in perceiving or recalling their children's overt behavior.

Situational Factors

There appears to be a consensus that infant shaking occurs at times of high stress for the individual and in the home (Carty & Ratcliffe, 1995; Chiocca, 1995; Spaide et al., 1990) and even that the abusive behavior is best conceptualized in the moment as a response to overwhelming stress. This may suggest new lines of research, as analog situations of "overwhelming" stress may be an appropriate experimental paradigm for studying the latter stages of decision making and/or loss of impulse control that end in an infant being shaken.

The association between difficult infant temperament and caregiver behavior may depend on the balance of stress and support in the caregiver's life. Among factors that affect parenting, high stress and/or low support may impact caregiver behavior, especially when the caregiver-child pair is already at-risk via adverse caregiver or child characteristics (Crockenberg & McCluskey, 1986).

CONCLUSION

We are in the very early stages of understanding the parent, child, interactional, family system, and situational factors that determine risk for and protection from shaking for infants. We need to move rapidly to understand these risk factors, not only separately, but as they interact with one another in the lives of young families. Figure 1 displays a proposed heuristic model that integrates our current understanding of shaken infant risk factors, extrapolating potential risk factors from the broader domain of child physical abuse. Factors in double boxes are believed to be proximal risk factors directly related to triggering a shaking incident. The remaining, distal factors may be beneficial in identifying at-risk individuals or dyads.

Although some authors have proposed that infant shaking may sometimes be considered as a form of conscious or even planned discipline (Coody et al., 1994), the weight of evidence at this time suggests that it is much more likely to result from a moment of extreme stress and frustration, and takes the form of an unreasoned and impulsive act. If this is confirmed by further research, it ob-

FIGURE 1

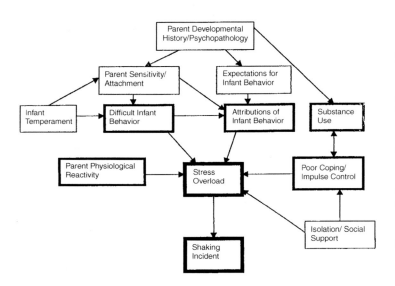

viously has important implications for intervention, and highlights the need for identifying reliable measures of risk based on predisposing factors so that preventive interventions can be aggressively and efficiently targeted.

Research Needs

The model laid out it Figure 1 suggests a number of research questions that deserve to be aggressively pursued, especially given the relatively large number of potential areas of screening for risk and protective factors. The model suggests that screening of areas such as knowledge of normal infant behavior, perception of infant temperament, expectations for interactions with the infant, impulse control, social support, and the parent's developmental history may be fertile areas to assess. The feasibility of paper-and-pencil risk assessments (perhaps similar to the Child Abuse Potential Inventory (Milner, 1986, 1994)) needs to be investigated.

We also need to return research efforts to the area of physiological reactivity to infants' cries. This was a fruitful area of research in the 1970s and 1980s, but has received scant attention recently. The possibility of developing physiological screens that could identify caregivers who would benefit from preventive interventions has much potential, although there are a number of ethical questions that must be carefully considered. Again, we need to consider the reactivity risk in the context of the cries/other behavior of a particular child, and protocols for such screening on individual adults have not yet been developed. Careful longitudinal research is needed in this area.

Much work is needed with the focused support of agencies that fund research into these potential areas of screening and prevention activities. We also need to take advantage of the scientific opportunities presented by convicted or confessed perpetrators in understanding the temporal and distal factors that create a risk for infant shaking.

Implications for Prevention

A public health prevention model is needed to address universal, selective, and specific prevention of Shaken Baby Syndrome. In the realm of universal prevention, we must more aggressively put out the message that shaking an infant is not acceptable behavior. Materials such as the "Never Never Never Never Shake a Baby" program of SBS Prevention Plus must become more visible in more arenas. The hope is, of course, that we can begin to instill a taboo against the behavior that may afford the only protection that is possible when a caregiver is losing control in a stressful situation (Thomas, 1994). These messages must become part of the bulwark of preventive education in prenatal classes, pediatricians' well child visits, and programming for families at risk.

Selective prevention will become more practical as research supports or refutes the various factors proposed in the risk and protective model. As noted above, some combination of paper-and-pencil and physiological measurement may be feasible for screening large numbers of new parents and/or parents-to-be for factors that may place them at risk for shaking or other loss of control with their infant. The best targets for intervention should remain an empirical question, but all of the attitudinal, parent-child interaction, and psychopathology factors in the proposed model are at least theoretically modifiable through education and treatment. Given the tremendous medical and social expenses associated with shaken infant victims, considerable public health spending will be justifiable as effective programming is developed.

Prevention aimed at recidivism is also indicated given the (currently) anecdotal evidence that numerous incidents of Shaken Baby Syndrome were preceded by substantiated or alleged child abuse on this or another child, or even by a previous suspicious death of a child. Obtaining well-grounded estimates of the relative risk increase associated with these types of incidents will certainly speak to the intensity of services that are indicated when an infant comes into an environment already suspected of being unsafe. This risk nexus will also be more clearly delineated as we gain clearer understanding of the similarities and dissimilarities in risk profiles for shaking versus other forms of child physical abuse.

Although our current knowledge base is woefully inadequate, the field is positioned to rapidly acquire information about identifying caregivers and caregiver-child dyads at risk for shaking. A model of risk cumulation makes clear that risks are potentially measurable, while many of the risk factors are potentially modifiable. The prospects for significantly impacting the occurrence of shaken infant syndrome are good assuming we can sustain the scientific, clinical, and policy initiatives that are indicated.

REFERENCES

Bates, J. E., & Bayles, K. (1988). Attachment and the development of behavior problems. In J. Belsky & T. Nezworski (Eds.), *Clinical implications of attachment* (pp. 253-299). Hillsdale, N.J: Erlbaum.

Belsky, J., & Isabella, R. (1988). Maternal, infant and social-contextual determinants of attachment security. In J. Belsky & T. Nezworski (Eds.), *Clinical implications of attachment* (pp. 41-94). Hillsdale, N.J: Erlbaum.

Braungart-Rieker, J., Garwood, M. M., Powers, B. P., & Notaro, P. (1998). Infant affect and affect-regulation during the still-face paradigm with mothers and fathers: The role of infant characteristics and parental sensitivity. *Developmental Psychology, 34,* 1428-1437.

Brenner, S. L., Fischer, H., & Mann-Gray, S. (1989). Race and the shaken baby syndrome: Experience at one hospital. *Journal of the National Medical Association, 81,* 183-184.

Caffey, J. (1974). The Whiplash Shaken Infant Syndrome: Manual shaking by the extremities with whiplash-induced intracranial and intraocular bleedings, linked with residual permanent brain damage and mental retardation. *Pediatrics, 54,* 396-403.

Campbell, S. B. (1990). *Behavior problems in preschool children: Clinical and developmental issues.* New York: Guilford Press.

Carty, H., & Ratcliffe, J. (1995). The shaken infant syndrome: Parents and other carers need to know of its dangers. *British Medical Journal, 310,* 344-345.

Chiocca, E. M. (1995). Shaken baby syndrome: A nursing perspective. *Pediatric Nursing, 21,* 33-38.

Cicchetti, D., & Rizley, R. (1981). Developmental perspectives on the etiology, intergenerational transmission, and sequelae of child maltreatment. In R. Rizley & D. Cicchetti (Eds.), *Developmental perspectives on child maltreatment* (pp. 31-55). San Francisco: Jossey-Bass.

Cohn, J. F., & Tronick, E. Z. (1983). Three-month-old infants' reaction to simulated maternal depression. *Child Development, 54,* 185-193.

Coody, D., Brown, M., Montgomery, D., Flynn, A., & Yetman, R. (1994). Shaken baby syndrome: Identification and prevention for nurse practitioners. *Journal of Pediatric Health Care, 8*, 50-56.

Crittenden, P. M. (1985). Maltreated infants: Vulnerability and resilience. *Journal of Child Psychology and Psychiatry, 26*, 85-96.

Crockenberg, S. B. (1981). Infant irritability, mother responsiveness, and social support influences on the security of infant-mother attachment. *Child Development, 52*, 857-865.

Crockenberg, S., & McCluskey, K. (1986). Change in maternal behavior during the baby's first year of life. *Child Development, 57*, 746-753.

Crowe, H. P., & Zeskind, P. S. (1992). Psychophysiological and perceptual responses to infant cries varying in pitch: Comparison of adults with low and high scores on the Child Abuse Potential Inventory. *Child Abuse & Neglect, 16*, 19-29.

Disbrow, M. A., Doerr, H., & Caulfield, C. (1977). Measuring the components of parents' potential for child abuse and neglect. *Child Abuse & Neglect, 1*, 279-296.

Donate-Bartfield, E., & Passman, R. H. (1985). Attentiveness of mothers and fathers to their baby's cries. *Infant Behavior and Development, 8*, 385-393.

Downey, G., & Coyne, J. C. (1990). Children of depressed parents: An integrated review. *Psychological Bulletin, 108*, 50-76.

Friedrich, W. N., Tyler, J. D., & Clark, J. A. (1985). Personality and psychophysiological variables in abusive, neglectful, and low-income control mothers. *Journal of Nervous and Mental Disease, 173*, 449-460.

Frodi, A. M., & Lamb, M. E. (1980). Child abusers' responses to infant smiles and cries. *Child Development, 51*, 238-241.

Howard, M. A., Bell, B. A., & Uttley, D. (1993). The pathophysiology of infant subdural haematomas. *British Journal of Neurosurgery, 7*, 355-365.

Hubbard, F. O. A., & van Ijzendoorn, M. H. (1991). Maternal unresponsiveness and infant crying across the first 9 months: A naturalistic longitudinal study. *Infant Behavior and Development, 14*, 299-312.

Jacobs, B. S., & Moss, H. A. (1976). Birth order and sex of sibling as determinants of mother-infant interaction. *Child Development, 47*, 315-322.

Kaufman, K. L., Hilliker, D. R., & Daleiden, E. L. (1996). Subgroup differences in the modus operandi of adolescent sexual offenders. *Child Maltreatment, 1*, 17-24.

Kropp, J. P., & Haynes, O. M. (1987). Abusive and nonabusive mothers' ability to identify general and specific emotion signals of infants. *Child Development, 58*, 187-190.

Lamb, M. E. (1978). Qualitative aspects of mother-and-father-infant attachment. *Infant Behavior and Development, 1*, 265-275.

Lazoritz, S., Baldwin, S., & Kini, N. (1997). The Whiplash Shaken Infant Syndrome: Has Caffey's syndrome changed or have we changed his syndrome? *Child Abuse & Neglect, 21*, 1009-1014.

McBride, J. (1998, July 9). Weight lifter charged with pressing baby to death. *Milwaukee Journal Sentinel*, p. 3B.

McCanne, T. R., & Milner, J. S. (1991). Physiological reactivity of physically abusive and at-risk subjects to child-related stimuli. In J. S. Milner (Ed.), *Neuropsychology of aggression* (pp. 147-166). Boston: Kluwer Academic.

Milner, J. S. (1986). *The Child Abuse Potential Inventory: Manual* (2nd ed.). Webster, NC: Psytec.

Milner, J. S. (1994). Assessing physical child abuse risk: The Child Abuse Potential Inventory. *Clinical Psychology Review, 14*, 547-583.

Milner, J. S., & Dopke, C. (1997). Child physical abuse: Review of offender characteristics. In D. A. Wolfe, R. J. McMahon, & R.D. Peters (Eds.), *Child abuse: New directions in prevention and treatment across the lifespan* (pp. 27-54). Thousand Oaks, CA: Sage.

Muller, R. T. (1995). The interaction of parent and child gender in physical child maltreatment. *Canadian Journal of Behavioural Science, 27*, 450-465.

Munger, C. E., Peiffer, R. L., Bouldin, T. W., Kylstra, J. A., & Thompson, R. L. (1993). Ocular and associated neuropathologic observations in suspected whiplash shaken infant syndrome. *American Journal of Forensic Medicine and Pathology, 14*, 193-200.

Parke, R. D., & Collmer, C. W. (1975). Child abuse: An interdisciplinary analysis. In E. M. Hetherington (Ed.), *Review of child development research* (vol. 5, pp. 509-590). Chicago: University of Chicago Press.

Pruitt, D. L., & Erickson, M. T. (1985). The Child Abuse Potential Inventory: A study of concurrent validity. *Journal of Clinical Psychology, 41*, 104-111.

Schmidt, B. D. (1980). The child with non-accidental trauma. In C. H. Kempe & R. E. Helfer (Eds.). *The battered child* (3rd ed., pp. 134-146). Chicago: University of Chicago Press.

Spaide, R. F., Swengel, R. M., Scharre, D. W., & Mein, C. E. (1990). Shaken baby syndrome. *American Family Physician, 41*, 1145-1152.

Sroufe, L. A., & Waters, E. (1979). Attachment as an organizational construct. *Child Development, 48*, 1184-1199.

Thomas, A., Chess, S., & Birch, H. (1986). *Temperament and behavior disorders in children.* New York: New York University Press.

Thomas, A., Chess, S. & Korn, S. J. (1982). The reality of difficult temperament. *Merrill-Palmer Quarterly, 28*, 1-19.

Thomas, N. (1994). Shaking infants: A case for public education? *Professional Care of the Mother & Child, 4*, 59-60.

Watkins, H. D., & Bradbard, M. R. (1982). The social development of young children in day care: What practitioners should know. *Child Care Quarterly, 11*, 169-187.

Wiesenfeld, A. R., Malatesta, C. Z., & DeLoach, L. L. (1981). Differential parental response to familiar and unfamiliar infant distress signals. *Infant Behavior and Development, 4*, 281-295.

Wolfe, D. A., Fairbank, J. A., Kelly, J. A., & Bradlyn, A. S. (1983). Child abusive parents' physiological responses to stressful and non-stressful behavior in children. *Behavioral Assessment, 5*, 363-371.

Zucker, R. A., Fitzgerald, H. E., & Moses, H. (1995). Emergence of alcohol problems and the several alcoholisms: A developmental perspective on etiologic theory and life course trajectory. In D. Cicchetti & D. Cohen (Eds.), *Manual of developmental psychopathology: Vol. 2. Risk, disorder, and adaptation* (pp. 677-711). New York: Wiley.

Chapter Five

Biomechanics of Abusive Head Trauma

Betty S. Spivack

SUMMARY. The chapter provides a reference to the basic concepts of physics and the biomechanics necessary to the understanding of the mechanism of injury in abusive head trauma. Specific attention is given to the whiplash shaken-infant syndrome and shaken-impact models of abusive head trauma. The mechanical implications of falls from low heights are analyzed. The concluding section highlights unresolved problems in our understanding of these injuries and provides direction for future research.*[Article copies available for a fee from The Haworth Document Delivery Service: 1-800-342-9678. E-mail address: <getinfo@haworthpressinc.com> Website: <http://www.HaworthPress.com> © 2001 by The Haworth Press, Inc. All rights reserved.]*

KEYWORDS. Biomechanics, inflicted cerebral trauma, brain injury, subdural hematoma, rotational forces, impact

"How did it happen?" and "Could it have happened that way?" are the two questions most frequently asked of physicians by child protection workers or law enforcement officers who are investigating a case of possible child abuse. These questions are also the most difficult questions for a physician to answer.

[Haworth co-indexing entry note]: "Biomechanics of Abusive Head Trauma." Spivack, Betty S. Co-published simultaneously in *Journal of Aggression, Maltreatment & Trauma* (The Haworth Maltreatment & Trauma Press, an imprint of The Haworth Press, Inc.) Vol. 5, No. 1(#9), 2001, pp. 55-78; and: *The Shaken Baby Syndrome: A Multidisciplinary Approach* (ed: Stephen Lazoritz, and Vincent J. Palusci) The Haworth Maltreatment & Trauma Press, an imprint of The Haworth Press, Inc., 2001, pp. 55-78. Single or multiple copies of this article are available for a fee from The Haworth Document Delivery Service [1-800-342-9678, 9:00 a.m. - 5:00 p.m. (EST). E-mail address: getinfo@haworthpressinc.com].

　　　55

We derive our understanding of mechanism of injury in two ways. We can analyze the outcomes of well-described incidents of trauma and note what sorts of injuries occur in those settings. We can extrapolate from variables noted in those clinical reports and identify patterns of injuries, which may occur under varying circumstances. Alternatively, we can develop experimental models for different types of trauma and identify the forces, which come into play and the types of injuries which occur under different experimental settings. Such experimentation generates the theoretical basis for understanding the patterns of injuries noted in clinical reports.

Clinical investigations into the mechanism of injuries resulting from child maltreatment are hampered by false or non-existent histories of the incident, which are frequently provided to medical personnel when the child presents for medical care. Our understanding of these injuries can; therefore, only come from a comparison of these injuries to those incurred in well-described accidental settings, from experimental data concerning the generation of such injuries, and from confessions freely and fully given.

In this article we will examine what is known about the biomechanics of abusive head trauma. Biomechanics is the science of the physical properties of biological tissues, that is, their response to the application of physical forces. In order to understand the features commonly seen in cases of abusive head trauma, we will first review basic linear and rotational mechanics and properties of some biological tissues. We will then look at the basic science experiments which have illuminated our understanding of traumatic brain injury. This data will be the basis for a paradigm for understanding the features of abusive brain injury which will provide a structure for giving an accurate answer to "How did it happen?" Finally, we will examine the limitations of our current understanding and indicate the areas which require further research.

BASIC CONCEPTS OF BIOMECHANICS

The Physics of Linear Motion

Mass (m) is an inherent property of matter, reflecting its inertia or resistance to change of its motion. In the scientific (M-K-S) system of measurement, mass is measured in kilograms (kg).

Velocity (v) is a measure of distance covered per unit of time. In the M-K-S system, distance is measured in meters (m) and time is measured in seconds (sec); velocity is measured in meters per second (m-sec^{-1}).

Acceleration (a) is the rate of change (positive or negative) of velocity over time; it is measured in meters per second per second (m-sec^{-2}).

Newton's First Law of Motion states: *In the absence of externally applied forces, an object will move with constant linear velocity.* Changes in velocity or direction, i.e., acceleration or deceleration, occur only when external forces act upon the object. The degree of force necessary to cause an observed acceleration (or change in velocity) is proportional to both the object's mass and the observed acceleration of the object after the application of the force. This is expressed by the equation: $F = ma$. *Force* is measured in Newtons, equivalent to kg-m-sec^{-2}.

Gravity is also an inherent property of matter and governs the interactions between two objects. A gravitational field generates an accelerative force on an object within its field. On the surface of the earth the strength of that gravitational field *(g)* causes an acceleration of 9.8 m-sec^{-2}.

Weight is the downward force caused by gravity-induced acceleration acting upon an object; weight is measured in Newtons. It is incorrect to say that one kilogram (a unit of mass) is equivalent to 2.2 pounds (a unit of weight or force); that is only true on Earth where an object massing one kilogram would have a weight of 9.8 Newtons, equivalent to 2.2 pounds in the English system of measurement.

Work (W) is done by applying a force over a distance. It is measured in joules, equivalent to Newton-meters or kg-m^2-sec^{-2} and is described by the equation: $W = FD$.

Energy (E) is the capacity to do work and therefore is also described in joules. In the context of traumatic injury, the work, which is being done is the disruption of body tissues. Such work requires the input of energy.

Energy is described as *kinetic* (associated with a moving object) or *potential* (associated with position of an object). Total energy (kinetic plus potential energy) within a system is constant, but potential energy can be converted into kinetic energy and back again.

Two equations describe the energy states of an object:

Kinetic energy $= 1/2\ mv^2$
Potential energy $= mgh$ where *h* is the height of the object above the surface of the earth.

When a 5 kg bowling ball sits upon a shelf 2 meters above the floor it has no kinetic energy as v = 0, but considerable potential energy (98 joules). If a tremor shakes the shelf and dislodges the bowling ball, the potential energy will be progressively converted into kinetic energy as the bowling ball is accelerated by gravity. At the moment that the bowling ball strikes the ground, it will have no remaining potential energy (h = 0), but considerable kinetic energy (98 joules). Much of the kinetic energy of the bowling ball may be expended in doing destructive "work" upon the surface of the floor; some may be converted again (temporarily) into potential energy if the bowling ball bounces upward after the initial impact.

The Physics of Rotational Motion

By Newton's first law, any object which does not experience a force acting upon it will continue with constant linear motion. Rotational motion requires the application of a force acting in a direction different from the initial motion of the object. *Rotational Inertia* is the equivalent of mass in equations describing rotational motion. It represents the resistance of an object to initiation or change of rotatory motion, and it is a function both of the mass of the object and the distance over which the force is exercised. Therefore it is harder to swing an object on a long string than on a short one.

Torque is the rotational equivalent of force and measures the rotational impact of the exerted force. It is equal to the force exerted multiplied by the lever arm or perpendicular distance of the pivot point from the line of application of that force (see Figure 1). For this reason, when we are using a wrench to turn (tighten or loosen) a bolt, the wrench is positioned horizontally while the force is directed downward which maximizes the torque exerted upon the bolt. Once the wrench has rotated to reach the bottom of its arc reducing its torque to zero, it is repositioned.

FIGURE 1. Torque Dependence upon Force and Lever Arm

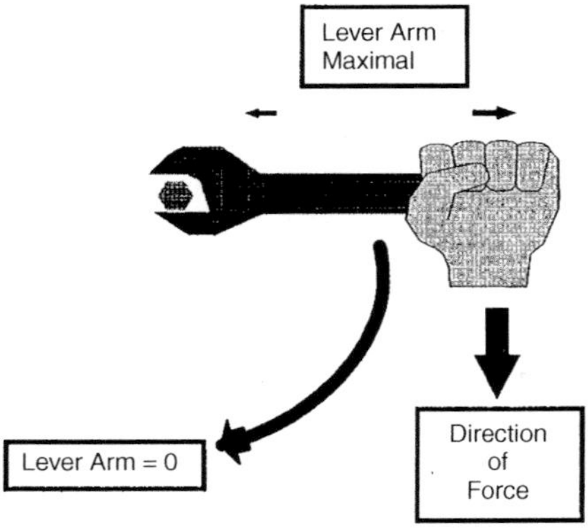

Rotational velocity and *acceleration* are described in terms of radians or degrees per unit of time (rotational velocity), or per unit of time-squared (rotational acceleration). An object which is rotating has both rotational velocity and acceleration and an instantaneous linear velocity. If the force which is causing the rotation is discontinued, as for example if the string to which a twirling object was attached breaks, the object will fly off in a straight line tangent to the arc through which it had been rotating; its velocity in that direction will be equal to its linear velocity at the time the string snapped.

During rotation, there is conservation of *angular momentum*, which is the product of rotational inertia and rotational velocity. It is for this reason that a spinning ice-skater slows down when the arms are extended. The rotational inertia of the body has increased because more of the mass is farther from the axis of rotation and rotational velocity decreases to preserve angular momentum; the reverse is seen when the arms are brought in toward the body.

RESPONSES OF MATERIALS TO MECHANICAL LOADING

Types of Loading

Loading is the application of a force to an object. Loads (see Figure 2) may be tensile (acts to stretch the material), compressive (acts to compress the material) or shearing (acts to change the angular relationship of portions of the material). Loads may exist in combination. Bending (see Figure 3) causes both

FIGURE 2. Types of Load

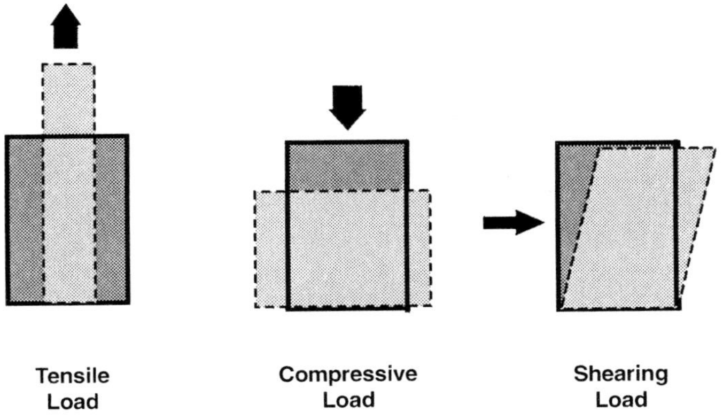

Tensile
Load

Compressive
Load

Shearing
Load

tensile and compressive forces in different areas of an object; torsion (see Figure 4) causes tension, compression and shearing.

Stress or *pressure* is a measure of force or load applied per unit area of application. It is measured in Pascals, equivalent to Newtons per square meter or kg-m^{-1}-sec^{-2}. The *ultimate strength* of a material is the maximum stress, which it can experience without rupture. If a given stress is tolerable, Newton's Second Law of Motion expresses the reciprocal nature of force: *Every action has an equal and opposite reaction.* A book with a mass of one kilogram and 0.1 m^2 in surface area which is resting upon a table, exerts a downward force on the table equivalent to its weight (9.8 Newtons downward) and a stress of 98

FIGURE 3. Effects of Bending

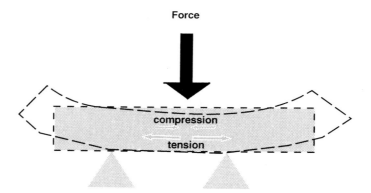

FIGURE 4.Effect of Torsion

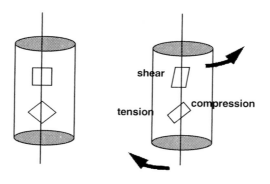

Pascals. The table pushes up on the book with an equal and opposite force (9.8 Newtons upward). If the book is resting not upon a wooden table, but upon a long, unsupported sheet of paper which has an ultimate strength less than 98 Pascals, the paper will tear and the book will fall.

Strain is the fractional change (increase or decrease) in the dimension of an object as the result of a load. It is a pure number having no dimension, since it is the ratio of post-load size to original size ($\Delta L/L$). Some strain may be temporary, lasting only as long as the force is applied; such a strain is called *elastic* (see Figure 5). An example of elastic strain is the stretching of a rubber band, which returns to its original length when the stretching ceases. If the strain is excessive, the object may rupture; in this case the strain has exceeded the *breaking strain* of the material. This is what happens when a rubber band is stretched too far; the breaking strain is exceeded and the rubber band breaks.

In an elastic deformation, the amount of deformation is proportional to the applied load. The energy utilized in causing the deformation is stored in the

FIGURE 5. Elasticity

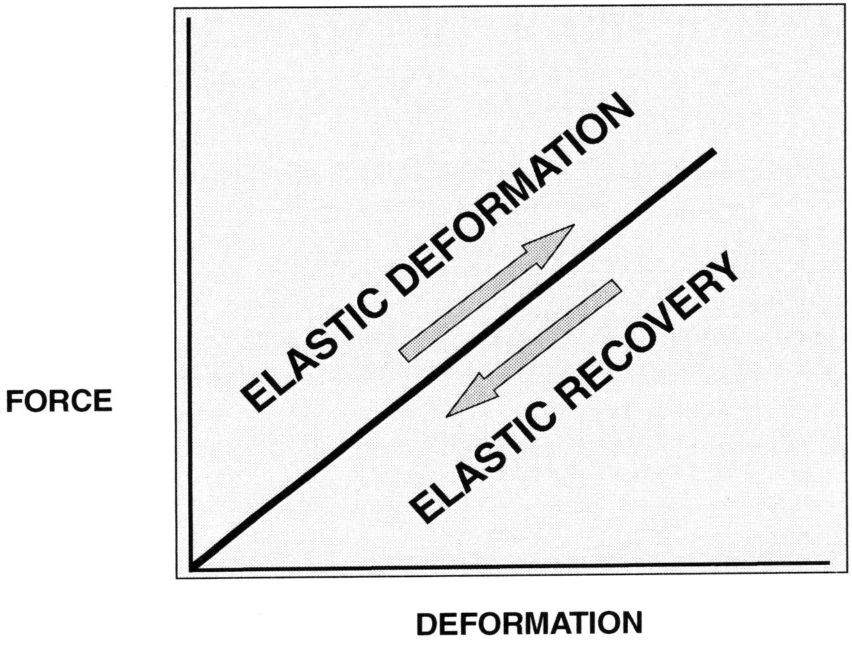

FORCE

DEFORMATION

material and is fully released after elastic recovery. In a fully elastic collision, kinetic energy is completely converted back into potential energy (i.e., the object will bounce back to its original height). In a purely elastic deformation or collision no work is done as no energy is expended; the situation at the end of the application of the force is exactly as it was before the force was applied. In the real world, there are no purely elastic deformations or collisions; some energy is always lost either in work and converted to heat or other energy due to friction or because of non-elastic properties of the material.

The ratio of stress to strain at levels in elastic or partially elastic materials is constant in the elastic region of the material; this ratio is the *modulus of rigidity* or *Young's modulus*. A high modulus of rigidity is found in very stiff materials; a low modulus of rigidity indicates that a material yields readily in response to loading.

Materials may be permanently deformed without rupture; such a property is called *plasticity*. A good example of plastic deformation (see Figure 6) is the mark left by pushing one's thumb into wet clay or Silly Putty®; the material is not torn but a permanent deformation has occurred. In a plastic deformation, no deformity occurs until the *yield point* is reached; thereafter, the amount of deformation is dependent upon the length of time in which the force is operating.

Pure plasticity is uncommon in biological materials, but many materials exhibit *elastoplastic* behavior (see Figure 7). In such a situation, some of the deformation (and associated energy) may be recoverable, while the remainder

FIGURE 6. Plastic Deformation

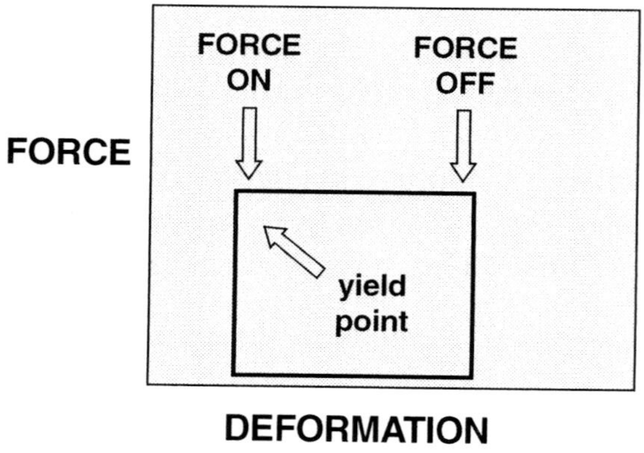

DEFORMATION

FIGURE 7. Elastoplastic Deformation

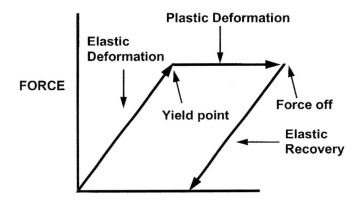

DEFORMATION

has led to permanent deformation (and expenditure of energy). Most biological materials demonstrate elastoplastic properties.

Some materials are highly responsive to the rate at which a force is applied; such deformations are described as *viscous* (see Figure 8). Viscous substances are stiff when a force is applied rapidly, but yield readily when a force is slowly and steadily applied. Biologic materials are unlikely to be "purely" viscous, though liquids such as blood have more viscous properties than plastic or elastic properties. Most body tissues can be described as *viscoelastic* (see Figure 9) with time and rate dependence seen in their susceptibility to injury. In a viscoelastic material exposed to a relatively short loading event, deformation or strain will be proportional to the length of time that the load is applied. This time factor makes short duration events dependent upon velocity rather than acceleration levels. In longer duration or quasistatic events, the elastic properties of a viscoelastic material predominate, and the strain will be dependent only on the magnitude of the loading force, and therefore on acceleration rather than velocity. Viscoelastic substances, then, have critical thresholds for both velocity and acceleration depending upon the manner in which a load is being applied. In particular, the viscoelastic properties of the brain are very important in its response to traumatic forces. As we shall see, different patterns of brain injury result from impact loading (1-30 msec), impulse loading (50-200 msec) and compressive loading (> 200 msec).

FIGURE 8. Viscous Deformation

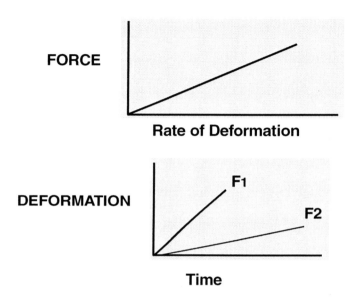

Scaling is an important consideration in our understanding and prediction of the result of exposure to traumatic forces. Some body dimensions increase linearly (e.g., proportional to length), others increase in a squared (e.g., proportional to surface area) or cubed (e.g., proportional to volume, mass or weight) manner relative to length. This has importance both for body structure and response to injury. The strength of a support structure, such as a leg bone, relative to a compressive load is dependent upon the cross-sectional area of the bone, while the compressive load it must bear is dependent upon the weight of the individual. However weight increases as the cube of length, while cross-sectional area increases as the square (i.e., less quickly). One result of this is that an elephant has different body proportions than a mouse; its legs must be proportionately thicker to be able to support the increased weight. Whenever susceptibility to injury is dependent upon the surface area of some body part (but is being described in terms of volume, mass or weight of the individual or the body part), we will expect to see the exponent of change to be 2/3, the ratio of the power of growth of the area to the power of growth of volume. We will see this as the predicted and demonstrated exponent in susceptibility to brain injury.

FIGURE 9. Viscoelastic Deformation

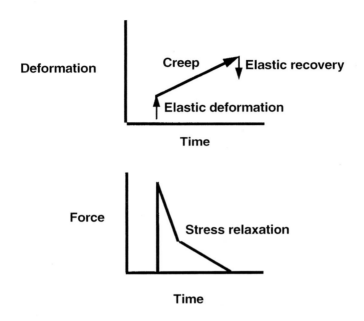

BIOMECHANICS OF ABUSIVE BRAIN TRAUMA

Early Experimental Background

We can only begin to comprehend the mechanism of abusive brain trauma in the context of understanding the pathogenesis of brain trauma in general. The first advance in our understanding of the biomechanics of brain injury came in 1943 when Holbourn, an Oxford physiologist, began to analyze the properties of cerebral tissue and speculate about the nature of forces which could cause cerebral injury (Holboum, 1943). He started with five basic assumptions about the nature of the brain.

1. The brain has comparatively uniform density.
2. The brain is roughly as incompressible as water. (This means that it would require a pressure of more than 10,000 tons per square inch to reduce its volume by 50%.)
3. The brain has a small modulus of rigidity. (This means that it changes shape easily in response to an applied force.)
4. The rigidity of the skull is much greater than that of the brain.

5. The shape of the skull and brain are important determinants of patho-
    logic results of injury.

Holbourn (1943) recognized that when a material is highly incompressible
(but not very rigid) that tension and compressive forces do not cause much injury. Instead, deformation is proportional to shearing load. He concluded that
skull distortion caused only local deformation due to shearing, and the waves
of tension and compression, which it generated would not result in a diffuse injury. Local injuries such as subdural, subarachnoid and extradural hemorrhages could result. However, rotation generates greater shearing forces, and
Holbourn concluded that rotational injury was important in producing concussion and significant brain injury.

He also recognized that the brain is a highly viscoelastic structure, and
therefore effects would differ depending upon the duration of the rotational
force. In events of "short duration" strain due to a shearing load would be proportional to both the force and duration of the event, and hence it would be proportional to angular velocity (force = mass × acceleration, velocity =
acceleration × time). In events of "long duration," the shearing strain would be
independent of duration, and therefore, it would be proportional to acceleration. Holbourn speculated that the transition from events of short duration to
events of long duration would occur somewhere in the interval between 2 and
200 milliseconds.

Based upon this conceptual framework, Holbourn molded gelatin into the
shape of the brain, and subjected this material to rotation in various planes
caused by impact, studying the relative degree of shear noted throughout the
model. Sagittal rotation caused by a blow to the "occiput" resulted in shearing
deformation, which was maximal in the parasagittal region, the frontal lobes
and the occipital lobes just above the cerebellum. Holbourn performed no *in
vivo* experiments nor did he study the effects of rotation without impact. Nevertheless, most of his speculations have been abundantly confirmed over the
last half-century and still form the theoretical underpinnings for understanding
all traumatic brain injury.

It was 25 years before significant progress was made on the nature of brain
biomechanics and its response to trauma. Ommaya, a neurosurgeon at the University of Pennsylvania, published his first paper on experimental brain injury
(Ommaya, Faas, & Yarnell, 1968). Ommaya and others (Gennarelli, Thibault, &
Ommaya, 1972; Hirsch & Ommaya, 1970) used a primate-mechanical model capable of generating a reproducible force due to head impact or non-impact rotation in
a single plane. In these studies many of Holbourn's speculations were corroborated. Specifically, they found a durational dependence of shearing injury in events

of short duration (< 20 msec), but independence from duration in events of long duration. This established minimal critical values of both angular velocity and angular acceleration. The areas of observed brain injury correlated closely with the areas of shearing predicted by Holboum's experiments with gelatin.

Ommaya and his colleagues found no pathology except when loss of consciousness had occurred, and resistance to injuries when forces were purely translational (i.e., the head was not free to rotate). Ommaya and his colleagues documented that significant brain injury could occur due to whiplash alone, although rotational accelerations needed to be twice as high as in equivalent injuries with impact.

Whiplash-Shaken Infant Syndrome

In the early 1970s, a hypothesis concerning the origin of abusive head trauma, which became known as the "whiplash-shaken infant" or "shaken baby" syndrome was formulated (Caffey, 1972; Guthkelch, 1971). These landmark papers were predicated upon the work of Holbourn and Ommaya. Guthkelch and Caffey recognized that the clinically identified pattern of parasagittal subdural hematoma and frontal and occipital cortical injury in these infants replicated the maximal shear strain areas identified by Holbourn in response to occipital impact, and that the intracranial pathology was similar to the lesions noted by Ommaya resulting from whiplash phenomena. These authors postulated that rotational acceleration injury was the fundamental mechanical determinant of diffuse brain injury in abused infants. This provided a paradigm to explain the severity of injury seen in these abused children, in stark contrast to the minor injuries suffered by infants falling from household heights (Kravitz, Driessen, Gomberg, & Korach, 1969 and subsequently confirmed by Helfer, Slovis, & Black, 1977; Lyons & Oates, 1993; Nimityongskul & Anderson, 1987), which was the most frequently proffered explanation of the injuries. Neither Guthkelch nor Caffey ever asserted that shaking was the sole cause of the noted injuries, but offered it as the instigator of the rotational forces involved during the traumatic event. In fact, in Caffey's original series of patients, one child was both shaken and beaten to death with a stick, and another suffered a bruise to the forehead when his head struck the crib while being shaken. The important concept in their understanding of this phenomenon was the importance of rotational forces and shearing injury and the possibility of shaking as an initiator of the rotational acceleration.

Further Experimental Work in Head Trauma

Ommaya had speculated that the critical angular acceleration or velocity would decrease at an exponential rate of 2/3 as the mass of the brain increased

(Ommaya et al., 1968). This reflects the dependence of mass on the volume of the brain, but the area of shearing forces being applied over the surface area of the brain. His later work confirmed this scaling factor (Ommaya, Fisch, & Mahone, 1970; Ommaya & Hirsch, 1971). Using the data obtained from squirrel monkeys, rhesus monkeys and chimpanzees, Ommaya proposed critical tolerances for concussion, subdural hematoma and diffuse axonal injury in adult humans.

Subsequent work has identified differences in tolerance to skull and brain injury dependent upon the axis of rotation and site of impact (Gennarelli, Thibault, & Ommaya, 1987; Kikuchi, Ono, & Nakamura, 1982; Marguiles, Thibault, & Gennarelli, 1990; Shatsky, Alter, & Evans, 1974). This work indicates that coronal rotational events are more injurious than similar rotations in a sagittal or horizontal plane. High-speed cinefluorography of impact events indicates that coronal impact leads to transient skull deformation, which does not occur with occipital impact. Skull deformation raises the potential for local, underlying brain contusion; hence, this data explains the predilection of coup injuries with coronal impacts and contra-coup injuries commonly seen after occipital impacts. Deformation of the skull implies higher bone strain; hence, it is not surprising that experimental temporo-parietal impacts showed significant brain injury only in association with fracture while occipital or frontal impacts often produced isolated brain injury. The differing nature of side-impact events has its correlate in abusive head trauma as the "tin-ear" injury (Hanigan, Peterson, & Njus, 1987). A difference has also been noted in mechanical effects of falls and blows (Yanagida, Fujiwara, & Mizol, 1989) in a mechanical model. Both types of events caused a positive pressure zone at the site of impact and a negative pressure zone in contra-coup regions. However, the negative pressure effect was brief with a blow and prolonged after a simulated fall; this correlates with the clinical observation that coup injuries are commonly seen after severe blows and contra-coup injuries are more common after falls (Lindenberg, 1973). This has implications for evaluation of childhood head injuries attributed to falls.

The development of diffuse axonal injury is dependent upon the duration of trauma as well as the axis of rotation (Gennarelli et al., 1982; Gennarelli et al., 1987). More prolonged rotational events, with higher angular velocity, result in increased likelihood of diffuse axonal injury in preference to more rapid decelerations with lower angular velocity, which are more likely to result in subdural hematomas (Gennarelli & Thibault, 1982). Diffuse axonal injury occurs with lower thresholds when rotation is coronal rather than sagittal.

Shaken-Impact Syndrome

In the decade following the publication of Guthkelch (1971) and Caffey's (1972) papers, it became increasingly evident that many children with brain injuries indistinguishable or highly similar to the injuries described by Caffey had evidence of impact injury to the head or elsewhere; we have already alluded to two children in Caffey's original series with concomitant blunt trauma. Hahn (1983) reported on 77 abused children with head trauma ranging from concussion to death. He found skull fracture to be common; 37 children (48%) had 72 skull fractures. Other evidence of blunt trauma was even more frequent. Finally, he obtained delayed histories after legal proceedings, which revealed "pure" shaking in only 8% of his cases. Similar data was noted at other centers during this interval.

Duhaime, a pediatric neurosurgeon, published a provocative two-part study in collaboration with her neurosurgical colleagues at the University of Pennsylvania. (Duhaime et al., 1987) They reviewed 48 children with abusive head trauma and found data consistent with Hahn's previous report; 30 children (63%) had evidence of blunt impact to the head, an additional six (13%) had evidence of extra-cranial impact. All thirteen fatal cases showed evidence of cranial impact injury, although this was only found on autopsy in six cases. A history, which was felt to be reliable was ultimately obtained in 40 cases (83%); only one such history implicated shaking alone as the source of injury.

Duhaime et al. (1987) linked this clinical study with an experimental model in which accelerometers were attached to various sites in and around a doll's head; the doll was appropriately weight-distributed and three different models of neck were utilized. Rotational acceleration and velocity was measured during shaking alone and during shaking followed by impact against a hard or soft surface; these results were compared to the critical threshold's generated by the work of Ommaya and Gennerelli. None of the shakes reached expected threshold levels for concussion, subdural hematoma, or diffuse axonal injury; many of the shakes associated with impact did surpass these thresholds, even when the impact was against a soft surface such as a mattress (see Figure 10). Impact caused a thirty-fold greater decelerative force than shaking alone (see Figure 11). It must be clear, that the impacts described in this paper are in the context of a freely moving, rotating, head at the end of a shaking episode, leading to significant rotational deceleration; these are not impacts resulting from a dropped "infant" or immobile infant.

This paper led to reassessment and controversy as to whether shaking alone was sufficient to cause abusive head injuries or whether impact was required, even if no overt evidence of impact was discernible. Indeed, there is one published report of death caused to a small adult by repetitive shaking by much larger adults as a means of torture (Pounder, 1997). Hence, it is not clear that Duhaime et al.'s (1987) conclusion that impact is required is true. Nevertheless, the high frequency of blunt trauma injuries of the head in children with abusive brain injury, Ommaya's observation that pure whiplash injuries have an injury threshold twice as high as rotation with impact, and Duhaime's data reflecting the achievable rotational accelerations and velocities in her infant model make it clear that any observed blunt head trauma should not be dismissed as coincidental but should be considered as important indicators of mechanism of injury.

The Modern Synthesis

In the past twenty years, there has been a steady increase in our understanding of brain injury from studies, which have linked gross and histological pathologic response and metabolic derangements to quantifiable, replicable experimental trauma. In 1982, Gennarelli, a student, colleague and successor of Ommaya, identified the node of Ranvier as the site of histological damage in diffuse axonal injury (Gennarelli, 1982a). Subsequently, he and his colleagues have identified the metabolic changes, which occur in axonal membranes and microglia after rotational trauma (McIntosh et al., 1996; Thibault & Gennarelli, 1985). This has led to an improved understanding of the relationship between traumatic mechanism, visible contusion, laceration and hemorrhage and associated axonal injury and cerebral edema. Several global reviews have consolidated this wealth of information (Gennarelli, 1993; Hymel, Bandak, Partington, & Winston, 1998; Viano, 1988). In these paradigms, traumatic mechanisms have been described as impact, impulse and compressive loading based upon duration of event and cerebral pathology has been described as focal or diffuse, and primary or secondary in nature.

Impact injuries range in duration from 1-30 msec. In impact events, focal injuries are due to contact processes; the degree and nature of the focal injuries are dependent upon the site of impact, degree of force and the anatomy of the structures. Diffuse injuries and loss of consciousness are due to head motion preceding or following the impact; the degree and nature of these injuries is dependent upon rotational velocity, rotational acceleration and duration of impact.

Impulse or whiplash events range in duration from 50-200 msec. In this setting, translational acceleration or deceleration is of little importance. Diffuse injury, including loss of consciousness, is the result of shearing forces as the brain rotates relative to the skull. The threshold for injury is dependent upon brain mass, duration of the impulse, and the geometry of the skull and brain in the axis of rotation.

Quasi-static compressive events occur with forces that are applied for longer than 200 msec. In this setting, focal injuries predominate, especially skull

FIGURE 10

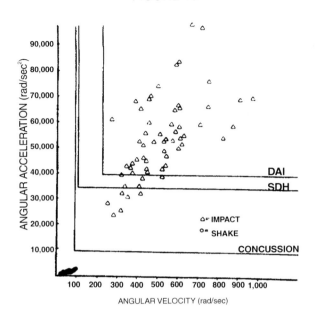

Adapted from Duhaime 1987

fracture and laceration and contusion of the cerebral tissues directly underlying the fracture. Loss of consciousness is a late and uncommon finding; when it does occur it is associated with direct injury of brainstem regions. These features of compressive loading have been corroborated in childhood as well (Duhaime, Eppley, Margulies, Heher, & Bartlett, 1995).

Hymel et al. (1998) have incorporated this framework into a paradigm for analysis of childhood brain injuries. Hymel advocates starting with the observed injuries and deriving the mechanism of injury from the constellation of focal and diffuse lesions, while differentiating primary and secondary pathology, and comparing these with the proffered history. This approach is most likely to result in a secure, scientifically-based analysis. Interestingly, he does not take a firm position on shaking alone versus shaking plus impact. Instead, he notes that diffuse injuries with impact imply that the head was free to move and rotate, either rotating prior to impact (as in shaking followed by impact) or set into motion by the impact itself (e.g., when hit by a "roundhouse" punch). This is consistent with what is currently known and avoids many of the pitfalls associated with a dogmatic approach to the question of impact. This important paper deserves the reader's thorough review.

FIGURE 11. Representative tangential acceleration traces for infant models undergoing shake (upper) and impact (lower) manipulations. While manipulations of the infant models were performed as described, with a series of shakes followed by an impact, the magnitude of the impact accelerations was so much greater than that associated with the shakes that different scales are used to display the respective acceleration traces.

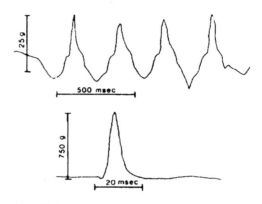

Adapted from Duhaime 1987

Falls

Any biomechanical analysis of abusive head trauma must include a review of the physics of falling since this is the most common explanation provided for the injuries at the time of presentation. There is a wide clinical literature indicating the safety of short falls in childhood, chief among them the articles by Helfer, Barlow and Chadwick (Barlow, 1983; Chadwick, Chin, Salerno, Landsverk, Kitchen, 1991; Helfer et al., 1977). Nevertheless, there exist papers in the medical literature, which support the possibility that severe or fatal brain injury can occur from household heights. Some, such as the article by Aoki (1984) are exceptionally credulous of parental history and require no further examination in this setting. However, the article by Reiber (1993) is more disturbing in its implications, and its assertions must be examined for validity. Reiber, a forensic pathologist, presents data on 22 children who died after reported falls. Three were publicly observed falls of 15-25 feet. Of the 19 children with reported falls of 1-5 feet, 14 were identified by the pathologist as homicides and three were felt to have indications of battering but were not ruled homicides. The remaining two deaths occurred in settings, which may have added increased rotational forces to the fall. This clinical portion of his paper is in agreement with the general clinical impression of the safety of short falls. However, Reiber cites a paper by Reichelderfer, Overback, and Greensher (1979) in his discussion as "compelling" and as giving good reason to believe that falls from as little as three inches could be fatal. The information, which proved so convincing to Reiber is summarized in Table 1 below. The data derives from studies performed at the Franklin Institute Research Laboratories (Philadelphia, PA) at the request of the Consumer Product Safety Commission-however no date or title of the report is given. An exhaustive search has failed to turn up the principal report describing how these studies were performed. The Franklin Institute Research laboratory is no longer in operation.

Table 1 lists the following g forces (i.e., deceleration rates) in drops onto various surfaces. The Reichelderfer summary does not indicate what has been dropped, nor the mechanical properties of that substance in comparison to that of the adult or infant human body. This table is accompanied by a statement saying that decelerations in excess of 50g can be associated with serious head injury (no reference given). The clear implication is that a fall of three inches onto concrete, of six or 12 inches onto asphalt, or four feet onto packed earth is not only possible but highly likely to cause severe head injury. This is not consistent either with clinical or practical experience. The assertions in this paper misrepresent the risk of significant head injury from short falls in three ways. First, whatever substance was used to derive these deceleration results, behaved in a manner very different from animal or human tissues. Calculation of the interval of deceleration time (i.e., the duration of impact) from the known heights of these "falls" indicates unrealistically short durations of impact (see Table 2).

In contrast, biological models of impact events show durations of 1-3 msec for hard impacts, such as a fall on concrete, and 15-30 msec for moderate impacts, such as a fall onto packed earth, two to twelve times longer than in the cited paper. It must be concluded that whatever object was dropped, it was far more rigid than an animal or human body. Substituting more reasonable impact durations drops all of these decelerations well below the supposed fatal threshold of 50g.

The second major flaw is in Reiber's failure to recognize the importance of viscoelasticity in brain trauma. Viscoelastic materials, such as the brain, have injury criteria dependent upon velocity rather than acceleration for short duration events. With short falls starting from rest, linear velocity is very low, and angular velocity is almost non-existent. High accelerations (or decelerations) are possible, but only if impact times are extremely small. The angular velocity thresholds for significant, non-contact brain injury cannot be met in this setting.

The third major misunderstanding in this paper is the assumption that all decelerative events have identical results. The type of deceleration reflected here is all translational, with no rotational component. As we have seen previously, the primate brain is very resistant to translational injury. Short falls, especially the extremely short falls hypothesized by Reiber, allow little or no possibility of significant rotational velocity or accelerative changes. Therefore the impact events predominantly result in contact phenomena such as ecchymosis, linear skull fracture, and perhaps, subdural or epidural hematoma immediately underlying the site of impact. This analysis is consistent with the mass of clinical information regarding the rarity of significant injuries resulting from falls of household height.

What Remains to Be Learned

1. How does the biomechanics of the infant brain differ from that of the adult? Is this difference important?

One possible flaw in Duhaime et al.'s (1987) analysis is that the predicted thresholds for injury were based upon data obtained from adult primates of various sizes, and extrapolated to human infants. No experimental data exists

TABLE 1. G Forces sustained from various heights onto various surfaces

Surface Material	Drop Height (feet)			
	0.25(3")	0.5(6")	1.0(12")	4.0 (48")
concrete	150-200g	250-300g	475-525g	
asphalt	40-45	60-65	140-160	
packed earth				175-225

(adapted from Reichelderfer)

TABLE 2. Impact times necessary to achieve the stated decelerations in milliseconds (0.001 seconds)

	3 inches	12 inches	48 inches
terminal velocity (m/sec)	1.22 m/sec	2.44m/sec	4.89 m/sec
concrete	0.6 msec	0.5 msec	
asphalt		1.65 msec	
packed earth			2.5 msec

for injury thresholds in the immature brain. Does this matter? Is the immature brain mechanically different from that of an adult?

The best answer to this question is that we don't know but there is reason to believe that the immature brain is different. As we have seen, the Node of Ranvier is the site of axonal shearing. This implies that the myelin sheath may be protective; if so, the relatively un-myelinated, infant brain may be more susceptible to shearing injury than an adult brain. There has been an interesting, recent paper supporting this premise (Thibault & Margulies, 1998). Comparison of freshly obtained, frontal lobe material from neonatal and adult porcine brains indicated that shear modulus increased from infancy to adulthood. This would imply an increased tendency to shearing in the more immature brain. The authors presented data to show several measures of equivalence between the 2-3 day old porcine brain constituents and one-month-old human brain. Other possible differences from the adult brain include rigidity of the attachment of the meninges; such differences can affect the degree of movement of the brain within the skull.

2. Is shaking the same as whiplash?

Shaking is an inherently cyclical event; whiplash is isolated. Can a rotational event, which is apparently below the threshold necessary to produce brain injury, cause injury if it is repeated frequently in a short period of time? If there is an additive effect of quickly repeated rotational injuries, this may explain the persistent small percentage of infants with abusive head trauma who show no signs of impact injury.

3. What is the mechanism of injury for retinal hemorrhage?

The high correlation of retinal hemorrhages with abusive head injury implicates a common mode of causation; presumably, rotational injury. However, none of the researchers studying experimental brain injury have examined the retinas of their experimental animals. The relative importance of transient increases in intra-cranial pressure, direct shearing effects, and dissection of blood along neural pathways has not been adequately studied.

4. Can computer models improve our understanding?

Exciting work is going on now in developing computer models of the head-neck complex (Bandak, 1995; King, Ruan, Zhou, Hardy, & Khalil, 1995; Krabbel & Appel, 1995; Lighthall, Melvin, & Ueno, 1989; Marguiles & Thibault, 1989; Marguiles & Thibault, 1992; Ruan & Prasad, 1995; Voo,

Kumaresan, & Pintar, 1996). However, caution must be exercised in interpreting this data; minor changes in the model can have a major impact upon the apparent outcome of modeled events (Kuijpers, Claessens, & Sauren, 1995; Kumaresan & Radhakrishnan, 1996). Appropriate models for the infant must await better delineation of biomechanical data for this age group.

REFERENCES

Aoki, N., & Masazuwa, H. (1984). Infantile acute subdural haematomata: Clinical analysis of 26 cases. *Journal of Neurosurgery, 61*, 273-280.

Bandak, F.A. (1995). On the mechanics of impact neurotrauma: A review and clinical synthesis. *Journal of Neurotrauma, 12*, 635.

Barlow, B. (1983). Ten years of experience with falls from a height in children. *Journal of Pediatric Surgery, 18*, 509.

Caffey, J. (1972). On the theory and practice of shaking infants. *American Journal of Diseases of Children, 124*, 161.

Chadwick, D.L., Chin, S., Salerno, C., Landsverk, J., & Kitchen, L. (1991). Deaths from falls in children: How far is fatal? *Journal of Trauma, 31*, 1353

Duhaime, A.C., Eppley, M., Margulies, S., Heher, K.L., & Bartlett, S.P. (1995). Crush injuries to the head in children. *Neurosurgery, 37*, 401.

Duhaime, A.C., Gennarelli, T.A., Thibault, L.E., Bruce, D.A., Margulies, S.S., & Wiser, R. (1987). The shaken baby syndrome: A clinical, pathological and biomechanical study. *Journal of Neurosurgery, 66*, 409.

Gennarelli, T.A. (1993). Mechanisms of brain injury. *Journal of Emergency Medicine, 11*(supp 1), 5.

Gennarelli, T.A., & Thibault, L.E. (1982). Biomechanics of acute subdural hematoma. *Journal of Trauma: Injury, Infection, and Critical Care, 22*, 680-686.

Gennarelli, T.A., Thibault, L., Adams, J.H., Graham, D.I., Thompson, C.J., & Marcincin, R.P. (1982). Diffuse axonal injury and traumatic coma in the primate. *Annals of Neurology, 12*, 564.

Gennarelli, T.A., Thibault, L.E., & Ommaya, A.K. (1972). Pathophysiological response to rotational and translational accelerations of the head. Proceedings of the 16th Stapp Car Crash Conference, SAE NY 296-308. Reprinted in *Biomechanics of impact injury and injury tolerances of the head neck complex* (pp. 411-423).

Gennarelli, T.A., Thibault, L.E., & Tomei, G. (1987). Directional dependence of axonal brain injury due to centroidal and non-centroidal acceleration. SAE reprinted in *Biomechanics of impact injury and injury tolerances of the head neck complex* (pp. 595-599).

Guthkelch, A.N. (1971). Infantile subdural haematoma and its relationship to whiplash injuries. *British Medical Journal, 2*, 430.

Hahn, Y.S., Raimondi, A.J., McLone, D.G., & Yamanouchi, Y. (1983). Traumatic mechanisms of head injury in child abuse. *Child Brain, 10*, 229.

Hanigan, W.C., Peterson, R.A., & Njus, G. (1987). Tin ear syndrome: Rotational acceleration in pediatric head injuries. *Pediatrics, 80*, 618.

Helfer, R.E., Slovis, T.L., & Black, M. (1977). Injuries resulting when small children fall out of bed. *Pediatrics, 60*, 533.

Hirsch, A.E., & Ommaya, A.K. (1970). Protection from brain injury: The relative significance of translational and rotational motions of the head after impact. SAE reprinted in *Biomechanics of impact injury and injury tolerances of the head neck complex* (pp. 275-282).

Holboum, A.H.S. (1943). Mechanics of head injuries. *Lancet, 2*, 438.

Hymel, K.P., Bandak, F.A., Partington, M.D., & Winston, K.R. (1998). Abusive head trauma? A biomechanical approach. *Child Maltreatment, 3*(2), 116.

Kikuchi, A., Ono, K., Nakamura, N. (1982). Human head tolerance to lateral impact deduced from experimental head injuries using primates. SAE reprinted in *Biomechanics of impact injury and injury tolerances of the head neck complex* (pp. 361-371).

King, A.I., Ruan, J.S., Zhou, C., Hardy, W.N., Khalil, T.B. (1995). Recent advances in biomechanics of brain injury research: a review. *Journal of Neurotrauma, 12*, 651.

Krabbel, G., & Appel, H. (1995). Development of a finite element model of the human skull. *Journal of Neurotrauma, 12*, 735.

Kravitz, H., Driessen, G., Gomberg, R., & Korach, A. (1969). Accidental falls from elevated surfaces in infants from birth to one year of age. *Pediatrics, 44*(suppl), 869.

Kuijpers, A.H., Claessens, M.H., & Sauren, A.A. (1995). The influence of different boundary conditions on the response of the head to impact: A 2-dimensional finite element study. *Journal of Neurotrauma, 12*, 715.

Kumaresan, S., & Radhakrishnan, S. (1996). Importance of partitioning membranes of the brain and the influence of the neck in head injury modeling. *Medical and Biological Engineering and Computing, 34*, 27.

Lighthall, J.W., Melvin, J.W., & Ueno, K. (1989). Toward a biomechanical criterion for functional brain injur. SAE reprinted in *Biomechanics of impact injury and injury tolerances of the head neck complex* (pp. 621-627).

Lindenberg, R. (1973). Mechanical injuries of brain and meninges. In W.V. Spiz, & R.S. Fisher (Eds.), *Medicolegal investigation of death* (pp. 447-456). Springfield, IL: Charles C. Thomas.

Lyons, T.J. & Oates, R.K. (1993). Falling out of bed: A relatively benign occurrence. *Pediatrics, 92*, 125.

Margulies, S.S., & Thibault, L.E. (1989). An analytical model of traumatic diffuse brain injury. *Journal of Biomechanics Eng, 111*, 241.

Margulies, S.S., & Thibault, L.E. (1992). A proposed tolerance criterion for diffuse axonal injury in man. *Journal of Biomechanics, 25*, 917.

Margulies, S.S., Thibault, L.E., & Gennarelli, T.A. (1990). Physical model simulations of brain injury in the primate. *Journal of Biomechanics, 23*, 823.

McIntosh, T.K., Smith, D.H., Meaney, D.F., Kotapka, M.J., Gennarelli, T.A., & Graham, D.I. (1996). Neuropathological sequelae of traumatic brain injury: Relationship to neurochemical and biomechanical mechanisms. *Lab Invest, 74*, 315.

Nimityongskul, P., & Anderson, L.D. (1987). The likelihood of injuries when children fall out of bed. *Journal of Pediatric Orthopedics, 7*, 184.

Ommaya, A.K., Faas, F., & Yarnell, P. (1968). Whiplash injury and brain damage. *Journal of the American Medical Association, 204*, 285.

Ommaya, A.K., Fisch, F.J., & Mahone, R.M. (1970). Comparative tolerances for cerebral concussion by head impact and whiplash injury in primates. SAE reprinted in S. Backaitis (Ed.) *Biomechanics of impact Injury and injury tolerances of the head neck complex* (pp. 265–274).

Ommaya, A.K., & Hirsch, A.E. (1971). Tolerances for cerebral concussion from head impact and whiplash in primates. *Journal of Biomechanics, 4*, 13.

Pounder, D.J. (1997). Shaken adult syndrome. *American Journal of Forensic Medicine, 18*, 37.

Reiber, G.D. (1993). Fatal falls in childhood: How far must children fall to sustain fatal head injury? Report of cases and review of the literature. *American Journal of Forensic Medicine and Pathology, 14*, 201.

Reichelderfer, T.C., Overback, A., & Greensher, J. (1979). Unsafe playgrounds. *Pediatrics, 64*, 962.

Ruan, J.S., & Prasad, P. (1995). Coupling of a finite element human head model with a lumped parameter Hybrid III Dummy model: Preliminary results. *Journal of Neurotrauma, 12*, 725.

Shatsky, S.A., Alter, W.A. III, & Evans, D.E. (1974). Traumatic distortions of the primate head and chest: Correlation of biomechanical, radiological and pathological data. SAE reprinted in *Biomechanics of impact injury and injury tolerances of the head neck complex* (pp. 105-121).

Thibault, K.L., & Margulies, S.S. (1998). Age-dependent material properties of the porcine cerebrum: effect on pediatric inertial head injury criteria. *Journal of Biomechanics, 31*, 1119-1126.

Thibault, L.E., & Gennarelli, T.A. (1985). Biomechanics of diffuse brain injury. SAE reprinted in *Biomechanics of impact injury and injury tolerances of the head neck complex* (pp. 555-561).

Viano, D.C. (1988). Biomechanics of head injury-Toward a theory linking head dynamic motion, brain tissue deformation and neural trauma. SAE reprinted in *Biomechanics of impact injury and injury tolerances of the head neck complex* (pp. 601-620).

Voo, K., Kumaresan, S., & Pintar, F.R. (1996). Finite-element models of the human head. *Medical and Biological Engineering and Computing, 34*, 375.

Yanagida Y, Fujiwara S, Mizol Y, "Differences in the intracranial pressure caused by a 'blow' and/or a 'fall'–an experimental study using physical models of the head and neck," 1989 *For Sci Int, 41,*135.

Chapter Six

Neurologic Sequelae
of Shaken Baby Syndrome

Kenneth W. Reichert
Meic Schmidt

SUMMARY. Shaken infant syndrome is commonly associated with injuries to the central nervous system. Non-accidental cerebral trauma has been implicated in 10 percent of children under age two with injury. Cranial vault fractures, subdural hematomas, localized parenchymal hemorrhages, diffuse axonal injury and spinal cord injury can be part of the shaken infant syndrome. This review will outline the neurosurgical aspects of the multidisciplinary team approach in cases of children with neurological sequelae from the shaken infant syndrome. *[Article copies available for a fee from The Haworth Document Delivery Service: 1-800-342-9678. E-mail address: <getinfo@haworthpressinc.com> Website: <http://www.HaworthPress.com> © 2001 by The Haworth Press, Inc. All rights reserved.]*

KEYWORDS. Cerebral trauma, intracranial pressure, hydrocephalus, subdural hematoma, diffuse axonal injury, brain swelling

---

[Haworth co-indexing entry note]: "Neurologic Sequelae of Shaken Baby Syndrome." Reichert, Kenneth W., and Meic Schmidt. Co-published simultaneously in *Journal of Aggression, Maltreatment & Trauma* (The Haworth Maltreatment & Trauma Press, an imprint of The Haworth Press, Inc.) Vol. 5, No. 1(#9), 2001, pp. 79-99; and: *The Shaken Baby Syndrome: A Multidisciplinary Approach* (ed: Stephen Lazoritz, and Vincent J. Palusci) The Haworth Maltreatment & Trauma Press, an imprint of The Haworth Press, Inc., 2001, pp. 79-99. Single or multiple copies of this article are available for a fee from The Haworth Document Delivery Service [1-800-342-9678, 9:00 a.m. - 5:00 p.m. (EST). E-mail address: getinfo@haworthpressinc.com].

INTRODUCTION

Non-accidental cerebral injury has been implicated in ten percent of head trauma to children less than two years of age (Bruce, 1990). In half of abused patients, head injury will be present. The mechanism of cerebral injury involves to and from shaking of the child's body producing a whiplash motion to the cervical region (Caffey, 1972, 1974). Duhaime et al.'s (1987) work documents the need for blunt head trauma as well as shaking to produce the syndrome in its most severe form. Traumatic injuries of the CNS may be classified as primary or secondary. Primary damage occurs at the moment of injury whereas secondary damage results from the processes that complicate the injury. Primary injury may be due to impact, with resulting fracture, epidural hemorrhage, brain contusion or laceration, or intracerebral hemorrhage, or to acceleration/deceleration injuries, resulting in subdural hemorrhage, diffuse axonal injury or diffuse vascular injury (Graham, Adams, Nicoll, Maxwell, & Gennarelli, 1995). Recent studies also demonstrate delayed consequences of primary injury owing to free radicals, receptor dysfunction, calcium-mediated damage, or inflammation (Miller, 1993; Teasdale, 1995). Secondary damage results from hypoxia/ischemia, edema, infection or increased intracranial pressure following head trauma (Graham, 1996; Graham & Gennarelli, 1997).

The goal of this chapter is to provide health care workers with an overview and a reference that can be used in the recognition of common child abuse syndromes involving neurosurgical care, the management of acute injuries and an outcome review of neurological damage. Many health care institutions use a team approach to cases of suspected non-accidental trauma. This provides an organized means of addressing the frequently complex disturbing and time-consuming issues involved in caring for the abused pediatric patient.

EVALUATION OF CHILD ABUSE

The history after suspected abuse is useful in a paradoxical way. Non-accidental injury is increasingly likely as the history diverges from the clinical and radiographic findings or with inconsistent histories from the supposed witnesses.

While not pathognomonic, retinal hemorrhages occur in a majority of abused head-injured children, and when present, abuse must be considered. Retinal hemorrhages are present in 65 to 100 percent of abused head injured patients (Caffey, 1974; Wilkinson, Han, Rappley, & Owings, 1989; Zimmerman et al., 1979). Furthermore, the severity of neurological insult correlates with the degree of retinal hemorrhage (Zimmerman et al., 1979).

Skull fractures crossing suture lines, multiple fractures and bilateral fractures are found more often in abused than accidentally-injured children (Merservy, Towbin, McLaurin, Myers, & Ball, 1987). Findings on CT scan include subdural hemorrhage, particularly acute interhemispheric subdural; intracerebral shear hemorrhage; or localized parenchymal hemorrhage (Zimmerman et al., 1979). Magnetic resonance imaging (MRI) of infant child abuse will show convexity and intrafalcine subdural hematoma, cortical contusions, and shearing injuries (Sato et al., 1989). Newton contrasts accidental with non-accidental trauma (Newton, 1989). After accidents, subdural hemorrhage occurred in less than 0.2 % of infants. Skull fractures were generally simple, unilateral and non-diastatic. Injury to the child's body was unlikely; prolonged loss of consciousness was rare. Overall the incidence of serious or life-threatening injury is lower after accidental than non-accidental trauma. Severe injury is common after abuse.

In a clinical and biomechanical study, Duhaime et al. (1987) concluded that, in its most severe form, the shaken baby usually also receives a blunt impact to the head to generate the force necessary to produce the observed clinical features. However, Hadley, Sonntag, Rekate, and Murphy (1989) identified a subset of critically injured abused patients without evidence of cranial impact who had the intracranial injury described above. Hadley also observed in five of six children, spinal cord injury at the cervicomedullary junction resulting in subdural or epidural hematoma formation. Spinal cord contusions were also identified in these five patients.

TIMING OF THE INJURY

The history given after a suspected child abuse case is often unreliable. Information about the timing of the injury must be extrapolated from data and knowledge of accidental trauma. Acute subdural hematoma associated with severe neurological decompensation, cerebral edema, or death occurs in the setting of an injury involving a major mechanical force followed by immediate or rapid onset of neurological symptoms (Gennarelli, 1983). In a series of 95 patients who died from accidental head injury, all but one of the children had an immediate decrease in the level of consciousness; the exception was a patient with an extracerebral, intracranial hemorrhage (Willman, Bank, Senac, & Chadwick, 1997). This type of injury, generated by contact forces to the skull and dura, is usually not associated with a primary brain injury. It is rarely associated with child abuse (Shugermann, Paez, Grossman, Feldman, & Grady, 1996). Other reports of delayed deterioration after pediatric head injury have primarily involved the onset of seizures, followed by recovery (Snock,

Minderhoud, & Wilmink, 1984). On the basis of data presented above, it can be discerned that there is no evidence of a prolonged interval of lucency between the injury and onset of symptoms in children with acute subdural hematoma and brain swelling. This injury is seen in all severe cases of child abuse associated with coma or death. Thus, an alert well-appearing child has not already sustained a devastating acute injury that will become clinically obvious hours to days later.

Timing of the traumatic event is more difficult to establish in patients with mild neurological injuries. The determination of this type of injury is based on general physical and radiographic findings. Unfortunately these methods can only indicate a general time frame of onset. A separate set of events is the serial minor trauma, which leads to acute urgent deterioration. Such rare events have been reported in older children, usually in the setting of repetitive concussive events in sports activity. These subarachnoid or subdural hemorrhages and associated brain swelling lead to a deterioration (Cantu, 1992; Kelly et al., 1991). This pattern of injury, with a clear time-line and rapid, well-described acute deterioration, stands in contrast to the vague histories of previous episodes of trivial trauma that are sometimes suggested as the cause of neurological injury in child abuse. There is no evidence that traumatic acute subdural hematoma, particularly that leading to death, occurs in an otherwise healthy infant in an occult or subclinical manner.

PHYSICAL ABUSE IN THE OLDER CHILD

Most older children brought to medical attention suffer from soft tissue or visceral injuries from direct blows. Intracranial injuries, although rare, can occur and be serious or even fatal. Most of these events involve behavioral management with physical punishment, such as beating. The reported motive is to prevent a child from becoming a social deviant in society.

Evaluation includes taking a careful history. The child should be questioned apart from the parents. A general trauma evaluation including urinalysis is recommended. Skeletal survey is usually limited in older children because the typical injuries of metaphyseal and rib fractures are not seen in older children. Careful review of the previous trauma history, including that of any fractures and physical examination, is usually more helpful than skeletal survey in detecting collaborating physical findings of child abuse in this age category.

Head injuries may include soft tissue lesions; linear, depressed or basilar skull fractures; and the range of intracranial lesions usually seen in low impact trauma. Management is guided by the specific injury. Counseling as well as a neuropsychologic evaluation may be required in children with acute or chronic brain injury. Behavioral disturbances can be associated with these injuries and should be evaluated in a multi-disciplinary team approach to help the child in social skills and education.

MANAGEMENT OF HEAD INJURIES
RESULTING FROM CHILD ABUSE

The initial treatment of infants with markedly impaired consciousness includes endotracheal intubation, ventilation, fluid resuscitation and consideration of anti-convulsant therapy. Surgical evacuation should be considered in cases of large acute intracranial hematomas. The value of aggressive management of intracranial hypertension has been questioned on the basis of outcome studies. These studies show infants who present with poor prognostic indicators, especially bilaterally diffuse hypodensity on CT scans, have dismal outcomes regardless of treatment. Less severely injured infants are treated with anticonvulsant agents and closely observed; recovery is variable in such cases (Duhaime, Christian, Moss, & Seidl, 1996; Johnson, Boal, & Baule, 1995).

In infants who succumb, the cause of death is uncontrollable intracranial hypertension. Severe cortical and white matter atrophy is consistently identified on follow-up radiographic studies in survivors with diffuse hypodensity during the acute period.

ACUTE SUBDURAL HEMATOMA IN CHILD ABUSE

The peak incidence of child abuse resulting in intracranial hemorrhages is six months, and most cases occur before the age of two years. The infant's head during this age is disproportionately large, with poor muscular support of the neck; the cerebrum is fragile because of its high water content and poor myelination, and the subarachnoid space is relatively large, all making the brain relatively mobile. Children with acute subdural hematomas are usually seriously ill at presentation but trauma is not always obvious. The obtunded or unconscious infant who is evaluated with a bulging fontanelle and history of respiratory arrest or seizures must be considered as a possible child abuse victim. An urgent cerebral CT scan and careful ophthalmologic assessment for retinal hemorrhages must be performed. The differential diagnosis for a child presenting with the above history includes meningitis, encephalitis, status epilepticus, and intoxication. The presence of retinal hemorrhages is virtually diagnostic of the violently shaken infant in the absence of severe accidental trauma (Greenwald, 1990; Luerssen, Huang, McLone, Walker, & Hahn,

1991). Retinal hemorrhages rarely occur following severe accidental trauma (Luerssen et al., 1991), spontaneous intracranial hemorrhage (McLellan, Prasad, & Punt, 1986), or vigorous cardiopulmonary resuscitation (Goetting & Sowa, 1990; Kanter, 1986). For all practical purposes, however, retinal hemorrhages in association with acute subdural hemorrhaging means that a violent shaking with or without impact occurred.

The cerebral injury resulting from the acceleration-deceleration force is severe. A combination of factors is involved since most intracranial hemorrhages are relatively minor and the ultimate cerebral destruction is major and widespread. At initial presentation, there is often a description of arrest or apneic event. An ischemic or hypoxic insult may add to the primary shaking injury. In this setting, it is known that severe cerebral injuries may be associated with injuries to brain regions important to respiratory function at the craniocervical junction (Hadley et al., 1989). The primary cerebral injury results in cerebral white matter shearing, cerebral cortical contusions and intracranial hemorrhage (Lindenberg & Freytag, 1969; Ordia, Strand, Gilles, & Welch, 1981). The hemorrhage usually arises from disrupted bridging veins leading to the posterior interhemispheric and tentorial hemorrhages. This is the reason why most interhemispheric subdural hematomas occur in this location. Cerebral arteries may also be injured. Subarachnoid hemorrhage is common and vasospasm may further lead to secondary cerebral injury from ischemia. As the brain swells or is compressed by an expanding intracranial hematoma, the intracranial pressure increases and cerebral perfusion pressure falls. This fall in cerebral perfusion pressure contributes to widespread ischemia. As intracranial pressure rises, cerebral herniation with a subsequent shift compresses arteries on the cerebral surface and along the tentorial incisura leading to infarction in arterial distributions. This complicated chain of events results in acute subdural hematomas, cerebral white matter shearing, subarachnoid hemorrhage and widespread cerebral cortical necrosis.

The cerebral injury is severe even if the subdural hematoma is relatively small. Occasional large subdural hematomas will require craniotomy for removal; only rarely is a subdural tap useful in the setting of an acute subdural hemorrhage. More commonly, neurosurgical involvement is limited to intracranial pressure monitoring with CSF drainage via a ventricular catheter. The severe cerebral ischemia/hypoxic insult must be managed medically in an intensive care unit until cerebral swelling can be controlled. After cerebral swelling is controlled, neurosurgical intervention may again be required. As the bulk of the brain diminishes, the subarachnoid and subdural spaces enlarge and the subdural space requires long-term drainage via a subdural to peritoneal shunt. The prognosis in acute subdural hematomas in infants is dismal. A mortality rate of 20% and a 50% morbidity rate in most series are reported (Alexander, Sato, Smith, & Bennett, 1990; Hahn, Raimondi, McLone, & Yamanouchi, 1983; Ludwig & Warman, 1984).

Diffuse Cerebral Swelling

Two mechanisms can account for enlargement of the brain after injury: cerebral edema and diffuse cerebral swelling. In the former, the extracellular space of the brain is distended by proteinaceous-rich fluid (Klatzo, 1979). Although the formation of edema has been reasonably well characterized in many settings, cerebral edema is not found in head injured children except as a reaction to focal brain injuries such as contusion or intracerebral hematoma. On the other hand, diffuse cerebral swelling (DCS) is an unusual response in adults after head injury, but occurs frequently after head injury in children. This entity was originally described as a common post-mortem finding in children dying from head injury and consisted of obliteration of the CSF spaces, venous congestion, and enlargement of the cerebral hemispheres (Lindenberg, Risher, & Durlacher, 1955).

CT evidence of DCS can be found in 29% of conscious head injured children and in over 40% of comatose children (Bruce et al, 1981). CT scanning demonstrates small ventricles and subarachnoid cisterns with compression or absence of the perimesencephalic cisterns in the absence of a focal brain lesion. Repeat imaging performed 7-10 days later shows that the ventricles and cisterns return to normal size. In severely head injured children, extracerebral collections of fluid may develop as the swelling diminishes. These collections usually resolve spontaneously and do not require treatment (Bruce et al., 1981). This is in contrast to the chronic subdural collections of abuse, which are more likely to require surgical treatment.

The higher CT density of cerebral parenchyma sometimes seen soon after injury has been interpreted as evidence that cerebral hyperemia causes DCS (Bruce et al., 1981). Increased cerebral blood volume has been demonstrated in some children by using Technetium-labeled red blood cells (Kuhl et al., 1980). When DCS is accompanied by diffuse axonal injury with small, deep-seated intraparenchymal foci or intraventricular hemorrhage, uncontrollable intracranial hypertension is frequently seen (Cordobes et al., 1987).

Diffuse cerebral swelling as a cause of increased intracranial pressure is thought to occur from cerebral hyperemia. Treatment measures, which would decrease cerebral blood flow, such as hyperventilation, play a role in controlling this type of intracerebral mass.

TREATMENT OF INTRACRANIAL HYPERTENSION

Most children with severe non-accidental injury will have markedly elevated intracranial pressure documented at the time of insertion of the monitoring device. In our experience, these children have a "pressure-passive" system in which ICP rises and falls in response to changes in systemic blood pressure. We have never successfully controlled ICP in these children; all have died. However, when intracranial hypertension can be controlled by a variety of methods, useful recovery is still questionable due to the diffuse cerebral injury present in this clinical entity.

The first issue to address in treating ICP is to define intracranial hypertension. Normal CSF pressure in young children may be only 2-10 mmHg (Welch, 1980). The lower normal systemic blood pressures found in children imply that the range for effective cerebral perfusion pressure (CPP) in children is probably narrower. With mass lesions and diffuse causes of raised ICP in children, relative systemic hypertension occurs early, perhaps in response to compromised cerebral perfusion with only modest elevations of ICP. For these reasons, ICP in head-injured children should be kept below 15-20 mmHg. Usually the initiation of ICP monitoring and treatment of intracranial hypertension are begun simultaneously. Obtaining a consistent and reliable tracing of intracranial pressure without intubation and paralysis via intravenous medication is usually impossible. The child may be mildly hyperventilated to a $PaCO_2$ of 30-35 torr, along with elevation of the head. Despite studies showing that the cerebral vasculature becomes less responsive to continued hypocarbia over one to two days, most clinical evidence indicates that continuous hyperventilation produces beneficial effects on ICP for a much longer period of time. This beneficial effect is presumed to happen via diminishing cerebral blood volume (Kuhl et al., 1980). In contrast to adults, profound hyperventilation in children with reduction of $PaCO_2$ to 17 torr can lower the ICP without compromising CBF (Bruce, 1982).

If these initial measures are not adequate, treatment advances in a stepwise fashion. After a ventricular catheter to monitor intracerebral pressure is inserted, CSF can be removed to lower pressure. The ventricles of head injured children are usually small. A 1-2 ml reduction of CSF can dramatically lower the ICP because of the steep pressure-volume curve found in children. If continuous CSF drainage does not control intracranial ICP, other modalities should be added.

The next step should be directed towards reducing brain volume by reducing extracellular fluid. This can be accomplished via diuretic therapy. Renal loop diuretics such as furosemide do not lower intracranial pressure rapidly, if at all (Wilkinson & Rosenfeld, 1983). Subsequently we use Mannitol (0.5-1.0 gm/kg/dose). Children can develop fluid and electrolyte difficulties after osmotic diuretics. Therefore it is essential that the excess urine output beyond the volume of Mannitol administered and the expected basal output of urine be replaced with appropriate intravenous solutions. Serum osmolarity should be measured frequently, especially when Mannitol is given more often than every 6-8 hours. In our experience, children requiring Mannitol more than every three or four hours can rapidly develop serum osmolarities over 300 mosm and may have renal and central nervous system toxic effects. To avoid this complication, some practitioners use intravenous glycerol (Bruce, 1983). We only use glycerol in very refractory patients.

The steps outlined above will successfully manage intracranial hypertension in the majority of head injured children. However, children of abuse will more likely require additional therapy to maintain ICP below 20 mmHg. In general, control of ICP may be achieved by using barbiturates, but this often must be supplemented with diuretics and drainage of CSF.

The best choice of barbiturate is presently unclear. Phenobarbital has the least effect on the systemic circulation, but may have less effect on ICP than thiopental or pentobarbital. Pentobarbital is probably the most frequently used agent, but it causes systemic hypotension by decreasing peripheral vascular resistance. Therefore the loading dose should be given slowly while monitoring systemic blood pressure and maintained at the lowest level that controls ICP. The initial dose of pentobarbital varies from 3-5 mg/kg. A continuous infusion is then begun at 1-2 mg/kg/hour. Blood levels of pentobarbital are measured. The endpoint is control of ICP or serum level of 25-35 mg/dl. In this group of patients, hypovolemia is more likely to be present because of the recurrent use of osmotic diuretics. Hemodynamic monitoring with an arterial catheter and central venous or pulmonary artery catheter is a necessary part of pentobarbital administration. If hypotension occurs, volume expansion, not vasoconstricting agents should be instituted promptly.

The recovery phase following head injury is a catabolic period. Early nutrition with total parenteral nutrition or enteral feedings is essential (Phillips, Ott, Young, & Walsh, 1987). We do not employ corticosteroids in treating head injured children because no beneficial effects on outcome have been proven. Furthermore, the use of corticosteroids carries a higher nutritional cost and is associated with medical complications such as pneumonia and sepsis (Cooper et al., 1979; Fanconi, Kloti, Meuli, Zaugg, & Zachmann, 1988).

CHRONIC SUBDURAL HEMATOMA

Chronic subdural hematomas of infancy, in contrast to acute subdural hematomas, which present a dramatic clinical picture with severe brain injury, often present simply as megalocephaly. The differential diagnosis includes hydrocephalus, benign extra-axial fluid collections of infancy, and brain tumor. Chronic subdural collections during infancy, for reasons not well understood, have a male predominance. Chronic subdural collections are regarded as post-traumatic lesions in a great majority of cases. Severe birth trauma is sometimes implicated but this is not likely in most cases. Rather, it seems that "minor" injuries during infancy or even more violent injuries such as infant shaking and/or cranial impact are the inciting events. In many cases a clear history of injury is not forthcoming. If a suspicion of trauma arises, the opportunity for a child abuse investigation with an initial social service screening, skeletal survey, bone scan and ophthalmologic assessment should be employed.

Congenital cerebral anomalies such as arachnoid cysts may predispose one for subdural hematoma formation (Cappelen & Unsgaard, 1986; Page, Paxton, & Mohan, 1987; Pozzati, Giuliani, Gaist, Piazza, & Vergoni, 1986). Subdural collections do occasionally follow meningitis (Goodman & Mealey, 1969; Rabe, Flynn, & Dodge, 1962). Haemophilus influenza and streptococcus pneumonia are two bacteria known to cause chronic subdural fluid collections. Pertussis, in association with violent coughing, is also reported to cause subdural fluid collections. Coagulopathy as a consequence of Vitamin K deficiency, leukemia or hemophilia are all well known to predispose infants to developing subdural fluid collections. An extremely rare case of subdural hematomas in infancy was related to Osteogenesis Imperfecta, a genetic condition that affects collagen metabolism and results in bone fragility (Tokoro, Nakajima, & Yamataki, 1988). Despite its rarity, this condition is occasionally invoked to defend an alleged perpetrator of child abuse in criminal proceedings. The condition is sporadic in about 2/3 of cases and an absence of a family history of the disease does not exclude it. The clinical signs of blue sclera, hypoplastic teeth and auditory abnormalities should alert the clinician to this diagnosis and biochemical abnormalities of Type I collagen may be demonstrated (Kooh, 1986).

Another common cause of subdural fluid collection on a neurosurgical service is cranial-cerebral disproportion resulting from CSF shunting. This may result in large accumulations of subdural/subarachnoid fluid as the cerebrum collapses from overshunting. Fortunately this type of subdural is relatively benign. These accumulations seem less likely to enlarge and the thick restrictive membranes rarely develop. The important message is that subdural collections of infancy should be considered as traumatic lesions and they have a tendency to increase in size.

Post-traumatic subdural hematomas are different in that many do progress. As a reaction to the opening of the potential subdural space, the surface of the dura mounts an inflammatory and neovascular response that then resembles granulation tissue (Glover & Labadie, 1976; McLone, Gutierrez, Raimondi, & Wiederhold, 1981). As a result of recurrent hemorrhage from this fragile, vascular membrane, subdural collections tend to increase in size often with multiple hemorrhages. These multiple hemorrhages can be documented either on CT scan or MRI imaging. Over time, a tendency for the reactive appearance of the membrane to resolve as recurrent hemorrhages cease and subdural fluid disappears is observed.

The clinical presentation of macrocephaly is usually subtle. Bilateral subdural fluid collections must be differentiated from benign enlargement of the subarachnoid spaces (Ment, Duncan, & Geehr, 1981). This diagnosis is usually best differentiated on the basis of contrast on CT scans or MRI studies. Clinically, these toddlers are usually less than two years of age and will present with a history of a moderate irritability and vomiting. The head size is usually just above the normal range and the anterior fontanelle is still patent and can be full to even sunken. A history of generalized seizures is common and in fact can be the presenting complaint. Physical examination carries with it few real diagnostic signs. It is not common to find papilledema, sunsetting of the eyes, or prominent frontal bossing with dilated scalp veins as is seen in hydrocephalus. A careful search should be made for retinal hemorrhages, which may reflect the underlying nature of the inciting event. Typically retinal hemorrhages will resolve within two to three weeks and may not be a common finding with this entity.

The combination of CT and MRI images is usually diagnostic. These radiographs document bilateral fluid collections that are distinct from the underlying subarachnoid space. Although chronic subdural collections can extend into the interhemispheric fissure, they are often limited by the adherence of the dura to the arachnoid in the region of the superior sagittal sinus.

The management of chronic subdural fluid collections of infancy is surgical. Controversy remains whether serial subdural tapping or subdural to peritoneal shunt insertion should be used as the initial treatment, but removal of the subdural fluid and avoidance of intracranial hypertension are the most important clinical considerations. Craniotomy for excision of membranes is no longer advocated as the primary approach. Occasionally this is still required when previous intervention fails. The major area of controversy is subdural tapping; some believe this bedside procedure is dangerous and carries the risk of hemorrhage and infection, and is not as effective as subdural shunting procedures. The technique is carried out via placing an angiocatheter through the anterior fontanel either in the lateral edge or through the coronal suture. The angiocatheter is inserted into the subdural space until the fluid is identified. Using the subdural catheter prevents laceration of the underlying cortical vessels once the inserting needle is removed. Over the last six years we have performed over 100 subdural taps using this technique. Only one hemorrhagic event was induced. This hemorrhage occurred in the interhemispheric fissure from brain shift with subdural fluid removal. Fluid should be drained until the fontanel sinks. As a general rule, removal of 25 ml from each side of the subdural can be performed. In most situations, the chronic subdurals over both convexities are in communication and only tapping one side is sufficient to control these fluid collections. Removal until the fontanel is sunken will eliminate the propensity for recurrent hemorrhage. The tap can always be repeated. Multiple taps are required in most cases, and the progress of the subdural collection must be followed closely by repeated CT scans or ultrasound in conjunction with daily head circumferences. I typically will perform two to three subdural taps. If protein levels are less than 1 gm/dl, consideration of a subdural to peritoneal shunt is performed. A shunt system that has an anti-clog mechanism and low resistance is best for this type of procedure. I use a Blake drain (Johnson & Johnson) in association with a Heyer-Schulte no-pressure on/off flushing valve and a PS Medical open-ended peritoneal catheter (Figure 1). This system allows for easy removal of the subdural catheter when it is no longer required. The valve can also be pumped if a clot occludes the valve. The valve can also be turned off after completion of brain re-expansion into the subdural space to assess whether the accumulation recurs with the valve turned off. Even bilateral collections can usually be drained with a unilateral shunting procedure (Aoki & Masuzawa, 1988; Aoki, Mizutani, & Masuzawa, 1985). This form of management works best when the brain is growing because in two or three months the subdural space is obliterated by a combination of fluid drainage and brain growth. If the underlying brain is injured and atrophic or if a ventricular shunt is in place, the subdural space persists longer and can be a surgical challenge for management. In this situation, a more long-term shunt is required and occasionally a combination of a ventricular and subdural shunt may be needed. Most infants (50-75%) have a favorable prognosis with chronic subdural collections using pediatric catheter drainage (Figures 1 and 2).

Subdural hygromas refers to collections of CSF in the subdural space. These fluid collections are managed in a fashion similar to the subdural hematomas. They are best considered post-traumatic lesions. The forces that tear bridging veins may tear the arachnoid where it attaches to the parasagittal dura. Both CSF and blood can collect in the subdural space. The clinical presentation is similar as is the management strategy. The main difference is that of less urgency with a subdural hygroma. Subdural membranes are not well formed and rebleeding is not as big of a concern. Subdural tapping or bur hole drainage seems to improve the clinical presenting signs in most subdural hygromas. An occasional subdural to peritoneal shunt may be required.

FIGURE 1

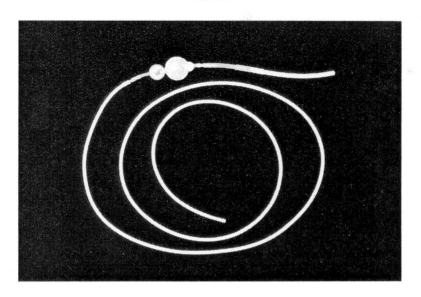

FIGURE 2

EX VACUO CEREBRAL SPINAL FLUID COLLECTIONS

Young children who suffered a documented severe closed head injury due to child abuse who develop extracerebral fluid collections weeks or months after injury pose a separate clinical problem. The pathophysiology of the extracerebral collection remains poorly understood but is in association with severe infarct of the brain. This black, low-density lesion progresses to frank infarction in most instances (Duhaime, Sutton, & Schut, 1988; Whyte & Pascoe, 1989). Serial CT scan or MRI evaluation performed several months after the injury shows severe atrophy with a prominent sulci pattern, loss of white matter and massive extracerebral collections of proteinaceous or cerebral spinal fluid density. These findings are the result of brain necrosis with atrophy and are usually associated with severe neurological damage. The head circumference may decrease somewhat but tends to plateau over time. In general, surgical drainage of this post-traumatic collection does not result in clinical improvement. In rare cases, drainage can be considered if there is clinical deterioration consistent with the time course in which the collections appeared or if there are overt signs and symptoms of intracranial hypertension present.

SKULL FRACTURES

Skull fractures are common during infancy. The bone is relatively thin and breaks easily after impact. Most simple linear skull fractures of infancy are not associated with underlying brain injury. However, diastasis of the fractured skull may indicate raised intracranial pressure or brain swelling. Fractures in infants may be associated with epidural hematomas caused by arterial or venous bleeding remote from the usual middle fossa location. The hemorrhage may be enough to produce anemia, especially in children less than one year of age. This anemic potential makes it policy in our institution to admit all infants with a skull fracture under one year of age for observation. In contrast to most simple fractures in infancy from falls, skull fractures crossing suture lines, multiple fractures and bilateral fractures are found more often in abused than accidentally injured children (Meservy et al., 1987).

Fractures in infancy can be associated with two unusual complications. A subepicranial hygroma occurs when the fracture extends into a suture line with laceration of the dura matter that is fixed to the suture. Rupture of the underlying arachnoid ensues (Epstein, Epstein, & Small, 1961). CSF dissects underneath the periosteum, which limits its expansion. These "pseudomeningoceles" usually subside spontaneously and rarely require primary operative repair. Another complication unique to infants is the growing skull fracture or leptomeningeal cyst. These are usually delayed complications of injury, but occasionally an acute growing fracture can be seen after a particularly severe head injury. The malleable skull is forced inward, lacerating the underlying dura mater. Because the subjacent brain is badly contused, it swells and herniates through the torn dura mater, separating the bones along the fracture (Tandon, Banerji, Bhatia, & Goulatia, 1987). Repair consists of separating the brain-dura and repairing the dura with a pericranial graft. Bone will usually not grow over this defect and I place a full thickness rotated cranial graft over the pericranial graft.

In contrast to acute injuries, the usual growing fracture appears insidiously weeks or months after injury. These children, most of whom are less than one year of age and rarely over three, sustain a diastatic skull fracture. Later the child presents with one or more physical findings: a skull defect with pulsatile swelling of the scalp, persistent or progressive neurological deficit, or seizures. AP and lateral skull films show a skull defect with scalloped edges. The margin may be everted, sclerotic or expanded due to type of underlying pathology of the dural opening. The CT scan shows porencephaly, ventricular diverticula and hypodensity of the brain beneath the growing fracture (Kingsley, Til, & Hoare, 1978; Tandon et al., 1987). Growing fractures occur during the period of rapid growth of the brain. Expansion of the fracture line is most likely caused by pulsations from the growing brain, which expands the dural tear and erodes the edges of the fracture. The operative findings include erosion of the inner table of the skull and a dural defect larger than the bony defect. The gliotic-exposed brain is devoid of the pia-arachnoid and thus the term leptomeningeal cyst is probably more of a misnomer (Roy, Sarkar, Tandon, & Banerji, 1987).

SPINAL INJURY DUE TO CHILD ABUSE IN YOUNG CHILDREN

In young children, a significant proportion of spinal cord trauma occurs above the level of C3. In child abuse, the whiplash to the cervical spine should result in a high incidence of cervical spine injuries. Surprisingly little attention has been devoted to the spine and spinal cord injury in clinical and autopsy series on this subject. The elastic ligaments which stretch more than the spinal cord, the horizontal orientation of the facets and the anterior vertebral body wedging along with a relatively large head compared to the underdeveloped neck musculature should all predispose the cervical region to injury. The true incidence of spinal cord injury in the setting of child abuse is probably underestimated. The severe cerebral injury warrants intervention and the cervical spine injury is easily overlooked. In most autopsy series, the brain is also transected at the cervical medullary junction with the spinal cord not necessarily being examined. It is important to remind an inexperienced medical examiner to closely evaluate the cervical spinal cord in cases of child abuse.

Autopsy series do report a significant percentage of fatally injured abused infants demonstrating subdural and epidural hemorrhages along with contusions of the cervical spinal cord. These findings may contribute to the morbidity and mortality associated with this pathophysiologic process (Hadley et al., 1989). Since most reports of spinal cord injury in child abuse come from autopsy series, it may be that these injuries are usually fatal and that survivors are unlikely to be affected. Indeed, it is rare to have a clinically detected spinal cord injury in a child who survives brain injury. Nonetheless it is conceivable that apnea from spinal cord concussion or compression in association with the impact might contribute to the cerebral insult that is prominent in child abuse patients. Vascular compression of the vertebral basilar system is also considered, but the posterior circulation distribution is usually spared in child abuse victims with widespread infarction. Spine fractures and spinal ligamentous instability appear to be uncommon aspects of nonaccidental trauma to infants (McGrory & Fenichel, 1977). Although the incidence may be under-recognized, it is appropriate to immobilize the neck and obtain screening cervical spine radiographs as part of the evaluation of any suspected child abuse victim. If an MRI of the brain is performed, a screening study of the upper cervical spinal cord region can also be obtained at the same time. The principles of management of unstable spine injuries to young children can be extrapolated from adult and older children care. The biggest challenge in the young child is stabilizing the cervical spine in cervical traction or in external orthosis. Size, especially in infants, of external orthoses is limited. Typically, if an external orthosis is not an appropriate size, I will wrap a rolled towel with tape to give slight axial traction as well as neck stability. If cervical fusion is required, reduction with immobilization can be performed through the standard anterior or posterior approaches.

NEUROLOGIC OUTCOME OF CHILD ABUSE

The outcome in shaken impact syndrome is notably poor with 7-30% mortality, 30-50% severe cognitive or neurologic deficits, and 30% potential full recovery. At the Children's Hospital of Wisconsin, 78% of head injury deaths in the zero to two-year old age group result from non-accidental trauma. Nationally, several thousand children per year die from child abuse. This is one-third of all deaths from head injury in childhood (Bruce, 1990). In several studies, the trend observed for improved outcome after head trauma with increasing age breaks down with infants and very young children; this observation can be attributed to the poor outcome after non-accidental trauma (Alberico, Ward, Choi, Marmarou, & Young, 1987; Kriel, Krach, & Panser, 1989). Several mechanisms have been proposed to explain the vulnerability of infants and toddlers to diffuse brain injury. Kriel et al. (1989) summarized these findings nicely:

> Impact injury to the immature brain is more likely to produce a shearing injury compared to contusions found in older children and adults; incomplete myelination, which predisposes to shearing injury is the proposed anatomic substrate; infants and toddlers may show increased cerebral edema because of increased metabolic rates and vasoreactivity; because of the relatively large head, less powerful neck and thin compliant bones of the skull, force is more effectively transferred to the brain; and the developmental sequence of the cerebrum is interrupted creating a compound effect of intellectual loss to the child as maturation occurs. (p. 297)

CONCLUSION

This reviews the neurologic sequelae of Shaken Baby Syndrome. Although neurosurgical input is required for children with severe cerebral or cervical spinal injury, most children do not require surgery and multidisciplinary team management is essential. With increasing awareness of this complex process, early prevention may help decrease the number of children who suffer from the devastating effects of this major cause of injury and mortality.

ACKNOWLEDGMENT

The authors wish to thank Marilyn Anderson and Anne Matthews for transcription and editorial assistance.

REFERENCES

Alberico, A.M., Ward, J.D., Choi, S.C., Marmarou, A., & Young, H.F. (1987). Outcome after severe head injury, relationship to mass lesions, diffuse injury, and ICP course in pediatric and adult patients. *Journal of Neurosurgy, 67*, 648-665.

Alexander, R., Sato, Y., Smith, W., & Bennett, T. (1990). Incidence of impact trauma with cranial injuries ascribed to shaking. *American Journal of Diseases in Children, 144*, 724-729.

Aoki, N., & Masuzawa, H. (1988). Bilateral chronic subdural hematoma without communication between the hematoma cavities: Treatment with unilateral subdural-peritoneal shunt. *Neurosurgery, 22*, 911-913.

Aoki, N., Mizutani, H., & Masuzawa, H. (1985). Unilateral subdural-peritoneal shunting for bilateral chronic subdural hematomas in infancy. *Journal of Neurosurgery, 63*, 134-137.

Bruce, D.A. (1982). Treatment of intracranial hypertension. In R. McLaurin, L. Schut, J.L. Venes, & F. Epstein (Eds.), *Pediatric neurosurgery: Surgery of the developing nervous system* (pp. 245-254). New York: Grune and Stratton.

Bruce, D.A. (1983). Clinical care of the severely head injured child. In K. Shapiro (Ed.), *Pediatric head trauma* (pp. 27-44). New York: Futura Publishing.

Bruce, D.A. (1990). Scope of the problem: Early assessment and management. In M. Rosenthal, E.R. Griffith, M. Bond, & J.D. Miller (Eds.), *Rehabilitation of the adult and child with traumatic brain injury* (pp. 521-537). Philadelphia: F.A. Davis Company.

Bruce, D.A., Alavi, A., Bilaniluk, L., Dolinkskas, C., Obrist, W., & Uzzell, B. (1981). Diffuses cerebral swelling following head injuries in children: The syndrome of "malignant brain edema". *Journal of Neurosurgery, 54*, 170-178.

Caffey, J. (1972). On the theory and practice of shaking infants. *American Journal of Diseases in Children, 124*, 161-169.

Caffey, J. (1974). The whiplash shaken infant syndrome: Manual shaking by the extremities with whiplash-induced intracranial and intraocular bleedings, linked with residual permanent brain damage and mental retardation. *Pediatrics, 54*, 396-403.

Cantu, R.C. (1992). Cerebral concussion in sport: Management and prevention. *Sports Medicine, 14*, 64-74.

Cappelen, J., & Unsgaard, G. (1986). Arachnoid cysts of the middle cranial fossa and traumatic complications. *Childs Nervous System, 2*, 225-227.

Cooper, P.R., Moody, S., Clark, W.K., Kirkpatrick, J., Maravilla, K., Gould, AlL., & Drane, W. (1979). Dexamethasone and severe head injury: A prospective double-blind study. *Journal of Neurosurgery, 51*(3), 301-316.

Cordobes, F., Lobato, R.D., Rivas, J.J., Portillo, J.M., Sarabia, M., & Munoz, M.J. (1987). Post-traumatic diffuse brain swelling: Isolated or associated with cerebral axonal injury. Clinical course and intracranial pressure in 18 children. *Childs Nervous System, 3*, 235-238.

Duhaime, A.C., Christian, C.W., Moss, E., & Seidl, T. (1996). Long-term outcome in infants with the shaking-impact syndrome. *Pediatric Neurosurgery, 24*, 292-298.

Duhaime, A.C., Gennarelli, T.A., Thibault, L.E., Bruce, D.A., Marguiles, S.S., & Wiser, R. (1987). The shaken baby syndrome. A clinical pathological and biomechanical study. *Journal of Neurosurgery, 66*, 409-415.

Duhaime, A.C., Sutton, L.N., & Schut, L. (1988). The "shaken baby syndrome": A misnomer? *Journal of Pediatric Neuroscience, 4*, 77-86.

Epstein, J.A., Epstein, B.S., & Small, M. (1961). Subepicranial hydroma. A complication of head injuries in infants and children. *Journal of Pediatrics, 59*, 562-566.

Fanconi, S., Kloti, J., Meuli, M., Zaugg, H., & Zachmann, M. (1988). Dexamethasone therapy and endogenous cortisol production in severe pediatric head injury. *Intensive Care Medicine, 14*, 163-166.

Graham, D.I. (1996). Neuropathology of head injury. In R.K. Narayan, J.E. Wilberger, & J.T. Povlishock (Eds.), *Neurotrauma* (pp. 43-54). New York: McGraw-Hill.

Graham, D.I., Adams, J.H., Nicoli, J.A.R., Maxwell, W.L., & Gennarelli, T.A. (1995). The nature, distribution and causes of traumatic brain injury. *Brain Pathology, 5,* 397-406.

Graham, D.I., & Gennarelli, T.A. (1997). Trauma. In D.I. Graham, & P.L. Lantos (Eds.), *Greenfield's neuropathology*. (6th ed.) (pp. 197-204). New York: Oxford University Press.

Gennarelli, T.A. (1983). Head injury in man and experimental animals: Clinical aspects. *Acta Neurochir Suppl (Wien), 32,* 1-13.

Glover, D., & Labadie, E.L. (1976). Physiopathogenesis of subdural hematomas. *Journal of Neurosurgery, 45,* 393-397.

Goetting, M.G., & Sowa, B. (1990). Retinal hemorrhage after cardiopulmonary resuscitation in children: An etiologic reevaluation. *Pediatrics, 85,* 585-588.

Goodman, J.M., & Mealey, J. (1969). Postmeningitic subdural effusions: The syndrome and its management. *Journal of Neurosurgery, 30,* 658-663.

Greenwald, M. (1990). The shaken baby syndrome. *Semin Ophthalmology, 5,* 202.

Hadley, M.N., Sonntag, V.K.H., Rekate, H.L., & Murphy, A. (1989). The infant whiplash-shake syndrome: A clinical and pathological study. *Neurosurgery, 24,* 536-540.

Hahn, Y.S., Raimondi, A.J., McLone, D.G., & Yamanouchi, Y. (1983). Traumatic mechanisms of head injury in child abuse. *Childs Brain, 10,* 229.

Johnson, D.L., Boal, D., & Baule, R. (1995). Role of apnea in nonaccidental head injury. *Pediatric Neurosurgery, 23,* 305-310.

Kanter, R.K. (1986). Retinal hemorrhage after cardiopulmonary resuscitation or child abuse. *Journal of Pediatrics, 108,* 430-432.

Kelly, J.P., Nicholas, J.S., Filley, C.M., Lillchei, K.O., Rubinstein, D., & Kleinschmdt-DeMasters, B.K. (1991). Concussion in sports: Guidelines for the prevention of catastrophic outcome. *The Journal of the American Medical Association, 266,* 2867-2869.

Kingsley, D., Til, K., & Hoare, R. (1978). Growing fractures of the skull. *Journal of Neurology, Neurosurgery, and Psychiatry, 41,* 312-318.

Klatzo, I. (1979). Brain edema. In G.L. Odon (Ed.), *Central nervous system trauma research status report* (pp. 110-112). Bethesda, MD: National Institute of Neurological and Communicative Disorders and Stroke, National Institutes of Health.

Kooh, S.W. (1986). Metabolic abnormalities of the skull and axial skeleton. In H. Hoffman, & F. Epstein (Eds.), *Disorders of the developing nervous system: Diagnosis and treatment* (pp. 449-463). Boston: Blackwell Scientific.

Kriel, R.L., Krach, L.E., & Panser, L.A. (1989). Closed head injury: Comparison of children younger and older than 6 years of age. *Pediatric Neurology, 5,* 296-300.

Kuhl, D.E., Alavi, A., Hoffman, E.J., Phelps, M.E., Zimmerman, R.A., Obrist, W.D., Bruce, D.A., Greenberg, J.H., & Uzzell, B. (1980). Local cerebral blood volume in head-injured patients. *Journal of Neurosurgery, 52,* 309-320.

Lindenberg, R., & Freytag, E. (1969). Morphology of brain lesions from blunt trauma in early infancy. *Archives of Pathology, 87,* 298-305.

Lindenberg, R., Risher, R.S., Durlacher, S. (1955). The pathology of the brain in blunt head injuries of infants and children. In *Second International Congress of Neuropathology* (pp. 477-479). Amsterdam: Excerpta Medica.

Ludwig, S., & Warman, M. (1984). Shaken baby syndrome. *Annals of Emergency Medicine, 13,* 104-107.

Luerssen, T.G., Huang, J.C., McLone, D.G., Walker, M.L., & Hahn, Y.S. (1991). Retinal hemorrhages, seizures, and intracranial hemorrhages: Relationships and outcomes in children suffering traumatic brain injury. *Concepts in Pediatric Neurosurgery, 11,* 87-94.

McGrory, B.E., & Fenichel, G.M. (1977). Hangman's fracture subsequent to shaking in an infant. *Annals of Neurology, 2,* 82.

Mclellan, N.J., Prasad, R., & Punt, J. (1986). Spontaneous subhyaloid and retinal hemorrhages in an infant. *Archives of Diseases in Children, 61*(11), 1130-1132.

McLone, D.G., Gutierrez, F.A., Raimondi, A.J., & Wiederhold, M. (1981). Ultrastructure of subdural membranes of children. *Concepts in Pediatric Neurosurgery, 1,* 174-188.

Ment, L.R., Duncan, C.C., & Geehr, R. (1981). Benign enlargement of the subarachnoid spaces in the infant. *Journal of Neurosurgery, 54,* 504.

Meservy, C.J., Towbin, R., McLaurin, R.L., Myers, P.A., Ball, W. (1987). Radiographic characteristics of skull fractures resulting from child abuse. *American Journal of Neuroradiology, 149,* 173-175.

Miller, J.D. (1993). Head injury. *Journal of Neurology, Neurosurgery, and Psychiatry, 56,* 440-447.

Newton, R.W. (1989). Intracranial hemorrhage and non-accident injury. *Archives of Diseases in Children, 64,* 188-190.

Ordia, I.J., Strand, R., Gilles, F., & Welch, K. (1981). Computerized tomography of contusional clefts in the white matter in infants. *Journal of Neurosurgery, 54,* 696-698.

Page, A., Paxton, R.M., & Mohan, D. (1987). A reappraisal of the relationship between arachnoid cysts of the middle fossa and chronic subdural hematoma. *Journal of Neurology, Neurosurgery, and Psychiatry, 50,* 1001-1007.

Phillips, R., Ott, L., Young, B., & Walsh, J. (1987). Nutritional support and measured energy expenditure of the child and adolescent with head injury. *Journal of Neurosurgery, 67,* 846-851.

Pozzati, E., Giuliana, G., Gaist, G., Piazza, G., & Vergoni, G. (1986). Chronic expanding intracerebral hematoma. *Journal of Neurosurgery, 65,* 611-614.

Rabe, E.F., Flynn, R.E., & Dodge, P.R. (1962). A study of subdural effusions in an infant. *Neurology, 12,* 79-92.

Roy, S., Sarkar, C., Tandon, P.A., & Banerji, A.K. (1987). Craniocerebral erosion (growing fractures of the skull in children). Part I: Pathology. *Acta Neurochir (Wien), 87,* 112-118.

Sato, Y., Yuh, W.T.C., Smith, W.I., Alexander, R.C., Kao, S.C., Ellerbroek, C.J. (1989). Head injuries in child abuse: Evaluation with MRI imaging. *Pediatric Radiology, 173,* 653-657.

Shugermann, R.P., Paez, A., Grossman, D.C., Feldman, K.W., & Grady, M.S. (1996). Epidural hemorrhage: Is it abuse? *Pediatrics, 97,* 664-668.

Snock, J.W., Minderhoud, J.M., & Wilmink, J.T. (1984). Delayed deterioration following mild head injury in children. *Brain, 107,* 15-36.

Tandon, P.N., Banerji, A.K., Bhatia, R., & Goulatia, R.K. (1987). Craniocerebral erosion (growing fracture of the skull in children). Part II. Clinical and radiologic observations. *Acta Neurochir, 88,* 1-9.

Teasdale, G. (1995). Head injury. *Journal of Neurology, Neurosurgery, and Psychiatry, 58,* 526-539.

Tokoro, K., Nakajima, F., & Yamataki, A. (1988). Infantile chronic subdural hematoma with local protrusion of the skull in a case of osteogenesis imperfecta. *Neurosurgery, 22,* 595-598.

Welch, K. (1980). The intracranial pressure in infants. *Journal of Neurosurgery, 52,* 693-699.

Whyte, K.M., & Pascoe, M. (1989). Does "black" brain mean doom? Computed tomography in the prediction of outcome in children with severe head injuries: "Benign" vs "malignant" brain swelling. *Australas Radiology, 33,* 344-347.

Wilkinson, H.A., & Rosenfeld, S. (1983). Furosemide and mannitol in the treatment of acute experimental intracranial hypertension. *Neurosurgery, 12,* 405-410.

Wilkinson, W.S., Han, D.P., Rappley, M.S., & Owings, C.L. (1989). Retinal hemorrhage predicts neurologic injury in the shaken baby syndrome. *Archives of Ophthalmology, 107,* 1472-1474.

Willman, K.Y., Bank, D.E., Senac, M., & Chadwick, D.L. (1997). Restricting the time of injury in fatal inflicted head injuries. *Child Abuse & Neglect, 21,* 929-940.

Zimmerman, R.A., Bilaniuk, L.T., Bruce, D.A., Schut, L., Uzzell, B., & Goldberg, H.I. (1979). Computed tomography of craniocerebral injury in the abused child. *Radiology, 130,* 687-690.

Chapter Seven

Radiographic Evaluation

Brian Lundeen

SUMMARY. One of the essential parts of the evaluation of victims of traumatic head injury is the radiographic evaluation of SBS, which includes computerized tomographic scans, magnetic resonance images and plain x-rays. This chapter discusses the role of radiologists starting with John Caffey, and examines our current understanding of bone injury and healing, dating fractures and intracranial blood and intracranial injury. The appropriate tests and the common findings in this syndrome are also reviewed. *[Article copies available for a fee from The Haworth Document Delivery Service: 1-800-342-9678. E-mail address: <getinfo@haworthpressinc.com> Website: <http://www.HaworthPress.com> © 2001 by The Haworth Press, Inc. All rights reserved.]*

KEYWORDS. Child abuse, fractures, subdural hemorrhage, magnetic resonance imaging, metaphyseal

INTRODUCTION

In 1946, John Caffey, MD, a pediatric radiologist, was the first to recognize the association between multiple long bone fractures and chronic subdural hematomas in abused infants (Caffey, 1946). Further work by Silverman

[Haworth co-indexing entry note]: "Radiographic Evaluation." Lundeen, Brian. Co-published simultaneously in *Journal of Aggression, Maltreatment & Trauma* (The Haworth Maltreatment & Trauma Press, an imprint of The Haworth Press, Inc.) Vol. 5, No. 1(#9), 2001, pp. 101-135; and: *The Shaken Baby Syndrome: A Multidisciplinary Approach* (ed: Stephen Lazoritz, and Vincent J. Palusci) The Haworth Maltreatment & Trauma Press, an imprint of The Haworth Press, Inc., 2001, pp. 101-135. Single or multiple copies of this article are available for a fee from The Haworth Document Delivery Service [1-800-342-9678, 9:00 a.m. - 5:00 p.m. (EST). E-mail address: getinfo@haworthpressinc.com].

(1953) and Kempe and Silverman (1962) delineated the radiographic findings of injuries to the long bones and recognized them as manifestations of the "battered child." In the early 1970s, Caffey (1974) and Guthkelch (1971) emphasized the prevalence and pathogenesis of the CNS injury associated with the whiplash-shaken infant syndrome. The development and refinement of computerized cross sectional imaging in the past three decades has allowed numerous other investigators to further describe the characteristic findings and often the devastating consequences of the shaken baby syndrome.

SKELETAL INJURIES

Caffey (1946) described a number of skeletal injuries in an infant who had bilateral subdural hematomas. Although unexplained subdural hematomas in infants had been noted before, it was Caffey who identified the association of subdural hematomas with certain patterns of bone injuries that popularized the importance of radiographs in the diagnosis of child abuse. It is now well established that certain characteristic skeletal injuries can occur in shaken infants. The type, location, and age of these skeletal injuries are important factors in establishing the diagnosis of non-accidental trauma. One must recognize, however, that many shaken infants do not have radiographic evidence of skeletal trauma. Therefore, a normal imaging work-up should never in and of itself be considered to exclude the diagnosis of child abuse.

SUBPERIOSTEAL HEMORRHAGE/PERIOSTEAL NEW BONE

Subperiosteal hemorrhage is common in child abuse and may or may not be associated with an underlying fracture of the bone. The periosteum, which circumferentially surrounds the long bones, comprises two layers: (1) a thick inner osteogenic layer, and (2) a thin, outer fibrous layer. With trauma, the periosteum is stripped from bone and blood accumulates between the cortex of the bone and the surrounding periosteum. The osteogenic layer responds by laying down a thin layer of periosteal new bone (Figure 1). In adults, the periosteum is securely attached to the shaft of the bone. Although the periosteum is more loosely attached in the infant, severe tractional or torsional forces are still necessary to cause stripping of the periosteum from the shaft of the bone. Such forces can occur as the child is held by an extremity and the extremity is pulled or twisted or when the extremities are grasped during violent shaking. These injuries, however, do not require direct application of force to the extremity. Identical injury of the long bones can occur in infants who are shaken while being gripped around the thorax. Vio-

FIGURE 1

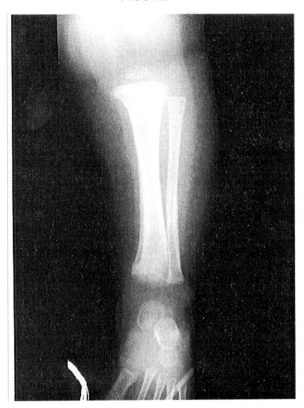

lent acceleration and deceleration forces develop as the extremities flail and are thought to account for most periosteal injuries (Caffey, 1946).

If the injury of the periosteum is severe, subperiosteal hemorrhage may become clinically apparent due to soft tissue swelling. This may be demonstrated as soft tissue prominence on standard radiographs. Subsequently, a thin layer of subperiosteal new bone develops in one to two weeks. In contrast, isolated subperiosteal new bone formation along the diaphysis of the long bones may not be clinically evident. Radiographic findings in these latter cases are often subtle, and radionuclide bone imaging may be quite useful. Bone scintigraphy shows increased activity along the margins of the involved bone during both the tissue phase and delayed images. Skeletal scintigraphy has greater sensitivity for detecting this injury (Sty & Starshak, 1983).

Focal or generalized periosteal new bone formation, although a frequent finding in shaken/abused infants, is itself nonspecific. Accidental trauma, infection, metastatic disease, and metabolic abnormalities may all result in periosteal new bone (LaCroix, 1951). Additionally, periosteal new bone resembling that seen in abused infants frequently occurs in neonates after traumatic delivery (Snedecor, Knapp, & Wilson, 1935). The differentiation from non-accidental periosteal injury in these instances is obtained from the appropriate clinical and laboratory findings.

METAPHYSEAL INFRACTIONS

Metaphyseal infractions (injuries to the metaphysis and cartilaginous growth plate) of the long bones are virtually pathognomonic of child abuse. Radiographically, these are the classic "corner" and "bucket handle" fractures. The metaphyseal injuries vary in location, extent, and degree of separation, but the fundamental anatomic alterations are relatively constant (Merten & Carpenter, 1990).

Shearing forces generated by rapid acceleration-deceleration or torsion of the limbs during violent shaking produce metaphyseal corner fractures. Simple falls or other accidental forms of trauma cannot generate the force necessary to produce these fractures. Because the plane of injury extends to the margin of the bone, the metaphyseal fragment may become separated as an isolated peripheral bone fragment. The peripheral portion of this fracture fragment is thicker than the central portion. This causes the fragment to have a disk-like shape that is thin centrally and thick peripherally. A different radiographic projection may reveal an ovoid fragment (bucket handle fracture). These fractures have variable radiographic appearances; some are visible only in one projection and not detectable in other views. The radiographic projection also influences the appearance of the disk-like metaphyseal fragment. Seen on tangent, the fragment may appear as a dense round segment that is separated from the metaphysis. Incomplete injuries may result in a fragment that appears as a corner fracture or radiolucency that extends across a portion of the metaphysis (Figure 2).

The healing process has a significant impact on the radiographic appearance of metaphyseal fractures. New bone formation and bony resorption may cause the fracture margins to become indistinct and the fracture plane to become obscure as reactive sclerosis takes place. In most cases of metaphyseal injury, the cartilage of the physis is preserved; therefore, there is no growth disturbance. Often there is little periosteal new bone formation associated with metaphyseal corner fractures. When present, however, the periosteal new bone may produce

FIGURE 2

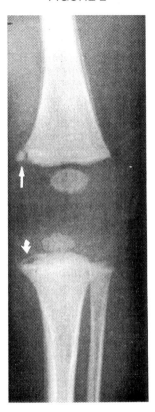

a subtle hazy appearance of the cortical border. As discussed above, associated subperiosteal hemorrhage may result in displacement of the fracture fragment. In most cases, the radiographic appearance returns to normal within several weeks unless there is repeated injury, in which case, and angular deformity may develop.

In addition to metaphyseal infractions, any other type of skeletal injury can occur in child abuse (Merten & Carpenter, 1990). Diaphyseal fractures, such as a spiral fracture of a major long bone (e.g., the femur or humerus) in the nonmobile infant are highly suggestive of abuse. Distal clavicular or acromial fractures result from traction or twisting forces applied to the arm and are considered corner fracture equivalents.

RIB FRACTURES

Rib fractures can result from an adult violently compressing or squeezing the infant's chest. Until callus develops at the site of trauma, acute rib fractures may not be detected immediately on radiographs unless separation or displacement is present. Callus develops at the site of trauma within 10 to 14 days. These fractures are commonly located posteriorly and may involve several contiguous ribs (Figure 3). Frontal or oblique radiographs of the ribs are often necessary for complete demonstration. Radionuclide bone imaging is again more sensitive than radiography for detecting rib fractures, especially acutely (Figure 4).

SKELETAL SURVEY VS. SCINTIGRAPHY

The American College of Radiology has established standards for skeletal surveys in children (American College of Radiology, 1997). High detail film screen combinations, along with tightly collimated views of each anatomic re-

FIGURE 3

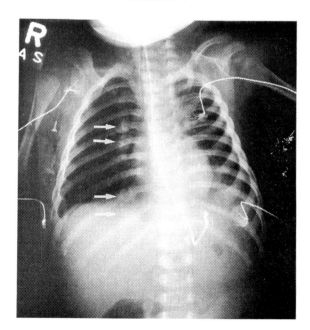

FIGURE 4

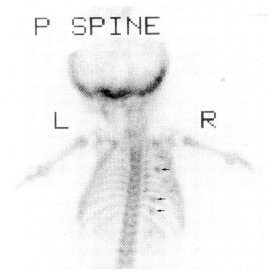

gion are necessary. Each extremity, including the hands and feet, should be radiographed in at least the frontal projection. Radiographs of the axial skeleton should be obtained in two projections. Additional projections of areas of suspected clinical injury, or as suggested by the initial radiographs, are often helpful. An AP and lateral projection of the skull should be included in the skeletal survey as well as obtained in conjunction with skeletal scintigraphy. Kleinman et al. (1996) have also shown the usefulness of a follow-up skeletal survey two weeks after the initial examination. In their series additional information regarding skeletal injury was identified in 61% of cases. The recommended follow-up skeletal survey is identical to that of the initial examination with the exception of deletion of views of the skull.

Radionuclide bone scans (scintigraphy) involve injection of a radiopharmaceutical intravenously and subsequently obtaining images with a gamma camera to evaluate for abnormal areas of radiopharmaceutical distribution. Scintigraphy can be used to demonstrate clinically occult fractures in cases where routine radiographs are either indefinite or initially normal. A radionuclide bone scan in an area of injury may become abnormal within several hours; it is always almost abnormal within 24 hours. Scintigraphy is far more sensitive than radiography in the assessment of rib fractures, nondisplaced long bone fractures, and periosteal injury. The shortcomings of scintigraphy are its inability to predict the type of fracture and determining the stages of healing or repair. Radionuclide imaging in infants is difficult and requires meticulous attention to detail and may necessitate the use of sedation. Additionally, the availability of technicians and physicians experienced in the acquisition and interpretation of bone scintigraphy is variable. Therefore, in infancy, the skeletal survey has remained the principle modality in evaluation of suspected shaken and abused infants. There is, however, no question that skeletal scintigraphy, either as initial evaluation or is addition to a skeletal survey, can add additional information or may be the only indication of abuse. In most instances, radionuclide bone imaging is a complementary rather than a competitive image modality (Conway, 1983).

DATING FRACTURES

The timing of skeletal injury as judged from the radiographic findings is important. Fractures of differing ages and those that do not correlate with the timing of the given clinical history are highly suggestive of non-accidental trauma. The normal radiographic progression from acute injury to healing is as follows: 0-5 days: radiolucent fracture line without reactive bone formation; 5-10 days: visible periosteal new bone formation; 10-14 days: soft callus formation; 14-21 days: hard callus formation. Metaphyseal fractures (bucket handle or corner fractures) as well as skull fractures often do not produce periosteal new bone formation; these fractures are dated by the loss of definition of the margins.

CRANIAL TRAUMA

Computed tomography of the head remains the exam of choice in initial evaluation of the shaken/abused infant. The exam can be easily performed on an unstable acutely injured child without the use of sedation. CT is readily available and has the highest sensitivity and specificity for detecting acute hemorrhagic injury. Cranial CT is effective at excluding intracranial injury that requires surgical therapy. The routine inclusion of images in bone window settings will also detect the majority of associated skull fractures if direct or impact injury has occurred (Merten, Osborne, Radkowski, & Leonidas, 1984).

Skull radiographs serve an important function in documentation of the inflicted injury and may demonstrate fractures not appreciated by cranial CT (Saulsbury & Alford, 1982). Such fractures often lie parallel to the plane of scan of an axial CT. At a minimum, an AP and lateral radiograph should be obtained as part of the skeletal survey or in conjunction with bone scintigraphy (ACR, 1997). A Townes and opposite lateral view may be necessary depending on the findings on the initial films.

Magnetic resonance imaging has been found valuable in the assessment of victims of suspected child abuse (Ball, 1989; Hesselink et al., 1988; Sato et al., 1989). Injuries of the brain, especially acute nonhemorrhagic contusions, shear injuries and secondary hypoxic-ischemic damage, are better depicted with MR imaging. As noted by Sato et al., even when CT images depict the same lesion, MR images often are more definitive allowing for a more confident diagnosis. It has been established that MR imaging is superior to CT in evaluation of subacute or chronic injuries, especially extra-axial hemorrhage. The addition of FLAIR, gradient echo, and gadolinium enhanced sequences to the standard T1 and T2 weighted MR images may add further evidence of injury (Kleinman et al., 1996; Kleinman & Barnes, 1998).

SHAKE VS. IMPACT

Duhaime et al. (1992) reviewed the clinical information in 48 cases (ages one month to two years) of suspected shaken baby syndrome. In addition to intra-cranial injuries of the type previously reported with shaken baby syndrome, 30 children (63%) showed evidence of blunt impact to the head. Pathologic examination revealed evidence of blunt trauma in all 13 fatal cases. In addition, experimental studies were conducted by duhaime using a doll model in an attempt to measure the force generated with shaking and impact injuries. Based on these studies and the clinical cases, the authors concluded that "shaken baby syndrome, at least in its most severe form is usually not caused by shaking alone. Although shaking may in fact be part of the process, it is more likely that such infants suffer blunt impact" (p. 410).

Subsequent studies have supported duhaime and colleagues conclusions that the shaking is usually associated with impact (alexander, sato, smith, & bennett, 1990). Many reports, however, have also provided evidence that shaking alone can produce life-threatening injuries in infants (alexander et al., 1990; Duhaime et al., 1992; Gilliland & folberg, 1996; lazoritz & baldwin, 1997; merten et al., 1984). The relative incidence of brain injury due to the shaking or the impact injury remains unknown; in many cases both forms of injury may be present.

SKULL AND SCALP INJURIES

Children with significant impact injury to the head frequently exhibit swelling of a portion of the scalp. The point of impact can usually be readily identified on CT scans as abnormal extracranial soft tissue. The radiographic demonstration of one or more skull fractures either on CT or plain radiographs provides firm documentation that a significant impact force has been applied to the calvaria. While the demonstration of skull fracture is not in and of itself proof of abuse, correlation with the alleged mechanism of injury and radiographic findings is essential. It should be remembered, however, that the presence or absence of a fracture correlates poorly with associated intracranial injury. In a study of 45 abused children by Tsai, Zee, Apthorp, and Dixon (1980), 17 skull fractures were identified. Intracranial injury was present in 65% of those with skull fractures and 78% of those with normal skull films.

The great majority of skull fractures in abused children occur during infancy; 80 to 85% occur in children younger than two years of age. Most skull fractures related to physical abuse are single linear fractures of the parietal bone (Figure 5) (Merten, Osborne, Radkowski, Leonidas, 1985). This, however, is also the most common skull fracture that occurs with accidental trauma. Meservy, Towbin, McLaurin, Myers, and Ball (1987) found no significant differences in the pattern of skull fractures between abused and accidentally injured children. This included depressed, complex, nonparietal, and diastatic fractures. Meservy et al.'s results, however, agreed with earlier investigators who found that multiple fractures, bilateral fractures, and fractures across suture lines are significantly associated with abuse. These fractures suggest severe or unusual trauma and indicate the need for close correlation with the alleged mechanism of injury.

Skull fractures do not heal by callus formation; thus dating an injury based on the radiographic appearance is difficult. If the edges of the fracture are rounded and smooth, the injury is more than two weeks old. Skull fractures normally heal in two to three months and typically disappear on radiographs by six months (Brown & Minns, 1993). A growing skull fracture (leptomeningeal cyst) is a unique type of fracture most commonly seen in infants (Figure 6). These fractures are usually associated with prior complex or diastatic fractures. Herniation of dura or a dural tear may prevent fracture healing and the fracture may enlarge gradually with time. Hobbs (1984) found that the presence of a growing fracture had a strong association with abuse.

EXTRA-AXIAL HEMORRHAGE

Inside the skull, three membranes surround the infant's brain. Immediately covering the surface of the brain is the pia arachnoid. Cerebral spinal fluid is

FIGURE 5

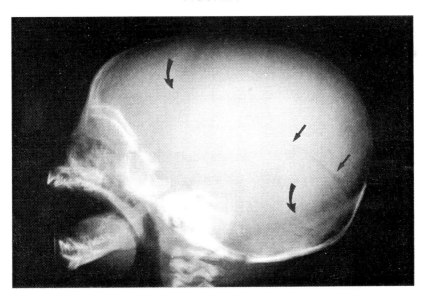

contained within the subarachnoid space, which lies between the pia arachnoid, and the next adjacent membrane, the dura arachnoid. The subarachnoid space is normally larger in infants than in older children and adults (Figure 7). This provides "cushioning" of the brain from minor trauma but also allows more movement of the brain within the skull with greater degrees of trauma. Finally, the outermost layer is the double-layered dura matter. Thus, there are two potential spaces defined by the dura matter, the epidural space between the inner table of the skull and the outer dural layer and the subdural space between the dura matter and adjacent dura arachnoid. The leaves of the dura matter split to enclose the dural venous sinuses and also form the falx cerebri and tentorium. Small cortical veins originating from the surface of the brain cross the subarachnoid and potential subdural space to enter these venous sinuses. It is the tearing of these bridging cortical veins in response to the sudden acceleration and deceleration of the head in the shaken infant that results in subdural hemorrhage. Subdural hematomas may also result from direct impact.

In several studies, subdural hemorrhage has been the most common acute intracranial abnormality found in shaken infants (Merten et al., 1984; Zimmerman et al., 1979). CT adequately demonstrates acute subdural hemor-

FIGURE 6

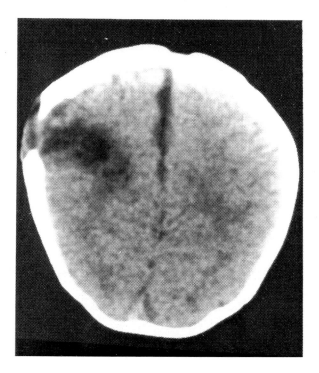

rhage in most of these cases as a crescentic peripheral zone of high attenuation adjacent to the brain surface without interdigitation into the sulci (Figure 8). There is a tendency for subdural hemorrhage to accumulate between the cerebral hemispheres as the result of shaking and shaking impact injury. On CT, these interhemispheric subdural hematomas are almost exclusively located in the parieto-occipital region and are seen as a high attenuation blood collection in the parasagittal region. The blood collection has a flat medial border where it is in contact with the falx and the lateral border tends to be convex (Figure 9). Coronal images, if tolerated, can be of assistance in demonstrating the subdural hemorrhage in the interhemispheric fissure (Figure 10). A small interhemispheric subdural hematoma may be quite subtle on CT and maintaining a high index of suspicion is important. Serial CT examinations may help confirm the presence of hemorrhage by documenting its normal decrease in attenuation over time. Even the presence of a small area of hemorrhage indicates

FIGURE 7

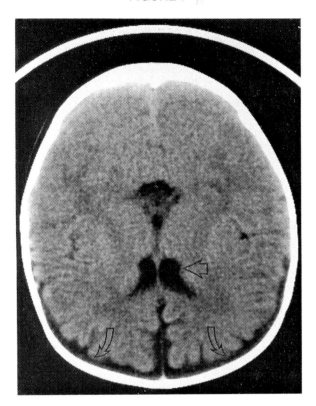

that significant intracranial trauma has occurred and severe neurologic sequela may ensue.

MRIs offer superior contrast resolution relative to a CT scan and its multiplanar capabilities lead to increased visualization of subdural hematomas. Magnetic resonance imaging has revealed that most interhemispheric subdural hematomas are usually associated and continuous with convexity subdural hematomas. The lack of signal from the overlying cortical bone on MRI (black) also leads to increased visualization of extra-axial hemorrhage (Figures 11a and b). MR is also superior to CT in detecting subacute or chronic injuries. Because the signal appearance of hemorrhage on MR images changes with time, MR provides guidelines for the dating of extra-axial hemorrhage. Extra-axial hemorrhage within the first few hours (hyperacute) is composed of

FIGURE 8

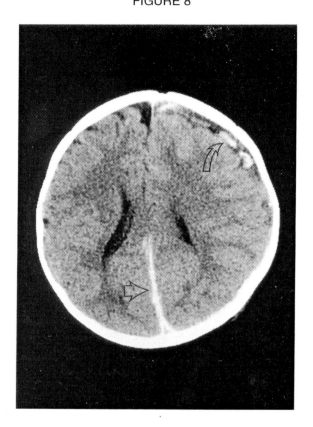

oxyhemoglobin and is isointense on T1 weighted images and is often of increased signal on T2 weighted images. Within hours (acute), the
oxyhemoglobin changes to deoxyhemoglobin with the resultant signal remaining isointense on T1 weighted images but becoming markedly hypointense on
T2 weighted images. The oxyhemoglobin becomes methemoglobin within the
intact red blood cell by the third or fourth day (early subacute) and becomes
hyperintense on T1 weighted images and hypointense on T2 weighted images.
With rupture of the red blood cells (late subacute), the extracellular
methemoglobin becomes hyperintense on both the T1 and T2 weighted sequences. With further maturation (chronic), the globin molecule is broken

FIGURE 9

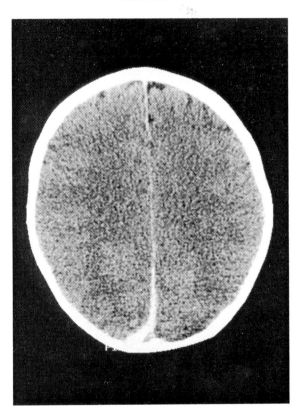

down and the T1 weighted signal becomes less intense but remains brighter than that of CSF (Zimmerman & Bilaniuk, 1994). Therefore, chronic extra-axial hemorrhage, which often appears similar to CSF on CT, can be differentiated as a result of prior hemorrhage by its appearance on the MR images (Figures 12a and b). There can be, however, considerable variability in the appearance of the hemorrhage on MR images due to its size, location, and stage of degradation. Repetitive trauma associated with hemorrhage or re-hemorrhage into an older subdural collection can further complicate the evaluation.

Subarachnoid and epidural hemorrhage are both relatively uncommon in child abuse. Subarachnoid hemorrhage usually occurs in association with parenchymal brain injury. Large amounts of subarachnoid hemorrhage can be

FIGURE 10

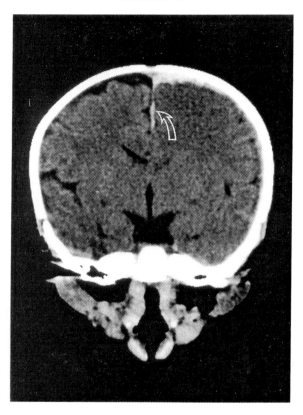

demonstrated on CT as blood accumulating within the cerebral cisterna and extending into the cerebral sulci. Smaller amounts of subarachnoid hemorrhage may be manifested only as high attenuation blood in the interhemispheric fissure. Delineation from an interhemispheric subdural hematoma or a normal hyperdense falx may be difficult on CT. Subarachnoid blood in the interhemispheric fissure usually has a wider and more irregular appearance than a normal falx and extends into the adjacent cortical sulci (Figures 13a and b) (Dolinskas, Zimmerman, & Bilaniuk, 1978). Unfortunately, magnetic resonance imaging is relatively poor in detecting the presence of acute subarachnoid hemorrhage. Recent studies, however, have reported an improved MRI detection of subacute and chronic subarachnoid hemorrhage when FLAIR imaging techniques are used (Ogawa et al., 1995). An acute

FIGURE 11a

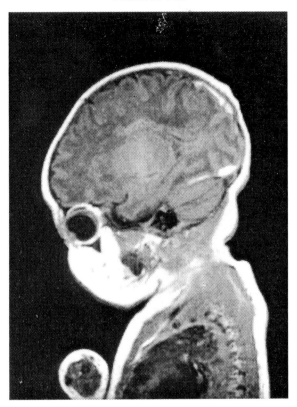

epidural hematoma is usually the result of a direct blow and is often associated with a skull fracture. Large epidural hematomas typically have a lenticular shape on axial CT or MRI. Epidural blood in smaller amounts, however, may be indistinguishable from a subdural hematoma.

BRAIN INJURIES

A number of parenchymal brain injuries may result from head trauma in the shaken/shaken impact syndrome. These include shear injuries, contusions, cerebral edema, and intraparenchymal hematomas. Shear injury of the white

FIGURE 11b

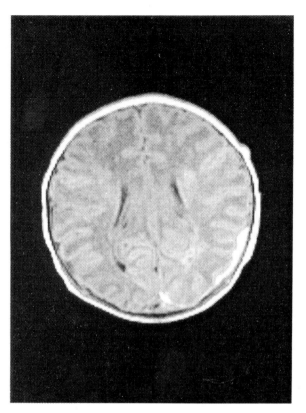

matter can result from angular acceleration during shaking or from blunt impact. The lesions are common within the cerebral hemispheres at the gray/white junctions, and within the corpus callosum and brainstem. These lesions are usually associated with little or no hemorrhage and can be difficult to appreciate on CT evaluations (Figure 14) (Ordia, Strand, Gilles, Welch, 1981). Both non-hemorrhagic and hemorrhagic shear injuries are more easily detected by MRI. T2* gradient echo and FLAIR imaging represent MRI techniques with the greatest sensitivity for the detection of diffuse axonal injury.

Cerebral contusions or hematomas may be produced by impact injury or from shearing of superficial or deep cerebral tissues induced by severe rotational forces during shaking. In shaken infants they are commonly identified in the frontal and anterior temporal lobes where the brain strikes the inner table of

FIGURE 12a

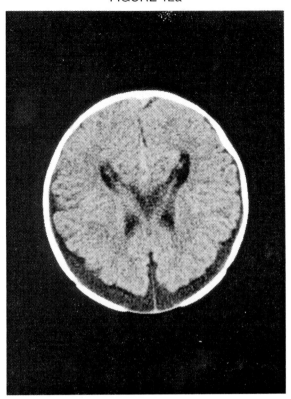

the skull. The appearance of a cerebral contusion on CT is somewhat variable depending on the presence and degree of petechial hemorrhage. Nonhemorrhagic contusions appear as heterogeneous decreased attenuation usually involving both the gray and white matter. When large enough, there may be signs of adjacent mass effect. Hemorrhagic contusions are identified as focal cortical areas of high attenuation (Figure 15). After the first 24 hours post-injury, the high attenuation component progressively decreases as the hemorrhage resolves (Ellison, Tsai, & Largent, 1978). Contusions are particularly well demonstrated on MRI. The signal characteristics vary depending on the amount of associated edema and/or hemorrhage.

Cerebral swelling in the shaken infant may result from various mechanisms but in many cases, it is probably an indirect pathophysiologic response to head

FIGURE 12b

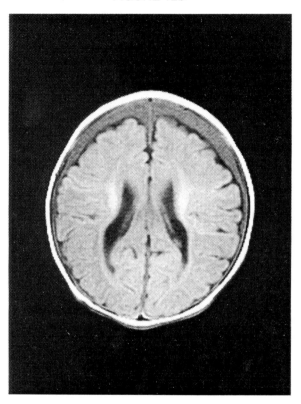

trauma (Aldrich et al., 1992; Bruce et al., 1981; Zimmerman et al., 1978). A study by Johnson, Boal, and Baule (1995) explored the role of hypoxic-ischemic injury in the shaken and shaken impact injured infant. They found 16 of 28 infants who suffered significant inflicted head injury had a history of apnea. Diffuse cerebral edema was noted on the initial CT in 71% of cases. Diffuse cerebral edema secondary to hypoxic-ischemic injury offers a grave prognosis. Post-traumatic cerebral swelling may be focal, multifocal, or diffuse. CT demonstrates area of decreased attenuation, which may be subtle. Localized edema may produce mass effect; diffuse edema usually causes decrease in the size of the ventricular system and obliteration of the extra-axial cerebral spinal fluid spaces (Figures 9 and 13). MR is often more sensitive than CT for the demonstration of focal edema but may not be practical in the acutely injured child. In cases of diffuse edema, the differentiation on CT between

FIGURE 12c

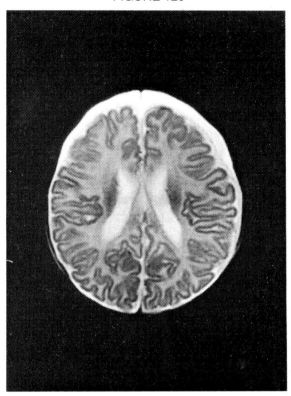

gray and white matter becomes less evident. The more normal attenuation of the thalamus, brainstem, and cerebellum may be preserved leading to the "reversal sign" because of the relatively higher attenuation of the central regions of the brain compared with the peripheral aspects of the hemispheres (Figures 16a and b) (Cohen, Kaufman, Myers, & Towbin, 1956).

CT evaluation performed immediately after injury may not show evidence of swelling or edema. Edema may become apparent on CT within two to three hours (perhaps sooner) or may not become evident until one to two days after the injury (Zimmerman & Bilaniuk, 1994). Therefore, the initial CT findings may be unreliable in predicting the extent of brain damage. If diffuse cerebral edema ensues, intracranial pressure may exceed the mean systolic arterial pressure resulting in hypoperfusion and secondary hypoxic ischemic injury. It is this progression of injury that is responsible for the death of the majority of

FIGURE 13a

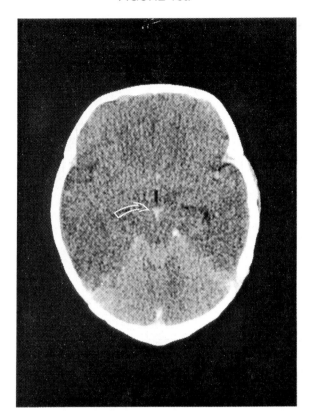

shaken infants. Findings of compressed or absent cisterns, intraventricular hemorrhage, significant subarachnoid hemorrhage, or shift of the midline structures are often associated with poor outcome, regardless of the initial clinical presentation (Kleinman & Barnes, 1998).

LONG TERM SEQUELAE

Subacute and chronic subdural hematomas are the result of previous acute subdural hematomas. On CT images, these appear as isodense or low-density collections and tend to be bilateral (Figure 17). Magnetic resonance imaging is the exam of choice for the evaluation of suspected subacute or chronic subdural hematomas (Figures 12a,b,c) (Ball, 1989). Subdural collections with

FIGURE 13b

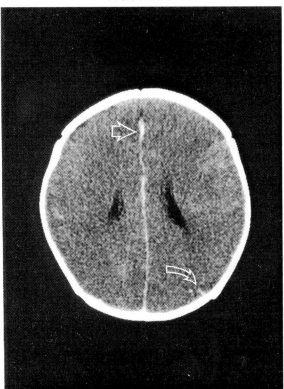

varying attenuation or signal characteristics on CT or MR most often indicate injuries of differing ages and therefore highly suggestive of abuse (Figures 18a,b and c). Patients with chronic subdural hematomas, however, are thought to be more susceptible to episodes of re-bleeding with minor trauma which can complicate the imaging findings. These patients, however, are usually asymptomatic. Therefore acute neurologic deterioration associated with re-hemorrhage into a subdural hematoma is generally the consequence of another episode of abuse and is often associated with acute parenchymal injury and/or retinal hemorrhages which are not otherwise present in chronic subdural hematomas (Kleinman & Barnes, 1998).

Atrophy and encephalomalacia are often the end result of traumatic brain injury in the shaken infant. This may be focal and associated with prior contusion or shear injury. Diffuse atrophy may accompany diffuse axonal injury or hypoxic

FIGURE 14

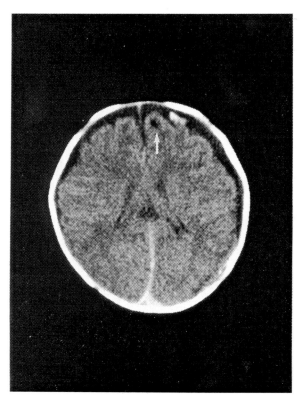

ischemic injury. Diffuse atrophy may be surprisingly rapid when the initial injury is severe (Figure 16). Post-traumatic hydrocephalus is also occasionally identified. Computed tomography shows atrophy and encephalomalacia as a loss of brain parenchyma and resultant enlargement of the sulci, fissures, and ventricles (Brown & Minns, 1993; Zimmerman & Bilaniuk, 1994; Zimmerman et al., 1979). MRI more exquisitely demonstrates focal areas of encephalomalacia, porencephaly, and diffuse cerebral atrophy (Figures 19a and b) (Mendelsohn et al., 1992).

THE ROLE OF THE RADIOLOGIST

Radiologists play an important role in the multidisciplinary approach to the shaken baby. The radiologic findings may be the only evidence of non-acci-

FIGURE 15

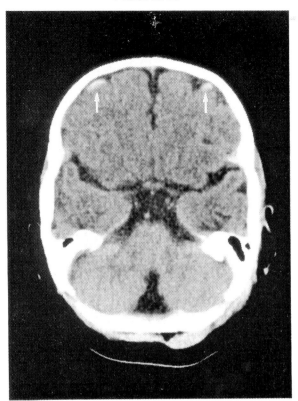

dental trauma. In these cases, the radiologist is relied upon to not only make the diagnosis but also to educate the medical and legal community as to the significance of these findings. Often called upon as an expert witness in court, the radiologist will be asked to establish expertise in the medical aspects of child abuse to ensure that the studies obtained for evidence are actually of the child in question and, most importantly, to establish that the studies are indicative of child abuse (Miller, 1982). An understanding of the common and characteristic findings of the shaken/abused infant underlies the ability of the radiologist to fulfill his role on the child abuse team, and knowledge of the radiologic approach to the evaluation of shaken baby syndrome can greatly improve the diagnosis, treatment and outcomes of SBS.

FIGURE 16a

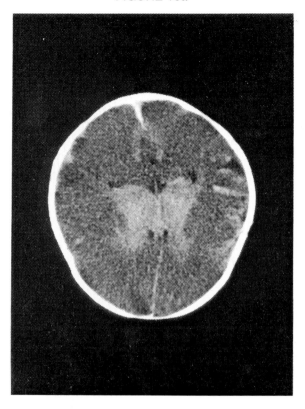

FIGURE 16b

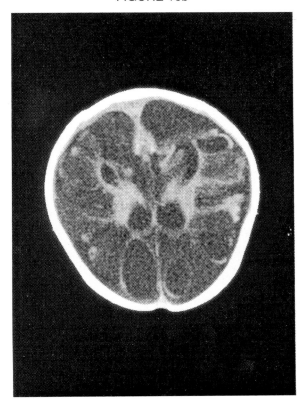

FIGURE 17

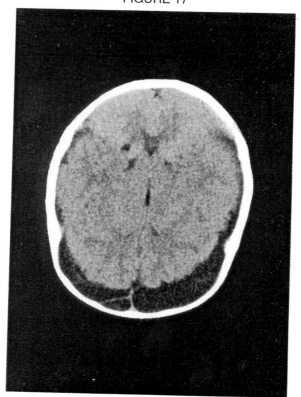

FIGURE 18a

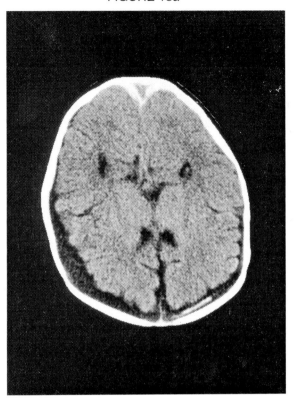

FIGURE 18b

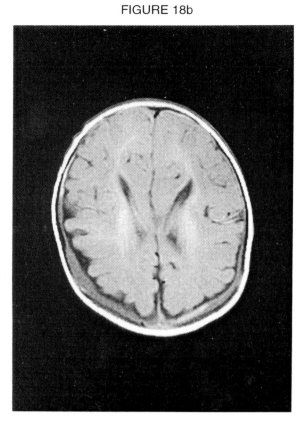

FIGURE 18c

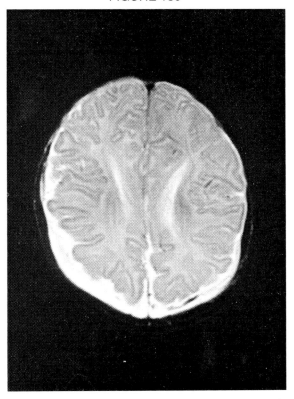

FIGURE 19a

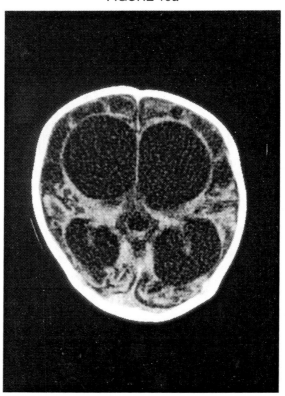

FIGURE 19b

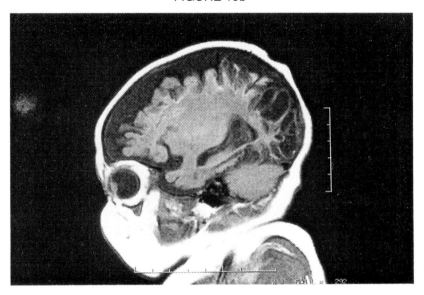

REFERENCES

Aldrich, E.F., Eisenberg, H.M., Saydjari, C., Luerssen, T.G., Foulkes, M.A., Jane, J.A., Marshall, L.F., Mormarou, A., & Young, H.F. (1992). Diffuse brain swelling in severely head-injured children. *Journal of Neurosurgery, 76,* 450-454.

Alexander, R., Sato, Y., Smith, W., & Bennett, T. (1990). The incidence of impact trauma with cranial injuries ascribed to shaking. *American Journal of Diseases in Children, 144,* 724-726.

American College of Radiology. (1997). ACR Standards, Standards for skeletal survey in children. *Research, 22-25,* 27-30.

Ball, W.S. (1989). Nonaccidental craniocerebral trauma (child abuse): MR Imaging. *Radiology, 173,* 609-610.

Brown, J.K., & Minns, R.A. (1993). Non-accidental head injury with particular reference to whiplash shaking injury and medico-legal aspects [review]. *Developmental Medicine and Child Neurology, 35*(10), 849-869.

Bruce, D.A., Alavi, A., Bilaniuk, L.T., Dolinskas, C., Obrist, W., & Uzzell, B. (1981). Diffuse cerebral swelling following head injuries in children: The syndrome of "malignant brain edema." *Journal of Neurosurgery, 54,* 170-178.

Caffey, J. (1946). Multiple fractures in the long bones of infants suffering from chronic subdural hematoma. *American Journal of Rontgenology, 56,* 163-173.

Caffey, J. (1974). The whiplash shaken infant syndrome: Manual shaking by the extremities with whiplash-induced intracranial and intraoccular bleedings, linked with residual permanent brain damage and mental retardation. *Pediatrics, 54*(4), 396-403.

Cohen, R.A., Kaufman, R.A., Myers, P.A., & Towbin, R.B. (1956). Cranial computed tomography in the abused child with head injury. *American Journal of Rontgenology, 146*(1), 97-102.

Conway, J.T. (1983). Should the radionuclide skeletal survey be used as a screening procedure in suspected child abuse victims? Letters to the Editor. *Radiology, 148,* 574-575.

Dolinskas, C.A., Zimmerman, R.A., & Bilaniuk, L.T. (1978). A sign of subarachnoid bleeding in cranial computed tomograms of pediatric head trauma patients. *Radiology, 126,* 409-411.

Duhaime, A.C., Alario, A.J., Lewander, W.J., Schut, L., Sutton, L.V., Seidl, T.S., Nudelman, S., Budenz, D., Hertle, R., Tsiaros, W., & Loporchio, S. (1992). Head injury in very young children: Mechanisms, injury types, and ophthalmologic findings in 100 hospitalized patients younger than 2 years of age. *Pediatrics, 90*(2), 179-184.

Ellison, P.H., Tsai, F.Y., & Largent, J.A. (1978). Computed tomography in child abuse and cerebral contusion. *Pediatrics, 62,* 1151-1154.

Gilliland, M.G.F., & Folberg, R. (1996). Shaken babies: Some have no impact injuries. *Journal of Forensic Science, 41,* 114-116.

Guthkelch, A.N. (1971). Infantile subdural hematoma and its relationship to whiplash injuries. *British Medical Journal, 2,* 430-431.

Hesselink, J.R., Dowd, C.F., Healy, M.E., Hajek, P., Baker, L.L., & Luerssen, T.G. (1988). MR imaging of brain contusions: A comparative study with CT. *American Journal of Neuroradiology, 9,* 269-278.

Hobbs, C.J. (1984). Skull fracture and the diagnosis of abuse. *Archives of Disease in Childhood, 59,* 246-252.

Johnson, D.L., Boal, D., & Baule, R. (1995). Role of apnea in nonaccidental head injury. *Pediatric Neurosurgery, 23,* 305-310.

Kempe, C.H., & Silverman, F.N. (1962). The battered child syndrome. *The Journal of the American Medical Association, 181,* 17-24.

Kleinman, P.K., & Barnes, P.D. (1998). Head trauma. In P.K. Kleinman (Ed.), *Diagnostic imaging of child abuse* (pp. 285-342). St. Louis, Missouri: Mosby.

Kleinman, P.K., Nimkin, K., Spevak, M.R., Royder, S.M., Modansky, D.L., Shelton, Y.A., & Patterson, M.M. (1996). Follow-up skeletal surveys in suspected child abuse. *American Journal of Rontgenology, 167,* 893-896.

LaCroix, P. (1951). Origin of the perichondrial osseous ring. First example of a phenomenon of induction in skeletal development. In P. LaCroix (Ed.), *The organization of bones* (pp. 90-97). Philadelphia: Blakiston.

Lazoritz, S., & Baldwin, S. (1997). The whiplash shaken infant syndrome: Has Caffey's syndrome changed or have we changed his syndrome? *Child Abuse and Neglect, 21,* 1009-1014.

Mendelsohn, D., Levin, H.S., Bruce, D., Lilly, M., Harvard, H., Culhane, K.A., & Eisenberg H.M. (1992). Late MRI after head injury in children: Relationship to clinical features and outcome. *Child's Nervous System, 8,* 445-452.

Merten, D.F., & Carpenter, B.L.M. (1990). Radiologic imaging of inflicted injury in the child abuse syndrome. *Pediatric Clinics of North America, 37*, 815-837.

Merten, D.F., Osborne, D.R., Radkowski, M.A., & Leonidas, J.C. (1984). Craniocerebral trauma in the child abuse syndrome: Radiological observations. *Pediatric Radiology, 14*(5), 272-277.

Meservy, C.J., Towbin, R., McLaurin, R.L., Myers, P.A., & Ball, W. (1987). Radiographic characteristics of skull fractures resulting from child abuse. *American Journal of Neuroradiology, 149*, 173-175.

Miller, T.Q. (1982). The role of the radiologist on the child abuse team. *Journal of the National Medical Association, 74*(7), 647-651.

Ogawa, T., Innagami, A., Fujita, H., Hatazawa, J., Shimosagawa, E., Noguchi, E., Okudera, T., Kamo, I., Vermua, T., & Suzuki, A. (1995). MR diagnosis of subacute and chronic subarachnoid hemorrhage: Comparison with CT. *American Journal of Rontgenology, 165*, 1257-1262.

Ordia, I.T., Strand, R., Gilles, F., & Welch, K. (1981). Computerized tomography of contusional clefts in the white matter of infants. *Journal of Neurosurgery, 54*, 696-698.

Sato, Y., Yuh, W.T.E., Smith, W.L., Alexander, R.C., Kao, S.C.S., & Ellerbroek, C.J. (1989). Head injury in child abuse: Evaluation with MR imaging. *Radiology, 173*, 653-657.

Saulsbury, F.T., & Alford, B.A. (1982). Intracranial bleeding from child abuse: The value of skull radiographs. *Pediatric Radiology, 12*(4), 175-478.

Silverman, F.M. (1953). The roentgen manifestations of unrecognized skeletal trauma in infants. *American Journal of Rontgenology, 69*, 413-426.

Snedecor, S.T., Knapp, R.E., & Wilson, H.B. (1935). Traumatic ossifying periostitis of the newborn. *Surgical and Gynecological Obstetrics, 61*, 385-387.

Sty, J.R., & Starshak, R.J. (1983). The role of scintigraphy in the evaluation of suspected abused child. *Radiology, 146*, 369-375.

Tsai, F.Y., Zee, C.S., Apthorp, J.S., & Dixon, G.H. (1980). Computed tomography in child abuse head trauma. *Journal of Computed Tomography, 4*(4), 227-286.

Zimmerman, R.A., & Bilaniuk, L.T. (1994). Pediatric head trauma [Review]. *Neuroimaging Clinics of North America, 4*(2), 349-366.

Zimmerman, R.A., Bilaniuk, L.T., Bruce, D., Dolinskas, C., Obrist, W., & Kuhl, D. (1978). Computed tomography of pediatric head trauma: Acute general cerebral swelling. *Radiology, 176*, 403-408.

Zimmerman, R.A., Bilaniuk, L.T., Bruce, D., Schut, L., Uzzell, B., & Goldberg, H.I. (1979). Computed tomography of craniocerebral injury in the abused child. *Radiology, 130*(3), 687-690.

Chapter Eight

Ophthalmic Manifestations
of Shaken Baby Syndrome

Jane D. Kivlin

SUMMARY. Retinal hemorrhages are the most common ocular finding in shaken baby syndrome. Retinal hemorrhages cannot be dated clinically or histopathologically. Non-ophthalmologists have great difficulty in seeing RH when limited by direct ophthalmoscopy and undilated pupils. There are many other causes, but ophthalmologists are not always aware of shaken baby syndrome in the differential of RH. While retinal injuries can cause loss of vision, the most common cause of blindness in SBS is direct bilateral injury to the visual pathways of the brain. *[Article copies available for a fee from The Haworth Document Delivery Service: 1-800-342-9678. E-mail address: <getinfo@haworthpressinc.com> Website: <http://www.HaworthPress.com> © 2001 by The Haworth Press, Inc. All rights reserved.]*

KEYWORDS. Ocular trauma, retinal hemorrhage, retinopathy, retinoshesis, cataract

Previous articles on the ocular manifestations of child abuse tend to cover the entire range of findings from those due to direct traumatic impact with the

[Haworth co-indexing entry note]: "Ophthalmic Manifestations of Shaken Baby Syndrome." Kivlin, Jane D. Co-published simultaneously in *Journal of Aggression, Maltreatment & Trauma* (The Haworth Maltreatment & Trauma Press, an imprint of The Haworth Press, Inc.) Vol. 5, No. 1(#9), 2001, pp. 137-153; and: *The Shaken Baby Syndrome: A Multidisciplinary Approach* (ed: Stephen Lazoritz, and Vincent J. Palusci) The Haworth Maltreatment & Trauma Press, an imprint of The Haworth Press, Inc., 2001, pp. 137-153. Single or multiple copies of this article are available for a fee from The Haworth Document Delivery Service [1-800-342-9678, 9:00 a.m. - 5:00 p.m. (EST). E-mail address: getinfo@haworthpressinc.com].

eye, to those in the child who has only been shaken and has had no impact even to the head. Those child abuse patients whose first medical encounter was with an ophthalmologist were almost always those who had signs of direct traumatic impact such as retinal detachments, cataracts, or glaucoma (Friendly 1971; Jensen, Smith, & Olson, 1971; Kiffney & Hill, 1964; Tseng & Keys, 1976; Weindenthal & Levin, 1976). The injuries from direct impact that have been reported have been the very late sequela of the trauma and the acute signs had resolved.

The number of patients reported with these direct ocular injuries has been very small. Ophthalmologists are more likely to think of metabolic disorders in the face of cataracts or conditions such as Coats' disease (Mushin, 1971), Stickler syndrome or Marfan syndrome in the face of retinal detachment and lens dislocation than to think of trauma. Yet in these situations, the ophthalmologist who recognizes scarring from trauma may help a child who has already survived serious trauma to the globe from suffering fatal injury. Knowledge among ophthalmologists about the importance of considering abuse in the differential diagnosis of a child's eye problem is still not complete.

It is extremely rare that a child with a shaking or shaking-impact injury would present initially to the ophthalmologist. Some children who are shaken clearly have had more than one injury which they have survived without medical attention at home. It is possible that one of these children could be seen for an eye examination after a milder injury which has caused retinal hemorrhages but has not caused prolonged loss of consciousness. However, young infants are not routinely examined by an ophthalmologist unless they have a health issue such as a history of significant prematurity or retinopathy of prematurity. Even though premature babies are at a greater risk for abuse, the possible number of abuse patients presenting this way is small.

The ophthalmologist is much more likely to serve as a consultant when abuse has been suspected. Retinal hemorrhages may have already been observed or suspected. The child may show other suspicious signs such as subdural hematoma or fractures. In view of the fact that some patients can even have prior admissions for lethargy, possible sepsis or previous fractures, it would be very interesting to do dilated fundus examinations on infants with these types of admissions to see if some of them do show retinal hemorrhages. The yield would probably be very small but could be life saving. To my knowledge, this study has not been done.

The most common ocular finding for the diagnosis of shaken baby syndrome is retinal hemorrhages (RH), occurring in 50 to 100 percent of patients (Figure 1) (Duhaime et al., 1992, Gilliland, Luckenback, & Chenier, 1994). Our experience at the Children's Hospital of Wisconsin is given in Table 1. These can take all forms depending on which layer of the retina is affected,

FIGURE 1. Retinal hemmorrhages in SBS

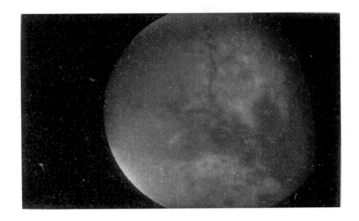

TABLE 1

Children's Hospital of Wisconsin – Eye examinations in SBS 1987-1998
Preliminary Experience
Patients identified – 95
Those examined by an ophthalmologist – 80
Those with retinal hemorrhages – 65 (81% of examined)
  Bilateral hemorrhages – 57 (88% of those with hemorrhages)
  Unilateral hemorrhages – 8 (12% of those with hemorrhages)
Vitreous hemorrhage – 15
Circinate retinal folds – 3
SBS inclusion criteria: Subdural hematoma due to abuse in a child less than 3 years of age.

varying from splinter hemorrhages to dot-blot hemorrhages to large boat shaped pre-retinal hemorrhages between the retina and the vitreous. Some may have white centers. The white center is a non-specific feature most likely due to the formation of a fibrin and platelet plug or due to retinal ischemia with resulting infarct of the nerve fiber layer (Kapoor et al., 1997).

Large dome-like hemorrhages have been observed particularly in the macular area (Greenwald, Weiss, Oesterle, & Friendly, 1986; Guarnaschelli, Lee, & Pitts, 1972; Mushin & Morgan, 1971; Riffenburgh & Sathyavagiswaran, 1991). They are often described clinically as subhyaloid hemorrhages, appearing to lie between the vitreous and the retina, but they may actually be underneath the internal limiting membrane of the retina or be contained within a raised circinate fold of the retina (Figure 1).

There is no reliable way to clinically date a retinal hemorrhage. I and others have observed small hemorrhages to resolve in two to three weeks (Giangiacomo & Barkett, 1985; Greenwald et al., 1986; Mushin & Morgan, 1971; Tomasi & Rosman, 1975). Large hemorrhages, particularly those between the retina and the vitreous, can remain for weeks to months gradually reducing in size. Small hemorrhages that have some clearing of the hemoglobin centrally are probably at least two weeks old and as little as one week old (Hollenhorst & Stein, 1958). This has not been rigorously documented, however. Retinal hemorrhages can evolve as well. Large pre-retinal hemorrhages, which broke out into the vitreous obscuring the view of the fundus, have been observed to be present on the initial examination (Greenwald, 1990). Vitreous hemorrhages can take months to resolve, causing concern about a developing child's vision. Severe amblyopia can be induced if a clear image is not received by the brain from that eye in a child less than seven years of age.

Even after death retinal hemorrhages cannot be dated. Histologically, hemosiderin appears as early as three days after an injury, but is more obvious afterfive to seven days. It can persist for as long as 20 years. Thus the presence of hemosiderin can indicate a minimum of three days between the injury and death, but not indicate a maximum time interval (Elner, Elner, Albert, & Arnall, 1991; Elner, Elner, Arnall, & Albert, 1990; Gilliland, Luckenback, Massicotte, & Folberg, 1991). It is unknown how many infants can have hemosiderin in their retinas from birth hemorrhages. From the carefully studied eyes from Sudden Infant Death (SIDS) patients, it appears to be unlikely to occur (Marcella F. Fierro, M.D., personal communication).

Retinal hemorrhages by themselves are non-specific findings. One cannot look at a hemorrhage and say this is definitely due to a particular diagnosis. One can say that it is consistent with that diagnosis but it is the constellation of all physical abnormalities in the child that will eliminate medical doubt as to the cause of the hemorrhage. However, the likelihood of severe intentional trauma is extremely high in a young child who has extensive retinal hemorrhages. Bilateral hemorrhages are often seen in deceased patients (Betz, Puschel, Miltner, Lignitz, & Eisenmenger, 1996; Gilliland et al., 1994).

Yet some patients with clear signs of abuse such as bilateral subdural hematomas (SDH) and rib fractures can have only one hemorrhage in one eye (Betz et al., 1996) or only a few hemorrhages in both eyes (Buys et al., 1992; Hadley, Sonntag, Rekate, & Murphy, 1989) or even no RH (Duhaime et al., 1992) (Table 1). Unilaterality versus bilaterality of a hemorrhage is frequently not given in the published series of abused children, so the respective frequencies are not accurately known. Unilateral hemorrhages have been observed in infants with clear signs of abuse such as multiple rib and long bone fractures (Betz et al., 1996; Buys et al., 1992; Hadley et al., 1989, Tyagi, Willshaw, &

Ainsworth, 1997; Wilkinson, 1989). We observed unilateral RH in 12% of infants who were examined (Table 1). Some patients with a unilateral hemorrhage may have had bilateral hemorrhages which resolved in one eye by the time of the examination. Asymmetric speed of resolution has been observed by this author.

The retinal hemorrhages are often clustered around the major retinal vessels in the posterior pole of the eye (Greenwald, 1990). While Gilliland and Folberg (1996) frequently found peripheral retinal hemorrhages, clinically one has the answer upon the first look at the posterior pole of the eye with an indirect ophthalmoscope.

There are many other causes of retinal hemorrhages, which look identical to those in SBS. Hemorrhages due to birth are the most problematic. They are extremely common, occurring in as many as 50% of infants on the first day of life (Egge, Lyng, & Maltau, 1981; Kaur & Taylor, 1992). The incidence is greatly influenced by the age of the infant, the type of delivery, parity of the infant's mother, the type of examination technique used, and experience of the examiner (Kaur & Taylor, 1992). They are rarely as massive as the classic SBS patient but can be with a traumatic delivery. (This author has seen two cases.) They appear to be less frequent in premature infants, while premature infants are at higher risk for abuse. It is generally agreed that once the infant is three weeks of age, the likelihood that the retinal hemorrhages are due to birth trauma is extremely low unless there was a particularly traumatic birth. However bleeding dyscrasias such as vitamin K deficiency in newborns (Lane, Hathaway, Githens, Krugman, & Rosenberg, 1983; Wetzel, Slater, & Dover, 1994), hemophilia (Kaur & Taylor, 1992), glutaric acidemia (Greenberg et al., 1995), protein C deficiency (Pulido, Lingua, Cristol, & Byrne, 1987), and vonWillebrand's disease (Kaur & Taylor, 1992) can cause retinal hemorrhaging identical to that in SBS; however, these occurrences are rare. With the coagulopathy that can occur with subdural hematomas, sorting out the hematologic status can take some time and effort to accomplish (Hymel, Abshire, Luckey, & Jenny, 1997). Other bleeding dyscrasias, such as leukemia and sickle cell disease, are rarely manifested in infants' eyes. Anemia appears to cause retinal hemorrhages in children less often than in adults (Merin & Freund, 1968). The combination of anemia and thrombocytopenia appears to be more likely to cause hemorrhages than either condition alone (Rubenstein, Yanoff, & Albert, 1968).

Extra corporeal membranous oxygenation (ECMO) has been reported to cause retinal hemorrhages (Sethi, 1990). Recent birth, heparinization, alterations in cerebral blood flow, major vessel ligation, mechanical ventilation and hypoxia are factors which could contribute to these hemorrhages (Sethi, 1990). This author observed one patient with a retinal hemorrhage in five years of screening ECHO patients. Other pediatric ophthalmologists have had a similar low yield for this type of screening (Pollack & Tychsen, 1996).

Other causes of central nervous system bleeding, such as from an arteriovenous malformation or aneurysm (Clark, Orr, Atkinson, Towbin, & Pang, 1995; McLellan, Prasad, & Punt, 1986; Vapalahti, Schugk, Tarkkanen, & Bjorkesten, 1969) of the brain or the spine, have caused a very similar picture to SBS both from the eye and neurologic examinations.

Meningitis has also been described as a cause of retinal hemorrhages (Eisenbrey, 1979; Fraser, Horgan, & Bardavio, 1995; Friendly, 1971; Gilliland et al., 1994). The number of reports is small and those reports without spinal fluid cultures are less convincing. The term pachymeningitis has been used in the older literature to simply indicate inflammation of the dura and subdural hematoma (SDH). Reading these older reports regarding SDH and RH in young infants, one has to think that many of these patients were also shaken babies simply reported prior to the recognition of that entity (Govan & Walsh, 1947; Hollenhorst & Stein, 1958; Sherwood, 1930).

Accidental trauma very rarely causes retinal hemorrhages (Betz et al., 1996; Buys et al., 1992; Duhaime et al., 1992; Eisenbrey, 1979; Johnson, Braun, & Friendly, 1993; Koser, 1995; Riffenburgh & Sathyavagiswaran, 1991). The severity of the trauma in these reported cases was usually marked, for example, fatal motor vehicle accidents or two story falls. Minor trauma such as falling out of a bed appears to be very unlikely to cause SDH or RH. The number of hemorrhages in these patients has tended to be much less than in the clearly shaken patients (Betz et al., 1996) and bilateral RH occurs much less frequently. The Japanese patients reported by Aoki and Masuzawa (1984) who fell onto mats at home but had SDH and RH were most likely SBS patients. This author has seen one patient who fell on his forehead before many witnesses resulting in a localized cerebral contusion under the bruised skin and a small number of RH in both eyes. The reliable, consistent history and the localized injury allowed the conclusion that only accidental injury occurred. Well-intentioned folk remedies causing SDH have caused RH also (Guarnaschelli et al., 1972). Evaluation by a child abuse expert is needed to sort out this type of injury.

Retinal hemorrhages can also occur as a result of chest trauma, such as being run over by a tractor (Purtscher's retinopathy). Many patients also have soft exudates or cotton wool spots (Madsen, 1972). Purtscher's retinopathy has raised the issue as to whether cardiopulmonary resuscitation (CPR) could have caused the retinal hemorrhages in a baby suspected of having non-accidental trauma. A few retinal hemorrhages have been observed in patients who had documented professional CPR in a hospital setting and in those patients with non-professional CPR in a situation not suspicious for child abuse (Goetting & Sowa, 1990; Kanter, 1986; Kirschner & Stein, 1985; Kramer &

Goldstein, 1993; Riffenburgh & Sathyavagiswaran, 1991). However exudates have not been reported. The vast majority of patients who have had CPR, even those with desperate non-professional CPR leading to rib fractures, have not had retinal hemorrhages. No patient who has had traumatic or atraumatic CPR has been found to have the extensive number and degree of hemorrhages that shaken babies commonly have. Thus extensive, numerous hemorrhages, particularly with large subhyaloid hemorrhages or a vitreous hemorrhage are very unlikely to have been caused by CPR. Only a few abused children have been found to have exudates in addition to retinal hemorrhages (San Martin, Steinkuller, & Nisbet, 1981; Tomasi & Rosman, 1975). Two were sexually abused as well so the type of force applied to the thorax was probably different from that operating in SBS. It is possible that other direct chest trauma could occur from abuse and thus cause retinal hemorrhages and exudates, but this has not been reported to my knowledge.

Some patients with persistent retinopathy of prematurity (ROP) in which the abnormal new vessels have not regressed promptly may have retinal hemorrhages and even vitreous hemorrhages. However in these patients the lingering neovascular tissue is apparent to the ophthalmologist. A vitreous hemorrhage, which obscures most fundus detail, could make the ROP impossible to see but the patient's history, possibly the findings in the other eye, and previous eye records will sort out most situations. This author has seen two patients with small round hemorrhages in the posterior pole in one eye each which were probably caused by the previous ROP examinations.

Valsalva maneuvers, high attitude hypoxia, bungee cord jumping and whiplash injuries in motor vehicle accidents have been reported to cause retinal hemorrhages in adults (David, Mears, & Quinlan, 1994; Duane, 1973; Haslett, Duvall-Young, & McGalliard, 1994; Kelley, 1972; Lubin, Rennie, Hackett, & Albert, 1982; Schipper, 1991). Most patients have had small numbers of hemorrhages and some have had exudates. All have had a clear history of a precipitating event, usually a significant injury, unlike most abused children. Sudden Infant Death Syndrome (SIDS) is extremely unlikely to cause retinal hemorrhages by itself or with CPR efforts (Betz et al., 1996).

Another distinctive but infrequent ocular finding in SBS is the circular retinal fold around the macula. (Figure 2) (Elner et al., 1990; Gaynon, Koh, Marmor, & Frankel, 1988; Lambert, Johnson, & Hoyt, 1986; Massicotte, Folberg, Torczynski, Gilliland, & Luckenbach, 1991; Mills, 1998; Munger, Peiffer, Bouldin, Kylstra, & Thompson, 1993; Rao, Smith, Choi, Xiaohu, & Kornblum, 1988; Rohrbach, Benz, Friedrichs, Thiel, & Wehner, 1997). There is still some controversy over the cause of these folds. The two possibilities are vitreous traction on the retina versus intra retinal bleeding as in Terson syndrome (Keithan, Bennett, Cameron, & Mieler, 1993; Massicotte et al., 1991;

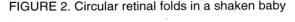

FIGURE 2. Circular retinal folds in a shaken baby

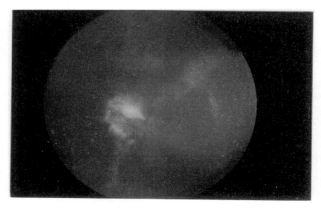

Morris, Kuhn, & Witherspoon, 1994). In the vitreous traction theory, the shaking has a direct effect on the vitreous and retina. In the hemorrhage theory, there is bleeding underneath the internal limiting membrane of the retina. Clinically this looks identical to subhyaloid hemorrhage between the retina and vitreous and is often labeled as such. The edge of the dome like hemorrhage is actually at the edge of the retinoschisis cavity or split in the retina.

In these folds, the retina can be tented up at the edge of the cavity and the underlying pigmented epithelium can be disrupted causing a circular pigmentary change later (Gaynon et al., 1988; Spaide, Swengel, Scharre, & Mein, 1990). The macular area is most often affected but splitting of the retina with hemorrhage can occur elsewhere also (Greenwald et al., 1986, Munger et al., 1993). The fold can flatten out over a few weeks to six months (Mark Greenwald MD, personal communication; Mills, 1998). At the Children's Hospital of Wisconsin, circular retinal folds have been found infrequently (Table 1).

Vision is quite variably affected by the injury causing the dome like hemorrhages and retinal folds. In some patients, vision is quite good (Alex Levin MD, personal communication) and in others vision is badly affected (Greenwald et al., 1986 and personal communication). Those patients with diminished electroretinogram responses must have had deeper retinal splitting than the internal limiting membrane (Fishman, Dasher, & Lambert, 1998). Clinically, deeper injury is difficult to recognize acutely. In only one of

Fishman's three cases was extensive subretinal hemorrhage noted. The other two had pre-retinal and intraretinal hemorrhages.

Like most clinical findings first felt to be pathognomonic for a condition, these retinal folds and dome like hemorrhages have been shown to occur in another condition, specifically Terson syndrome after severe head trauma (Keithahn et al., 1993; Morris et al., 1994). Internal limiting membrane was found to span the macula and attach to the apices of the fold. A peripheral circular fold in an adult motor vehicle accident victim was also reported by Wolter (1965).

With our current understanding of the evolution of dome like hemorrhages and retinal folds, it is interesting to speculate whether the round hypopigmented peripheral lesions observed late in French patients represent the same phenomenon (Aron, Marx, Blanch, Duval, & Luce, 1970; Blanck, 1973; Maroteaux & Lamy, 1967). However Harcourt has observed patches of chorioretinal atrophy which were not always related to previously observed hemorrhage (Harcourt, 1973). Peripheral fundus examinations can be very difficult in young children. Very few other reports of late pigmentary changes have been made.

The success of finding retinal hemorrhages and other fundus abnormalities is very dependent on the technique used. Figure 3 demonstrates the difference in field of view of the indirect ophthalmoscope versus the direct ophthalmoscope. The indirect ophthalmoscope, most often a head mounted unit with a condensing lens, provides a wide-angle binocular view which can include nearly all the areas within the temporal vascular arcades at once. By directing the view toward different parts of the fundus, much of the periphery can be easily seen. For the far peripheral retina, light indentation of the globe through the eyelids is necessary but essentially impossible in an awake child less than 12 years old. In a struggling child the fundus picture may flash past the viewer as the child's eyes move around. The indirect ophthalmoscope allows much easier chasing of the fundus details and the larger field makes it more likely that important structures such as the disk will pop into view.

The hand-held direct ophthalmoscope used by all physicians provides a slightly more magnified but much more limited view of the fundus, little more than one disk diameter. It is very easy to miss small retinal hemorrhages with this type of examination (Carter & McCormick, 1983; Levin, 1990). Even in a comatose child with dilated pupils, scanning of the retina is tedious and the periphery is not seen well or completely. However in severely injured children, particularly those with spontaneously dilated and fixed pupils because of neurologic injury, the massive retinal hemorrhages in the posterior pole of the fundus can be obvious with a direct ophthalmoscope. Yet, non-ophthalmologists missed the retinal hemorrhages in 53% of the children in whom ophthalmologists later found them at our institution.

FIGURE 3 (A and B). View of same fundus through (a.) direct and (b.) indirect ophthalmoscopes. Hemorrhage is not visible with the smaller field.

A

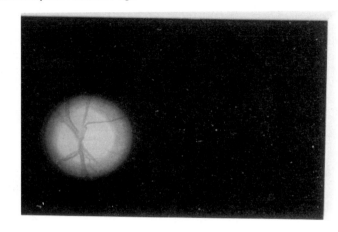

B

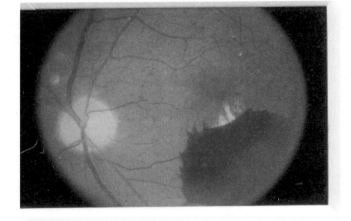

A dilated pupil is essential, particularly for peripheral lesions (see Table 2). If the child has been sedated or treated with barbiturates, the resulting pupillary constriction can make a fundus examination almost impossible even with an indirect ophthalmoscope. The value of a fundus examination and photographs using dilating drops must be weighed against the inability to monitor pupillary reaction for several hours.

TABLE 2. Dilating Drops* Recommended for Fundus Examination for SBS

Name	Efficacy Advantages	Duration of large pupil[†]	Disadvantages
Tropicamide (Mydriacyl®) ½ or 1%	Good in less pigmented eyes	4-6 hours	Works less well in brown eyes
Cyclopentolate (Cyclogyl®) ½ or 1%	Good in all eyes	1-2 days	Long duration 2% solution can cause hallucinations
Phenylephrine 2.5%	Poor by itself Very helpful combined with tropicamide or cyclopentolate	3-4 hours	Systemic hypertension in higher strengths Used alone, pupil still constricts during exam
Cyclomydril® (0.2% cyclopentolate and 1% phenylephrine; Alcon laboratories)	Good in less pigmented eyes Commonly used for ROP exams Convenient combination drop	3-4 hours	Often needs to be re-peated for darker eyes
*Generically available, so little information is available, even in the separate Physicians' Desk Reference for Ophthamology®. A hospital pharmacy is a good source of information.			
[†]Repeat dosage will prolong duration by up to 50%			

Photographs of retinal hemorrhages can be very useful in building a medical or legal case of abuse. Most fundus cameras, which can be taken to the bedside, have the same limitations as a direct ophthalmoscope of small view and relative immobility compared to a struggling child's eye. Anesthetic or sedation episodes for other care, such as SDH drainage, are opportunities to obtain good photographs. Hemorrhages and retinal folds can be elevated from the surface of the retina, yielding pictures that are partly out of focus. Video fundus photography with a hand held probe (RetCam®) offers promise for wide view pictures at the bedside but the current price of $60,000 is prohibitive for most institutions. Dilating the pupils is essential. Taping the eyelids for a few hours instead of using lubricating ointment in the eyes is necessary for clear pictures. A topical anesthetic and a lid speculum are almost always needed.

There is the impression in the eye literature that fatally abused infants have more extensive retinal hemorrhages. However the largest series of patients have been from autopsy experience. Clinical series of survivors from the same patient population or geographic area have not been done (Gilliland et al., 1994). Not all reported patients have had eye exams.

Some attempts have been made to correlate the eye findings with severity of neurologic injury and outcome in abused children. The series of patients with confirmed abuse have ranged from only 5 to 23 patients, being consecutive hospital admissions, consecutive autopsy cases which included the eyes or vitrectomy cases (Green, Lieberman, Milroy, & Parsons, 1996; Matthews & Das, 1996; Mills, 1998; Wilkinson, 1989). The exact mode of injury in an abused child is rarely known and could be a factor in how extensive the retinal hemorrhages are. Coma scores and other neurologic assessments have been quantitatively correlated with death and neurologic outcome in large series of patients (Hennes, Lee, Smith, Sty, & Losek, 1988; Raimondi & Hirschauer, 1984). CT or MRI scans will also give a more complete view of the extent and location of the brain injury than an eye exam.

For the past 60 years, retinal hemorrhages have been noted to be present extremely often when a child has a subdural hematoma (Govan & Walsh, 1947; Hollenhorst & Sty, 1958; Sherwood, 1930). Subdural hematoma is still often a fatal condition, most likely reflecting the severity of the injury that caused it. Therefore retinal hemorrhages are often found in children who die of their injuries. Predictions of outcome based on an eye examination when MRI and CT scanning are available do not seem very productive.

The visual outcome of SBS has not been extensively examined. Many series mentioned that a few of their surviving patients were blind but the particular reason is often not given. Splitting of the layers of the retina or retinoschisis can cause interruption of the nerve conduction within the retina and thus cause loss of vision on an ocular basis with a poor electroretinogram (Fishman et al., 1998; Greenwald et al., 1986). Optic atrophy can occur secondary to retinal injury or possibly due to optic nerve sheath hemorrhage with nerve compression. Pigmented fundus lesions, particularly in the periphery, have been described but are fairly rare (Aron et al., 1970; Maroteaux & Lamy, 1967). In our institution, cerebral visual impairment secondary to injury of the visual system posterior to the chiasm appears to be the most common cause of visual loss in survivors (Table 3). These patients have very poor vision and yet have normal pupillary response and normal fundi. We rarely see retinal scarring.

In conclusion, extensive RH are the most common ocular finding in SBS. They are not pathognomonic for SBS but raise a very high suspicion for it. One third of surviving infants with SBS at our institution have had cerebral visual impairment.

TABLE 3. Vision outcome for 95 SBS patients at the Children's Hospital of Wisconsin

95 patients
67 survived
47 had follow up
32 had normal vision for age
14 had cerebral visual impairment
1 homonymous hemianopsia
1 optic atrophy
3 strabismus and amblyopia
1 anisometropic

REFERENCES

Aoki, N., & Masuzawa, H. (1984). Infantile acute subdural hematoma. *Journal of Neurosurgery, 61*, 273-280.

Aron, J.J., Marx, P., Blanck, M.F., Duval, R., & Luce, R. (1970). Signes oculaires observes dans le syndrome de silverman. *Annals of Oculism, 203*, 533-546.

Betz, P., Puschel, K., Miltner, E., Lignitz, E., & Eisenmenger, W. (1996). Morphometrical analysis of retinal hemorrhages in the shaken baby syndrome. *Forensic Science International, 78*, 71-80.

Blanck, M.F. (1973). A propos de deux cas de syndrome de silverman avec decollement de retine. *Bulletin Des Societes D Ophtalmologie De France, 73*, 881-885.

Buys, Y.M., Levin, A.V., Enzenauer, R.W., Elder, J.E., Letourneau, M.A., Humphreys, R.P., Mian, M., & Morin, J.D. (1992). Retinal findings after head trauma in infants and young children. *Ophthalmology, 99*, 1718-1723.

Carter, J.E., & McCormick, A.Q. (1983). Whiplash shaking syndrome: Retinal hemorrhages and computerized axial tomography of the brain. *Child Abuse & Neglect, 7*, 279-286.

Clark, R., Orr, R.A., Atkinson, C.S., Towbin, R.B., & Pang, D. (1995). Retinal hemorrhages associated with spinal cord arteriovenous malformation. *Clinical Pediatrics, 34*, 281-283.

David, D.B., Mears, T., & Quinlan, M.P. (1994). Ocular complications associated with bungee jumping. *British Journal of Ophthalmology, 78*, 234-235.

Duane, T.D. (1973). Valsalva hemorrhagic retinopathy. *American Journal of Ophthalmology, 75*, 637-642.

Duhaime, A.C., Alario, A.J., Lewander, W.J., Schut, L., Sutton, L.N., Seidl, T.S., Nudelman, S., Budenz, D., Hertle, R., Tsiaras, W., & Loporchio, S. (1992). Head injury in very young children: Mechanisms, injury types, and ophthalmologic findings in 100 hospitalized patients younger than two years of age. *Pediatrics, 90,* 179-185.

Egge, D., Lyng, G., & Maltau, J.M. (1981). Effect of instrumental delivery on the frequency and severity of retinal hemorrhages in the newborn. *Acta Obstetrics and Gynecology Scandinavia, 60,* 153-155.

Eisenbrey, A.B. (1979). Retinal hemorrhage in the battered child. *Child's Brain, 5,* 40-44.

Elner, S.G., Elner, V.M., Albert, D.M., & Arnall, M. (1991). Letter. *Archives of Ophthalmology, 109,* 322.

Elner S.G., Elner V.M., Arnall M., & Albert D.M. (1990). Ocular and associated systemic findings in suspected child abuse. *Archives of Ophthalmology, 108,* 1094-1101.

Fishman, C.D., Dasher, W.B., & Lambert, S.R. (1998). Electroretinographic findings in infants with the shaken baby syndrome. *Journal of Pediatric Ophthalmology and Strabismus, 35,* 22-26.

Fraser, S.G., Horgan, S.E., & Bardavio, J. (1995). Retinal hemorrhage in meningitis. *Eye, 9,* 659-660.

Friendly, D.S. (1971). Ocular manifestations of physical child abuse. *Proceedings of American Academy of Ophthalmology & Otolaryngology, 75,* 318-352.

Gaynon, M.W., Koh, K., Marmor, M.F., & Frankel, L.R. (1988). Retinal folds in the shaken baby syndrome. *American Journal of Ophthalmology, 106,* 423-425.

Giangiacomo, J., & Barkett, K.J. (1985). Ophthalmoscopic Findings in occult child abuse. *Journal of Pediatric Ophthalmology & Strabismus, 22,* 234-237.

Gilliland, M.G.F., & Folberg, R (1996). Shaken babies–some have no impact injuries. *Journal of Forensic Science, 41*(1), 114-116.

Gilliland, M.G.F., Luckenbach, M.W., & Chenier, T.C. (1994). Systemic and ocular findings in 169 prospectively studied child deaths: Retinal hemorrhages usually mean child abuse. *Forensic Science International, 68,* 117-132.

Gilliland M.G.F., Luckenbach, M.W., Massicotte, S.J., & Folberg R. (1991). Letters. *Archives of Ophthalmology, 109,* 321-322.

Goetting, M.G., & Sowa, B. (1990). Retinal hemorrhage after cardiopulmonary resuscitation in children: An etiologic reevaluation. *Pediatrics, 85,* 585-587.

Govan Jr., C.D., & Walsh, F.B. (1947). Symptomatology of subdural hematoma in infants and in adults. *Archives of Ophthalmology, 37,* 701-715.

Green, M.D., Lieberman, G., Milroy, C.M., & Parsons, M.A. (1996). Ocular and cerebral trauma in non-accidental injury in infancy: Underlying mechanisms and implications for paediatric practice. *British Journal of Ophthalmology, 8,* 282-287.

Greenberg, C.R., Booth, F.A., DeGroot, W., Reggin, J.D., Greene, C.L., & Goodman, S.I. (1995). Intracranial hemorrhage and glutaric acidemia Type I (GAI). *Pediatric Research, 37,* 379A.

Greenwald, M.J. (1990). The shaken baby syndrome. *Seminars in Ophthalmology, 5*(4), 202-215.

Greenwald, M.J., Weiss, A., Oesterle, C.S., & Friendly, D.S. (1986). Traumatic retinoschisis in battered babies. *Ophthalmology, 93,* 618-625.

Guarnaschelli, J., Lee, J., & Pitts, F.W. (1972). "Fallen Fontanelle" (Caida de Mollera). *Journal of the American Medical Association, 222,* 1545-1546.

Hadley, M.N., Sonntag, V.K.H., Rekate, H.L., & Murphy, A. (1989). The infant whiplash-shake injury syndrome: A clinical and pathological study. *Neurosurgery, 24*(4), 536-540.

Harcourt, B. (1973). The role of the ophthalmologist in the diagnosis and management of child abuse. *Ophthalmic Surgery, 4,* 37-40.

Haslett, R.S., Duvall-Young, J., & McGalliard, J.N. (1994). Traumaticretinal angiopathy and seat belts: Pathogenesis of whiplash injury. *Eye, 8,* 615-617.

Hennes, H., Lee, M., Smith, D., Sty, J.R., & Losek, J. (1988). Clinical predictors of severe head trauma in children. *American Journal of Diseases of Children, 142,* 1045-1047.

Hollenhorst, R.W., & Stein, H.A. (1958). Ocular signs and prognosis in subdural and subarachnoid bleeding in young children. *Archives of Ophthalmology, 60,* 187-192.

Hymel, K., Abshire, T., Luckey, D., & Jenny, C. (1997). Coagulopathy in pediatric abusive head trauma. *Pediatrics, 99,* 371-375.

Jensen, A.D., Smith, R.E., & Olson, M.I. (1971). Ocular clues to child abuse. *Journal of Pediatric Ophthalmology, 8,* 270-272.

Johnson, D.L., Braun, D., & Friendly, D. (1993). Accidental head trauma and retinal hemorrhage. *Neurosurgery, 33*(2), 231-235.

Kanter, R.K. (1986). Retinal hemorrhage after cardiopulmonary resuscitation or child abuse. *Journal of Pediatrics, 108,* 430-432.

Kapoor, S., Schiffman, J., Tang, R., Kiang, E., Li, H., & Woodward, J. (1997). The significance of white-centered retinal hemorrhages in the shaken baby syndrome. *Pediatric Emergency Care, 13,* 183-185.

Kaur, B., & Taylor, D. (1992). Fundus hemorrhages in infancy. *Survey of Ophthalmology, 37,* 1-17.

Keithahn, M.A.Z., Bennett, S.R., Cameron, D., & Mieler, W.F. (1993). Retinal folds in Terson syndrome. *Ophthalmology, 100,* 1187-1190.

Kelley, J.S. (1972). Purtscher's retinopathy related to chest compression by safety belts. *American Journal of Ophthalmology, 74,* 278-283.

Kiffney Jr., G.T., & Hill, C. (1964). The eye of the "battered child." *Archives of Ophthalmology, 72,* 231-233.

Kirschner, R.H., & Stein, R.J. (1985). The mistaken diagnosis of child abuse. *American Journal of Diseases of Children, 139,* 873-875.

Koser, M. (1995). The association of vision-threatening ocular injury with infant walker use. *Archives of Pediatric and Adolescent Medicine, 149,* 1275-1276.

Kramer, K., & Goldstein, B. (1993). Retinal hemorrhages following cardiopulmonary resuscitation. *Clinical Pediatrics, 32,* 366-368.

Lambert, S.R., Johnson, T.E., & Hoyt, C.S. (1986). Optic nerve sheath and retinal hemorrhages associated with the shaken baby syndrome. *Archives of Ophthalmology, 104,* 1509-1512.

Lane, P.A., Hathaway, W.E., Githens, J.H., Krugman, R.D., & Rosenberg, D.A. (1983). Fatal intracranial hemorrhage in a normal infant secondary to vitamin K deficiency. *Pediatrics, 72,* 562-564.

Levin, A.V. (1990). Ocular manifestations of child abuse. *Ophthalmology Clinics of North America, 3*(2), 249-263.

Lubin, J.R., Rennie, D., Hackett, P., & Albert, D.M. (1982). High altitude retinal hemorrhage: A clinical and pathological case report. *Annals Ophthalmology, 14,* 1071-1076.

Madsen, P.H. (1972). Traumatic retinal angiopathy (Purtscher). *Ophthalmologica, 165,* 453-458.

Maroteaux, P., & Lamy, M. (1967). Fundi of battered babies. *The Lancet, 2*(7531), 829.

Massicotte, S.J., Folberg, R., Torczynski, E., Gilliland, M.G.F., & Luckenbach, M.W. (1991). Vitreoretinal traction and perimacular retinal folds in the eyes of deliberately traumatized children. *Ophthalmology, 98,* 1124-1127.

Matthews, G.P., & Das, A. (1996). Dense vitreous hemorrhages predict poor visual and neurological prognosis in infants with shaken baby syndrome. *Journal of Pediatric Ophthalmology and Strabismus, 33,* 260-265.

McLellan, N.J., Prasad, R., & Punt, J. (1986). Spontaneous subhyaloid and retinal hemorrhages in an infant. *Archives of Disease in Childhood, 61,* 1130-1132.

Merin, S., & Freund, M. (1968). Retinopathy in severe anemia. *American Journal of Ophthalmology, 66,* 1102-1106.

Mills, M. (1998). Funduscopic lesions associated with mortality in shaken baby syndrome. *Journal of the American Academy of Pediatric Ophthalmologic Surgery, 2,* 67-71.

Morris, R., Kuhn, F., & Witherspoon, C.D. (1994). Hemorrhagic macular cysts. *Ophthalmology, 101,* 1.

Munger, C.E., Peiffer, R.L., Bouldin, T.W., Kylstra, J.A., & Thompson, R.L. (1993). Ocular and associated neuropathologic observations in suspected whiplash shaken infant syndrome. *American Journal of Forensic Medicine and Pathology, 14,* 193-200.

Mushin, A.S. (1971). Ocular damage in the battered-baby syndrome. *British Medical Journal, 14,* 402-404.

Mushin, A., & Morgan, G. (1971). Ocular injury in the battered baby syndrome. *British Journal of Ophthalmology, 55,* 343-347.

Pollack, J. & Tychsen, L. (1996). Prevalence of retinal hemorrhage in infants after extracorporeal membrane oxygenation. *American Journal of Ophthalmology, 121,* 297-303.

Pulido, J.S., Lingua, R.W., Cristol, S., & Byrne, S.F. (1987). Protein C deficiency associated with vitreous hemorrhage in a neonate. *American Journal of Ophthalmology, 104,* 546-547.

Raimondi, A.J., & Hirschauer, J. (1984). Head injury in the infant and toddler. *Child's Brain, 11,* 12-35.

Rao, N., Smith, R.E., Choi, J.H., Xiaohu, X, & Kornblum, R.N. (1988). Autopsy findings in the eyes of fourteen fatally abused children. *Forensic Science International, 39,* 293-299.

Riffenburgh, R.S., & Sathyavagiswaran, L. (1991). Ocular findings at autopsy of child abuse victims. *Ophthalmology, 98,* 1519-1524.

Rohrbach, J.M., Benz, D., Friedrichs, W., Thiel, H.J., & Wehner, H.D. (1997). Ocular pathology of child abuse (German). *Klinische Monatsblatter fur Augenheilkunde, 210*, 133-138.

Rubenstein, R.A., Yanoff, M., & Albert, D.M. (1968). Thrombocytopenia, anemia, and retinal hemorrhage. *American Journal of Ophthalmology, 65*, 435-439.

San Martin, R., Steinkuller, P.G., & Nisbet, R.M. (1981). Retinopathy in the sexually abused battered child. *Annals Ophthalmology, 13*, 89-91.

Schipper, I. (1991). Valsalvamanover: Nicht immer gutartig. *Klinische Monatsblatter fur Augenheilkunde, 198*, 457-459.

Sethi, S.K. (1990). Retinal hemorrhages after extra corporeal membranous oxygenation. *North Carolina Medical Journal, 51*, 246-248.

Sherwood, D. (1930). Chronic subdural hematoma in infants. *American Journal of Diseases of Children, 39*, 980-1021.

Spaide, R.F., Swengel, R.M., Scharre, D.W., & Mein, C.E. (1990). Shaken baby syndrome. *American Family Physician, 41*, 1145-1152.

Tomasi, L.G., & Rosman, N.P. (1975). Purtscher retinopathy in the battered child syndrome. *American Journal of Diseases in Childhood, 129*, 1335-1337.

Tseng, S.S., & Keys, M.P. (1976). Battered child syndrome simulating cogenital glaucoma. *Archives of Ophthalmology, 94*, 839-840.

Tyagi, A.K., Willshaw, H.E., & Ainsworth, J.R. (1997). Unilateral retinal haemorrhages in non-accidental injury. *The Lancet, 349*, 1224.

Weidenthal, D.T., & Levin, D.B. (1976). Retinal detachment in a battered infant. *American Journal of Ophthalmology, 81*, 725-727.

Wetzel, R.C., Slater, A.J., & Dover, G.J. (1994). Fatal intramuscular bleeding misdiagnosised as suspected nonaccidental injury. *Pediatrics, 94*, 771-773.

Wilkinson, W.S. (1989). Retinal hemorrhage predicts neurologic injury in the shaken baby syndrome. *Archives of Ophthalmology, 107*, 1472-1474.

Wolter, J.R. (1965). Circular fixed fold of the retina. *American Journal of Ophthalmology, 60*, 805-811.

Vapalahti, P.M., Schugk, P., Tarkkanen, L., & Bjorkesten, G. (1969). Intercranial arterial aneurysm in a three-month-old infant. *Neurosurgy, 30*, 169-171.

Chapter Nine

Medical Management of the Shaken Infant

Rainer G. Gedeit

SUMMARY. The medical management of the Shaken Infant is challenging and frustrating. Severe traumatic and hypoxic-ischemic injuries commonly occur in these patients, resulting in significant central nervous system injury. The medical management of these children depends mostly on the severity of central nervous system injury. The infant with isolated traumatic brain injury may benefit from aggressive management of increased intracranial pressure. Otherwise, the major thrust of care for these infants is supportive in nature, maintenance of normal hemodynamic and respiratory parameters, and treatment of seizures. Recognition of SBS is important so that appropriate diagnostic tests can be done and therapies initiated. Because of the devastating nature of these injuries, numerous resources are required to care for survivors. The outcome of infants with severe brain injury is dismal; therefore, prevention is required. *[Article copies available for a fee from The Haworth Document Delivery Service: 1-800-342-9678. E-mail address: <getinfo@haworthpressinc.com> Website: <http://www.HaworthPress.com> © 2001 by The Haworth Press, Inc. All rights reserved.]*

KEYWORDS. Head trauma, brain injury, intracranial pressure, apnea, seizures, cerebral edema, cardiac arrest

---

[Haworth co-indexing entry note]: "Medical Management of the Shaken Infant." Gedeit, Rainer G. Co-published simultaneously in *Journal of Aggression, Maltreatment & Trauma* (The Haworth Maltreatment & Trauma Press, an imprint of The Haworth Press, Inc.) Vol. 5, No. 1(#9), 2001, pp. 155-171; and: *The Shaken Baby Syndrome: A Multidisciplinary Approach* (ed: Stephen Lazoritz, and Vincent J. Palusci) The Haworth Maltreatment & Trauma Press, an imprint of The Haworth Press, Inc., 2001, pp. 155-171. Single or multiple copies of this article are available for a fee from The Haworth Document Delivery Service [1-800-342-9678, 9:00 a.m. - 5:00 p.m. (EST). E-mail address: getinfo@haworthpressinc.com].

155

INTRODUCTION

The medical management of the victim of Shaken Baby Syndrome is a challenging and frustrating job. Significant brain injuries occur in these infants resulting in life-long physical and cognitive abnormalities, or death. When the shaken infant presents for medical care, the history of the illness is often inaccurate, and significant delay in obtaining medical care has most likely occurred. This causes a delay in treatment, and allows complications to occur which will worsen the brain injury, and the prognosis for the infant. Thus, when the infant is brought to medical care, the injury must be recognized and steps taken to prevent further complications from occurring.

This discussion will cover topics surrounding the medical management of the shaken infant. The initial presentation, management and work-up of the shaken infant will be described and the differential diagnosis discussed. Strategies used for managing these patients in the Intensive Care Unit will be outlined with a brief description of the pathophysiology of brain injury in these patients. Finally the prognosis of the shaken infant who is severely brain-injured will be discussed.

INITIAL PRESENTATION

The victims of Shaken Baby Syndrome present to medical care with a variety of complaints, and a varying severity of illness, which is most dependent on the degree of brain injury they have suffered (Table 1). Vague or non-specific complaints such as irritability, somnolence, or poor feeding are common in infants with less severe injuries, whereas, the infant with devastating injury can present moribund or with cardiorespiratory arrest (Duhaime, Christian, Moss, & Seidl, 1996). In each of these scenarios, the personnel who first come

TABLE 1. Clinical Presentation of the Shaken Infant

Irritability
History of minor trauma
Seizures
Lethargy
Apnea
Poor feeding
Excess sleepiness
Respiratory arrest
Cardiac arrest

in contact with the victim (physician, nurse, paramedic, EMT, police officer or firefighter) must be able to recognize the illness and begin appropriate therapy.

There are numerous clues that should raise the suspicion that the infant has been a victim of abuse. The history given to explain the illness may not fit the clinical situation and will often involve an explanation of minor trauma (Duhaime et al., 1987; Ludwig & Warman, 1984). Additionally, timing of the incident does not correspond to the type or severity of the presenting signs and symptoms. The history will often change depending on who asks the questions and how persistent they are about noting the discrepancies in the history and the findings on exam. The physical examination of the patient may reveal bruises of varying ages and retinal hemorrhages may be seen about 70% of shaken infants (Duhaime et al., 1987; Hadley, Sonntag, Rekate, & Murphy, 1989). These types of findings in the presentation should alert the medical team to the possibility of Shaken Baby Syndrome.

The clinical condition of the shaken infant depends on the degree of brain injury that has occurred. The infant may be irritable, lethargic, have altered muscular tone, vomiting, or poor feeding (Hahn, Roimondi, McLone, & Yamanouchi, 1983). In more severe injury, the infant can demonstrate abnormalities in respiration and manifest apnea. The apnea, if prolonged, will result in significant hypoxia and effect cardiovascular function, resulting in cardiovascular collapse and eventually cardiac arrest. The clinical presentation will determine the type of care required.

Differential Diagnosis

The differential diagnosis of the shaken infant includes few other disease processes. The Shaken Baby Syndrome is diagnosed by obtaining a history that does not fit the clinical findings in an infant who presents with significant neurological abnormalities. Other diagnoses can usually be omitted on the basis of a good history and physical examination.

Accidental trauma is the most common diagnosis with similarities to the Shaken Baby Syndrome. In this instance a history of significant trauma such as a motor vehicle collision or fall from a significant height is obtained. The infant is usually brought to medical care soon after these types of injuries, and no unexplained injuries are identified. Retinal hemorrhages are generally not present in these patients.

Coagulopathies such as hemophilia or vitamin K deficiencies can present with CNS hemorrhages. Infants with Shaken Baby Syndrome may frequently have clotting abnormalities secondary to disseminated intravascular coagulation with severe brain injury. However, this coagulopathy will correct over time. The infant who presents with Shaken Baby Syndrome and coagulopathy needs follow-up laboratory studies performed to document correction of the coagulopathy. These infants often receive replacement therapy with blood products to correct the coagulopathy. However, if the infant has a congenital coagulation abnormality, blood products will not correct the coagulopathy permanently. Any recurring or persistant abnormalities in coagulation need further investigation and treatment.

Other problems such as intracranial bleeding from arteriovenous malformations and infectious diseases such as meningitis and encephalitis may present with signs and symptoms similar to the shaken infant. Initial assessment and resuscitation of these infants will be similar to that of the shaken infant.

Meningitis and encephalitis need to be considered in the critically ill infant, and appropriate culture and antibiotics started. Intracranial bleeding from arteriovenous malformations can be seen on CT scanning performed on these patients. If arteriovenous malformation is suspected, angiography or magnetic resonance angiography can be performed to delineate the presence of vascular abnormalities. Infectious and other central nervous system pathology can be excluded from the differential diagnosis by obtaining an in depth history, performing a complete physical examination, and obtaining appropriate laboratory and radiographic data.

Pathophysiology

To understand the treatment and the limitations of medical therapy of the shaken infant, it is important to understand the pathophysiology of the brain injury that occurs. By definition, the Shaken Baby Syndrome occurs in the infant and young child. It is a major cause of traumatic brain injury in infancy accounting for up to 40% of traumatic injury in this age group, with a mortality of 15-24% (Duhaime et al., 1987; Ludwig & Warman, 1984). The injuries that occur as a result of the Shaken Baby Syndrome are unique since they tend to be diffuse and multiple, and are often complicated by secondary injury related to hypoxia and hypotension that occurs from delayed medical care. This differs significantly from head trauma related to motor vehicle or sports related injuries where medical care is usually sought immediately (Johnson, Boal, & Baule, 1995).

Brain injury resulting from shaking can be divided into three categories: (1) injury caused by direct trauma, (2) hypoxic-ischemic injury, and (3) secondary injury that occurs as a result of the traumatic and hypoxic-ischemic injury. These injuries are not exclusive of one another. Infants will manifest varying degrees of injury from traumatic and hypoxic/ischemic injury that are complicated by secondary injuries which result from abnormalities in blood flow, disturbances of capillary permeability, and inflammatory activation.

The primary insult suffered by the shaken infant is from direct trauma. The forces caused by severe shaking and impact cause disruption of bridging veins resulting in subdural hematomas. Fractures can occur secondary to impact resulting in epidural bleeding from disruption of arteries, most commonly the middle meningeal artery. The forces involved will also disrupt axonal connections and small intraparenchymal vessels resulting in cerebral edema and intraparenchymal bleeding.

The most common findings in the infant with diffuse brain injury is cerebral swelling (Kazan, Tuncer, Karasoy, Rahat, & Saveren, 1997). Diffuse cerebral swelling is characterized by a primary injury that consists of diffuse axonal injury or shearing which results from a stretching or transection of axons, leading to a widespread disconnection of neurons. The infant is highly susceptible to this type of injury because of weak neck musculature, head to body ratio and lack of myelination. This diffuse swelling is manifest in the CT scan by the loss of gray-white differentiation, compressed or obliterated cisterns and other cerebrospinal fluid spaces. Enlargement of the fontanelle and widening of the suture because of the swelling and increased intracranial pressure may also develop. There is no surgical intervention possible to relieve cerebral swelling. Significant intracranial bleeding from subdural or epidural bleeding needs to treated aggressively. Subdural or epidural bleeding resulting in compression of the brain parenchyma and shifting of intracranial structures will result in further damage to the brain secondary to impairment of blood flow.

Hypoxic-ischemic injury occurs in many shaken infants. This manifests as apnea, a common finding in the history of these infants, or in respiratory or cardiorespiratory arrest. The hypoxic injury is devastating to the brain since it is exquisitely sensitive to lack of oxygen. Neuronal cell death can occur within minutes in the ischemic brain. The reperfusion of the ischemic brain will paradoxically result in more injury through activation of the same cellular pathways activated by the traumatic injury (Greenwald, Ghajaar, & Notterman, 1995). The child who suffers from a cardiorespiratory arrest will have poorer outcome due to worsening of the secondary injury.

The initial traumatic and hypoxic/ischemic injury to the brain begins a cascade of cellular responses that leads to secondary injury, which worsens the initial insult. Secondary injuries occur as a result of numerous cellular events that worsen cerebral swelling. Current studies have shown that local and global ischemia, abnormalities in glucose metabolism, autoregulatory mechanisms that regulate cerebral blood flow, and abnormal permeability of the blood brain barrier may increase brain edema (Adelson & Kochanek, 1998). Other important factors such as inflammation, free radical formation and calcium influx will cause cell damage resulting in worsening edema. These responses can result in a cycle in which continued damage occurs and becomes irreversible.

INITIAL MANAGEMENT

Respiratory and Cardiovascular Management

The key to the management of brain injury is to institute therapies that will prevent or reduce secondary injury in a timely manner (Adelson & Kochanek, 1998). Traumatic head injuries that occur secondary to most other types of trauma are usually brought to medical care early and will not suffer significant periods of hypoxia or ischemia prior to obtaining medical care. Shaken infants may not be brought to medical care for hours or days, and the window of opportunity to begin treatment that may reduce or prevent secondary injuries is lost. If hypoxic or ischemic injury occurs on top of the traumatic injury, this will worsen the injury and limit treatment, since there is no effective therapy of hypoxic-ischemic injury (Spack, Gedeit, Splaingard, & Havens, 1997).

Whether the injured infant presents at home, to the physician's office or to the emergency room, the primary goal of initial therapy is the same as in any critically ill infant. The first priority is to ensure that the infant has adequate respiratory and cardiovascular function. The ABC's of emergency medical care apply here as it does in every life-threatening situation: airway, breathing, circulation. Maintenance of the airway is performed by careful positioning, remembering in the infant the occiput is larger than the adult and that care must be taken not to cause an airway obstruction. Mouth to face, mouth to mask, or bag mask ventilation is required for those infants demonstrating inadequate respiratory effort. Endotracheal intubation and mechanical ventilation should be performed in those infants with a modified Glasgow Coma Score of ≤ 8 (Table 2), apnea or cardiorespiratory arrest. Hypoxia and hypercarbia should be avoided through the use of supplemental oxygen and controlled ventilation, since even mild to moderate hypoxia or hypercarbia can affect cerebral blood flow and result in further brain injury (Forbes, Hendrick, & Shidling, 1996; Skippen et al., 1997). Hemodynamics need to be carefully assessed by monitoring vital signs, heart rate and blood pressure as well as using laboratory investigations and physical assessments to determine the severity of other organ injury or dysfunction. Patients with signs of impaired cardiac output such as tachycardia or borderline or low blood pressures should receive a bolus of isotonic fluid intravenously to ensure adequate circulating volume to maintain blood flow to the compromised brain. The patients who continue to demonstrate hemodynamic compromise despite 40-60 cc/kg of fluid should receive

TABLE 2. Modified Glasgow Coma Score

Eye Opening
Response

Score	> 1 year	< 1 year
4	Spontaneous	Spontaneous
3	To verbal command	To shout
2	To pain	To pain
1	None	None

Motor Response

Score	> 1 year	< 1 year
6	Obeys commands	Spontaneous
5	Localizes pain	Localizes Pain
4	Withdraws to pain	Withdraws to pain
3	Abnormal flexion to pain (decorticate)	Abnormal flexion to pain (decorticate)
2	Abnormal extension to pain (decerebrate)	Abnormal extension to pain (decerebrate)
1	None	None

Verbal Response

Score	> 5 years	2-5 years	0-2 years
5	Oriented and converses	Appropriate words and phrases	Babbles, coos appropriately
4	Confused conversation	Inappropriate words	Cries but is consolable
3	Inappropriate words	Persistent crying or screaming to pain	Persistent crying or screaming to pain
2	Incomprehensible sounds	Grunts or moans to pain	Grunts or moans to pain
1	None	None	None

inotropic/vasoactive support with dopamine or epinephrine by continuous infusion, to maintain a normal to slightly elevated blood pressure to support cerebral circulation. The neurological status of the patient needs to be assessed during the initial period of resuscitation. The modified Glasgow Coma Score is used to assess severity of brain injury and can be used to clinically follow the response of the infant to therapy. Seizures are common after traumatic and hypoxic brain injury and should be treated with benodiazepines, phenytoin, and phenobarbital as needed.

Physical Examination

After initial assessment and stabilization of the patient are complete a more thorough examination of the patient is in order. A full head to toe examination needs to be performed. The examiner needs to look for other injuries, or clues to the underlying disease process. The examination should focus on the search for trauma to the head, looking for bruising, or palpating skull fractures, as well as the skin to assess for other evidence of injury (bruises, burns, unusual scarring, bites). All findings should be clearly documented, using a diagram as well as narrative description, and photographs if available. Examination of the eyes is crucial, since the presence of retinal hemorrhages raises suspicion significantly. All abnormalities found on the physical examination need to be accurately documented and appropriate treatment begun.

RADIOGRAPHIC AND LABORATORY INVESTIGATIONS

Initial laboratory investigations are performed to assist in determining the extent of end organ dysfunction or injury and to identify any significant abnormalities that could worsen secondary injury in these patients (Table 3). Serum glucose measurement is imperative since the infant may become hypoglycemic secondary to a lack of oral intake and limited glucose stores. Hypoglycemia should be corrected and glucose concentrations followed carefully, since hypo and hyperglycemia adversely effect the injured brain. Disseminated intravascular coagulation (DIC) can also occur secondary to severe brain, and hypoxic-ischemic injury (Hymel, Abshire, Luckey, & Jenny, 1997). Laboratory investigations into coagulation status are needed in order to treat significant abnormalities, especially in the face of intracranial bleeding, and to assist in diagnosis of underlying bleeding disorders as a part of the work up, and to begin appropriate treatment with transfusion of blood products. A complete blood count is needed to determine if anemia or thrombcytopenia are present. Significant anemia should be corrected with a transfusion of packed red blood cells to ensure adequate oxygen delivery. Liver function tests, amylase, and lipase are performed to determine the extent of intraabdominal pathology. Abnormalities in these studies should direct radiographic investigations into intraabdominal injuries that can also occur in these children (Camerron, Lazoritz, & Calhoun, 1997).

Radiographic assessment should include a chest x-ray to assess endotracheal tube placement and to assess pulmonary pathology which secondary to aspiration that can occur as a result of the cardiorespiratory arrest or seizures. Bony injuries such as rib fractures may also be seen which would substantiate the diagnosis of child abuse. A CT scan of the head is mandatory once the initial

TABLE 3. Initial Laboratory and Radiographic Investigations

Complete blood count (CBC) including platelet count
Prothrombin time
Partial thromboplastin time
Fibrinogen concentration
Serum glucose
Liver function tests (AST, ALT)
Amylase
Lipase

CT Scan of the head
Chest x-ray
CT Scan of the abdomen
Skeletal survey/Bone scan (when medically stable)

evaluation and stabilization have been completed and the patient can safely be transported to the Radiology department. If abdominal pathology is suspected either by physical examination or laboratory evaluation, a CT scan of the abdomen should be obtained as well. After the patient has been stabilized a more methodical search for other bony injuries needs to be undertaken, using radiographs and/or nuclear medicine techniques.

ADMISSION AND CONSULTATION

The radiographic and laboratory investigations and clinical status of the patient will determine care from this point. Infants with mild brain injury (GCS ≥ 12) can be admitted to a regular hospital ward for further observation and treatment. Those children with a GCS < 12 or other visceral injuries need to be admitted to a Pediatric Intensive Care Unit due to their potential for worsening neurological or hemodynamic function (Greenwald et al., 1995). Significant intracranial hemorrhage, or severe cerebral edema identified by CT scan or need for placement of an intracranial pressure monitor requires the consultation of a Pediatric Neurosurgeon. If intraabdominal pathology such as a ruptured viscus, hepatic or splenic hematomas or other significant injuries are present, a Pediatric Surgery consultation is required. Ophthalmology consultation is required to verify the presence of retinal hemorrhages and document their presence with photographs. Child advocacy team and social work consultations should be called whenever abuse is suspected.

INTENSIVE CARE UNIT TREATMENT

The goal of therapy in brain injury is to support cardiac, respiratory and metabolic function in order to prevent any further secondary insults caused by hypotension and hypoxemia. This includes maintenance of adequate blood pressure, oxygenation and cerebral perfusion. In the patient with isolated traumatic injury, aggressive therapies aimed at controlling intracranial hypertension should be considered. Conversely, in those patients who have had a significant hypoxic-ischemic injury, i.e., cardiorespiratory arrest, these therapies are avoided since they have shown not to be efficacious (Le Roux, Jardine, Kaney, & Loeser, 1991).

The discussion that follows will outline therapies to be considered in the shaken infant. The infant who has suffered cardiorespiratory arrest with resultant hypoxic-ischemic injury is treated with supportive therapies aimed at maintaining normal hemodynamics and oxygenation. Those therapies that are aimed at reducing intracranial pressure should be reserved for the patient who has predominant traumatic brain injury. These therapies will be discussed separately. This is done with the understanding that delineating the extent of hypoxic versus traumatic injury in the individual patient can be difficult.

TREATMENT OF THE INFANT WITH TRAUMATIC BRAIN INJURY

Traumatic brain injury is treated aggressively in patients involved in motor vehicle collisions or with other acute traumatic brain injuries (Adelson & Kochanek, 1998). The goal of therapy is to maintain cerebral perfusion and minimize intracranial pressure; this can be accomplished with aggressive therapy including CSF drainage, sedation, osmolar therapy and maintenance of adequate blood pressure. This type of management has led to decreased morbidity and mortality and improved functional outcomes for victims of traumatic head injury. These interventions attempt to lessen the secondary injuries that occur from ongoing hypoxia or inadequate perfusion.

Maintenance of normal or slightly increased blood pressures is needed to ensure adequate cerebral perfusion, with hypotension being avoided at all costs to reduce the chance of any further ischemic injury. This is maintained by ensuring there is adequate intravascular volume, which needs to be monitored with a central venous pressure monitor that can be placed via a central venous line via the femoral , subclavian or internal jugular venous catheter. Fluid administration is weighed against the need for maintenance of hyperosmolality to reduce cerebral edema in traumatic brain injury. The blood pressure should never suffer in order to maintain relative fluid restriction due to the dire consequences of prolonged hypotension on secondary cerebral injury. In order to maintain blood pressure, inotropic or vasoactive support may be needed. Both dopamine and epinephrine may be needed to maintain blood pressure in the moribund patient. However these should not be given in high doses in the face of hypovolemia, since they may potentiate vasoconstriction and worsen ischemic injury.

The control of breathing is also important in the management of patients with traumatic brain injury. Changes in carbon dioxide concentrations in the blood have a profound effect on cerebrovascular responses. With hyperventilation, cerebral blood flow decreases in response to cerebrovascular vasoconstriction and thereby reducing intracranial pressure. Until recently, hyperventilation was a mainstay of intracranial pressure control; however, its use has now come into question. The use of random hyperventilation was shown to worsen outcome in adults with head trauma (Muizelaar, Marmarou, & Ward, 1991). The adverse effects of prolonged hyperventilation may result from the loss of buffering ability of the cerebrospinal fluid after prolonged hyperventilation as well as the reduction in cerebral blood flow that occurs secondary to hyperventilation (Fortune, Feustel, Graca, Hasselbarth, & Keuhker, 1995). Therefore routine prolonged hyperventilation is no longer recommended. Patients should be maintained with carbon dioxide concentrations in the low normal range and hyperventilation being reserved for times when acute reduction of intracranial pressure is needed as with acute increases in intracranial pressure (ICP) and threatened herniation. Hypercapnia should likewise be avoided since this may increase cerebral blood flow abnormally and result in acute increases in ICP.

Just as important is the maintenance of normal oxygenation in the patient with head trauma. Hypoxemia contributes to secondary injury and thereby worsens brain injury. Hypoxemia may also increase cerebral blood flow thereby increasing ICP and also worsening brain edema. Adequate oxygenation needs to be ensured through the use of supplemental oxygen and the use of continuous pulse oximetry.

Head positioning in a neutral and elevated position is often used as a method of maintaining adequate venous drainage from the cranium, via the jugular venous system. The patient is frequently placed at 15-30 degrees to optimize venous return and lower intracranial pressure. There is no data regarding the effect of head positioning on intracranial pressure in children with traumatic injury, but the practice is probably prudent. Placing the patient in a head neutral position and slightly elevating the head to 5-15% is, at least, probably not harmful and may be helpful.

Sedation is a mainstay of therapy in the head-injured patients. It is important to reduce the noxious stimulus of intubation, suctioning and other factors related to care of the patient, which can cause increases in intracranial pressure. The use of short acting narcotics and benzodiazepines can allow for adequate sedation and control of intracranial pressure. In difficult cases, non-depolarizing neuromuscular blockers can be used to reduce ICP. Adequate sedation is imperative with the use of these agents, and the use of continuous sedation is required.

Intracranial pressure management is a mainstay of therapy for traumatic brain injury with cerebral swelling (Fortune et al., 1995; Greenwald et al., 1995; Le Roux et al., 1991). There is no conclusive data regarding the use of intracranial pressure monitoring in infants and young children. However, the use of intracranial pressure monitors has been shown to be safe and should therefore be strongly considered (Pople, Mulbauer, Sanord, & Kirk, 1995; Shankaran et al., 1994). The importance of intracranial pressure monitoring comes from the fact that it can reduce intracranial pressure through the use of cerebrospinal fluid drainage, and thereby improve cerebral perfusion. Monitoring can also guide therapy by allowing the clinician to see the results of specific therapies and to maintain an adequate cerebral perfusion pressure by manipulating ICP and systemic blood pressures. The ideal method of monitoring pressure would be through the use of an intraventricular catheter since it can be used to measure pressure and drain fluid to reduce pressure. The use of intracranial pressure monitoring in infancy is not widely used since the infant is often felt to have some protection due to the presence of the open fontanelle, and sutures. The older infant with significant traumatic head injury and a small or closed fontanelle should seriously be considered for placement of an intracranial pressure monitor.

Osmotic therapy through the use of mannitol has been shown to reduce intracranial pressure. The mechanisms by which mannitol achieves are twofold; mannitol (1) reduces blood viscosity acutely which can reduce intracranial pressure within moments after infusions, and (2) reduces intravascular volume by increasing serum osmolality and thereby reducing brain edema and intracranial pressure. Mannitol can be given every 4 to 6 hours or more frequently to maintain optimal intracranial pressure and osmolality. The use is limited by serum osmolality that should be maintained in the 300-310 mosm/l range. Care must be taken to not reduce intravascular volume to the point where hypovolemia occurs since this will potentiate secondary injury to the brain.

Barbiturates have been used in the treatment of brain injury because of their ability to reduce cerebral metabolism. The reduction of cerebral metabolism reduces blood flow and lowers ICP. Reduction of metabolic demand also allows the brain to tolerate periods of decreased perfusion that occurs with elevated ICP. This therapy is controversial and is usually reserved as an option of last resort. Barbiturate induced coma has been used as a method of maximally reducing cerebral metabolism and is generally achieved by seeing a pattern of burst suppression monitored at the bedside by EEG. The therapy can be limited by systemic hypotension since barbiturates are vasodilators and negative inotropes. Careful attention must be paid to hemodynamic parameters during this therapy. Both pressors and fluid support may be needed. The use of an ICP monitor is required to evaluate the effect since the neurological exam is invalid.

Seizures occur frequently in patients with Shaken Baby Syndrome. They may be part of the presenting complaint or occur later on in the hospital course. The use of anticonvulsant is required for those patients who have even a brief seizure. Seizures can increase intracranial pressure by increasing metabolic demand, through the release of excitatory neurotransmitters, and by causing hypertension, hypoxemia or hypercarbia. Therefore aggressive treatment of seizures with phenytoin and/or phenobarbital is important. These infants often need long-term anticonvulsant therapy because of repeated seizures.

Other therapies for reduction of ICP and secondary cerebral injury have also been used but are not effective. Corticosteroids have been shown to be of no use in adults with traumatic injury and no studies in children have been performed. Their use in hypoxic brain injury has also shown no improvement in outcome. Therefore the use of steroids in the shaken infant is not recommended. Temperature manipulation to treat brain injury was first reported in the 1950s. The use of hypothermia in children was reported and suggested some benefit. A clinical trial of early, short duration hypothermia showed a reduction of ICP but no significant differences in outcome at six months (Marion et al., 1997). These studies were performed in patients with traumatic brain injury and not Shaken Baby Syndrome, and therefore the use of hypothermia is not recommended. However, further clinical trials are underway to study the effects of hypothermia on outcome of children with traumatic brain injury. Decompressive craniotomy for traumatic injury and in shaken infants has been described but cannot be recommended (Cho, Wang, & Chi, 1995; Hieu, Sizun, Person, & Besson, 1996).

THERAPIES IN INFANTS WITH HYPOXIC-ISCHEMIC INJURY

The infant who has suffered significant hypoxic-ischemic injury is managed differently than the patient with isolated head trauma. This fact lies in the dismal outcome of these infants despite the use of aggressive therapies (Greenwald et al., 1995; Le Roux et al., 1991; Shankaran et al., 1994). The primary reason for this is that the process that leads to cardiac arrest in these infants is primarily hypoxia from apnea caused by the brain injury. Prolonged hypoxia eventually results in cardiovascular collapse and cardiorespiratory arrest. The infant has already suffered a prolonged episode of hypoxia even before reaching medical attention (Johnson et al., 1995).

After resuscitation, the goal of therapy is supportive care through the maintenance of normal hemodymanics and oxygenation, along with prevention of secondary insults that can worsen outcome. Treatment of children with hypoxic-ischemic brain injuries includes the maintenance of normal or slightly increased blood pressure to promote adequate cerebral perfusion. Hypotension needs to be avoided at all costs to reduce the chance of any further ischemic injury. Monitoring of central venous pressure and arterial blood pressure using indwelling catheters is recommended to ensure adequate maintenance of hemodynamics. In order to maintain blood pressure, dopamine or epinephrine may be needed to counteract the effects of end organ dysfunction caused by hypoxic-ischemic injury. Glucose concentrations should be followed closely since both hypoglycemia and hyperglycemia may be detrimental to the injured brain. Seizure control is also important due to the increases in cerebral oxygen demand that occurs. Hypoxemia is treated aggressively with supplemental oxygen and controlled mechanical ventilation to prevent hypoxic injury.

OUTCOME

The prognosis for infants with Shaken Baby Syndrome who present with coma, apnea or status epilepticus is dismal (Bonnier, Nassogne, & Evrard, 1995; Goldstein, Kelly, Brutton, & Cox, 1993; Haviland & Ross-Rissel, 1995). Shaken Baby Syndrome is the most common cause of mortality in some series of infants with central nervous system injury. Mortality ranges 15-27%. The combination of severe trauma, hypoxic-ischemic injury, multiple episodes of injury and delay in seeking medical treatment contribute to the poor outcome of these infants (Alexander, Crabbe, Sto, Smith, & Bennett, 1990). The factors that worsen the primary and secondary injury will also worsen outcome. Those infants who die soon after the injury succumb to untreatable intracranial hypertension due to massive cerebral swelling (Duhaime et al., 1987).

The survivors of Shaken Baby Syndrome suffer significant abnormalities that will continue and become more apparent over time. On CT scan, initial diffuse swelling that is seen initially is replaced by significant cortical and white matter atrophy. Premorbid factors such as prematurity, or other preexisting neurological abnormalities, environmental factors such as family instability and socioeconomic conditions may also contribute to the poor prognosis of these infants, and may influence the child's outcome both before and after the injury. The majority of survivors have significant disability and even those children with good outcome have problems as well. Common long term disabilities include seizures, blindness, deafness, hemiparesis, motor delays, significant speech problems and learning disabilities. Some of these disorders present soon after the injuries but the more subtle abnormalities such as learning problems often do not show up for many years (Klein & Stern, 1971; Sills, Thomas, & Rosenbloom, 1977). Unfortunately, the medical management during the acute phase does not seem to influence outcome, especially among those with more severe injury. Long term care of these patients requires speech, physical, and occupational therapists, social workers, neurologists, surgeons and a primary care physician to coordinate the complex medical and social problems that the survivors will face.

CONCLUSION

In summary, the effectiveness of treatment in the shaken infant relies on the early recognition of its presence. Prevention of secondary insults and reduction of secondary injury can only be accomplished if treatment is instituted soon after the trauma occurs. This often does not occur in the shaken infant and worsens their chance of a good outcome. Children who suffer from severe hypoxic-ischemic injury have an even more dismal outcome and will not benefit from delayed institution of therapies aimed at treatment of traumatic brain injury. Those infants with isolated traumatic brain injuries may benefit from therapies aimed at preserving cerebral perfusion and reducing cerebral metabolic need, but there is no clear evidence that this type of therapy improves outcome in these patients. The care of the shaken infant involves a wide variety of physicians, surgeons, nurses and therapists that illustrates the complex nature of the disease and the resultant morbidities. The only effective treatment for the shaken infant is prevention. The causes and prevention of Shaken Baby Syndrome should be the focus of research and education.

REFERENCES

Adelson, P.D., Kochanek, P.M. (1998). Head injury in children. *Journal of Child Neurology, 13*, 2 15.

Alexander R., Crabbe, L., Sto, Y., Smith, W., & Bennett, T. (1990). Serial abuse in children who are shaken. *American Journal of Diseases of Children, 144*, 58-60.

Bonnier, C., Nassogne, M.C., & Evrard, P. (1995). Outcome and prognosis of whiplash shaken infant syndrome: Late consequences after a symptom free interval. *Developmental Medicine and Child Neurology, 37*, 943-956.

Camerron, C.M., Lazoritz, S., & Calhoun, A. (1997). Blunt abdominal injury: Simultaneously occurring liver and pancreatic injury in child abuse. *Pediatric Emergency Care, 13*, 334-336.

Cho, D.Y., Wang, Y.C., & Chi, C.S., (1995). Decompressive craniotomy for acute shaken/impact baby syndrome. *Pediatric Neurosurgery, 23,* 192-198.

Duhaime, A.C., Christian, C., Moss E., & Seidl, T. (1996). Long term outcome in infants with the shaking-impact syndrome. *Pediatric Neurosurgery, 24,* 292-298.

Duhaime, A.C., Gennarelli, T.A., Thibault, L.E., Bruce, D.A., Margulies, S.S., & Wiser, R. (1987). The shaken infant syndrome: A clinical pathological and biomechanical study. *Journal of Neurosurgery, 66,* 409-415.

Forbes, M.T., Hendrich, K.S., & Shidling, K.K. (1996). Perfusion weighted MRI assessment of cerebral blood flow on carbon dioxide reactivity after controlled cortical impact in rats. *Journal of Neurotrauma, 12,* 988.

Fortune, J.B., Feustel, P.J., Graca, L., Hasselbarth, J., & Keuhker, D.H. (1995). Effect of hyperventilation, mannitol, and ventriculostomy drainage on cerebral blood flow after head injury. *The Journal of Trauma: Injury, Infection, and Critical Care, 39,* 1091-1099.

Goldstein, B., Kelly, M.M., Brutton, D., & Cox, C. (1993). Inflicted versus accidental head injury in critically injured children. *Critical Care Medicine, 21,* 1328-1332.

Greenwald, B.M., Ghajar, J., & Notterman, D.A. (1995). Critical care of children with acute brain injury. *Advances in Pediatrics, 42,* 47-89.

Hadley, M.N., Sonntag, V.K.H., Rekate, H.L., & Murphy, A. (1989). The infant whiplash-shake syndrome: A clinical and pathologic study. *Neurosurgery, 24,* 536-540.

Hahn, Y.S., Raimondi, A.J., McLone, D.G., & Yamanouchi, Y. (1983). Traumatic mechanisms of head injury in child abuse. *Child's Brain, 10,* 229-241.

Haviland, J., & Ross-Rissel, R.I. (1995). Outcome after severe non-accidental head injury. *Archives of Diseases in Children, 77,* 504-507.

Hieu, P.D., Sizun, J., Person, H., & Besson, G. (1996). The place of decompressive surgery in the treatment of uncontrollable post-traumatic intracranial hypertension in children. *Child's Nervous System, 12,* 270-275.

Hymel, K.P., Abshire, T.C., Luckey, D.W., & Jenny, C. (1997). Coagulopathy in pediatric abusive head trauma. *Pediatrics, 99,* 371-375.

Johnson, D.L., Boal, D., & Baule, R. (1995). Role of apnea in nonaccidental head injury. *Pediatric Neurosurgery, 23,* 305-310.

Kazan, S., Tuncer, R., Karasoy, M., Rahat, O., & Saveren, M. (1997). Post-traumatic bilateral diffuse cerebral swelling. *Acta Neurochirurgica, 139,* 295-302.

Klein, M., & Stern, L. (1971). Low birth weight and the battered child syndrome. *American Journal of Diseases of Childhood, 122,* 15-18.

Le Roux, P.D., Jardine, D.S., Kaney, P.M., & Loeser, J.D. (1991). Pediatric intracranial pressure monitoring in hypoxic and non-hypoxic brain injury. *Child's Nervous System, 7,* 34-39.

Ludwig, S., & Warman, M., (1984). Shaken baby syndrome: A review of 20 cases. *Annals of Emergency Medicine, 13,* 104-107.

Marion, D.W., Penrod, L.E., Kelsey, S.F., Obrist, W.D., Kochanek, P.M., Palmer, A.M., Wisniewski, S.R., & Dekosky, S.T. (1997). Treatment of traumatic brain injury with moderate hypothermia. *New England Journal of Medicine, 336,* 540-546.

Muizelaar, J.P., Marmarou, A., & Ward, J.D. (1991). Adverse effects of prolonged hyperventilation in patients with severe head injury: A randomized clinical trial. *Journal of Neurosurgery, 75,* 731-739.

Pople, I.K., Mulbauer, M.S., Sanord, R.A., & Kirk, E. (1995). Results and complications of intracranial pressure monitoring in 303 children. *Pediatric Neurosurgery, 23*, 64-67.

Shankaran, S., Woldt, E., Bedard, M.P., Delaney-Black, V., Zakalik, K., & Canady, A. (1994). Feasibility of invasive monitoring of intracranial pressure in term neonates. *Brain and Development, 16*, 121-125.

Sills, J.A., Thomas, L.J., & Rosenbloom, L. (1977). *Developmental Medicine and Childhood Neurology, 19*, 26-33.

Skippen, P., Seear, M., Posskitt, K., Kestle, J., Cochrane, D., Annich, G., & Handel, J. (1997). Effect of hyperventilation on regional cerebral blood flow in head-injured children. *Critical Care Medicine, 25*, 1402-1409.

Spack, L., Gedeit, R., Splaingard, M., & Havens, P. (1997). Failure of aggressive therapy to alter outcome in pediatric near-drowning. *Pediatric Emergency Care, 13*, 98-102.

Chapter Ten

Brain Injury Rehabilitation in Children with Non-Accidental Trauma

Mark Splaingard

SUMMARY. Brain injuries commonly occur in children who suffer non-accidental trauma. Survivors of shaking-impact syndrome are especially prone to develop a myriad of problems related to brain damage. Understanding the clinical prognostic indicators and their limitations is critical to providing appropriate care for these children. Critical non-neurological complications involving breathing and feeding are discussed in depth to help avoid further morbidity and mortality. Rehabilitation is essential for these children. Techniques to control muscle spasticity, protect skin and joints and provide emotional support for the caregivers of the brain-injured child are outlined. A well designed, comprehensive, coordinated rehabilitation program will reduce initial hospitalization and train caregivers to reduce the likelihood of future hospitalization for preventable conditions and will provide the educational framework for the ongoing care of the injured child. *[Article copies available for a fee from The Haworth Document Delivery Service: 1-800-342-9678. E-mail address: <getinfo@haworthpressinc.com> Website: <http://www.HaworthPress.com> © 2001 by The Haworth Press, Inc. All rights reserved.]*

KEYWORDS. Traumatic brain injury, rehabilitation, functional outcomes, prognosis

[Haworth co-indexing entry note]: "Brain Injury Rehabilitation in Children with Non-Accidental Trauma." Splaingard, Mark. Co-published simultaneously in *Journal of Aggression, Maltreatment & Trauma* (The Haworth Maltreatment & Trauma Press, an imprint of The Haworth Press, Inc.) Vol. 5, No. 1(#9), 2001, pp. 173-198; and: *The Shaken Baby Syndrome: A Multidisciplinary Approach* (ed: Stephen Lazoritz, and Vincent J. Palusci) The Haworth Maltreatment & Trauma Press, an imprint of The Haworth Press, Inc., 2001, pp. 173-198. Single or multiple copies of this article are available for a fee from The Haworth Document Delivery Service [1-800-342-9678, 9:00 a.m. - 5:00 p.m. (EST). E-mail address: getinfo@haworthpressinc.com].

173

INTRODUCTION

Significant advances in the treatment of acute pediatric brain injury have resulted in increased survival over the past two decades. Improved pulmonary management with endotracheal intubation, mechanical ventilation, cardiovascular support, and application of techniques to monitor and treat intracranial hypertension have evolved with resulting decreases in mortality of severely injured children (Kumar, West, Quirke, Hall, & Taylor, 1991). While there appears to be differences in adult and pediatric centers deciding which patients benefit from osmotic diuretics, intracranial pressure monitoring, and intubation with or without hyperventilation (Harari, Narayan, Iacona, Ishman, & Ghajar, 1992), all physicians share a common goal of reducing morbidity and optimizing the functional outcome of severely head-injured children.

Three concepts define the consequences of a severe traumatic brain injury:

1. Impairment (the loss of physiologic function or anatomic structure)
2. Disability (the limitation in functional performance resulting from an impairment)
3. Handicap (the disadvantage experienced as a result of impairments and/or disabilities, which limit interaction of the child with the physical and social environment) (CDC, 1994).

The ultimate goals in the treatment of pediatric brain injury are to:

1. Improve quality of life
2. Optimize functional performance
3. Decrease the costs of injury and subsequent disability.

Studies have shown the benefits of early rehabilitation involvement in adults with cerebrovascular accidents (Johnston & Keister, 1984) and head injury (Cope & Hall, 1982; Grosswasser, Costef, & Tamir, 1985). Mackay, Bernstein, Chapman, Morgan, and Milazzo (1992) report improved functional outcomes in traumatic brain injuries with institution of early, aggressive rehabilitation strategies in the Intensive Care Unit. The involvement of multiple disciplines requires careful coordination to prevent inappropriate interventions and allow identification and documentation of a child's problems and progress. Identifying the responsibility of team members avoids duplication of effort and unnecessary expense since the goals of rehabilitation change as children evolve through stages of recovery. Each stage calls for a different strategy of intervention, yet the purpose of treatment is fourfold (Molnar, 1992):

1. To prevent complications from immobilization, disuse and neurologic dysfunction which interfere with functional neurological recovery.
2. To augment the abilities regained from central nervous system recovery.
3. To train children in adaptive compensation for abilities lost.
4. To alleviate the effects of chronic disability on the process of growth and development.

EPIDEMIOLOGY

In the United States, nearly five million children sustain a traumatic head injury each year with approximately 200,000 children injured severely enough to require hospitalization (Raphaely, Swedlow, Dounes, & Bruce, 1980). Head injuries account for 75% of all pediatric trauma admissions to hospitals and are the cause of 70% of all trauma deaths in children (Davis, Fan Tait, Dean, Goldber, & Rogers, 1992). Approximately 185 per 100,000 children under 15 years of age and 296 per 100,000 adolescents and young adults from 15 through 24 years of age are annually hospitalized for traumatic brain injuries (Kraus & Nourjah, 1988). While automobile collisions are the greatest cause of fatal head injures among adults, the most common cause of death in abused children is brain injury (Bellmire & Myers, 1985). Tepas (1990) reports an overall mortality rate from pediatric head injury of 6% based on records entered into the National Pediatric Trauma Registry of 4,400 children with head injuries (Tepas, DiScala, Ramenofsky, & Barlow, 1990). This is similar to the 6% mortality reported by Bruce, Schut, Bruno, Wood, and Sutton (1978).

The need for intubation before arrival or while in the emergency room is used as an indication of severe head injury since it equates with a degree of injury that mandates immediate intensive intervention, and also represents an essential first step in the management of a multiply-injured child. Children admitted with a Glasgow Coma Scale score of eight or lower are generally defined as severe traumatic brain injuries. Children with Glasgow Coma Scores of nine or greater are defined as moderate brain injuries if they have a hospital stay of at least 48 hours with a Glasgow Coma Score below 13, an abnormal brain computed tomographic scan, or required brain surgery. Kraus, Rock, and Hemyari (1990), extrapolating from San Diego County data, estimated that about 7,000 brain injury deaths occur annually in children under 20 years of age in the United States. This represents 29% of all injury deaths in this age group. Data from San Diego County from 1981 showed 5% of children with head injuries were dead at the scene of accident or on arrival at the emergency facility, 6% had severe brain injury, 8% had moderate level injury, and 82%

had mild brain injury (i.e., Glasgow Coma Score of 13-15). Among severely brain injured children, 28% were severely disabled or in a persistent vegetative state at the time of hospital discharge. Infants under one year of age had the highest percentage of moderate or severe head injuries with 18% sustaining moderate or severe injuries. Different authors have found that one quarter to one third of head injures occurring in children less than two years of age are a result of inflicted trauma (Bellmire & Myers, 1985; Duhaime et al., 1992). It is estimated that brain injuries in children under 19 years of age in the United States result in over 550,000 days of hospitalization and 29,000 children with a resultant disability annually (Kraus et al., 1990). A recent study found that median costs of moderate and severe pediatric brain injuries, using Glasgow Coma Scale criteria, were $12,022 and $55,332 respectively (Jaffe, Massagli, Martin, Rivara, & Fay, 1993). Rehabilitation accounted for 45% of total costs for children with the most serious injuries.

PREDICTORS OF OUTCOME FROM TRAUMATIC BRAIN INJURIES

A child's expected prognosis is a crucial factor in making decisions about management and counseling families. While multiple investigations have studied the relationship of a variety of factors such as length of coma, EEG, evoked potentials, CT scans and associated injuries, the ultimate functional recovery of an individual child with a severe pediatric head injury cannot always be accurately predicted. Flaccidity with no motor response is probably the most unfavorable prognostic sign in children and associated spinal cord injuries should always be suspected. Presence of abnormal muscle tone and pupillary light reflexes predicted an outcome of death or severe disability in traumatic brain injury with only 80% accuracy in a recent study by Grewal and Sutcliffe (1991), compared to 99% accuracy in the author's earlier study (Wagstyl, Sutcliffe, & Alpar, 1992). Presence of flaccidity or mid-line shift on CT scan was unhelpful in prognostication. Jennett (1979) found that a Glasgow Coma Scale of four or less was associated with poor outcome in adults, i.e., 87% dead or a persistent negative state. Yet, Bruce, Schut, Bruno, Wood, and Sutton (1978) reports much better outcomes for children with similar clinical indicators. All children with Glasgow Coma Scores greater than five recovered well, and five of seven children with GCS ≤ 4 with bilateral fixed pupils and absent caloric responses made either a good recovery or were only moderately disabled. Thakker et al. (1997) reported that Pediatric Risk of Mortality (PRISM) scores predicted survival and functional outcome at two years more specifically than Glasgow Coma Score in 105 children intubated in the Pediatric Intensive Care Unit after traumatic brain injury. At 24 months follow-up, 41% of patients with initial Glasgow Coma Scores less than or equal to five survived with normal or independent function in areas of self-care, locomotion and communication. However, seven of eight patients with brain injury as a result of child abuse either died or developed severe disability. Duhaime, Christien, Moss, and Seidl (1996) reported that 50% of a small group of infants under two years of age who survived hospitalization with shaking-impact syndrome were found to be either severely disabled or vegetative on follow-up on average of nine years after injury.

Exclusive use of clinical prognostic indicators is tempered by the fact that extraordinary recovery in children occasionally occurs in spite of the presence of negative prognostic indicators (Dean & Kaufman, 1981). A British study in an adult neurosurgical unit showed that the introduction of routine predictive services had a clear effect on provision of services to patients with high probability of poor outcome, leading to questions of selffulfilling prophesy (Murray et al., 1993). Nevertheless, Ruijs, Keyser, Gabreels, & Notermans (1993) reported that prolongation of somatosensory evoked potential P300 (SEPS) correlated with long-term deficits in school performance when measured in 17 children with mild and moderately severe traumatic brain injuries. Abnormalities in brain stem auditory evoked potentials (BAEPs) alone were associated with brain stem lesions in severe head injury but appeared to be a poor predictor of outcome (Drake & John, 1987; Lindsay et al., 1981). Lutsch, Pfenninger, Ludin, and Vassella (1983) reported that loss of BAEPs and somatosensory together was predictive of severe neurologic deficit or death in 43 comatose children. Beca et al. (1995) found absent SEPs in 45 or 49 children with death or persistent vegetative state at six months post injury (92% positive predictive power). SEPs were found to be unreliable with extracranial fluid collections, brainstem hemorrhages or after cranial decompressions. An advantage of somatosensory evoked potentials is that they are not affected by sedatives, analgesic drugs, or neuromuscular blockade typically used in the PICU making clinical evaluation impossible (Goodwin, Friedman, & Bellefleur, 1991).

In children with traumatic brain injury, head CT scan findings alone do not reliably predict outcome (Kraus et al., 1990; Narayan et al., 1981). Hahn et al. (1988) found in a study of young children with traumatic brain injuries that 75% of children with intracranial pressures greater than 40 torr died and 25% remained vegetative. Langfitt and Gennarelli (1982) reports experience in 140 children and states that an intracranial pressure greater than 40 torr was seen in each fatality. Humphreys, Jaimovich, Hendrick, and Hoffman (1984) however, reported no correlation between ICP levels and outcome.

Studies of long-term outcome in pediatric traumatic brain injury are limited by the perspective of the individual investigators. Neurosurgeons tend to be more interested in immediate survival and presence of severe dependency. Rehabilitationists tend to be more interested in degrees of functional impairment. Neuropsychologists tend to be interested in degrees of cognitive and behavioral abnormalities. For that reason, comparisons between studies becomes difficult and confounds any attempt at meta-analysis. It is clear from multiple studies, however, that children with severe brain injuries have potential for continued recovery and measurable improvements for years following a traumatic brain injury. Boyer and Edwards (1991) reporting on 220 children and adolescents who sustained traumatic brain injuries admitted to a pediatric rehabilitation facility over a six year period found that while a realistic appraisal of ultimate recovery could usually be made six months after injury, there was continued improvement in some children in mobility, activity of daily living, and cognitive function for up to three years. Jaffe et al. (1995) reports strong improvements in neuropsychological test scores over the first year in 15 severely brain-injured children with a negligible rate of change during the next two years in most areas. He describes a "plateauing effect" in the areas of most neurobehavioral deficiencies. Kriel, Kriel, and Sheehan (1998) studied 26 children who were comatose for at least 90 days after a traumatic injury and found 11 of the children able to communicate and five children (20%) able to ambulate by two years after injury. Minimal cerebral atrophy by computerized brain scan performed two months post injury was felt to be reliable in prognosticating improved recovery.

A direct correlation between the duration of coma and outcome after injury has been shown in two separate studies (Brink, Garrett, Hale, Wood-Sam, & Nichel, 1970; Brink, Inbus, & Wood-Sam, 1990). In the 1970 study, surviving children with a normal range of intelligence had the shortest duration of coma, i.e., average duration of coma for children under ten years of age was 1.7 weeks, and children with mild retardation had an average duration of coma of eight weeks. Children who were severely retarded had an average duration of coma of 11 weeks. For children older than ten years, the coma could be four weeks long with similar neurological results. In a comprehensive report of 344 patients under 18 years of age with severe traumatic brain injury who remained in coma for at least 24 hours, Brink et al. (1990) showed that a favorable prognosis for recovery of motor function could be made if the duration of coma was less than three months . Prolonged systemic hypertension, ventricular enlargement and seizures significantly decreased probability of achieving physical independence. The improved mortality was not associated with an increased percentage of severely disabled survivors in these studies. If the length of coma was less than six weeks, 94% of patients achieved independence in ambulation and self care by a year after injury. If the length of comas was between

6 and 12 weeks, 76% were independent in ambulation and self care in a year. If the length of coma was greater than 12 weeks, 38% of patients had a good recovery, but 38% remain totally dependent for all cares. Almost all children had some sequelae with the greatest impairments in the area of neuropsychological deficits. Those with injuries due to non-accidental trauma, i.e., child abuse, had poorer outcomes than accidental injuries.

Ruijs, Keyser, and Gabreels (1990) reported that 91% of children who had a length of coma greater than one week showed clear decline in intellectual performance related to concentration with or without memory impairment. All children had distinct personality changes. School problems occurred in 21% of patients in coma for less than 15 minutes. School problems were seen in 59% of children in coma for 15 minutes to seven days, and 29% with coma less than a week had distinct personality problems. A recent study by Fay et al. (1993), however, reports that children with mild traumatic brain injuries, i.e., initial Glasgow Coma Scores of 13-15 who achieved a Glasgow Coma Scale of 15 within three days, had no significant long-term deficits in intellectual, neuropsychological, academic or real-world functioning. Short-term mortality after hospital discharge has been reported as 6-14% of children and young adults with traumatic brain injuries (Brink et al., 1970; Eiben et al., 1984).

Prognostic indicators are probably of greatest assistance in communicating severity of injury and probably neurological outcome with the families. Families who are presented with guidelines and expectations for recovery early after injury can see progress for themselves when it occurs. If weeks pass without improvement, the families are able to start grieving appropriately. Once the family is informed about a child's most probable outcome, nursing and rehabilitation staff can intervene to assure that family members understand what has been explained and begin to mobilize support services, such as pastoral care, social services, and discharge planning early in the course of care for a child identified as a survivor with a risk for disability. Listening to family and caregiver concerns and providing emotional support is critical at this time.

NON-NEUROLOGICAL COMPLICATIONS
FOLLOWING TRAUMATIC BRAIN INJURY

Respiratory

Airway complications after traumatic brain injury are common in adults and complicate rehabilitation (Klingbeil, 1988; Nowak, Cohn, & Guidice, 1987). Lanza, Parnes, Koltai, and Fortune (1990) reported a 61% early complication rate for endotracheal tube intubation and a 20% complication rate for tracheostomy in 52 head injured adults studied in 1990. Citt-Pietrolungo, Alexander, Cook, and Padman (1993) reported 27 complications occurring in 21 of 30 children admitted to a rehabilitation unit with tracheostomies following traumatic brain injuries. Tracheal granulomas occurred in 30%, altered voice quality was noted in 23% and tracheal stenosis in 13% of children, with no age related differences for the various complications. Infections may be higher in pediatric traumatic patients because an immune defect involving antibody production to new antigens occurs in trauma patients and may contribute to the pulmonary infections seen in these children (Wilson, Ochs, Peterson, Hamburger, & Bastian, 1989).

Pulmonary embolism, while rare in pediatrics, has a higher incidence in certain subgroups of patients, i.e., 10% of pediatric patients awaiting heart transplant (Hsu, Addonizio, Hordof, & Gersong, 1991). Based on autopsy data, the incidents of pulmonary embolism in patients under 18 years of age is estimated to be one per 1,000 hospital admissions. About 30% are clinically significant. While a 50-year retrospective review of autopsy cases from Canada found only eight cases of pulmonary embolism in 17,500 autopsies (Byard & Cruz, 1990), a recent Canadian registry report found that the incidence of DVT/pulmonary embolism was 5.3 per 10,000 admissions in 15 tertiary care pediatric centers, i.e., 1 per 2,000 admissions (Andrew et al., 1994). DVT's were almost equal in upper and lower extremities in children. While pulmonary embolism alone was very rare, 2.2% of children with pulmonary embolism and deep-vein thrombosis died as a result of their thrombogenic disease. Cerebral tissue pulmonary embolism has been reported in up to 10% of autopsies following severe traumatic brain injuries (Collins & Davis, 1994). Radecki and Gaebler-Spira (1994) found that 2.2% of children admitted to a large rehabilitation center over a five year period had evidence of deep-vein thrombosis, most occurring in children with spinal cord injuries. Only one of 185 children with closed-head injuries had documented deep-vein thrombosis. Prophylactic treatment for deep-vein thrombosis in isolated pediatric brain injury is not routinely recommended.

Pneumonia is frequently seen in brain-injured patients. It is unclear whether aspiration of saliva or gastric secretions causes pulmonary infiltrates. Bacterial overgrowth in the stomach with aspiration may be the real causes of the high incidence of pneumonia in this patient population. Adams et al. (1986) compared TPN with jejunostomy feeding in trauma patients and found pneumonia in 35% of TPN patients and 48% of jejunostomy patients. Kiver, Hays, and Forten (1984) reported aspiration in 46% in gastric tube fed patients versus 6% of those fed in the duodenum. A prospective study by Saltzberg, Medhat, and Jaffe (1987) using technician sulfur colloid found evidence of aspiration in 89% of nasogastric-fed adults, compared with 32% fed via gastrostomy.

Chronic nasogastric intubation results in nasal irritation and may compromise pulmonary function in brain-injured patients (Wyllie, Kerns, O'Brien, & Hyatt, 1976). NG tubes in the pharynx and across the upper and lower esophageal sphincters may disrupt normal cough and swallowing mechanisms and predispose to gastroesophageal reflux. Attempted dislodgement of nasojejunal feeding tubes is common in children because of agitation and nasopharyngeal discomfort.

Children in the intensive care unit with brain injuries should be evaluated carefully for swallowing abnormalities before institution of oral feedings to prevent aspiration and further pulmonary compromise. A high-incidence of clinically "silent" aspiration has been found after brain injury in both adults and children (Arvedson, Rogers, Buck, Smart, & Msall, 1994; Splaingard, Hutchins, Sulton, & Chaudhuri, 1988). Aspiration generally occurred before or during swallowing liquids and was trace (i.e., less than 10% of bolus) in most children. Tanighchui and Moyer (1994) identified aspiration in 44% of neurologically compromised children studied by video-fluoroscopic swallowing studies. While children with traumatic brain injuries appeared at lower risk for pneumonia compared to other groups of neurologically impaired children with dysphagia, a history of pneumonia was documented in 35% within one year of study. The lack of a goal standard, i.e., autopsy or lipid laden macrophages on bronchoscopy inhibits the interpretation of studies reporting children with pneumonia due to aspiration. Given lack of clear clinical criteria to identify children at risk for oral aspiration, a modified barium swallow may be necessary in all children with dysphagia after head injury to detect silent aspiration.

Nutrition/Feeding Supplementation

Several authors have reported a beneficial affect of early parenteral feeding on survival in head injured patients (Grahm, Zadrozny, & Harrington, 1989; Rapp et al., 1983; Young et al., 1987). Achievement of full caloric replacement within three to five days by total parenteral nutrition (TPN) or jejunal feedings has been associated with more rapid neurological recovery and with reduced infectious complications. Experimental data suggests enteral feedings diminished the ability of bacteria and fungus to translocate out of the gut after brain injury reducing risk of infection (Inoue, Epstein, & Alexander, 1989). The primary obstacle to enteral feedings is delayed gastric emptying associated in part with increased intracranial pressure. Norton et al. (1988) showed a defect in gastric emptying in severely brain-injured adults lasting two weeks and inversely related to increased intracranial pressure, severity of brain injury, and unrelated to return of bowel sounds. Intolerance to enteral feedings occurred in 50% of patients at 10 days after injury with aspiration pneumonia in almost onequarter of patients fed gastrically. Graham et al. (1989) reported that small bore nasojejunal tube feedings allowed full caloric intake in head injured patients except those with serious abdominal trauma and those in barbiturate coma. He reported achieving as good or better nitrogen balance and caloric delivery in these patients than in patients receiving TPN or gastric enteral feedings. A few studies demonstrated a high rate of failure attempting to feed patients postpylorus i.e., beyond the second portion of the duodenum, because of failure either to achieve or maintain proper tube position (Kiver et al., 1984; Whatley, Turner, & Day, 1983).

Gauderer, Ponsky, and Izant (1980) reported a technique for endoscopically placed gastrostomy tubes for nutritional support of patients as an alternative to enteral feedings. Percutaneous endoscopic gastrostomy (PEG) has since become an accepted method of providing long-term enteral nutrition in both adults and children. Short-term studies have suggested that rate of PEG associated mortality, major and minor complications are low. Gauderer (1991) analyzed the outcome of 224 PEGs placed in 220 children and reported a mortality rate associated with PEG placement of less than 1%. Gastrostomy tube feedings may avoid the changes in the pulmonary dynamics and the increased work of breathing which results from increasing nasal secretions and resistance due to an indwelling nasogastric tube. Kirby (1992) has reported that early PEG placement with a feeding tube in the jejunum facilitates early feeding of head injured adults. Coben, Weintraub, Dimarino, and Cohen (1994) recently reported that gastroesophageal reflux and aspiration in patients fed by gastrostomy tube may be caused by lower esophageal sphincter relaxation secondary to reduced LES pressure caused by gastric fungal distension with bolus feedings. Slow continuous feedings did not alter LES pressures or show free gastroesophageal reflux by scintigraphy. Kocan and Hickish (1986), however, did not find a significant difference in the incidence of aspiration pneumonia between patients fed by gastrostomy with slow continuous enteral feedings or gravity feedings in a neurosurgical intensive care unit. Sartori et al. (1994) suggested the use of motility agents such as Cisapride may prevent aspiration pneumonia in patients fed by PEG gastrostomy. Allison, Morris, Park, and Mills (1992) reports the problem of long-term NG feedings in adults with stroke and the improved nutritional status and functional recovery following a PEG which allows more intensive physiotherapy.

While small bore NG or NJ tubes are suitable for short-term feeding of brain-injured patients, after four to six weeks, we routinely place PEG gastrostomy in children with abnormal swallowing mechanics. PEG tubes are less prone to displacement because they are securely anchored in the stomach and are less likely to interfere with rehabilitation. PEGs also have a low rate of blockage because their diameters are considerably larger than NG tubes so that medication tablets may be crushed and flushed with water through the tubes.

Pancreatitis

Acute traumatic brain injury may be associated with increased serum salivary amylase without elevation of serum lipase. Elevated intracranial pressure is a vagal stimulant resulting in a marked increase in circulatory pancreatic polypeptides. About 40% of normal serum amylase activity is derived from the pancrease. Diagnosis of pancreatitis is based on elevation of serum levels of pancreatic amylase and lipase as well as the constellation of clinical findings typically including abdominal pain, vomiting, abdominal distension, and feeding intolerance. Elevated serum amylase enzyme activity has been described in adults with severe head injury who did not show clinical signs or symptoms of pancreatitis (Vitale, Larson, Davidson, Bouwman, & Weaver, 1987). Justice, Dibenedetto, and Stanford (1994) recently described an association between elevation of both serum amylase and lipase and intracranial bleeding in adults with isolated brain injury. They reported only one of 25 patients with elevated lipase had clinical evidence of pancreatitis i.e., abdominal tenderness or pain, intolerance to enteral feeding, and/or paralytic ileus. One group found that symptomatic pancreatitis developed after seven days of injury in 6.6% of children with isolated head trauma had no evidence of associated abdominal trauma (Urban, Splaingard, & Werlin, 1994). Many children with head injury with intracranial bleeding may have elevation of pancreatic enzymes but unless correlated with clinical pancreatitis do not require further evaluation or limitation of feeding regimes.

REHABILITATION

Designing and executing an effective rehabilitation program requires a multidisciplinary team of specialists during the rehabilitation period (see Figure 1). Setting realistic goals, explaining possible complications, and approximate time tables for recovery are discussed early with a child's guardians so that they can begin to understand not only what is expected to be accomplished but what care will be expected of them during the child's rehabilitation. Consideration of the premorbid development status is critical in planning the rehabilitation program for brain-injured children since many have premorbid behavorial or cognitive problems preceding their injuries (Bijur, Brown, & Butler, 1986; Haas, Cope, & Hall, 1987). A positive effect of early mobilization and functional assistance appears in both brain-injured primates and man (Yu, 1976). Rehabilitation interventions for a child in a coma initially focus on reduction of muscle tone, maintenance of normal joint range of motion through passive exercises, positioning in bed, and orthotics. Assessment of a child's level of sensory awareness and arousal through the use of standard-

FIGURE 1. Members of a Multidisciplinary Rehabilitation Team

Pediatric Intensivist or Pediatrician
Pediatric Rehabilitationist or Neurologist
Primary Nurse
Rehabilitation Nurse Clinician
Dietician
Occupational Therapist
Physical Therapist
Speech Pathologist
Neuropsychologist
Social Worker
Discharge Planner

ized measures, such as the Glasgow Coma Scale (Figure 2) and later the Rancho Los Amigos Scale of Cognitive Functioning (Figure 3) is important. A pediatric version of Glasgow Coma Scale has been developed for the infant and young child (Figure 4) (Reilly, Simpson, Sprod, & Thomas, 1988). There is minimal evidence that structured sensory stimulation programs help children emerge from coma and are necessary or effective (Pierce et al., 1992). Neuromuscular problems seen in the PICU in brain-injured children fall into two general categories:

1. The direct consequences of brain damage including spasticity, joint contractures, and decubitus ulcers.
2. Concomitant orthopedic trauma to limbs and spine including spinal cord injury, brachial plexus injury, fractures and dislocations (Hoffer et al., 1971).

Spasticity

Spasticity is defined as a motor disorder, characterized by a velocity-dependent increase in tonic stretch reflexes with exaggerated tendon jerks resulting from hyperexcitability of the stretch reflex as one component of the upper motor neuron syndrome (Lance, 1980). While spasticity may be advantageous in some circumstances, (i.e., providing support for otherwise paretic muscles) it may be painful and can lead to assumption of abnormal postures that increase risk for decubitus ulcer formation and joint contractures. Avoidance of noxious stimuli, control of pain, treatment of fever and infections, proper skin care (including prevention of decubitus ulcers) and correct bed positioning are essential to the primary management of spasticity. Active and passive range of motion techniques applied in conjunction with proper positioning and splinting are necessary. A daily stretching program helps restore resting length of muscle, tendon and joint capsules and can prevent contractures. The effects of

FIGURE 2. Glasgow Coma Scale Score

Activity	Best response	Score
Eye opening	Spontaneous	4
	To verbal stimuli	3
	To pain	2
	None	1
Verbal	Oriented	5
	Confused	4
	Inappropriate words	3
	Nonspecific sounds	2
	None	1
Motor	Follows commands	6
	Localizes pain	5
	Withdraws in response to pain	4
	Flexion in response to pain	3
	Extension in response to pain	2
	None	1

stretching programs will often last for several hours with possible mechanisms of effect existing at the muscle, peripheral nerve and the spinal cord level (Odeen, 1981). Lying in bed causes feet to drop into plantar flexion and hips and knees to flex. Failure to counteract these postures by moving these joints through their full range of motion daily causes fixed joint contractures. Ankle plantar flexion and knee flexion contractures of only 15 degrees will make it impossible to later stand upright without assistance. Upper extremities are even more susceptible than lower extremities to contractures since even greater ranges of motion are necessary for normal activities. Cast and splints can help prevent or reduce contracted joints, reduce tonic stretch reflexes and improve joint range of motion. Bed rest and immobilization causes muscles to lose strength at approximately 1-5% per day (Mueller, 1970). The challenge is to plan a child's care so mobilization is undertaken as early as possible without compromising patient safety. Static or resting splints are most frequently used since dynamic splints may apply forces that lead to pressure ulceration of skin. Tone may be reproduced by "inhibitory" casting which provides prolonged stretch to relax spastic muscles of the distal upper or lower extremities (Connie, 1990). Serial "casts" are frequently used to gradually increase ranges of motion when fixed contractures of ankles, elbows, or wrists are present. Plaster casts are applied and changed once a week and are used until complete cor-

FIGURE 3. Rancho Los Amigos Levels of Cognitive Functioning

I. no response	patient is completely unresponsive to any environment
II. generalized response	patient reacts inconsistently and non-specifically to the enviroment; patient is awake but not aware
III. localized response	patient reacts specifically but inconsistently to stimuli; he may respond to discomfort by pulling at tubes and may seem to respond better to familiar persons such as family members
IV. confused, agitated	patient is confused and excited and cannot process all that is being said and done; if talking, what he says may not make sense to others; attention span is short, and patient may be unable to cooperate with treatment procedures; fatigues easily
V. confused, non-agitated	patient is alert and able to respond inappropriately to simple commands fairly consistently; responds best to familiar routines and people; needs a great deal of external structure; may wander; memory is impaired
VI. confused, appropriate	patient shows goal-directed behavior but still needs external structure; shows the ability to learn new information but may require frequent repetitions and may not generalize to new situations or people; has increased awareness of own needs and of the environment
VII. automatic, appropriate	patient may not function as well as before the injury but is alert and oriented and needs no supervision once he has learned a skill; is functional in society but may still have difficulty dealing with the unexpected or with stressful situations

rection of a joint deformity is obtained. Serial casts are well padded and gradually stretch soft tissues improving range of motion in contracted joints. Any reddened area is allowed to heal by creation of a window in the cast. Once the desired position of the limb has been achieved, the cast may be bivalved (split into two pieces attached by velcro straps) and worn intermittently during the day and night to maintain joint range of motion. A polypropylene brace may then be fabricated for joint position.

The three most commonly used drugs to treat spasticity are diazepam, baclofen and dantrolene, all of which have potential toxicities and various degrees of adverse effects (Martensson, 1981; Young & Delwaide, 1981). Benzodiazepines reduce spastically by enhancing the inhibitory effects of the

FIGURE 4. Modified Glasgow Coma Scale Score for Infants

Activity	Best response	Score
Eye opening	Spontaneous	4
	To speech	3
	To pain	2
	None	1
Verbal	Coos and babbles	5
	Irritable cries	4
	Cries to pain	3
	Moans to pain	2
	None	1
Motor	Normal spontaneous movements	6
	Withdraws to touch	5
	Withdraws to pain	4
	Abnormal flexion	3
	Abnormal extension	2
	None	1

central neurotransmitter gamma-amino-butyric acid (GABA) at multiple CNS levels (Verrier, Ashby, & MacLeod, 1976). Diazepam is most often prescribed, but lorazepam has also been used in the PICU to reduce spasticity and provide sedation. Accommodation to the sedative effects of benzodiazepines may occur over several days. Baclofen is an inhibitor of the excitatory pre-synoptic potential reducing stimulation of the anterior horn cell by the interneuron pool (Jones & Lance, 1976). Baclofen is less sedating than diazepam but generally has less effect on centrally mediated spasticity (Fodstad & Ljunggren, 1991; Glenn & Wroblewski, 1986). Dantrolene sodium decreases muscle tone by interfering with release of calcium from the sarcoplasmic reticulum, reducing the excitatory contraction coupling necessary for muscle contraction (Lietman, Haslam, & Walcler, 1974). It is the least likely of the three drugs to cause severe lethargy or sedation, but hepatotoxicity is a potentially severe complication. A combination of moderate doses of dantrolene sodium and a central acting agent such as diazepam or baclofen may be more effective than higher doses of a single medication. Clonidine is a central alpha adrenergic agent available for transdermal delivery that is useful in narcotic withdrawal in children who have been heavily sedated during hyperventilation for brain injuries. It has antispasticity effects reported in spinal cord injuries and is sometimes useful in patients with head injuries and hypertension (Donovan, Carter, Rossi, & Wilderson, 1988).

Local blocks of musculocutaneous, median, or ulnar nerves to reduce fixed flexion contractures of the upper extremity or tibial nerve for ankle plantar flexion contractures are occasionally required. Intramuscular neurolysis which is achieved by a series of local injections at individual myoneural junctions or "motor points" within a muscle may also be useful (Easton, Ozel, & Halpern, 1979). Surgical procedures to release contractures are generally not performed sooner than 12 months after injuries.

Early onset of dystonia after acute brain injury has been reported in children, and it is often associated with autonomic instability of central origin due to hypothalamic insult with hypertension, tachycardia and hyperthermia (Silver & Lux, 1994). Dystonia is a movement disorder characterized by slow assumption of abnormal and involuntary postures that may involve only one part or the entire body. The presumed etiology is injury to the thalamus and/or basal ganglion. Treatment for generalized dystonia includes dopaminomemetic drugs and high dose anticholinergic therapy.

In children with unusual spasticity or joint contractures after traumatic brain injury, it is common to find undiagnosed fractures even several weeks after injury. Sobus, Alexander, and Harcke (1993) reported that 16 of 60 children with traumatic brain injuries had a total of 25 newly detected fracture sites and 19 had 24 newly detected areas of soft tissue trauma after admission to rehabilitation. The largest number of undetected fractures was found in the ribs, clavicle, scapula, shoulder, tibia, ankle, and foot. Twenty-five percent of patients required alterations in their rehabilitation programs because of undiagnosed fractures or areas of heterotopic ossification. In patients with multiple trauma, bone scan may detect additional fractures not suspected clinically or seen on x-ray. Bone scans can also detect heterotopic ossification two to three weeks before traditional x-ray views. In one study of 183 trauma patients, 44 had abnormal scans revealing fractures not identified on initial x-ray (Deutsch & Gransman, 1983). Bone scan may be particularly useful at the time of transfer from ICU in detecting small bone fractures in the hands, feet, ribs, costochondral junctions, skull, and vertebra. Internal fixation of fractures in attempts to gain early mobility is often used in children with traumatic brain injuries.

Skin and Joint Protection

Pressure ulcers (also called decubitus ulcers, bed sores, or ischemic ulcers) are localized areas of cellular necrosis occurring when tissue is subjected to external force and excess capillary pressure for prolonged periods. They form when pressure, sheer or friction traumatizes the skin and underlying tissues with the greatest frequency over bony prominences covered only by skin and small amounts of muscle and subcutaneous tissue. Skin protection to prevent decubitus ulcer formation is a major problem in paralyzed or heavily-sedated children. Weight concentration and bone configuration are such that the sacrum and occiput in children are very vulnerable to pressure ulcers (Solis, Krouskop, Trainer, & Marburger, 1988). Skin viability depends on maintaining capillary patency with pressure less than 30 torr. When an area of reactive hyperemia without ulcer persists for more than 24 hours, it is defined as a Grade I pressure ulcer. If pressure is not relieved at this stage, tissue destruction progresses to surface ulceration. The visible ulcer, however, represents only the tip of the iceberg as liquefaction occurs over several days or weeks before the full extent of the ulceration becomes apparent. Elevating the head of the bed more than 30 degrees with the patient lying supine commonly produces sheer over the sacral and coccygeal regions. Immobilization after a neurologic injury causes skin irritated by moist heat from sweat, urine, or feces to become macerated and slough. Prevention is the key, with local pressure dressing, debridement and antibiotics used as treatment. Severe tissue injuries may require plastic surgical intervention (Yarkony, 1994). Fluidized bead beds were designed to prevent decubitus ulcers. Fluidization is the process of making granules behave like liquids (Thomson, Dunkin, Ryan, Smith, & Marshall, 1980). Tiny glass microspheres are suspended in a layer of warm air so that each bead is separated from its neighbor and is able to move about freely like a liquid. Children supported by the suspended particles float like an iceberg immersed in a warm, dry fluid with a stream of air flowing imperceptibly over the skin. These beds reduce pressure over bony prominences significantly and reduce risk of decubitus ulcers. Pressure ulcers develop in 4.5% of hospitalized patients in the United States (Herman & Rothman, 1989). Depending on severity, cost of treatment of a decubitus ulcer is between $5,000-$40,000 (Maklebust, 1987). Schmidt recently evaluated occipital decubiti in children receiving either conventional mechanical ventilation or high frequency oscillation for at least 24 hours (Schmidt, Berens, Zollo, Weisner, & Weigle, 1994). In spite of an average of four head turns per day, one-third of 64 children developed at least a Grade I decubitus ulcer. Length of PICU stay and not mode of ventilation was the major risk factor for development of an occipital decubitus ulcer. It is clear that systematic comprehensive preventative management is the best and most cost effective approach to decubitus ulcer. Studies have shown the clinical utility and cost effectiveness of air suspension beds in both the prevention (Inman, Sibbald, Rutledge, & Clark, 1993) and treatment (Ferrell, Osterweil, & Christenson, 1993) of pressure ulcers in critically-ill adults compared with traditional foam mattresses.

FAMILY SUPPORTIVE INTERVENTIONS

A traumatic brain injury from child abuse is an unfortunate family affair that represents a direct threat to the integrity of the family unit (Frohman, 1990; Rivara, 1994; Romano, 1989). Families frequently care for their brain-injured children with great interpersonal and emotional cost and endure anxiety, frustration, guilt, and despair. Pediatric brain injury places major stressors on families. Financial problems are common, and early interventions should ensure the families receive help from appropriate funding sources. Family support is critical to a brain-injured child since a family's ability to adequately support and care for their child clearly effects the functional outcome of the child (Clydesdale, Fahs, Kilgore, & Splaingard, 1990). A fundamental goal of a rehabilitation team is:

1. To educate and train the family to appropriately care for and support the independent living skills a child may gain during the rehabilitation program.
2. To prepare the family for the child's special needs as he/she grows and develops.

Most children with traumatic brain injuries, even with tracheostomies and gastrostomies, live with caregivers outside of institutions who assume the major responsibility for their long-term care (Splaingard, Gaebler, Havens, & Kalichman, 1989). Failure to include caregivers in the rehabilitation process is to neglect a critical aspect of care.

Caregivers of brain-injured children rate their need for accurate and consistent information as critical to their ability to cope (Mauss-Clum & Ryan, 1981; Sherburne, 1986). They require consistent information on a daily basis from nurses and physicians. Ensuring that caregivers are recognized as members of the treatment team can serve to avoid many potential conflicts. However, families of traumatically brain-injured children, especially those who are victims of abuse, are often in a state of emotional shock and are unable to fully understand either intellectually or emotionally what has happened to their child and their family. Ongoing and mandatory family education, shared decision making, and flexibility on the part of both the family and the medical and rehabilitation staff allow the development of viable treatment and discharge plans (Johnston & Higgens, 1987).

Rosenthal and Young (1988)proposed a "PLISSIT" model for interventions with families of traumatic brain-injured patients that has been found useful.

*   P = permission
*   L = limited information
*   SS = specific suggestions
*   IT = therapy

At the permission stage, family members are encouraged to express their hopes and fears regarding their child future recovery and to ask questions about medical status to staff who will refer them to appropriate team members. At the limited information level, basic information about brain injury is provided to families. This includes brochures, articles, as well as descriptions of the specific treatments being given to their child. During the specific suggestion stage, families are provided with detailed responses to questions, given opportunities to receive information about care activities, and may attend meetings with representatives from all disciplines treating their child, (i.e., family conferences). During family conferences, a small nucleus of professionals may effectively summarize a child's progress for the family thus avoiding large groups which can be overwhelming. Finally, in the intensive therapy stage, families may receive psychological counseling to help them facilitate their adjustments to their child's disability and to cope with its impact on their family. Family premorbid coping mechanisms was found to be the best predictor of ability to manage stress in the year following a child's traumatic brain injury (Rivara et al., 1992). Early psychological and social service intervention can help identify "high-risk families" that are poorly equipped to facilitate their child's recovery process. Presenting important information without "overloading" the caregivers with details requires wisdom since the medical/rehabilitation treatment team define their relationship and responsibilities by child's present condition, while the family often continues to respond to the child as they did before the brain injury. As an example, families and staff frequently diverge in their interpretation of "coma." This dichotomy is often a preview of emerging family/staff conflicts that can develop early in treatment (Frohman, 1990). Thus, the stage is set for disagreements and misinterpretations of actions by different parties. We have found that early family conferences, ongoing daily information sessions, and utilizing the principle of the PLISSIT system allows us to prevent or reduce disagreements that lead to antagonistic relationships which only hinder future rehabilitation efforts.

REFERENCES

Adams, S., Dellinger, E.P., Wertz, M.J., Oreskovich, M.R., Simonowitz, D., & Johansen, K. (1986). Enteral vs. parenteral nutritional support following laparotomy for trauma: A randomized prospective trail. *Journal of Trauma, 26*, 882-891.

Allison, M., Morris, A., Park, R., & Mills, P. (1992). Percutaneous endoscopic gastrostomy tube feeding may improve outcome of late rehabilitation following stroke. *Journal of the Royal Society of Medicine, 85*(3), 147-149.

Andrew, M., David, M., Adams, M., Ali, K., Anderson, R., Barnard, D., Berstein, M., Bresson, L., Cairney, B., DeSai, D., Grant, R., Israels, S., Luke, J., Massicotti, P., & Silva, M. (1994). Venous thromboembolic complications (VTE) in children: First analysis of the Canadian registry of VTE. *Blood, 83*(5), 1251-1257.

Arvedson, J., Rogers, B., Buck, G., Smart, P., & Msall, M. (1994). Silent aspiration prominent in children with dysphagia. *International Journal of Pediatric Otorhinolaryngology, 28*(2-3), 173-181.

Beca, J., Cox, P., Taylor, M., Bohn, D., Butt, W., Logan, W., Rutha, J., & Barker, G. (1995). Somatosensory evoked potentials for prediction of outcome in acute severe brain injury. *Journal of Pediatrics, 126*, 44-49.

Bellmire, M.E., & Myers, P.A. (1985). Serious head injury in infants–Accidental or abuse? *Pediatrics, 75*, 340-342.

Bijur, P., Brown, S., & Butler, N. (1986). Child behavior and accidental injury in 11,966 preschool children. *American Journal of Diseases in Children, 140*, 487-492.

Boyer, M.G., & Edwards, P. (1991). Outcome 1 to 3 years after severe traumatic brain injury in children and adolescents. *Injury, 22*(4), 315-320.

Brink, J., Garrett, A., Hale, W., Woo-Sam, J., & Nichel, V. (1970). Recovery of motor and intellectual function in children sustaining severe head injuries. *Developmental Medicine and Child Neurology, 12*, 565-571.

Brink, J., Inbus, C., & Wood-Sam, J. (1990). Physical recovery after severe closed head trauma in children and adolescents. *Clinical Neurology and Neurosurgery, 92*(4), 323-328.

Bruce, D.A., Schut, L., Bruno, L.A., Wood, J.H., & Sutton, L.N. (1978). Outcome following severe head injury in children. *Journal of Neurosurgery, 48*(5), 679-688.

Byard, R.W., & Cruz, E. (1990). Sudden and unexpected death in infancy and childhood due to pulmonary thromboembolism. *Archives of Pathology and Laboratory Medicine, 114*, 142-144.

CDC. (1994). Prevalence of disabilities and associated health conditions–United States, 1991-1992. *Mortality and Morbidity Weekly Report, 43*, 730-731, 737-739.

Citt-Pietrolungo, T.J., Alexander, M.A., Cook, S.P., & Padman, R. (1993). Complications of tracheostomy and decannulation in pediatric and young patients with traumatic brain injury. *Archives of Physical Medicine and Rehabilitation, 74*, 905-909.

Clydesdale, T.T., Fahs, I.J., Kilgore, K.M., & Splaingard, M.L. (1990). Social dimensions to functional gain in pediatric patients. *Archives of Physical Medicine and Rehabilitation, 71*, 469-472.

Coben, R., Weintraub, A., Dimarino, A., & Cohen S. (1994). Gastroesophageal reflux during gastrostomy feeding. *Gastroenterology, 106*, 13-18.

Collins, K.A., & Davis, G.J. (1994). A retrospective and prospective study of cerebral tissue pulmonary embolism in severe head trauma. *Journal of Forensic Science, 39*(3), 624-628.

Connie, T.A., Sullivan, T., Machie, T., & Goodman, M. (1990). Effect of serial casting for the prevention of equines in patients with acute head injury. *Archives of Physical Medicine and Rehabilitation, 71*, 310-312.

Cope, D.N., & Hall, K. (1982). Head injury rehabilitation: benefit of early intervention. *Archives of Physical Medicine and Rehabilitation, 63*, 433-437.

Davis, R.J., Fan Tait, W., Dean, J.M., Goldberg, A.L., & Rogers, M.C. (1992). Head and spinal cord injury. In M.C. Rogers (Ed.), *Textbook of pediatric intensive care* (2nd ed.) (pp. 805-857). Baltimore: Williams & Wilkins.

Dean, J.M., & Kaufman, N.D. (1981). Prognostic indicators in pediatric near-drowning: The Glasgow Coma Scale. *Critical Care Medicine, 9*(7), 536-539.

Deutsch, S.D., & Gransman, E.J. (1983). The use of bone scanning for the diagnosis and management of musculoskeletal trauma. *Surgery Clinics of North America, 58*, 799-816.

Donovan, W.H., Carter, R.E., Rossi, C.D., & Wilderson, M.A. (1988). Clonidine effect on spasticity: A clinical trial. *Archives of Physical Medicine and Rehabilitation, 69*, 193-194.

Drake, M., & John, K. (1987). Long latency auditory event related potentials in the post-concussive syndrome. *Clinical Evoked Potentials, 5*, 19-21.

Duhaime, A.C., Alario, A.J., Lewander, W.J., Schut, L., Sutton, L.N., Seidl, T.S., Nudelman, S., Budenz, D., Hertle, R., & Tsiaras, W. (1992). Head injury in very young children: Mechanisms, injury types, and ophthalmologic findings in 100 hospitalized patients younger than 2 years of age. *Pediatrics, 90*, 179-85.

Duhaime, A., Christien, C., Moss, E., & Seidl, T. (1996). Long term outcome in infants with the shaking impact syndrome. *Pediatric Neurosurgery, 24*, 292-298.

Easton, J., Ozel, T., & Halpern, D. (1979). Intramuscular neurolysis for spasticity in children. *Archives of Physical Medicine and Rehabilitation, 60*, 55-158.

Eiben, C.F., Anderson, T.P., Lockman, L., Matthews, D.J., Dryja, R., Martin, J., & Burrill, C. (1984). Functional outcome of closed head injury in children and young adults. *Archives of Physical Medicine and Rehabilitation, 65*(4), 168-170.

Fay, G., Jaffe, K., Polissar, N., Liano, S., Martin, K., Shurtleff, H., Rivara, J., & Winn, H. (1993). Mild pediatric traumatic brain injury: A cohort study. *Archives of Physical Medicine and Rehabilitation, 74*, 895-901.

Ferrell, B.A., Osterweil, D., & Christenson, P. (1993). A randomized trial of low-air-loss beds for treatment of pressure ulcers. *Journal of the American Medical Association, 269*, 494-497.

Fodstad, H., & Ljunggren, B.C. (1991). Baclofen and carbamazepine in supraspinal spasticity. *Journal of the Royal Society of Medicine, 84*(12), 747-748.

Frohman, S. (1990). Family response to the coma emerging patient. In M.E. Sandel, D.W. Ellis (Eds.), *The coma emerging patient. Physical medicine and rehabilitation: State of the art reviews* (pp 593-603). Philadelphia: Hanley & Belfus.

Gauderer, M. (1991). Percutaneous endoscopic gastrostomy: A ten year experience with 220 children. *Journal of Pediatric Surgery, 26*(3), 288-294.

Gauderer, M., Ponsky, J., & Izant, R. (1980). Gastrostomy without laparotomy: A percutaneous endoscopic technique. *Journal of Pediatric Surgery, 15*, 872-875.

Glenn, M.B., & Wroblewski, B. (1986). Anti-spasticity medications in the patient with traumatic brain injury. *Journal of Head Trauma Rehabilitation, 1*, 71-80.

Goodwin, S.R., Friedman, W., & Bellefleur, M. (1991). Is it time to use evoked potentials to predict outcome in comatose children and adults? *Critical Care Medicine, 19*, 518-524.

Grahm, T.W., Zadrozny, D.B., & Harrington, T. (1989). The benefits of early jejunal hyperalimentation in the head-injured patient. *Neurosurgery, 25*, 729-735.

Grewal, M., & Sutcliffe, A.J. (1991). Early prediction of outcome following head injury in children: An assessment of the value of Glasgow Coma Scale score trend and abnormal plantar and pupillary light reflexes. *Journal of Pediatric Surgery, 26*(10), 1161-1163.

Grosswasser, Z., Costef, H., & Tamir, A. (1985). Survivors of severe traumatic brain injury in childhood, I. Incidence, background, and hospital course. *Scandinavian Journal of Rehabilitation Medicine (Suppl), 12*, 6-20.

Haas, J.F., Cope, D.N., & Hall, K. (1987). Premorbid prevalence of poor academic performance in severe head injury. *Journal of Neurologic and Neurosurgical Psychiatry, 50*, 52-56.

Hahn, Y., Chyung, C., Barthel, M., Bailes, J., Flannery, A., & McLone, D. (1988). Head injury in children under 36 months of age. *Child's Nervous System, 4*, 34-40.

Harari, R.J., Narayan, R.K., Iacona, L., Ishman, R., & Ghajar, J. Marked variability in the management of severe head injury at trauma centres in the United States. *Journal of Neurosurgery, 76*, 397A.

Herman, L.E., & Rothman, K.F. (1989). Prevention, care and treatment of pressure (decubitus) ulcers in intensive care unit patients. *Journal of Intensive Care Medicine, 4*, 117-123.

Hoffer, M.M., Garrett, A., Brink, J., Perry, J., Hale, W., & Nichol, J. (1971). The orthopaedic management of brain injured children. *Journal of Bone Joint Surgery, 53*, 567-577.

Hsu, D.T., Addonizio, L.J., Hordof, A.J., & Gersong, W.M. Acute pulmonary embolism in pediatric patients awaiting heart transplantation. *Journal of the American College of Cardiology, 17*, 1621-1625.

Humphreys, R.P., Jaimovich, R., Hendrick, E., & Hoffman, H. (1984). Severe head injury in children. In *Concepts in pediatric neurosurgery* (Vol. 4) (pp. 230-242). Karger: Basel.

Inman, K.J., Sibbald, W.J., Rutledge, F.S., & Clark, B.J. (1993). Clinical utility and cost effectiveness of an air suspension bed in the prevention of pressure ulcers. *Journal of the American Medical Association, 269*, 1139-1143.

Inoue, S., Epstein, M., & Alexander, J.W. (1989). Prevention of yeast translocation across the gut by a single enteral feeding after brain injury. *Journal of Pediatric Enterology and Nutrition, 13*, 565-571.

Jaffe, K.M., Massagli, T.L., Martin, K.M., Rivara, J.B., Fay, G.C., & Polissar, N.L. (1993). Pediatric traumatic brain injury; acute and rehabilitation costs. *Archives of Physical Medicine and Rehabilitation, 74*, 681-686.

Jaffe, K., Polissar, N., Fay, G., & Liano, S. (1995). Recovery trends over three years following pediatric traumatic brain injury. *Archives of Physical Medicine and Rehabilitation, 76*, 17-26.

Jennet B. Severe head injury: prediction of outcome as a basis for management decisions. *International Anesthesiology Clinics, 17*(2-3), 133-152.

Johnson, J.R., & Higgins, L. (1987). Integration of family dynamics into the rehabilitation of the brain injured patient. *Rehabilitation Nursing, 12*(6), 320-322.

Johnston, M.V., & Keister, M. (1984). Early rehabilitation for stroke patients: A new look. *Archives of Physical Medicine and Rehabilitation, 65,* 437-441.

Jones, R., & Lance, J. (1976). Baclofen in the long-term management of spasticity. *Medical Journal of Australia, 1,* 654-657.

Justice, A., Dibenedetto, R., & Stanford, E. (1994). Significance of elevated pancreatic enzymes in intracranial bleeding. *Southern Medical Journal, 87*(9), 889-893.

Kirby, D. (1992). To PEG or not to PEG–That is the costly question. *Mayo Clinic Proceedings, 67,* 1115-1117.

Kiver, K.F., Hays, D.P., & Forten, D. (1984). Pre and postpyloric enteral feeding: Analysis of safety and complications. *Journal of Pediatric Enterology and Nutrition, 8,* 95.

Klingbeil, G. (1988). Airway problems in patients with traumatic brain injury. *Archives of Physical Medicine and Rehabilitation, 69,* 493-495.

Kocan, M.H., & Hickisch, S.M. (1986). A comparison of continuous and intermittent enteral nutrition in NICU patients. *Journal of Neuroscience Nursing, 18,* 333-337.

Kraus, J.F., & Nourjah, P. (1988). The epidemiology of uncomplicated brain injury. *Trauma, 29,* 1637-1643.

Kraus, J.F., Rock, A., & Hemyari, P. (1990). Brain injuries among infants, children, adolescents, and young adults. *American Journal of Diseases in Children, 144,* 684-691.

Kriel, R., Krach, L., & Sheehan, M. (1998). Pediatric closed head injury: Outcome following prolonged unconsciousness. *Archives of Physical Medicine and Rehabilitation, 69,* 678-681.

Kumar, R., West, C., Quirke, C., Hall, L., & Taylor, R. (1991). Do children with severe head injury benefit from intensive care? *Child Nervous System, 7,* 299-304.

Lance, J.W. (1980). Symposium synopsis. In R.G. Feldman, R.R. Young, & W.P. Koella (Eds.), *Spasticity: Disordered motor control* (485-494). Chicago: Yearbook.

Langfitt, T.W., & Gennarelli, T.A. (1982). Can the outcome from head injury be improved? *Journal of Neurosurgery, 56,* 19-25.

Lanza, D.C., Parnes, S.M., Koltai, P.J., & Fortune, J.B. (1990). Early complications of airway management in head-injured patients. *Laryngoscope, 9,* 958-961.

Lietman, P.S., Haslam, R., & Walcler, J. (1974). Pharmacology of dantrolene sodium in children. *Archives of Physical Medicine and Rehabilitation, 55,* 388-392.

Lindsay, K.W., Carlin, J., Kennedy, I., Fry, J., McInnes, A., & Teasdale, G.M. (1981). Evoked potentials in severe head injury: Analysis and relation to outcome. *Journal of Neurologic and Neurosurgical Psychiatry, 44,* 762-802.

Lutsch, G., Pfenninger, J., Ludin, H., & Vassella, F. (1983). Brain stem auditory evoked potentials and early somatosensory evoked potentials in neurointensively treated comatose children. *American Journal of Diseases in Children, 137,* 421-426.

Mackay, L.E., Bernstein, B.A., Chapman, P.E., Morgan, A.S., & Milazzo, L.S. (1992). Early intervention in sever head injury: long-term benefits of a formalized program. *Archives of Physical Medicine and Rehabilitation, 73,* 635-641.

Maklebust, J. (1987). Pressure ulcers: Etiology and prevention. *Nursing Clinics North America, 22,* 359-377.

Martensson A. (1981). Anti-spasticity medication. A review. *Scandinavian Journal of Rehabilitation Medicine, 13*(4), 143-147.

Mauss-Clum, N., & Ryan, M. (1981). Brain injury and the family. *Journal of Neurosurgical Nursing, 13,* 165-169.

Molnar, G.E. (Ed.) (1992). *Pediatric rehabilitation.* Baltimore, Williams & Wilkins.

Mueller, E.A. (1970). Influence of training and of inactivity on muscle strength. *Archives of Physical Medicine and Rehabilitation, 51,* 449-462.

Murray, L.S., Tasdale, G.M., Murray, G.D., Jennett, B., Miller, J.D., Pickard, J.D., Shaw, M.D.M., Achilles, J., Bailey, S., Jones, P., Kelly, D., & Lacey, J. (1993). Does prediction of outcome alter patient management? *Lancet, 341,* 1487-1491.

Narayan, R.K., Greenberg, R.P., Miller, J.D., Evans, G., Choi, S.C., Keshorep, R.S., Selhorst, J.B., Lutz, H.A., & Becker, D.P. (1981). Improved confidence of outcome prediction in severe head injury. A comparative analysis of the clinical examination, multi-modality evoked potentials, CT scanning and intracranial pressure. *Journal of Neurosurgery, 54,* 751-762.

Norton, J.A., Ott, L.G., McClain, C., Adams, L., Dempsey, R.J., Haack, D., Tibbs, P.A., & Young, A.B. (1988). Intolerance to enteral feeding in the brain-injured patient. *Journal of Neurosurgery, 68,* 62-66.

Nowak, P., Cohn, A., & Guidice, M.A. (1987). Airway complications in patients with closed-head injuries. *American Journal of Otolaryngology, 8*(2), 91-96.

Odeen, I. (1981). Reduction of muscular hypertonus by long-term muscle stretch. *Scandinavian Journal of Rehabilitation Medicine, 13,* 93-99.

Pierce, J.P., Lyle, D.M., Quine, S., Evans, N.J., Morris, J., & Fearnside, M.R. (1992). The effectiveness of coma arousal intervention. *Brain Injury, 6*(1), 95-100.

Radecki, R., & Gaebler-Spira, D. (1994). Deep vein thrombosis in the disabled pediatric population. *Archives of Physical Medicine and Rehabilitation, 75,* 248-250.

Raphaely, R., Swedlow, D.B., Dounes, J.J., & Bruce, D.A. (1980). Management of severe pediatric head injury. *Pediatric Clinics of North America, 27*(3), 715-727.

Rapp, R.P., Young, B., Twyman, D., Bivins, B.A., Haack, D., Tibbs, P.A., & Bean, J.R. (1983). The favorable effect of early parenteral feeding on survival in head-injured patients. *Journal of Neurosurgery, 58,* 906-912.

Reilly, P.L., Simpson, D.A., Sprod, R., & Thomas, L. (1988). Assessing the conscious level in infants and young children: A paediatric version of the Glasgow Coma Scale. *Child Nervous System, 4,* 30-33.

Rivara, J.M. (1994). Family functioning following pediatric traumatic brain injury. *Pediatric Annals, 23*(1), 38-43.

Rivara, J.M., Fay, G.C., Jaffe, K.M., Polissar, N.L., Shurtleff, H.A., & Martin, K.M. (1992). Predictors of family functioning one year following traumatic brain injury in children. *Archives of Physical Medicine and Rehabilitation, 73,* 899-910.

Romano, M.D. (1989). Family issues in head trauma. In L.J. Horn, & D.N. Cope (Eds.), *Traumatic brain injury and physical medicine and rehabilitation: State of the art reviews* (pp. 157-167). Philadelphia: Hanley & Belfus.

Rosenthal, M., & Young, T. (1988). Effective family intervention after traumatic brain injury: Theory and practice. *Journal of Head Trauma Rehabilitation, 3*, 42-50.

Ruijs, M., Keyser, A., & Gabreels, F. (1990). Long-term sequelae of brain damage from closed head injury in children and adolescents. *Clinical Neurology and Neurosurgery, 92*(4), 323-328.

Ruijs, M., Keyser, A., Gabreels, F., & Notermans, S. (1993). Somatosensory evoked potentials and cognitive sequelae in children with closed head injury. *Neuropediatrics, 24*, 307-312.

Saltzberg, D., Medhat, A., & Jaffe, I. (1987). Pulmonary aspiration during nasogastric feeding. *Journal of Pediatric Enterology and Nutrition, 11*, 205.

Sartori, S., Trevisani, L., Tassinari, D., Nielsen, I., Gilli, G., Donati, D., & Malacarne, P. (1994). Prevention of aspiration pneumonia during long-term feeding by percutaneous endoscopic gastrostomy: Might cisapride play a role? *Supplemental Care in Cancer, 2*(3), 188-190.

Schmidt, J., Berens, R., Zollo, M., Weisner, M., & Weigle, C. (1994). *Skin breakdown in children and high frequency oscillatory ventilation.* Symposium presented at the Eighth Pediatric Critical Care Colloquium, Seattle, WA, October 23-25.

Sherburne, E. (1986). Rehabilitation protocol for the neurosurgical intensive care unit. *Journal of Neurosurgical Nursing, 18*(3), 140-145.

Silver, J.K., & Lux, W.E. (1994). Early onset dystonia following traumatic brain injury. *Archives of Physical Medicine and Rehabilitation, 75*, 885-888.

Sobus, K.M., Alexander, M.A., & Harcke, P.T. (1993). Undetected musculoskeletal trauma in children with traumatic brain injury or spinal cord injury. *Archives of Physical Medicine and Rehabilitation, 74*(9), 902-904.

Solis, I., Krouskop, T., Trainer, N., & Marburger, R. (1988). Supine interface pressure in children. *Archives of Physical Medicine and Rehabilitation, 69*(7), 524-526.

Splaingard, M.L., Gaebler, D., Havens, P., & Kalichman, M. (1989). Brain injury: Survival in children with tracheostomies and gastrostomies. *Archives of Physical Medicine and Rehabilitation, 70*(4), 318-321.

Splaingard, M.L., Hutchins, B., Sulton, L., & Chaudhuri, G. (1988). Aspiration in rehabilitation patients; video fluoroscopy vs. bedside clinical assessment. *Archives of Physical Medicine and Rehabilitation, 69*, 637-640.

Taniguchi, M.H., & Moyer, R.S. (1994). Assessment of risk factors for pneumonia in dysphagic children: Significance of video fluoroscopic swallowing evaluation. *Developmental Medicine and Child Neurology, 36*(6), 495-502.

Tepas, J.J., DiScala, C., Ramenofsky, M.L., & Barlow, B. (1990). Mortality and head injury: The pediatric perspective. *Journal of Pediatric Surgery, 25*(1), 92-96.

Thakker, J., Splaingard, M.L., Zhu, J., Babel, K., Bresnalan, J., & Havens, P.L. (1997). Survival and functional outcome of children requiring endotracheal intubation during therapy for severe traumatic brain injury. *Critical Care Medicine, 25*, 1396-1401.

Thomson, C.W., Dunkin, L.J., Ryan, D.W., Smith, M., & Marshall, M. (1980). Fluidised-bead bed in the intensive care unit. *Lancet, 1*, 568-570.

Urban, M., Splaingard, M.L., & Werlin, S. (1994). Pancreatitis associated with remote traumatic brain injury in children. *Child Nervous System, 10*, 388-391.

Verrier, M., Ashby, P., & MacLeod, S. (1976). Effect of diazepam on muscle contraction in spasticity. *American Journal of Physical Medicine, 55*, 184-187.

Vitale, G.C., Larson, G.M., Davidson, P.R., Bouwman, D.L., & Weaver, D.W. (1987). Analysis of hyperamylasemia in patients with severe head injury. *Journal of Surgical Research, 43*, 226-233.

Wagstyl, J., Sutcliffe, A.J., & Alpar, E.K. (1987). Early prediction of outcome following head injury in children. *Journal of Pediatric Surgery, 22*(2), 127-129.

Whatley, K., Turner, W., & Dey, M. (1983). Transpyloric passage of feeding tubes. *Nutrition Supplemental Services, 3*, 18-21.

Wilson, N.W., Ochs, H., Peterson, B., Hamburger, R., & Bastian, J. (1989). Abnormal primary antibody responses in pediatric trauma patients. *Journal of Pediatrics, 115*(3), 424-427.

Wyllie, J., Kerns, E., O'Brien, P., & Hyatt, R. (1976). Alteration of pulmonary function associated with artificial nasal obstruction. *Surgical Forum, 27*, 535-537.

Yarkony, G. (1994). Pressure ulcers: A review. *Archives of Physical Medicine and Rehabilitation, 75*, 908-917.

Young, B., Ott, L., Twyman, D., Norton, J., Rapp, R., Tibbs, P., Haack, D., Brivins, B., & Dempsey, R. (1987). The effect of nutritional support on outcome from severe head injury. *Journal of Neurosurgery, 67*, 668-676.

Young, R.R., & Delwaide, P.J. (1981). Spasticity. *New England Journal of Medicine, 304*(1), 28-33.

Yu, J. (1976). Functional recovery with and without training following brain damage in experimental animals: A review. *Archives of Physical Medicine and Rehabilitation, 57*(1), 38-41.

Chapter Eleven

Pathological Findings in Fatal Shaken Impact Syndrome

Jeffrey M. Jentzen

SUMMARY. This article presents the pathological findings in fatal shaken impact syndrome which reflect the current state of knowledge and the majority opinion of practicing forensic pathologists. The discussion is limited to issues related to fatal cases of shaken impact syndrome with a review of the pathophysiology, autopsy, and neuropathologic findings. Pathophysiology, presentation and autopsy techniques are discussed, with special emphasis on findings specific to SBS. The article concludes with a review of current knowledge of the timing of injuries in inflicted cerebral trauma. *[Article copies available for a fee from The Haworth Document Delivery Service: 1-800-342-9678. E-mail address: <getinfo@haworthpressinc.com> Website: <http://www.HaworthPress.com> © 2001 by The Haworth Press, Inc. All rights reserved.]*

KEYWORDS. Autopsy, subdural hemorrhage, subarachnoid hemorrhage, diffuse axonal injury

INTRODUCTION

From the time Caffey (1972) first described the constellation of subdural hematoma, metaphyseal fractures, and retinal hemorrhages in the whip-

[Haworth co-indexing entry note]: "Pathological Findings in Fatal Shaken Impact Syndrome." Jentzen, Jeffrey M. Co-published simultaneously in *Journal of Aggression, Maltreatment & Trauma* (The Haworth Maltreatment & Trauma Press, an imprint of The Haworth Press, Inc.) Vol. 5, No. 1(#9), 2001, pp. 199-224; and: *The Shaken Baby Syndrome: A Multidisciplinary Approach* (ed: Stephen Lazoritz, and Vincent J. Palusci) The Haworth Maltreatment & Trauma Press, an imprint of The Haworth Press, Inc., 2001, pp. 199-224. Single or multiple copies of this article are available for a fee from The Haworth Document Delivery Service [1-800-342-9678, 9:00 a.m. - 5:00 p.m. (EST). E-mail address: getinfo@haworthpressinc.com].

199

lash-shaking of infants in the 1970s, forensic pathologists have attempted to further define the pathological findings of shaken impact syndrome. Due to the lack of adequate human controls, investigation into the mechanisms and pathological characterization of the shaken impact syndrome often has relied on descriptions of autopsy findings by forensic pathologists and correlation with the clinical presentation of the injured child.

Currently, the most controversy revolves around the mechanism of injury and the magnitude of force necessary to cause the type of injuries observed in shaking a child versus forcefully striking the child's head against a fixed object. This confusion is apparent in both the terminology used to describe the injuries as shaken baby, shaken infant or shaken impact syndrome and the evolving state of knowledge regarding the neuropathologic interpretation of injuries. For the sake of clarity, to the constellation of retinal hemorrhages, brain swelling and subdural hemorrhage will be referred to as the shaken impact syndrome.

In this article, the pathological findings in fatal shaken impact syndrome which reflect the current state of knowledge and the majority opinion of practicing forensic pathologists will be presented. The discussion will be limited to issues related to fatal cases shaken impact syndrome and refer the reader elsewhere in this volume for a more comprehensive discussion of specific organ systems, clinical presentation, and the related cultural and social aspects of the shaken impact syndrome.

PATHOPHYSIOLOGY OF SHAKEN IMPACT SYNDROME

The presentation of shaken impact syndrome originates from a mechanical injury, which results in angular rotation of the infant's head sufficient to create acceleration and deceleration forces of the type frequently encountered in major automobile collisions. The clinical presentations vary from a pure shaking incident, where the child is typically forcibly grasped about the thorax and violently shaken; blunt force injury, where the child is thrown or receives a blunt impact injury to the head; and finally, as a component of other injury in the battered child syndrome (Figure 1).

Duhaime et al. (1987) described the clinical, pathological, and biomechanical characteristics of shaken impact syndrome using a non-human model to evaluate the forces necessary to cause the injuries. The study supported the theory that shaking alone, at least a single shaking episode, was insufficient to cause serious injury or death but that an impact from blunt force trauma was required to generate the forces necessary to develop injuries associated with the shaken impact syndrome. Contrary to opinion of Duhaime, most forensic pathologists

FIGURE 1. The proposed mechanisms of injury in shaken impact syndrome. (A) The child is forcibly shaken from the chest area. (B) The child sustains a blunt impact associated with velocity. (C) As a result of a shaking incident, the child sustains blunt force trauma. (D) The child sustains blunt force trauma after being discarded following a shaking episode.

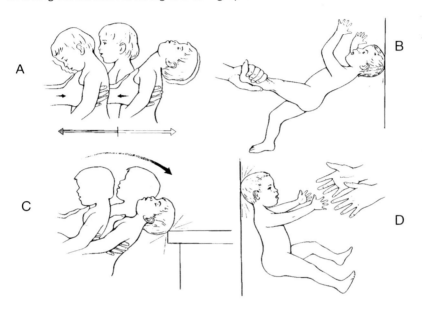

currently believe that pure shaking mechanism can result in these injuries (Alexander, Sato, Smith, & Bennett, 1990; Graham & Lantos, 1997). They support their claim using the statements of perpetrators and other witnesses, the lack of evidence of impact, and the presence of other injuries such as rib fractures. Despite the current debate over the exact mechanism of injury of shaken impact syndrome, the classical findings of retinal hemorrhages, subdural hematoma, and brain swelling cannot be fully explained by any other medical entity.

CLINICAL PRESENTATION

The initial history obtained during the investigation of fatal child abuse is frequently misleading or overtly fictitious. As a consequence, it is important to correlate the pathological findings obtained during the autopsy with the clinical history. Pathologists, similar to other medical practitioners, utilize clinical information in the form of witness statements, medical records, and a death scene investigation in order to arrive at a legally defensible determination of the cause and manner of death. For the death investigator, multiple and frequently changing stories inconsistent with the pathological findings strongly suggests a non-accidental origin of the injury. Infants frequently may have received emergency medical treatment in the days and weeks prior to the fatal injury. It is important that law enforcement personnel carefully document any statements obtained from the caregiver in order to preserve any historical discrepancies for future use during the investigation.

It is a common practice of death investigators to attribute fatal injuries to resuscitative techniques. Our experience, obtained by examining hundreds of routine pediatric autopsies, confirms the impression that fatal injuries are not caused by attempts at cardiopulmonary resuscitation, regardless of the level of the resuscitator's training.

The preliminary medical evaluation may detect injuries such as retinal hemorrhages or fractures which will alert the pathologist to the possibility of non-accidental injury. Prior to commencing the autopsy, full body radiographs should be obtained. At a minimum, a skeletal survey should contain full skeletal imaging of the chest, abdomen, and pelvis, with two views of the spine, anteroposterior-lateral skull views, and anteroposterior views of the extremities. Detailed radiological studies such as CAT or MRI scans may not be available if the child dies at the scene or shortly after arrival to the hospital. The death investigator should never assume that radiological studies have been completed by the treating physician prior to the death. Pathologists, even forensic pathologists who routinely examine and autopsy injured children, should obtain a radiological consultation by a radiologist experienced in interpreting pediatric injuries.

The pathologist should be provided with all available medical, social, and investigative information at the time of autopsy. All written medical records, law enforcement reports, copies of radiographs or other laboratory studies should be made available as soon as possible. All blood samples should be retained for possible toxicological analysis. If the child has been removed from the scene, a formal, law enforcement personnel in cooperation with other death scene investigators must perform retrospective scene investigation. Any information released before the death investigation is completed is speculative and must be avoided. The treating physician and medical staff should avoid releasing information regarding the investigation to family members or others that might jeopardize the future outcome of the investigation. It is equally important for medical personnel to refrain from unnecessary speculation in the medical record. This practice can unnecessarily jeopardize the outcome of an investigation (Kanda, Thomas, & Lloyd, 1985).

THE PEDIATRIC AUTOPSY

A complete forensic autopsy performed by a pathologist experienced in pediatric death investigation is essential to properly document and evaluate pediatric injuries. Death investigations may be jeopardized by an incomplete or poorly documented postmortem examination. Pathologists unaccustomed to performing detailed medicolegal autopsies should consult a pediatric or forensic pathologist to assist in the autopsy examination and interpretation.

A complete autopsy consists of a detailed external examination followed by an examination of all body cavities and internal organs (Table 1). Body diagrams should be utilized along with detailed photography and the autopsy protocol to document all significant injuries. All cutaneous lesions, both acute and chronic, must be described, photographed, and documented. The anal, oral, and genital orifices should be examined for the presence of injury. A formal sexual assault examination should be obtained in any case where the clinical or external examination suggests the potential of sexual assault. In order to avoid the possibility of artefactual hemorrhage, the dissection should begin with the thoracic cavity, followed by the abdominal, cranial, and neck compartments, respectively. Each organ should be inspected and tissue samples retained to microscopically document significant disease or trauma. Blood, other body fluids and hair should be retained for possible toxicological examination. Special attention to the quantity and characteristics of the stomach contents may facilitate the determination of the time of death. In suspicious cases, the autopsy should also include a posterior-midline neck dissection and removal and examination of the eyes to examine for the presence of hemorrhage or injury (Randall, Fierro, & Froede, 1998). Routine screening for metabolic diseases is obtained to rule out contributions of inborn errors of metabolism, an issue that frequently arises in the courtroom. Whenever possible, a neuropathologist experienced in the interpretation of cranial injuries should be consulted in cases where there is suspicious head trauma. The pathologist should personally examine the brain prior to the removal from the cranial cavity to evaluate the presence of a lacerated corpus callosum or posterior interhemispheric subdural hematoma (Table 2).

Due to the numerous experts involved in the investigation of a suspicious child death, autopsy results are frequently not immediately available. Preliminary results should be provided to authorized investigators when available to aid in the investigation. The use of a multidisciplinary child death review team

TABLE 1. Pediatric Autopsy–Milwaukee County Medical Examiner's Office

- Scene Investigation
- Complete dissection
- Full body radiographs
- Posterior midline neck and thorax incision
- Removal of eyes
- Complete toxicology
- Viral cultures
- Metabolic screen
- Multidisciplinary child death review

TABLE 2. Pathological Findings in Shaken Impact Syndrome

Primary:
- Retinal hemorrhages
- Subdural/subarachnoid hemorrhage
- Brain swelling
- Diffuse axonal injury
- Laceration of corpus callosum

Secondary:
- Rib fractures
- Metaphyseal fractures
- Contusions
- Cortical lacerations

is strongly recommended as a method to rapidly exchange information among agencies involved in investigating sudden deaths in children.

PATHOLOGICAL FINDINGS

The pathological changes noted during the autopsy examination are best understood as resulting from the primary effect of shearing injuries and secondary associated injuries. Injuries that are primarily due to the effects of shearing forces include subarachnoid and subdural hemorrhage, retinal hemorrhage, diffuse axonal injury, brain swelling, cortical lacerations and brain contusions. Secondary injuries associated with the shaken impact syndrome include rib fractures, contusions to the extremities, and cranial suture separation. Table 3 lists the injuries documented on eighteen consecutive cases of shaken impact syndrome at the Milwaukee County Medical Examiner's Office.

TABLE 3. Pathological Findings in 18 Consecutive Cases of Shaken Impact Syndrome–Milwaukee County Medical Examiner's Office

Mean age: 11.5 months **Types of injury**	
• Diffuse axonal injury	7/18
• Subdural hemorrhage	17/18
• Posterior intra hemisphere sudden hematoma	10/18
• Retinal hemorrhage	18/18
• Bilateral	16/18
• Unilateral	2/18
• Asymmetrical	4/18
• Skull fracture	6/18
• Scalp contusion	7/18
• Laceration of corpus callosum	10/18
• Remote injury (fracture, bitemarks, burns, malnutrition, etc.)	10/18
Mechanism of death	
• Shaking alone	6/18
• Blunt trauma associated with shaking	6/18
• Closed head trauma (probable shaking)	1/18
• Battered child syndrome with probable shaking episode	5/18

An impact to the infant brain is more likely to produce shearing injury. The under-developed myelination of the neuronal axons of the child's brain predisposes to laceration of long neurons. The infant skull also permits more rotation to the child's brain than an adult brain during acceleration-deceleration owing to the flat base and lack of well-developed fossae that typically hold the adult brain in place. As a result, an impact to the brain of a child is more likely to produce shearing injuries than the cortical contusions typically seen in the adult (Case, 2000).

RETINAL HEMORRHAGES

The presence of retinal hemorrhages is strongly suggestive of shaken impact syndrome. Retinal hemorrhages have been described in 70% to 80% of victims of shaken impact syndrome (Ludwig, 1984). The hemorrhages are bilateral in 80% of cases. The hemorrhages consist of a mixture of blot, flame-shaped, and smaller, pinpoint hemorrhages that involve the entire retina (Figures 2 and 3). The hemorrhages occur within all layers and are multi-layered

FIGURE 2. Normal appearance of infant eye sectioned horizontally above the optic nerve.

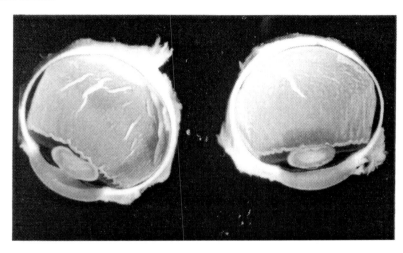

FIGURE 3. Retinal hemorrhages cover inner surface of retina in diffuse and peripheral distribution. Note flame and blot shape of hemorrhage.

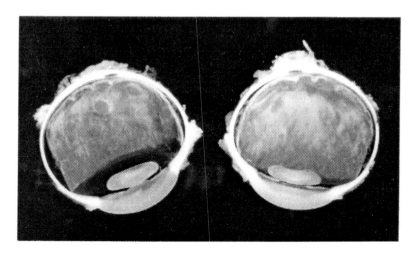

in the vast majority of cases. The significance of the asymmetrical distribution of the hemorrhage present in a small percentage of cases remains to be determined. The hemorrhages may also occur in the vitreous body. Subarachnoid and subdural hemorrhage is commonly present in the subdural space of the optic nerve which presents the strongest correlation with non-accidental injury (Figure 4) (Duhaime, Christian, Rorke, & Zimmerman, 1998). Other ocular injuries related to the shaken impact syndrome include macular folds and retinal detachment (Buys & Levin, 1992).

Gross examination of the eyes should be preformed in any case of unexplained or suspicious death of a child or in the presence of trauma. The eyes are easily removed by unroofing the orbital plate and cutting the conjunctival fold while applying gentile traction on the optic nerve. The eyes are fixed in 10% buffered formalin for a minimum of three days prior to examination. This allows for sufficient hardening of the globe for cutting. Internal examination of the retina can be performed by sectioning the globe in halves and visualizing the internal surface of each colote. Photographic documentation is best obtained by photographing the eyes while submerged in 80% alcohol on a black velvet background.

Microscopic examination of the retinal hemorrhage is important to further document the location of the hemorrhage and preserve the ocular evidence for

FIGURE 4. View of optic nerve demonstrating subarachnoid and subdural hemorrhage surrounding the nerve.

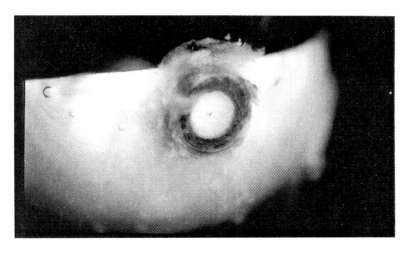

FIGURE 5. The retina overlying the fibrous sclera displays retinal hemorrhage. The hemorrhage extends throughout the inner and outer layers of the retina (insert).

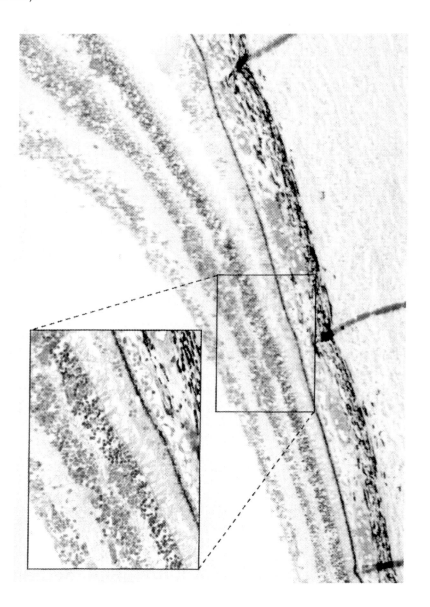

future examination (Figure 5). Because of the correlation of retinal hemorrhages with central retinal vein thrombosis, a cross section of the optic nerve should be included in the microscopic evaluation to exclude the possibility of thrombosis.

Despite the variability of the gross coloration and presence of positive iron staining for hemosiderin, dating of retinal hemorrhage currently cannot be obtained with precision. In our experience, the slight variation in the tinctorial qualities of retinal hemorrhages cannot be accurately used to interpret the time of injury. The use of microscopic iron-staining techniques to determine the age of these injuries is also unreliable and not sufficiently sensitive to support valid conclusions as to the exact time of the injury. Hemosiderin-laden macrophages may appear within a relatively short period of time (48-72 hours) and their presence cannot be interpreted as evidence of repeated episodes of trauma. The presence of positive iron staining in the eyes of abused children could be the result of residual hemorrhage during birth trauma and therefore should be interpreted with caution.

The pathogenesis and biomechanical mechanisms responsible for retinal hemorrhage are presently unknown. A possible mechanism includes an increase in intra-thoracic pressure in combination with traction and shearing of the retinal vessels. Retinal hemorrhages are present in 60% of infants following normal vaginal delivery. Most of these hemorrhages resolve in five to six days and all completely disappear by 14 days (Egge, Lyng, & Malta, 1981; Kaur & Taylor, 1992). Other causes of non-accidental retinal hemorrhage include bleeding disorders, increased intracerebral pressure, and central vein thrombosis. Some authors have attributed retinal hemorrhage to cardiopulmonary resuscitation, which is unsubstantiated. Most authors and practicing forensic pathologists agree that the presence of retinal hemorrhage associated with cardiopulmonary resuscitation or increased intracranial pressure is extremely rare and usually associated with prolonged assisted ventilation. In these cases, hemorrhages are pinpoint, not blot or flame-shaped. In Milwaukee County, after examining over 400 cases, we have seen only one case with unexplained retinal hemorrhage that consisted of a solitary petechial hemorrhage in a child on mechanical ventilation for hours following a negative initial examination.

SUBDURAL AND SUBARACHNOID HEMORRHAGE

Subdural hemorrhage is the most common acute intra-cranial injury present in the shaken impact syndrome. Although the quantity of hemorrhage is small (frequently less than 10 ml.) and does not usually result in a space occupying lesion, it provides a valuable marker of severe cranial injury. The hemorrhage is located in the dural space between the dura and subarachnoid membrane (Figure 6). Subdural hemorrhage is caused by laceration of the small bridging veins which span the dural space from the surface of the brain to the dura (Figure 7). Subdural hemorrhage that accumulates in the posterior inter-hemispheric fissure is generally acknowledged to be more common in cases of non-accidental trauma and characteristic of shaken impact syndrome (Sty, 1992). The antenatal CAT scan easily documents hemorrhage of this type. The pathologist should examine this area prior to removal of the brain to provide definitive evidence of the hemorrhage.

On gross examination recent subdural blood has a dark purple "grape-jelly" appearance (Figure 8). Acute hemorrhage may spontaneously dislodge from the cortical surface prior to becoming adherent to the dura. This process typically occurs in approximately four days. As the clot becomes organized, brown discoloration due to hemosiderin (iron) pigment begins to appear in one to two weeks. By two to four weeks a thin membrane begins to form over the surface of the clot. By six weeks, the clot has a thick, brown and black "motor-oil" quality. By eight weeks, the hematoma in completely encased in a

FIGURE 6. A schematic drawing of the coverings of the brain. The dura mater is adherent to the undersurface of the brain and lies superficial to the subarachnoid membrane and the pia mater that covers the neural tissue of the brain.

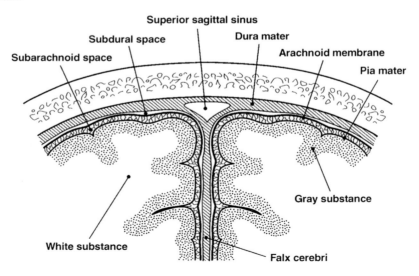

FIGURE 7. The delicate bridging veins traverse the subarachnoid space attaching to the meningeal vessels on the surface of the brain.

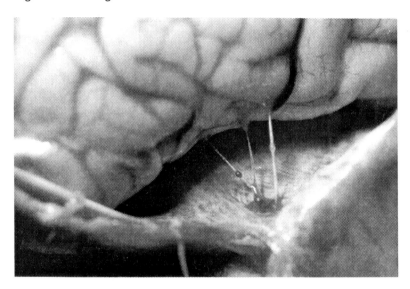

FIGURE 8. Subdural hemorrhage is adherent to the dura of the removed calvarium of an infant. Note the film-like thickness and characteristic "grape-jelly" appearance of a recent hemorrhage.

thick fibrous membrane. The chronic subdural hematoma appears as a rusty-brown membrane-like structure. There may be fusion of the cortical surface to the dura.

On microscopic examination, a recent subdural hematoma appears as simply clotted blood. Beginning in two to three days, fibroblasts on the dura swell and proliferate to form a thin membrane. By five days, a layer of fibrin and the layer of fibroblast are present. By ten days, red blood cells begin to degenerate and small capillaries begin to form on the outer edges of the clot. Highly vascularized granulation tissue develops over the inner dural membrane in two to four weeks (Figure 9). Eventually, depending upon the size of the hematoma, the membrane becomes a dense fibrous structure composed of hemosiderin-laden macrophages and connective tissue (Hirsch, 1990).

Subarachnoid hemorrhage is present to some degree in almost every case of shaken impact syndrome. The hemorrhage is located between the brain and thin subarachnoid membrane. Subarachnoid injury is caused by the same mechanism that results in subdural hemorrhage. Unlike the cortical contusions to the brain resulting from blunt force impact, the location and quantity of subdural and subarachnoid hemorrhage do not correlate to the direction, velocity, force, or site of the impact to the skull.

The presence of a chronic subdural hematoma has recently been used to explain the presence of acute subdural hematoma. The interpretation given by some implies that the recent hematoma is a result of a re-bleed following trivial trauma. Chronic subdural hematomas, however, typically occur in patients with low intracranial pressure and brain atrophy such as the elderly, alcoholics, or patients with hydrocephalus. Most pathologists agree that the thin subdural membranes that are found in children who do not have brain atrophy or have an intracerebral shunt are not at risk for rebleeding under any degree of trauma.

DIFFUSE AXONAL INJURY

Diffuse axonal injury is the most sensitive indicator of the acceleration-deceleration injuries sustained during a shaking episode. The presence of diffuse axonal injury is time dependent and its presence reflects the post-injury survival interval. During the course of the rapid angular and rotational acceleration, the long, poorly-myelinated axonal fibers tear. The resulting disruption of the axonal fiber impairs the transport of axoplasm that results in accumulation at the site of the tear, forming a bulbous enlargement. The axonal end develops the appearance of a retraction ball that can be visible by light microscopy on routine hematoxylin-eosin staining. The area of axonal injury corresponds to the regions of the brain under the most mechanical stress during angular accelera-

FIGURE 9. The figure depicts a chronic subdural hematoma. A thin layer of fibroblasts (above) covers the light colored space containing proliferating capillaries, fibroblasts and histiocytes. On higher magnification (insert) hemosiderin layden macrophages (arrows) cluster around blood vessels. Note the layer of fibroblasts that form the outer limit of the resolving hematoma.

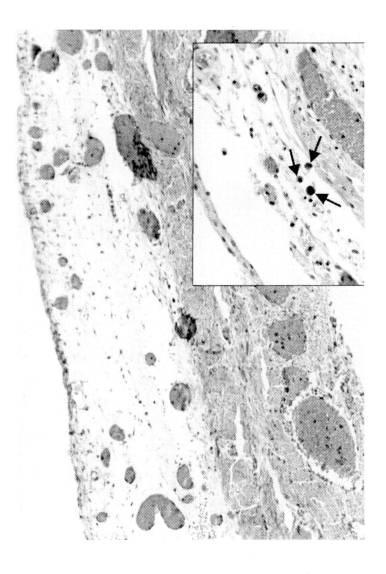

tion-deceleration. These areas are typically located in the subcortical–parasagittal white matter, corpus callosum, periventricular areas, and the dorsolateral quadrants of the rostral brainstem (Figure 10).

On microscopic examination, axonal swellings appear as eosinophilic bulbs on nerve fibers with hematoxylin-eosin staining (Figure 11). These lesions may not be readily visible microscopically until 18 to 24 hours following the injury. Additional sensitivity can be obtained using silver stains, which, in addition to the demonstration of retraction bulbs, can detect the subtle irregular beading of the axon which occurs with the accumulation of axoplasm.

The development of new immunohistochemical stains have greatly enhanced the ability of pathologists to detect diffuse axonal injury (Gleckman, Bell, Evans, & Smith, 1999; Grady et al., 1993). The development of ®-amyloid precursor protein (®-APP) has allowed for the detection of diffuse axonal injury in as early as two hours following the injury. The ®-APP staining currently is restricted to academic research centers, and the effectiveness of the stain cannot be determined until it can be widely commercially available to

FIGURE 10. A schematic illustration of a coronal brain section. The shaded areas represent regions where diffuse axonal injury is most likely to occur: the corpus callosum, preventricular white matter, and rostral brainstem.

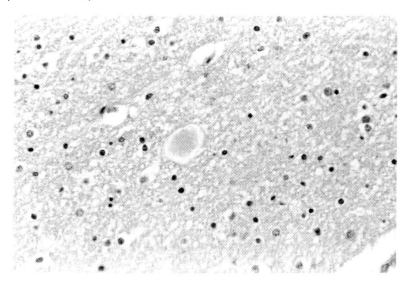

FIGURE 11. Microscopic view of retraction bulb in white matter region. Note the markedly expanded size and homogeneous appearance of the myelinated fiber.

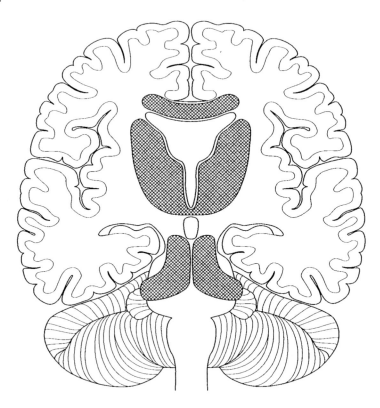

The crosshatched regions correspond to the areas of highest stress on shaken impact syndrome, corpus callosum, preventricular, and brainstem.

the forensic community. The absence of staining with ®-APP may occur for a number of reasons which include: survival time of less than two hours, lack of adequate cerebral blood perfusion, prolonged time period between injury and death, lack of adequate sampling, and the presence of other destructive lesions.

The clinical implication of the recognition of diffuse axonal injury is that there would have to be an immediate loss of consciousness. Lacerations of myelinated fibers deep in the periventricular and brainstem regions are incompatible with normal neurologic functions. These children can not survive for prolonged periods of time without supportive medical care. However, it is not currently possible to determine the exact time when the lethal injury was inflicted. The detection of diffuse axonal injury thus has considerable importance in the future evaluation of fatal child abuse.

CORTICAL CONTUSIONS AND LACERATIONS

In many instances, contusions or bruises caused by blunt force trauma to the scalp are not readily identifiable on external examination. Scalp trauma is often only identified after shaving of the scalp hair or reflection of the scalp and examination of the subgaleal region. The absence of a contusion or impact site does not preclude that there was an impact. For example, striking the head on a broad, soft surface may not result in an identifiable bruise at the point of contact (Graham & Hanzlick, 1997). In our experience, scalp contusions are identified in approximately one half of cases of shaken impact syndrome. Skull fractures are present in approximately one third of cases and typically are located over the posterior parietal bone. Fractures are considered strongly suggestive of non-accidental injury if they are complex (non-linear), depressed, cross suture lines, or have gaping dimensions of greater than one centimeter (Ludwig & Kornberg, 1992; Sty, 1994). Owing to the high water content of the brain, cortical contusions are rarely detected in cases of shaken impact syndrome. If present, these contusions are most commonly located on the orbital gyri that reflect the impact of the undersurface of the brain on the orbital plate of the skull.

Brain swelling or cerebral edema is a non-specific indicator of cell injury or death and a common finding in shaken impact syndrome. At autopsy, brain swelling is indicated by a tense or bulging anterior fontanel, separation of the cranial sutures, or brain herniation. As the brain becomes enlarged due to the increase in edema fluid, the brain is literally forced through the small foramen magna opening of the spinal cord canal. The compression of the respiratory and heart rate centers of the brainstem region of the brain and upper spinal cord by the cerebellum portion of the brainstem. This is the most common mechanism of death in the shaken impact syndrome.

MUSCULOSKELETAL INJURIES

In addition to injuries involving the brain and retina, many victims of shaken impact syndrome sustain injuries to the soft tissues and skeletal structures during an assault. These injuries are contusions and scratches that typically occur on the lateral portions of the chest. Contusions occur in this region as the child is forcibly grasped about the chest. The injuries may be subtle and not visible by external examination alone. The pathologist should carefully examine the anterior and posterior thorax for signs of injury. It is advisable to re-examine the body 12 to 24 hours after the initial autopsy for the presence of contusion. Contusions may become more apparent after drainage of the blood from the tissues. The extremities should also be carefully examined for superficial contusions. In sites where radiographs suggest the present of recent or remote skeletal injury, the area should be incised, examined, and fractured bones removed for examination with more detailed radiological and histological methods.

Dating contusions can be difficult. Recent bruises, as discussed above, may not be visible externally. Traditional teaching holds that a recent bruise appear purple-red in color (Wilson, Ochs, Peterson, Hamburger, & Bastian, 1989). After two to three days, a yellow color becomes evident as the red blood cells undergo degeneration into hemosiderin. By four to five days, the contusion develops a greenish hue due to accumulation of hematodin during the resorption of hemoglobin from degenerated red blood cells. Recent work has called into question the resolution of bruises in living children.

Hemorrhages into the soft tissues and epidural regions of the neck have been described in conjunction with the shaken impact syndrome. Our experience also suggests that epidural hemorrhage can occur artefactually without trauma. This is due to increased pressure applied to the venous drainage system of the internal vertebral plexus of veins and arteries contained in the epidural fat. However, this phenomenon is mostly restricted to the mid to high thoracic distribution. Our experience suggests that hemorrhage in the high-cervical epidural fat, subarachnoid hemorrhage, or hemorrhage into the soft tissue is strongly suggestive of a shaking episode. We recommend routine examination of the posterior cervical spine bone and soft tissues in suspicious child deaths.

RIB FRACTURES

Rib fractures are frequently present in children who have been shaken. The classic position of rib fractures associated with shaking impact syndrome is posterior near the articulation between the transverse process of the vertebral body and the rib tubercle (Figure 12). Radiographic visualization of injuries in this area is difficult to obtain on plain films. Radiologists, even under optimal conditions, can detect recent fractures in only seventy-five percent of cases

FIGURE 12a. Demonstrates rib fractures in an early state of repair. Note the sclerosis adjacent to the fracture site. The haziness and blurring of the fracture indicates early repair. The periosteal callous formation is not readily apparent (10 to 14 days).

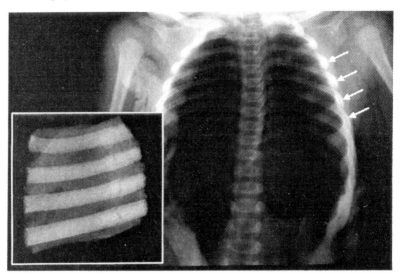

(Kleinman, 1989) (Figure 13). The position of these injuries is explained by the bending of the rib across a fulcrum created by the transverse processes of the vertebral bodies. Rib fractures are rare in the anterior or lateral position. Posterior rib fractures are not associated with cardiopulmonary resuscitation methods. In a review of skeletal surveys in 91 non-homicidal cases, Spevak, Kleinman, Belanger, Primack, and Richmond (1994) found no evidence of rib fractures in infants who had undergone cardiopulmonary resuscitation. In rare cases, we have encountered bending of the rib at the costo-chrondral junction that we interpreted as an association with resuscitation.

In our experience, healing posterior rib fractures are commonly seen in of shaken impact syndrome and indicate a prior shaking or injury episode. Rib fractures in infants heal more rapidly than similar fractures in adults. Protuberant periosteal callus formation allows the healing fractures to be more easily detected by the radiologist and pathologist at autopsy (Figure 13). Grossly recent fractures are accompanied by hemorrhage, which may persist for three to four weeks. The fracture may be only detected on manual palpation. During the course of repair, special connective tissue known as callus forms around the fracture site. The size of the callus does not appear to correlate with the age

FIGURE 12b. Rib fractures four to six weeks following the injury. Note the prominent callous formation, abundant sclerosis and lack of a discernable fracture, the result of endocortical and periosteal mature bone formation.

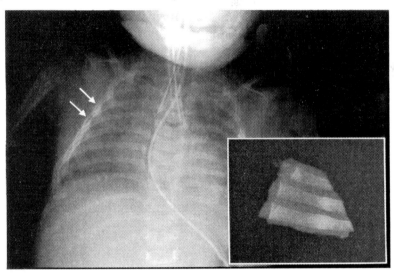

FIGURE 13. Recent fractures of the posterior perivertebral distribution are readily apparent using a posterior midline incision. Acute fractures may not be easily discernible by radiology alone.

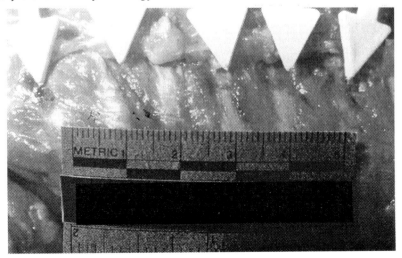

of injury but more with the amount of displacement of the rib fragments. Callus is generally palpable in seven to 10 days. We recommend that the pathologist manually palpate each rib for fractures following removal of the chest and abdominal organs. Our practice is to remove the fracture site to obtain more detailed radiographic images and microscopic analysis. Microscopic examination of the fracture site following decalcification of the bone allows for a more definitive determination of the age of the injury (Figure 14). New bone and cartilage is first microscopically visualized in four to five days following the injury (Table 4).

REMOTE INJURY OF SHAKEN IMPACT SYNDROME

In occasional cases where a moribund child has been resuscitated and maintained by mechanical means, the pathological findings of the initial assault may be altered or obliterated due to deterioration of the brain and resolution of the injuries. Unfortunately, the long delay in death frequently complicates the diagnosis of shaken impact syndrome. Cutaneous contusions resolve in days. Subdural and subarachnoid hemorrhage resolves and may only be identified by a honey-brown discoloration to the dura. The brain edema may resolve

TABLE 4. Gross, Radiologic, and Microscopic Landmarks in Healing Infant Rib Fractures

Landmark	Earliest appearance	Usual appearance
• Periosteal thickening	24 hours	2-3 days
• Medullary cell proliferation	24 hours	2-3 days
• Microscopic appearance of cartilage and new bone formation	4-5 days	7-14 days
• Radiologic appearance of new bone formation	4-5 days	7-14 days
• Palpable calcification in callus	10 days	2-3 weeks
• Microscopic bony union of fracture	18 days	3-6 weeks
• Solid uniting of fracture	4-6 weeks	6-10 weeks
• Disappearance of nuclei from necrotic bone fragments	1 week	2-4 weeks

R.E. Zumwalt and A.M Fanizza-Orphanos, "Dating of Healing Rib Fractures in Fatal Child Abuse" Advances in Pathology (St. Louis: Mosby Year Book, Inc., 1990)

leaving an atrophic or shrunken brain with dilated ventricular spaces. Retinal hemorrhages undergo resorption (Figure 15). Diffuse axonal injury may be difficult to identify due to the death of brain cells and resulting repair and cellular reaction known as gliosis. The resolution of injuries requires a diligent effort by the physician to document any and all injuries during life with photographs, detailed descriptions and drawings.

INJURY INTERVAL

Forensic pathologists are frequently requested by legal authorities to provide opinions regarding the interval between the injury and death. Estimates of the interval in fatal injuries relies on the clinical, radiologic, and autopsy findings. Clinically, infants who sustain eventually fatal head injuries most certainly develop immediate onset of symptoms (Duhaime et al., 1998; Williman, Bank, Senac, & Chadwick, 1997). In a prospective study of 76 fatal cases of head injury, Gilliland found that the interval of death was less than 24 hours in 80% of cases (Gilliland, 1998). Although the actual time of death may show some variability among victims of shaken impact syndrome, authors generally agree that in all cases where the child eventually died, the child would not have appeared normal, even to non-medically trained persons following the inflic-

FIGURE 14. Microscopic examination of the healing rib fracture four to six weeks following the injury. The fracture site is faintly discernible (arrows). There is evidence of endocortical and periosteal mature bone formation.

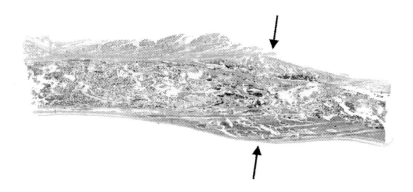

FIGURE 15. The shrunken brain of a victim of shaken impact syndrome three years following the injury. Note the dilated ventricles, "watershed-type" cortical necrosis and atrophic temporal lobes.

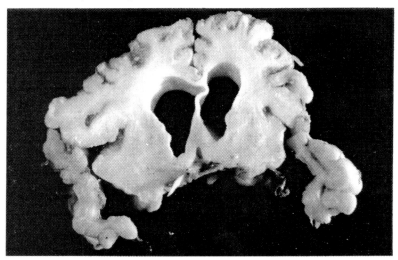

tion of the injury (Graham & Hanzlick, 1997). Radiologists can provide estimates of the interval by dating intracerebral hemorrhage and fractures. The presence of remote injuries, most commonly fractures, confirms the role of non-accidental injuries and provides the investigators additional information for the questioning of potential suspects. The pathological evidence for timing of injuries diminishes as the interval between injury and death increases. Gross examination of fractures and resolving injuries allows the pathologist to give opinions on the interval of the death. Microscopic examination of injuries for evidence of healing (inflammation, fibrosis, and vascularization) further enhances the precision in dating injuries.

Other less technical means can be of considerable assistance in determining the time of injuries. Evaluation of gastric contents may narrow the time frame since 4-8 oz feedings are normally cleared from the stomach in approximately two hours. Clinical information obtained from the scene may further aid in focussing the time of death. In our experience, children may sustain injuries in relatively brief periods of time when the perpetrator and victim are left alone.

CONCLUSION

The pathological evaluation of death due the shaken impact syndrome requires a detailed examination and documentation involving a complete investigation, autopsy, and correlation of findings. The investigation requires a multidisciplinary approach in which the pathologist needs to contact and interact with a myriad of investigators and may employ the use of experts in radiology, ophthamology, neuropathology and forensic pediatrics. Despite controversy over the exact mechanism of injury, the non-accidental nature of the classical injuries of shaken impact syndrome is accepted by almost the entire forensic pathology community. As detailed examinations and new investigative laboratory techniques allow for advances in the interpretation of injuries, the nature and mechanism of injuries sustained in shaken impact syndrome will become better understood.

REFERENCES

Alexander, R., Sato, Y., Smith, W., & Bennett, T. (1990). Incidence of impact trauma with cranial injuries ascribed to shaking. *American Journal of Diseases in Children, 144*, 724.

Buys, Y.M., Levin, A.V., Enzenauer, R.W., Elder, J.E., Letourneau, M.A., Humphreys, R.P., Mian, M., & Morin, J.D. (1992). Retinal findings after head trauma in infants and young children. *Ophthalmology, 99*(11), 1718-1723.

Caffey, J. (1972). On the theory and practice of shaking infants: Its potential residual effects on permanent brain damage and mental retardation. *American Journal of Diseases in Children, 124*, 161-169.

Case, M. (in press). National Association of Medical Examiners position paper on shaken infant syndrome. American Journal of Forensic Medicine and Pathology.

Duhaime, A.C., Christian, C.W., Rorke, L.B., & Zimmerman, R.A. (1998). Nonaccidental head injury in infants–The "Shaken-Baby Syndrome." *New England Journal of Medicine, 338*, 1822-1829.

Duhaime, A.C., Gennarelli, T.A., Thibault, L.E., Bruce, D.A., Margulies, S.S., & Wiser, R. (1987). The shaken baby syndrome: A clinical, pathological, and biomechanical study. *Journal of Neurosurgery, 66*, 409-415.

Egge, K., Lyng, G., & Malta, M. (1981). Effect of instrumental delivery on the frequency and severity of retinal hemorrhages in the newborn. *Acta Obstetrics and Gynecology of Scandinavia, 60*, 153-155.

Gilliland, M.G.F. (1998). Interval duration between injury and sever symptoms in nonaccidential head trauma in infants and young children. *Journal of Forensic Science, 43*, 723-725.

Gleckman, A.M., Bell, M.D., Evans, R.J., & Smith, T.W. (1999). Diffuse axonal injury in infants with nonaccidental craniocerebral trauma. *Archives of Pathology and Laboratory Medicine, 123*, 146-151.

Grady, M.S., McLaughlin, M.R., Christman, C.W., Valadka, A.B., Fligner, C.L., & Povlishock, J.T. (1993). The use of antibodies targeted against the neurofilament subunits for the detection of diffuse axonal injury in humans. *Journal Neuropathology and Experimental Neurology, 52,* 143-152.

Graham, D.I., & Lantos, P.L., (Eds.) (1997). *Greenfield's neuropathology.* New York: Oxford University Press.

Graham, M.A., & Hanzlick, R. (1997). *Forensic pathology in criminal cases.* California: Lexis Law Publishing.

Hirsch, C. (1990). Craniocerebral trauma. In R.C. Froede (Ed.), *Handbook of forensic pathology* (pp. 182-190). Northfiled, IL: College of American Pathologists.

Kanda, M., Thomas, J., & Lloyd, D. (1985). The role of forensic evidence in child abuse and neglect, *American Journal of Forensic Medicine and Pathology, 6,* 7-15.

Kaur, B., & Taylor, D. (1992). Fundus hemorrhages in infancy. Review. *Survey of Ophthalmology, 37*(1), 1-17.

Kleinman, P. (1989). Radiologic contributions to the investigation and prosecution of cases of fatal infant abuse. *New England Journal of Medicine, 320,* 507-511.

Ludwig, S. (1984). Shaken baby syndrome: A review of 20 cases. *Annals of Emergency Medicine, 13,* 104-107.

Ludwig, S., & Kornberg, A. (1992). *Child abuse: A medical reference.* New York: Churchill Livingston.

Randall, B.B., Fierro, M.F., & Froede, R.C. (1998). Practice guideline for forensic pathology. Members of the Forensic Pathology Committee, College of American Pathologists. *Archives of Pathology & Laboratory Medicine, 122*(12), 1056-64.

Spevak, M.R., Kleinman, P.K., Belanger, P.L., Primack, C., & Richmond, J.M. (1994). Cardiopulmonary resuscitation and rib fractures in infants: A postmortem radiologic-pathologic study. *Journal of the American Medical Association, 272,* 617-618.

Sty, J.R. (1992). *Diagnostic imaging of infants and children* (Vol. II). Gaithersburg Maryland: Aspen Publication.

Willman, K.Y., Bank, D.E., Senac, M., & Chadwick, D.L. (1997). Restricting the time of injury in fatal inflicted head injuries. *Child Abuse & Neglect, 21,* 929-940.

Wilson, N.W., Ochs, H.D., Peterson, B., Hamburger, R.N., & Bastian, J.F. (1989). Abnormal primary antibody responses in pediatric trauma patients. *Journal of Pediatrics, 115*(3), 424-427.

Chapter Twelve

The Medical Social Worker, Child Advocacy and the Shaken Baby

Jean M. Hudlett

SUMMARY. This chapter focuses on the medical social worker's role in the collaborative effort by the various professionals dedicated to identifying and treating cases of Shaken Baby Syndrome. Key topics include the interview with the attending parent or caregiver of the injured child, the nature of the information that is to be gathered from the interview, suggested techniques for the effective gathering of this information, and how to best advocate for the needs of the victim of SBS in a pediatric hospital. *[Article copies available for a fee from The Haworth Document Delivery Service: 1-800-342-9678. E-mail address: <getinfo@haworthpressinc.com> Website: <http://www.HaworthPress.com> © 2001 by The Haworth Press, Inc. All rights reserved.]*

KEYWORDS. Psychosocial, evaluation, support, family, home situation, interview

They bring us their babies, broken in subtle ways we can't explain. At that age they're so defenseless, so limited in strength and movement, they're virtually incapable of hurting themselves.

–Medical Social Worker (anonymous)

[Haworth co-indexing entry note]: "The Medical Social Worker, Child Advocacy and the Shaken Baby." Hudlett, Jean M. Co-published simultaneously in *Journal of Aggression, Maltreatment & Trauma* (The Haworth Maltreatment & Trauma Press, an imprint of The Haworth Press, Inc.) Vol. 5, No. 1(#9), 2001, pp. 225-236; and: *The Shaken Baby Syndrome: A Multidisciplinary Approach* (ed: Stephen Lazoritz, and Vincent J. Palusci) The Haworth Maltreatment & Trauma Press, an imprint of The Haworth Press, Inc., 2001, pp. 225-236. Single or multiple copies of this article are available for a fee from The Haworth Document Delivery Service [1-800-342-9678, 9:00 a.m. - 5:00 p.m. (EST). E-mail address: getinfo@haworthpressinc.com].

While no single profession claims child abuse and neglect as its sole field of practice, social work assumes the dominant role as its victim's protector. In this capacity, social workers have the legal responsibility and obligation to investigate and verify reports of maltreatment. As cases are confirmed, child protective services must develop and implement plans for intervention and treatment (Schene, 1996).

Recent history has brought us advances in medicine that make possible the ability to redefine certain pediatric injuries previously diagnosed simply as accidental and typical of childhood. That same injury today under the discerning eye of current medical technology is too often seen as only one in a series or history of injuries, possibly the result of non-accidental violence or trauma. In the past, as more of these suspicious cases were brought to light in hospital emergency units, the increasing caseloads requiring investigation gave rise to a team approach to cases of suspected child abuse. Over time this united front has become multidisciplinary, having added the participation of law enforcement investigators, legal representatives and the community's child protective service personnel to the hospital's medical team.

There is little doubt that while today's technologies save lives daily, they must also impose greater technical demands on the medical professionals who must know and understand them. This recent development has given rise to a practice by many hospitals to employ an in-house medical social worker as a case consultant to maintain comprehensive care and support for patients and their families. This chapter describes the specific duties and responsibilities of the medical social worker in a pediatric hospital in cases when shaken baby syndrome is suspected.

The social worker employed in a hospital environment needs to have a practical knowledge of the medical aspects, terminology and language relative to clinical pediatrics. He or she will confer and coordinate activities with hospital physicians, medical and technical staff; and act as hospital liaison with law enforcement investigators and child protective service personnel. Most importantly, the medical social worker will serve as an advocate on behalf of the child and family in the child welfare and health systems.

ROLE OF THE MEDICAL SOCIAL WORKER

Social work is the only profession practicing in health care that examines roles, relationships and resources, and their impact on life. Consequently, social work assessments are critical in identifying psychosocial factors that affect health care interventions. Whereas the hospital assessment necessarily assumes a medical model which tends to view abnormal behavior as the result of sickness or disease, the social model views behavior as the result of learned experiences and environmental conditions (Cayner & Jensen, 1993). These two assessments with their separate and distinct principles are used in conjunction and applied to cases of child abuse and provide a more balanced and comprehensive approach to the process of assessing the individual needs in each case and prescribing the appropriate treatment and follow-up.

Of all the duties and responsibilities the hospital medical social worker assumes, the one unifying principle upon which all decisions are based asks: "What is best for the child?" And in those cases where the victim is an infant and shaken baby syndrome is suspected, that pronouncement is profoundly critical. For here is a tiny victim, helpless, purely innocent and most deserving of justice and sadly unable to give witness to his or her own brief life's experience. Everything the social worker will research, observe, gather and take into account and analyze will culminate in an assessment that will set into motion the plans and process that will best reintegrate the broken child.

ASSESSMENTS

Great care must be taken when making the determination of abuse. The consequences of incorrect assessment may result in the victim's return to the source of trauma and the resumption of abuse (Alexander, Crabbe, Sato, Smith, & Bennett, 1990; Levy, Markovic, Chaudry, Ahart, & Torres, 1995). Conversely, a careless or loosely based assessment may cause irreparable damage to a whole family by the unwarranted removal of a child from its nurturing and rightful place.

Avoiding such tragedies demands careful and thorough reporting. Suspicious evidence uncovered by the medical staff must be considered along with the infant's medical history including the details of family and home environment. This collateral information is gathered by the medical social worker whose interviews with parents and caregivers will combine with all other findings to form the basis for an assessment that will affect the future of the victim and family.

INTERVIEW

Interviewing where shaken baby syndrome is suspected has special considerations. When a case of suspected abuse involves a child with even rudimentary verbal skills, statements obtained from the injured child may be compared with accounts obtained from others. This situation can find the abuser in the untenable position suspiciously at odds with the injured and typically presumed innocent child. This device, though effective when it's known that a child is able to testify, is sadly unavailable when the victim is an infant. While the notion of an adult brutalizing an infant is so intrinsically abhorrent, the abuser without this witness becomes increasingly difficult to identify. Obtaining the critical information and wisdom needed to process cases where helpless infants are severely injured presents one of the most difficult challenges in the career of a child advocate.

Shaken baby injuries are not usually witnessed and not necessarily obvious. Because its early symptoms are common to many infant disorders (fever, vomiting, lethargy, etc.) shaken baby syndrome is seldom readily identified, and parents who bring their child to the hospital believing their baby is sick are shocked when violence is considered a possible cause. While sickness might be socially accepted as inevitable, injury will insinuate careless or neglectful parenting. Parents can feel very defensive if they hadn't considered that their child's condition might have been inflicted. We certainly want them to understand that we are looking at all possible explanations. But when the tests show no blood disorders, no metabolic problems and no evidence of organic illness, we have to consider the possibility that their child may have been injured or hurt.

For the medical social worker preparing for the interview, it is a time to reconcile within oneself the often seemingly disparate definitions of what it means to be a professional and what it means to be human. Clearly the dispassionate focus distinguished by the medical social worker is essential for separating an account from a confused parent under stress versus a confusing account from an abuser under cover. While literature on the interview stresses the importance and technique of control, the effective interviewer as child advocate will demonstrate to the parent or caregiver a willingness to forego control when compassion is in the best interest of their child (Sattler, 1998).

While the interview may provide medical personnel with information vital for the victim's immediate survival; the same interview may provide law enforcement and child protective services with information equally vital for the victim's protection and future well-being. The gathering and reporting of information to the appropriate team, however, is not to be confused with doing their work. This precaution is especially pertinent for the medical social worker when information is useful to law enforcement investigators. For example, it may suddenly become apparent to the medical social worker, yet unbeknown to the person being interviewed, that this may be the person who has injured the child. And while it may be tempting to pursue this suspicion, it is not in the best interest of the child and, accordingly, is not the mission of the child advocate. In this case, the social worker who exposes his or her suspicions may be denied information critical for the child's survival. Instead, the child's advocate will note his or her suspicions and later notify the rightful authorities.

Shortly after an infant is admitted into the hospital emergency unit, the medical social worker will schedule an interview with the parent or caregiver that brought the child to the hospital. Prior to the interview, the infant's medical history will be reviewed and admitting medical personnel will be consulted regarding the nature of the infant's symptoms to identify any subject areas to be explored in the interview. This preparation will also convey to the parent a sense of concern on the part of the hospital and its staff. Finally, if there is a language barrier, a hospital translator will be scheduled.

In general, the medical social worker will begin the interview with two major objectives. The first matter will concern the immediate activities in the emergency room. Questions will be concise, direct, non-leading and convey a calm sense of urgency while emphasizing the importance of any information that may be useful to the attending medical personnel for their diagnosis and treatment of the infant. The attentive medical social worker will listen for any descriptions or language used by the parent to describe his or her baby's condition prior to admission that may indicate injury or trauma. Seemingly typical infant behavior like irritability or crankiness may be symptomatic of injury resulting from some trauma, and ordinary back-arching behavior in healthy babies might in fact be convulsive.

Second, if the parent or caregiver is guilty or has knowledge of foul play, the urgency of recent events may have preempted any collaboration or opportunity to prepare for anticipated questions. And while it's not the direct purpose of the medical social worker to exact a confession from a perpetrator, information obtained in the interview that may help identify an abuser should be discretely noted and reported.

For the skilled medical social worker, the initial questions will set the tone of the interview, and once underway, subsequent questions will derive from the information as it is gathered. Behavior and responses may indicate the individual's level of comfort with speaking and the nature of the questions. For example, a parent may appear distressed while following a line of questions that refer to their child's present circumstances in the nearby emergency room, other questions about their child in the context of less stressful circumstances may elicit a more relaxed response. This technique of leaving and later revisiting a potentially relevant area of questioning may confirm the sensitivity of that subject if the parent's uneasiness is again exhibited (Sattler, 1998).

These sensitive areas uncovered during the interview are very powerful and require special consideration. They may be uncomfortable for reasons that are personal, though unrelated to present circumstances. Conversely, they may have ties to abuse in the parent's own childhood and must not be overlooked.

Bear in mind these vulnerabilities were uncovered in the context of trust and deserve respect. Any subsequent questioning along the same lines as those that may have opened this seemingly painful area must be carefully orchestrated. Questioning that becomes too aggressive will suddenly convey to the unsuspecting parent the feel that the interview has become an interrogation or that they are being wrongfully suspected. If left unchecked, this will likely jeopardize the trust of the person interviewed and any rapport and candor developed to that point might be suddenly lost.

On the other hand, these same probing questions asked in the presence of a perpetrator may appear to provoke a similar response, which is masking a fear of discovery. In either case, these delicate areas are not to be ignored but rather explored with great care if it's considered critical or necessary to help the infant. If, however, subsequent attempts to reintroduce the subject are met each time with agitation or resistance, excursions into this area should be curtailed and noted in the assessment, perhaps to be explored more aggressively by others.

Apart from issues of criminality, the effective medical social worker proceeds with the interview assuming the parent or caregiver may have information that will help medical personnel understand the cause of the child's present condition. Indeed, this is the time to dispense with any direct or implicit accusatory or incriminating language. Questions posed in the context of working together and enlisting the help of the parent to determine how it happened is more effective than matters related to blame. This is the time to provide comfort and assurance, thereby enabling the parent to focus on the child. The intent here is to evoke the voices of the parents themselves, to elicit their stories, and to generate knowledge from the inside out (Beebe, 1993).

At the onset of the interview, it is important to introduce oneself, establish rapport and in calm, non-threatening terms underscore the serious and urgent nature of the interview. Generally, a medical social worker is viewed as an authority figure and job titles in these circumstances may inhibit open and free disclosure. It is important to try to make clear that one is employed by the hospital to assist parents when their children are ill. It is the job of the medical social worker to take part in the child's assessment in order to understand what has happened and assist the health care team in caring for the infant.

Following these preliminaries, questions are asked to address the baby's history, the details or occurrence of symptoms, changes in health, and the specific events just prior to admission. While this is often a repeat of the questions a parent will have been asked on admitting the infant, sufficient time will have lapsed allowing an opportunity for him or her to reconsider earlier responses or recall additional information or observations.

Questions are best framed in non-specific terms. For example, one may ask the parent if there is anything they may have thought of that can help us identify the problem or what he or she saw when they first noticed something was wrong with their baby. Any information relative to "What is the matter with the child?" may be helpful to the immediate concerns of the attending medical staff. "How did it happen?" addresses the mechanics causing the injury and may be useful in the final assessment. Without the mechanism causing the injury, assessing plans for the future safety of the infant are incomplete since there is no assurance that the injury will not be repeated. Whether or not such information is forthcoming, this first order of the interview serves to inform the parent that the child's immediate concerns are the first priority.

After searching for urgent information, the medical social worker will shift the emphasis to the other objective of the interview: the victim's background and environment. Here the parent may enjoy some respite insofar as this shift is off the subject of his or her child in crisis. However slight this change of subject may be will depend on the quality and circumstances of the infant's brief psychosocial history. Whereas information needed by emergency medical personnel will have been obtained from answers to key questions directly stated, questions at this next juncture of the interview are less interrogatory.

By this time, a relationship between the medical social worker and the parent will have been established. To the extent that the medical social worker has developed trust and understanding, this aspect of the interview will be open to the discussion of the child's world, the people who populate it and the episodes and events of his or her life. As an active listener, the inquirer will guide the interview with sensitivity and interest (Kadushin, 1997). The effectiveness of the medical social worker is often in terms of his or her level of neutrality–avoiding interruptions, with occasional pauses to think about what may have been said. Any questions to be asked will be in words sensitive to the parent's level of understanding.

Though this may seem a more relaxed period, the medical social worker will remain vigilant and recognize that these are still sensitive circumstances requiring questions that are no less sensitive or personal. Nor will this be lost on the parent or caregiver being interviewed. If the intention of the first part of the interview is to gather important, time-sensitive information for the attending physician, the objective of the second part is to identify underlying factors that may hinder the return of the infant to a safe environment.

In cases of suspected Shaken Baby Syndrome, the interview places the social worker in an environment charged with emotion. Parents who are shocked, bereaved or angry may cry uncontrollably, be highly anxious or emotional, and potentially violent. Compounding this, the purpose of the interview is to open to scrutiny matters that are very personal in their lives. Any question posed under these circumstances, however neutral or carefully framed, may be perceived as offensive, incriminating or insulting.

For the medical social worker, managing a crisis situation in an interview begins by recognizing the early signs of danger and applying appropriate pre-emptive techniques to deter its escalation. Besides content, the attentive interviewer will give equal consideration to the parent's physical and psychological demeanor in response to questions. These observable cues may reveal early signs of difficulties (Langsley & Kaplan, 1968).

Several techniques are suggested. Conduct the interview at a distance that is both considerate of the parent's personal space as well as the interviewer's personal safety. This will minimize tension and enable the person being interviewed to relax and speak freely. If the person interviewed becomes nervous or agitated, note the conditions or context just prior to the behavior, perhaps it was something said or implied, maybe it was a change of subject. Try a different or previous subject or fall back to a more general line of questioning. While direct eye contact is otherwise an important component in the interview, it should be used cautiously for its tendency to provoke or invite a challenge. If the individual challenges your position, training or policy, redirect his or her attention to the issue of their child's welfare. Attempting to answer these questions often fuels a power struggle. If the individual becomes belligerent, defensive, or disruptive, state limits and directives clearly and concisely.

Choose your words carefully and use them sparingly. Ambiguous words or medical jargon may be misunderstood and saying too much increases the likelihood of miscommunication. Often what the interviewer not say may be more effective than what is. Build your interview based on language that worked earlier in the session. Remain calm rational and professional. How you respond will directly affect the individual. Speak in moderate, even tones being aware not only of what you say to the person being interviewed, but how you say it. Inattention or failure to listen actively can signal a lack of concern. Only a small percentage of the messages we deliver are in the words. Keep your non-verbal cues non-threatening; hand gestures using clenched fists and desk thumping for emphasis are counter productive. Be aware of your body language, movement and tone of voice. The more an individual loses control the less he or she listens to your actual words, focusing instead on your nonverbal cues. So, when interviewing parents or calming an unstable or volatile situation, how the words are delivered are as essential as the words themselves.

Be alert to physical, behavioral changes, i.e., pacing, staring, fidgeting. Opening up communication at this point can be effective. Simply asking, "How are you feeling?" or, "Can I help you with any questions or concerns?" can often diffuse increasing anxiety in the parent. Above all, remember the child and have the courage to be focused and non-threatening in what can be a threatening situation.

ASSESSMENT AND FOLLOW-UP

Following the interview, the medical social worker will prepare a report from the notes and observations gathered during the interview. This report and a report from the medical department representing their findings and recommendations will be forwarded to child protective services who will then draw up the conditions for the treatment, placement and discharge of the infant and to law enforcement, if investigation is warranted.

In preparing this report, the medical social worker will be responsible for the assessment of the information he or she has gathered. The document must be complete with the details relevant to:

- the victim's and family's biological and psychosocial background;
- the particulars relative to the caregiver prior to and at the time of the injury;
- the caregiver's history of abuse as a child;
- the aspects of the injury;
- the history of injuries, and
- any delay in seeking medical attention for the victim.

Keep in mind that a child advocacy assessment may become part of the documents that the court subpoenas to evaluate the need for foster care or to decide who should get custody of the child. Under these circumstances, the content of the assessment and the care and accuracy with which it has been written could have long-term implications.

EXAMPLE OF COMPREHENSIVE ASSESSMENT REPORT (LUKAS, 1993)

Patient Identifying Data

NAME, DATE OF BIRTH, DATE: (on which you wrote or dictated the assessment).

Also the author's title and signature must be included at the end of the document.

In the narrative form the following questions will be addressed:

Presenting Problem

- When did the caregiver first notice the child was ill or injured?
- What exactly did they observe?
- What did they believe caused the illness or injury?

- Who was with the child at the time of the injury or when the child first appeared ill? (Cover as much time as necessary up to several days.)
- What was the child's health and activity level for the same period up to the time of illness?
- Does the child attend day care?

Household Description

- Who constitutes the family of origin?
- What are the parents' names?
- What is their marital status and employment history?
- Where does the child live?
- Who else lives there?
- What are the names and ages of other siblings?
- Who are the caregivers?

Historical and Developmental Data

- How is the child's health?
- When was the last time a physician was seen and for what reason?
- What is the child's developmental level?
- Are immunizations up to date?
- Prenatal and postnatal history?
- Has the child been hospitalized or treated for prior injuries or illness?
- If so what treatment was needed or what caused the injuries?

An assessment and plan should be written in narrative form, stating whether or not there is any suspicion of abuse requiring notification of child protective services or law enforcement personnel. Assessment should include a description of the parent's demeanor and overall levels of cooperation and concern.

Meanwhile, the primary focus of the child's medical and developmental needs continues. The role of liaison between the hospital and the child protective service agency is an ongoing function and yet another aspect of the child advocacy role. Referrals for the child and parents will be made and services for the medical care of the child must be coordinated. The post-injury medical needs of the SBS child are often complex and call for careful planning prior to discharge from the hospital. Additionally, referrals and resources will likely involve developmental programming, nursing home health care, in-home therapy services, primary pediatrician and referrals made as appropriate for state, county, federal insurance programs and Social Security benefits, as well as supportive services for the parents and families. In the case of the injured child who dies during hos-

TABLE 1. Social Work Skills Needed to Evaluate SBS

- Knowledge of child abuse and neglect and the State's regulations about reporting cases of child maltreatment

- Knowledge of medical, psychiatric and child development evaluative procedures pertinent to the area of child maltreatment

- Ability to conduct a comprehensive biopsychosocial assessment

- Skills in crisis intervention and grief counseling

- Ability to identify, co-ordinate, and utilize community resources to engage and mobilize family coping strengths

- Ability to educate professional staff and community providers regarding psychosocial factors and family responses to medical treatment

- Written and oral reporting skills

pitalization, the social worker would extend bereavement counseling, support and, as needed, notification of in-hospital or community clergy.

MEDICAL SOCIAL WORK

Whether the individual seeking a career in child advocacy is a social worker or a student in a social work curriculum, specific competencies will be required. A degree in social work and postgraduate work with medical competencies to include specific field experience in a hospital or clinical setting is recommended. Additionally, interpersonal skills will be required to communicate and consult with medical personnel, law enforcement agents, CPS (Child Protective Service) workers as well as interviewing a variety of people including parents, relatives and caregivers potentially guilty of child abuse. Within this context, some specific competencies associated with the hospital child advocacy role include those listed in Table 1. With these skills and dedication to the needs of children, the medical social worker can play a unique part in the multidisciplinary evaluation of the shaken baby and fulfill their historic role to support families in crisis and advocate for helpless children.

REFERENCES

Alexander, R., Crabbe, L., Sato, Y., Smith, W., & Bennett, T. (1990). Serial abuse in children who are shaken. *American Journal of Diseases of Children, 144*(1), 58-60.
Beebe, L. (1993). *Professional writing for the human services.* Washington DC: National Association of Social Workers Press.

Cayner, J., & Jensen, G. (1993). Discharge Planning Update, 13(3), 8-14.

Kadushin, A. (1997). *The social work interview: A guide for human service professionals* (4th ed.). New York: University Press.

Langsley, D.G., & Kaplan, D.M. (1968). *The treatment of families in crisis.* New York: Grune & Stratton.

Levy, H.B., Markovic, J., Chaudry, U., Ahart, S., & Torres, H. (1995). Reabuse rates in a sample of children followed for 5 years after discharge from a child abuse hospital assessment program. *Child Abuse and Neglect, 19*(11), 1363-1377.

Lukas, S. (1993). *Where to start and what to ask: An assessment handbook.* New York: W. W. Norton.

Sattler, J. (1998). *Clinical and forensic interviewing of children and families.* San Diego, CA: Jerome M. Sattler, Publisher.

Schene, P. (1996). Child abuse and neglect policy. In J. Briere, L. Berliner, J. Bulkley, C. Jenny, T. Reid (Eds.), *The APSAC Handbook on Child Maltreatment* (pp. 385-397). Thousand Oaks, CA.

Chapter Thirteen

Law Enforcement Investigative Issues

Michael Vendola

SUMMARY. The criminal investigation in the Shaken Baby Syndrome must remain objective and gather all available information to establish what occurred, whether multiple abusive incidents are involved, and the party(s) responsible. The four cornerstones of investigation are (1) medical and pathological findings, (2) recording the scene and the lawful seizure of evidence, (3) background investigation, and (4) statements, interviews and interrogations of witnesses and suspects. The criminal investigator is in a focal portion in that he/she is also responsible for chain of custody of evidence, documentation and collation of relevant facts and providing assistance to the prosecutor in evaluation cases for trial. *[Article copies available for a fee from The Haworth Document Delivery Service: 1-800-342-9678. E-mail address: <getinfo@haworthpressinc.com> Website: <http://www.HaworthPress.com> © 2001 by The Haworth Press, Inc. All rights reserved.]*

KEYWORDS. Law enforcement, police, criminal interrogation, background investigation, scene examination, timeline, battered child syndrome

[Haworth co-indexing entry note]: "Law Enforcement Investigative Issues." Vendola, Michael. Co-published simultaneously in *Journal of Aggression, Maltreatment & Trauma* (The Haworth Maltreatment & Trauma Press, an imprint of The Haworth Press, Inc.) Vol. 5, No. 1(#9), 2001, pp. 237-262; and: *The Shaken Baby Syndrome: A Multidisciplinary Approach* (ed: Stephen Lazoritz, and Vincent J. Palusci) The Haworth Maltreatment & Trauma Press, an imprint of The Haworth Press, Inc., 2001, pp. 237-262. Single or multiple copies of this article are available for a fee from The Haworth Document Delivery Service [1-800-342-9678, 9:00 a.m. - 5:00 p.m. (EST). E-mail address: getinfo@haworthpressinc.com].

The leading cause of death among abused children is head injury (Billmire & Myers, 1985). Violent shaking of an infant or young child, with or without impact, will be referred to as Shaken Baby Syndrome (SBS). These unfortunate incidents occur in all segments of society, irrespective of sociodemographic status. The criminal investigator must remain objective and not form any early opinion as to the person(s) responsible for inflicting the trauma. There is real injustice in an incomplete investigation. SBS incidents are tragic, but that tragedy is doubled when an innocent person is unjustly accused. An incomplete investigation may forever prevent identification and prosecution of the perpetrator. A multidisciplinary team with specific areas of expertise and timely communication is ideally suited for SBS cases.

The police investigation of an SBS episode must answer the questions of who, what, when, where, and why. This is no easy task, for the incidents are rarely witnessed, the victim is usually non-verbal, and there are few outward signs of trauma. The four cornerstones of a thorough SBS investigation are (1) the medical and pathological findings, (2) recording the scene and surroundings, and the lawful seizure of evidence, (3) the background investigation, and (4) the statements, interviews, and interrogations of witnesses and suspects.

THE MEDICAL AND PATHOLOGICAL FINDINGS

To optimally perform their work, it is important for the investigator to know the signs and symptoms associated with shaken baby syndrome. The typical injuries of SBS include subdural hematomas, subarachnoid hemorrhage, cerebral edema, and retinal hemorrhages (Brodeur & Moneleone, 1994; Smith, 1994). Infants can be grabbed and shaken in a variety of ways. Victims may be tightly held and squeezed by the ribs, legs, shoulders, neck, etc. A heavier child may be straddled while lying on the floor. There may be other less prominent injuries consistent with SBS, including bruising on the victim's outer body surfaces left by the perpetrator's fingertips and rib fractures from grabbing and squeezing the victim's torso. The rapid acceleration-deceleration of the head may occasionally cause vertebral compression fractures, upper cervical cord contusion, anterior vertebral notching, or spine dislocation. In a violent shaking incident, the infant's limbs flail about resulting in fractures. In moderate and severe shaking episodes, the airway protective reflexes are compromised and vomitus may be aspirated into the lungs. Other observable symptoms associated with SBS include bulging and/or spongy forehead, extreme irritability, vomiting, photophobia, poor muscle tone/increased lethargy, breathing irregularities, poor sucking or swallowing, high pitched cry, no smiling or vocalization, rigidity, arching and posturing, inability to lift head, inability to focus eyes and track movement, and unequal size of pupils (Brodeur & Monteleone, 1994).

Severe cases resulting in fatal outcomes involve a rapid progression of symptoms immediately following the shaking episode. These symptoms frequently include vomiting and respiratory impairment, followed by seizures, progressing to coma, then death. Depending on the type of medical intervention, some symptoms can linger for several days or weeks before they die. Some victims have presented with an impact injury to their scalp or face, other body surfaces, or a skull fracture (Bruce & Zimmerman, 1984; Duhaime et al., 1987). In these cases, not only are the victims shaken, they are forcefully released and propelled at great speeds, causing them to suffer the injuries discussed above, if a hard object is struck. Even if the victim strikes a soft object (sofa, mattress), the forces generated on impact can cause additional cerebral bruising, shearing, and bleeding (Duhaime et al., 1987). Knowledge of this potential scenario can assist in a more clear understanding of the mechanisms causing the injury and can alert the investigator as to what to expect in interviews.

The symptoms of SBS need to be known for several reasons. The classic symptoms of SBS (subdural hematoma, retinal hemorrhages and associated long bone fractures) are diagnosed by medical staff. The onset of these and other symptoms may be determined by careful interviewing, thus aiding to establish a time frame within which the shaking occurred. Secondly, earlier studies have shown that SBS symptoms have been initially misdiagnosed in as many as 31% of the cases reviewed (Jenny & Hymel, 1999). The misdiagnoses occur when a caretaker's explanation is accepted without scrutiny, the scene is incompletely investigated, and medical staff do not include SBS as a possible cause of symptoms. An investigator who recognizes the gamut of SBS symptoms and altered infant behaviors is in a more qualified position to suggest SBS as a causal mechanism to medical staff.

Investigators should consider the use of the following key questions for witnesses:

- Did the victim's eye track objects (explain and demonstrate what tracking means)
- Did the victim exhibit an unusual forced, high pitch or whiny cry?
- Did the victim exhibit breathing difficulties?
- Was the victim irritable for unusually long periods of time (depends on the infant's routine)
- Did the victim vomit? How many times over what time frame?

- Did the victim have seizures or exhibit posturing (arched back, rigid limbs)?
- What are the normal feeding habits? How did the victim feed most recently (with amounts consumed)?
- Did the victim become lethargic (easily confused with napping, illness, coma)?

In fatal incidents, there should be coordination between the investigator and the medical examiner's office. The chain of custody of the body must be maintained, for it is the most important piece of evidence. The investigator who accompanies the body can later testify that it was not altered in transportation. The investigator should furnish details of the scene, background information, and victim history to assist the pathologist in establishing the cause and manner of death. The autopsy should be performed by a forensic pathologist familiar with pediatrics. A complete forensic autopsy will not only help in establishing a cause and manner of death, but will eliminate other causes and identify other pre-existing medical conditions. Protocols should be followed which include preservation of specimens, toxicological testing, radiographs. Hair and blood samples from the victim may be necessary for comparison with possible trace evidence at the scene. In addition to skull, brain membrane, and brain substance examination, microscopic samples from multiple brain areas should be obtained to determine if diffuse axonal injury (DAI) is present (Perloff, 1998). The victim's outer body surfaces should be reexamined about 24 hours post-mortem, after blood has drained, for skin blanching indicative of bruising or other trauma. Photo-documentation and injury diagrams are needed to supplement the pathologist's report. If there is no evidence of skin bruises/contusions to outer body surfaces by the naked eye, trauma sites may be photographed using long wave ultraviolet (UV) light and an 18A filter. Imaging of bruising (usually fingertip marks) may be possible. This procedure applies to fatal and non-fatal cases. Short wave UV light can damage retinas, but long wave UV light poses no additional health hazards (Krauss & Warlen, 1985).

While the investigator may not have physical custody of the victim's blood samples, tissues, microscopic slides, etc., it is the investigator's duty to know the location, chain of custody and security of the items. In nearly all cases, the autopsy will be completed before the investigation. The continuing investigation is facilitated by a careful balance of what information is put on the death certificate, as well as when the death certificate is filed. It may be advantageous to list the manner of death as "pending" and the immediate cause of death as "sudden death-pending investigation." An amended death certificate can be filed after the critical phases of the investigation are completed. This is a guideline which can be adapted to the particular investigation.

SCENE INVESTIGATION AND SEIZURE OF EVIDENCE

The second cornerstone of a thorough SBS investigation is recording the scene and the lawful seizure of evidence. If a caregiver called 911 for emergency services, the original tape should be seized as evidence. Copies can be made and scrutinized. The caregiver's statements on the 911 call should be compared to subsequent caregiver statements. Are there other voices or background noises on the taped call? Does this information conflict with the caregiver's original account (presenting history)? Upon arrival at the scene (usually a dwelling), the investigator should lawfully conduct a search of the premises. Lawful searches include consent searches, search warrant services, and exigent circumstances searches. In most cases, caregivers are provided the option of endorsing a consent search. Many "consent to search" forms contain a blank line designating statutes violated and a verbal description of the crime suspected. The investigators should not cue the caregiver by inserting words and phrases clearly specifying the seizure of incriminating evidence of a possible child abuse/homicide offense. Instead, the investigator should list generic terms, i.e., searching for "items" regarding the "incident," "occurrence," "accident," etc. The investigator can do this in good conscience since, at this stage, the investigation is far from complete. Most caregivers will consent to a search.

While the consent search is executed, the investigator should document those activities and comments, which show the consent was given voluntarily and the caregiver was not in a custodial setting. The caregiver's freedom to move about, carry on household functions, or even leave the premises should be noted. Bathroom breaks, phone calls, cigarette smoking, obtaining food or drink, and taking medication all show the caregiver's freedom.

Careful consideration must be given to scene control, which necessitates several officers. There may be multiple scenes (e.g., the dwelling and an outdoor swing set), multiple caregivers, visits from family and significant others, siblings and other children, and media presence. Maximum scene control means minimal scene contamination. The scene is very likely to have been altered prior to the arrival of the investigator. Caregivers may have attempted resuscitation efforts, moved items, or attempted to stage the scene. EMT personnel, other investigators, or the coroner/medical examiner may have had contact with the victim and/or moved items. Careful interviewing will assist in the best possible reconstruction of the scene.

Small children are frequently overlooked at crime scenes. Youngsters are often frightened by the commotion at the scene, assume they did something wrong, go play somewhere else, or seek refuge with an adult. When the adults are asked who was present, they may not include the children's names because they think small children do not pay attention, the adult wants to spare the children, or the adult is fearful that the children will explain what they really observed. For all of these reasons, those children who can verbally communicate should be individually interviewed as soon as the scene is controlled. This maximizes the children's recall, minimizes confabulation from what they may hear later, and may aid in preventing rehearsed statements as instructed by caregivers. The children should be interviewed by CPS workers or officers familiar with juveniles in a coordinated fashion, away from caregivers, who may ultimately become defendants. These procedures involving children are an integral part of the scene control.

The scene should be recorded and scaled in four formats: schematic diagram, Polaroid or other instant film, 35mm film, and videotape. The schematic diagram integrates each floor and provides a top view of the relative positions of objects inside the dwelling. The Polaroid or other instant film provides immediate images for investigators doing follow up and for prosecutors assisting in those cases with rapid developments. The 35mm film provides detailed clear shots of specific areas and close ups as needed. The videotape is an eye level integration of the whole dwelling. All rooms (including closets) and all floors (including basement and attic) should be imaged. What at first seems like extraneous detail may prove to be the evidence which discredits a presenting history or negates an alibi.

It is nearly impossible for the responding officer to remember all relevant details. The use of a standardized death scene checklist is highly recommended, whether the scene involves fatal or non-fatal trauma (Michigan Public Health Institute, 1998; Missouri Department of Social Services, 1998). Special emphasis should be placed on areas/items involved in impacts. If the accidental fall explanation is provided, record the distance between the surface from which the child fell to the floor. Note any carpet, carpet padding, etc., where the child was alleged to have fallen and obtain samples of same.

The investigator at the scene should also collect everything in the immediate vicinity of the reported trauma. The investigator should search for and seize evidence of a triggering incident—the final, frustrating event which culminates in an explosive loss of control manifested in a shaking episode. The three most common triggering incidents are inability to control infant crying, feeding difficulties, and toileting issues. The triggering event may be very trivial and less common, such as the 29-year-old California man who fatally shook his girlfriend's toddler who blocked his view of a televised football game (Showers,

1994). Evidence of the triggering incident may consist of vomitus, colic, messes or spills, soiled diapers, splattered food, medication and administration procedures, monitors or devices for a special needs child, etc. The scene examination should include trash containers, laundry chutes and bins, and areas outside window wells. A suspect may hastily discard items in a location he/she hopes will be overlooked. A garbage examination may also provide evidence of stressors in a caregiver's life. A discarded job layoff notice, a bank statement listing NSF checks written, coupled with a crying infant, may culminate in a shaking episode. Knowledge of the possible stressors in the caregiver's life provides themes in subsequent interviews. What may be unpractical to seize (living room sofa, kitchen table, wall-to-wall carpet, flooring, or a wall) should be measured and scaled, with manufacturer name, identification number, and model being recorded.

Finally, a thorough scene examination should include seizing, or at least recording, medical and health care documentation. Pediatric child care books, baby books, journals, prenatal and postnatal records, medical assistance cards, physician and pediatrician names, public health nurse and volunteer agency visits, Lamaze classes, etc., attest to the general health of the child and knowledge of the caregivers. Photographs and videotapes of the victim show the child's appearance and developmental abilities. The investigator will save him/herself considerable time and work by recording/seizing this information while at the scene.

Whether at the scene, ambulance, or medical facility, the investigator should seize all medical devices and paraphernalia disposed of by EMT personnel. This may also include clothing cut away from the victim. If the child was on medication, seize all medicine containers and contents. The follow up investigation must determine if the medication was administered as prescribed, altered, substituted, or withheld, and if the pharmaceutical labels are identical to the pills, capsules, or liquids within medicine containers. Baby bottles, formula packages and baby foods should be seized and examined in a similar fashion. This not only rules out adulterants but also rules out other causes later offered to explain/complicate the victim's present condition.

The investigator usually has one opportunity to view the scene and surrounding area. This is also the best time to obtain written consents for release of the victim's medical records. Once obtained, the consents should be presented forthwith to health care providers for immediate compliance, as the consents can be revoked at any time. The suspect caregiver becomes less cooperative as the investigation intensifies. The thorough scene investigation maximizes the collection of data and evidence, helps to reconstruct the most accurate account of what really happened, minimizes defense options, and presents a more clear and understandable picture in court.

BACKGROUND INVESTIGATION

The third cornerstone of a thorough SBS investigation is the background investigation. Obtain the victim's complete and certified copies of medical records of the present hospitalization, including lab reports, imaging studies (CT, MRI, bone scan, skeletal survey), nurses' notes, discharge summaries, and photos taken by the hospital. Several nurses and physicians may have worked on the victim, with one nurse and one physician composing a written report. Other medical personnel who provided care should be interviewed for their impressions, especially if they had contact with caregivers and the victim's family. The nurses' notes are excellent sources of information detailing interaction and comments made by caregivers. Next, the complete medical history of the victim should be examined. These records are used as an objective base line of chronologizing the health of the child. Medical experts can then be consulted concerning the victim's pre-existing conditions, and whether those conditions impact on the SBS diagnosis. These records will detail whether appointments were kept, immunizations were obtained, and any incidents of earlier trauma. Prenatal questionnaires and polling forms sometimes yield startling results. The author is aware of fatal SBS cases wherein the previously pregnant mother stated the pregnancy was unwanted, placed a big stress on the family, or was the direct cause of marital discord. This may be one underlying motive for the SBS episode, and certainly provides another theme for subsequent interviews.

The investigator needs to determine the normal activities of the victim in the weeks prior to the SBS episode diagnosis, but especially 96 hours immediately prior to presentation, in order to frame the abusive event. This itinerary includes all people with whom the victim had contact. The victim's 96-hour schedule and routine combined with primary caregiver access may lead to a viable suspect. The victim's last 96 hours cannot be overemphasized, for the people who had contact with the victim are either (a) witnesses who can attest to the victim's behavior, including the onset of symptoms or (b) the defendant(s). Parents, day-care providers, baby sitters and close relatives can be rich sources of information. These people see the victim on a regular basis, clothed and unclothed. Not only can these witnesses help frame the SBS incident, but they may also identify symptoms of prior abusive incidents.

The investigator needs to know the developmental abilities of the victim. Answers to specific and detailed questions show what is normal and abnormal behavior for the victim. The Denver II Developmental Screening Test (DDST) (Frankenberg et al., 1990) involves a series of examinations and tests to assess personal-social, fine motor-adaptive, language, and gross motor skills for children from birth to six years of age. The DDST lists the typical age range these skills are developed and can help the investigator form a host of detailed questions.

The background investigation should be as comprehensive as possible in order to learn about suspects, their relationships, and their behaviors. A suspect with prior social service agency contact is a great source of information. A suspect or suspect's significant other on parole/probation will have a corrections file rich in information. Military records, employment records, welfare records, divorce files, and insurance records and claims should be identified and searched. Sheriff's department, police department, and social service agency records in previous and present areas of residency should be checked. Neighbors, former neighbors, friends, relatives, ex-spouses, and former significant others should be interviewed. These background sources may identify alcohol and drug involvement and degree of impairment, stressors, relationship dynamics, anger control and tendency toward physical violence, witnessing of prior abusive acts, educational and functional level, and coping strategies. The investigator must know as much as possible about the suspect. The background information provides interview/interrogation themes and may reveal "other crimes" evidence[1] (Appendix A).

Information about the victim may hold clues to his/her victimization. The victim may be the wrong gender desired by the parents. The victim may be the offspring of a failed relationship, and a constant reminder of that failure. The victim may be the last and unwanted child, and is perceived as dependent, may cry more frequently, and may need additional soothing. Through no fault of the child may present conditions that frustrate the caregiver, thereby making them susceptible to being abused.

Another valuable source of leads is long distance and local telephone detailing records. Subpoenas can be obtained for land-line and cellular phone companies to provide phone exchanges, connect times, and duration for both incoming and outgoing calls from the suspect's phone(s). The subpoenas should bracket several days on either side of the SBS episode. Follow up interviews of conversant parties may yield excited utterances about the SBS event, delays in seeking medical attention, different presenting histories, requesting medical advice from friends, etc. The final area of background information involves compiling data when a charged suspect claims total ignorance, misunderstanding of the damages of shaking, or shaking done in a panic situation. From repeated reviews of criminal cases, to include post-verdict juror polling and judges' sentencing comments, the above claims have been accepted as a valid or mitigating defense. In addition to the background sources previously cited, the following will assist in determining caregiver responsibility in SBS episodes:

a. What is the educational level of the caregiver? The higher level of education, the higher degree of responsibility.

b. Were childcare, nutrition and child development taught in the caregiver's school curriculum? Was the caregiver in attendance? What does the caregiver's teachers remember about the caregiver? What grades were received? Similar questions could be used for any support groups attended by the caregiver.

c. What type of prenatal care was sought? What type of information was provided? Did the parents follow medical advice? Did the expectant parents keep all scheduled appointments?

d. Were special needs identified after birth in the postnatal visits? What information was provided? Did the parents obtain needed immunizations or prescriptions? Did the parents keep their appointments?

e. Were parents involved in community programs such as "Right Start," "Healthy Start" or receive Maternal/Infant Support Services? What topics were covered and what information was provided?

f. Was any family member receiving nutritional supplements such as WIC, food stamps? What information was provided?

g. Did the caregiver receive any pamphlets, brochures or other material concerning proper childcare or Shaken Baby Syndrome?

h. Did any visiting nurse, public health or volunteer visiting program visit the family? What information did they provide? What was their perception of the family?

i. Did the caregiver have prior contact with fire or emergency services? What were the circumstances of those calls? What did third party professionals observe upon arrival at the scene?

j. Was there a history of "hospital shopping" or "doctor shopping"? Are there multiple visits not reported on medical insurance records? "Hospital shopping" is an intentional series of acts to conceal the complete medical history of the victim, and/or is an attempt to seek the least scrutinizing health care professional.

k. Are any of the caretakers on probation or parole? Are there stipulations regarding parenting classes or contact with children? Anger control? Did the caregiver attend?

l. Does the caregiver have current or prior Social Service contacts? What course of action occurred? Did the caretaker follow through with recommendations?

m. Did the caretaker exercise reason and common sense in child care and supervision? In other non-child related areas?

n. Was the caregiver provided information concerning proper child care? Was the caregiver asked if he/she read the printed material? Did other volunteer or church groups provide any assistance or health care items to the caregiver? What do the volunteers recall about the caregivers and the victim care?

o. Examine billing records for medical assistance cards and insurance policies purchased by the caregiver. Who is the insurance carrier, and what are the conditions for a beneficiary payout?

INTERVIEWS AND INTERROGATIONS

The fourth cornerstone of a thorough SBS investigation is the statements made by the caregivers. These include the initial accounts (presenting history), interviews and interrogations. One cardinal rule must be followed by the investigator during questioning: the investigator must never suggest an injury mechanism. If the presenting history involves a caregiver reporting an impaired or unconscious infant, the investigator can generally ask what, if anything, was done to revive the child. If the suspect admits to shaking the victim, the investigator must continue through the entire shaking episode, for there is frequently additional head trauma when the child is forcefully discarded. Knowing this combined mechanism allows for a clear presentation of facts to the jury, and removes the defense contention that the head trauma responsible for the child's death was not shaking.

The investigator must press onward. Two aggravating factors are the time delay between the SBS episode and seeking medical attention, and what the perpetrator did within that time frame. The investigator should seek out this information. The timing and nature of the presenting history can have grave consequences for the victim. After an SBS episode has occurred, the perpetrator often delays in seeking medical attention. This is done for two reasons: (1) the perpetrator has the false hope that the body will heal itself over time and (2) the perpetrator wants to distance himself from the abusive event. A perpetrator will sometimes wait for a spouse/significant other to arrive home, whereupon both adults and victim proceed to the hospital emergency room, only to have the non-offending adult provide a hearsay history. The history provided by the perpetrator is usually false in that the shaking is omitted, or grossly minimized.

It is the investigator's job to gather and compare all of the presenting histories, comparing 911 calls with accounts provided to emergency medical technicians, medical staff, emergency room nurses, police officers, spouses, relatives, friends, insurance agents, co-workers, and other relevant parties. Is the presenting history consistent with medical findings? Is the same presenting history provided to the aforelisted parties? Does the presenting history change after medical staff suggest non-accidental trauma to the caregivers?

After the SBS diagnosis is made and the perpetrator learns of the severity of the trauma, does the perpetrator change the presenting history and offer a more traumatic mechanism? Once SBS is diagnosed, medical, rescue, and social service disciplines must be cautioned not to be confrontational with the caretaker. This cuts off the flow of information once hostility is perceived and saddles those disciplines to a function for which they are not trained. Often the perpetrator will reverse the true order of events. The perpetrator may allege the victim had difficulty breathing, experienced seizures, etc., at which point, he/she shook the child in an effort to revive the victim. This explanation fails to explain the cause of the respiratory failure or seizures. The medical diagnosis of SBS, absent any presenting history of trauma, is also an inconsistent explanation of events. It is inconsistent because SBS is severe trauma. Caregivers who are responsible for and in the presence of infants cannot be unaware of at least some form of trauma offered as a causal mechanism.

The investigator should be cognizant of social dynamics. In the situation where the victim is shaken, there may be an abusive relationship between husband-wife or boyfriend-girlfriend (battered woman syndrome). If the male caregiver is the primary suspect, the spouse/girlfriend may initially provide a discrepant history. This false history is usually caused by a combination of fear and dependence of the male caregiver, the lack of a support system, and ignorance about available resources (Brodeur & Monteleone, 1994).

The initial, detailed statement of caregivers is instrumental in solving SBS crimes. The investigator must interview the caregivers with empathy, patience and in a totally non-accusatory manner. The information can be obtained in various interview formats. One format is a simple question and answer interview where the investigator takes notes. The interviewer pays scrupulous attention to detail and asks supplemental questions. The interviewee, answering questions from a subjective viewpoint, will provide incomplete answers–answers, which incorporate additional pieces of information and contain conclusions. The investigator must sort this out and clarify the information. After the information is obtained, the interviewer should repeat the answers back and allow for corrections, clarifications and additions. The goal is to "lock in" the interviewee to a detailed statement.

Near the completion of the interview, the investigator should ask about behavior shaping and coping mechanisms. Then the investigator should ask what the caregiver does when the coping mechanisms do not work. The investigator may be surprised at the responses. Exact words and phrases used by the caregiver may show masking the onset of symptoms or minimizing his actions. In one case, the suspect was the son of a physician whose father operated his own clinic. The suspect's mother was a registered nurse. The suspect clearly indicated medical knowledge over and above the average citizen, and went as far to correctly state some symptoms of head trauma. This suspect, providing care for his girlfriend's child, claimed the child fell out a crib and impacted a hard plastic toy. The suspect said the child was "soothed," put down for a nap, and then exhibited irregular breathing, with "yawning and sighing," and "arms held out." The suspect attempted to revive the child by "gentle shaking," and makes seven references to shaking the child, who subsequently expired. This suspect was attempting to mask a seizure the victim experienced, and the gross underestimation of "gentle shaking" was clearly refuted by clinical presentation and subsequent autopsy findings.

An extension of the simple interview format is a written statement taken by the interviewer. Some investigators prefer to have the interviewee write their own statement. The writer has found this to be ineffective after a lengthy interview. The interviewee is fatigued, and a handwritten statement omits relevant details. A better procedure is to have the interviewer write out a statement, simultaneously verbalizing what he/she is writing. The interviewee then reads each page, initials each page, and makes corrections, additions, and deletions. At the end of the written statement, the interviewee is encouraged to write anything else the interviewee feels is important. If possible, the veracity of the statement should be sworn to under oath. This further "locks in" the witness. If any of the information was falsified, the groundwork has been set for impeachment on the witness stand, with possible charges of false swearing, perjury, etc. One could also use a question/answer format, which is simultaneously recorded by a transcriber.

The investigator may wish to use a different technique, called "statement analysis," as an aid to screen for veracity (Adams, 1996). This process is used with adult witnesses and is not valid for young children. Witnesses/suspects are asked to detail, in a written statement, what they did the entire day from the time they woke up until the time they went to bed. This technique should be used prior to any interview so that the witness/suspect provides a subjective but untainted account. The technique is not an end in itself but a tool to secure a confession. The analysis involves parts of speech (pronouns, nouns, verbs), extraneous information, subject matter omitted, lack of conviction, and balance of statement. The writer is aware of two SBS cases where statement analysis provided by the FBI, Behavioral Science Unit, Quantico, Virginia has greatly assisted the investigation.

In those presenting histories where a caregiver is directly involved in a purported accident with the victim (e.g., the caregiver, carrying the child, fell on the stairway), the caregiver should be allowed to re-enact the incident. Allow the caregiver to physically show what happened without interruption. The investigator can then go over the re-enactment in detail, paying close attention to events and actions occurring simultaneously. It is difficult to lie in three dimensions. Later scrutiny of the account may reveal highly improbable body contortions, unnatural body movements, actions that are inconsistent with the laws of physics and mechanisms that are inconsistent with the nature and severity of the injuries. When possible, the re-enactment should be done where the accident was alleged to have occurred and under the same conditions. Apart from the plausibility of the alleged accident, the investigator should attempt to verify whether those conditions and objects existed as the caregiver described.

Other visual aids and props should be used to most accurately record the caregiver's version of the event. If the caregiver indicates roughhousing, shaking, or other motor activities with the child, the explanation will be greatly facilitated by providing a plastic or rubber doll (not a cloth doll) approximately the same size as the victim. In one Wisconsin case, an investigator provided a "Resuscitation Anne" doll to a suspect who clearly demonstrated how he shook the victim (who subsequently died). The doll can be a fantastic investigational tool. The doll is not animated and quickly becomes depersonalized from the suspect. Use of the doll more specifically demonstrates the suspect's version of events.

The most demonstrative reenactment is the videotaped interview. This may be impractical or ill advised during the early stages of the investigation because it may place the caregiver in a defensive posture. Not only is the videotape a permanent record, but it may alert the caregiver he/she is becoming a suspect. The use of the videotape is best reserved for the interrogation phase.

In different cases, the investigator may wish to have the caregiver repeat the account, or expand on portions of the original account. Multiple interviews should be spaced over a minimum of several days. So as not to unduly arouse caregiver suspicion, the investigator can always return on the premise of providing case update information. Multiple interviews test the consistency of the account. Again, the investigator should refrain from being accusatory.

THE SUSPECT

As the investigation progresses, it will usually focus on a single suspect. The last phase in taking statements is the formal interrogation. Prior to any interrogation, the investigator must be thoroughly familiar with the suspect's role, background, those portions of earlier statements which may have been refuted, and the medical evidence. The investigator controls the environment, provides Miranda Warnings if suspect is in custody, and uses the element of surprise. It is most advantageous if a second investigator(s) can monitor through a one-way glass and feed questions and comments through a concealed ear microphone. The suspect still must be treated with respect and the rapport must show sympathy. No incriminating admissions will be made unless two conditions are met: (1) the suspect must be allowed to express his actions in a manner morally acceptable to him and (2) the suspect believes the interrogator understands him. The suspect must be allowed to rationalize and minimize his behavior. The investigator can facilitate this by suggesting various themes and strategies (Walsh, 1999). SBS cases involve attempts to control the child's behavior, and reckless behavior, but rarely is there an intent to kill. Verbalizing this position will aid in eliciting incriminating admissions.

Some interrogation themes and strategies are:

a. Tell the truth and be fair to yourself and the victim. It will relieve your conscience and get the matter behind you, so that you can get on with your life.
b. Your conduct was a freak occurrence. This was an isolated incident and would never happen again, right?
c. This was your first mistake. We all make mistakes, right?
d. You never did this to a child before. You won't do it again, right?
e. You didn't mean to hurt the child, you were only trying to discipline him/her to not be spoiled. You only did what you thought would be good for the child, right?
f. Children are fragile and you don't know your own strength. You weren't trying to hurt the child, just stop him from crying.
g. Could you benefit from counseling? What behaviors should counseling discourage?
h. I bet you were physically disciplined/abused as a child. That's what you learned, isn't it? I know you didn't intentionally mean to hurt anyone.
i. I've checked your background and what you have done is not like you. If it wasn't for the alcohol/drugs you wouldn't have done it/lost control.
j. If the suspect has unrealistic expectations of the child, use this theme. This was the third time he urinated on you while you changed him. He didn't do that for his mother . . .
k. I need your account of what happened. Without your honest account, I am left with no alternative but to present this to the prosecuting attorney. Your side of the story may provide some mitigating circumstances.

There are various tools, which can aid in getting the suspect to elicit admissions. Bring the investigative folders or the "file." A thick, divided, and labeled file shows how much investigating was done, the thoroughness of which leads to the conclusion that the suspect was responsible. Another document is a draft of an unsigned criminal complaint. Allow the suspect to read the probable cause section and tell him this document or similar facsimile will be publicly filed without the benefit of the suspect's account contained therein.

If the suspect begins to make admissions, the investigator can build on these and flush out a more honest account. This may take several hours but, by this time, a good rapport has probably been developed. This is usually a prime opportunity to suggest a videotaped re-enactment, probably the most damaging piece of evidence. It is a confession permanently recorded, eliminating any claimed investigator bias. Cases with videotaped confessions are most always settled without trial.

INVESTIGATION DYNAMICS

SBS investigations are multi-disciplinary in nature, and each discipline hopefully knows their roles. Criminal investigators must carefully review the reports from rescue personnel, emergency room services, pediatric intensive care units and medical specialists. Investigators often do not know or understand medical terms, procedures, abbreviations and physicians' writing styles. Investigators ask many detailed questions, and the rescue and medical professionals may feel their actions are being scrutinized. This is an incorrect impression. The investigator simply wants to understand what was done. If the investigator is conducting a detailed interview with health care professionals who seem reserved or decline to give opinions, he should clear up this misunderstanding. It is absolutely necessary that the medical records and diagnosis be easily understood. While there are many reasons why an SBS prosecution fails, a major cause is the failure to reduce complex medical evidence, sometimes introduced through a variety of experts, to terms that lay persons (jury) can understand (Parrish, 1998).

Another important interdisciplinary link is between the police investigator and the social service agency. A victim's family with prior social service involvement yields a rich history of information. The investigation should be jump-started by accessing the social service file. Joint child protective service-police investigation teams have another advantage. Caregivers are more apt to provide information to social workers whom they view as less threatening. Social service agencies have the power to remove siblings from an unsafe home environment whether or not there is probable cause to make an arrest. If an abusive adult relationship dissolves, it is a social worker who finds out first. The remaining caretaker may now have the courage to tell everything she knows.

Police documentation must be diligent, complete, and timely. An investigation and prosecution takes weeks, months, and sometimes years to complete. From a practical standpoint, information that is not documented does not exist, for it is not retrievable. It is neither realistic nor fair to expect the prosecution to recall undocumented information verbally relayed to the prosecutor months later. The investigator should be familiar with all state laws designed to aid child abuse investigations. Two important features are in place in most states. First, there are no privileged communications between spouses in matters of child abuse/death. Secondly, many states have a "failure to protect" provision. A relative and sometimes an unrelated adult assuming caregiver responsibility has a presumed duty to protect the child. The non-offending relative can be criminally charged for failure to protect the child when the relative observes, or reasonably believes, the child is in imminent danger of abuse or needs immediate medical attention. Delay in seeking medical attention coupled with false information presented to EMS and hospital staff shows the caregiver acted with criminal recklessness.

One of the most significant exhibits in a SBS investigation is the "time line," a chronological synopsis of events prior and subsequent to the SBS episode. The time line is a graphic display, which dovetails with medical evidence. All SBS incidents are serious and potentially deadly. Some incidents are classified as being mildly symptomatic, with non-specific symptoms easily confused with other causes. The "mild" incidents are the most unrecognized, most underdiagnosed and most difficult to prove. Moderate incidents present with noticeable symptoms that may or may not be immediately manifested.

Severe incidents present with immediate loss of consciousness as well as other well-defined symptoms. The time line simply and graphically pulls together the core of the investigation findings, corroborated by the medical evidence. Although it may synopsize a wealth of data, it is easily understood by investigators, prosecutors, and the jury. The time line is a standard tool used in SBS cases (see Appendix B).

Since many SBS investigations span over a period of weeks or months, the investigator must maintain a rapport with suspects and witnesses. The investigator's professional demeanor must be maintained, even when he knows who the future defendant may be. Every opportunity to speak to the suspect is another occasion to obtain inconsistent statements. These are golden opportunities to strengthen the case. This leads to another cardinal rule: do everything reasonable and legal to keep the suspect talking. Periodic review of the early evidence (initial statements, 35mm photos and videotape of scene, 911 tape) may reveal minor details that are now inconsistent with the greater volume of information obtained through the course of the investigation.

A child may be the victim of a singular shaking episode, multiple shaking episodes and/or other forms of abuse. The Battered Child Syndrome (BCS) identified by Kempe, Silverman, Steele, Droegemueller, and Silver (1962) is the collection of injuries sustained by a child as a result of repeated mistreatment or beating. BCS evidence is recognized by a landmark case, Estelle v. McGuire (1991) and is admissible to prove intent, absence of mistake or accident, and identity. The case is significant for SBS investigations and prosecutions in that:

a. BCS "exists when a child has sustained repeated or serious injuries by non-accidental means . . . Evidence demonstrating BCS helps to prove a child died at the hands of another and not by falling off a couch; it also tends to establish that the 'other,' whoever that might be, inflicted the injuries intentionally" (116 L.Ed.2d 395-396).

b. "When offered to show that certain injuries are a product of child abuse rather than accident, evidence of prior injuries is relevant even though it does not purport to prove the identity of the person who might have inflicted the injuries" (116 L.Ed.2d 396).

c. "The proof of battered child syndrome itself has narrowed the group of possible perpetrators to the (defendant) and his wife . . . Only someone who is regularly 'caring' for the child has the continuing opportunity to inflict these types of injuries; an isolated contact with a vicious stranger would not result in this pattern of successive injuries stretching through several months" (116 L.Ed.2d 400).

Under Estelle v. McGuire guidelines, the meticulous and painstaking details of the investigation bear fruit. A variety of past injuries are admissible against the defendant provided the defendant had the opportunity to have caused them.

There are three ways to determine what happened to the child: (1) the background history, (2) medical diagnosis, and (3) autopsy. Police investigators have the most time consuming assignment and most ground to cover by obtaining everything they can from the background investigation. Simply put, SBS cases are circumstantial, and they are successfully prosecuted when investigators learn all of the circumstances. The investigator's briefcase contains a plethora of forms. SBS adds the child death scene checklist, medical records release form, consent to search, and child developmental ability assessment.

The media is replete with examples of very old child deaths originally believed to be accidental, SIDS or unexplained that are re-examined and ruled non-accidental SBS. Perhaps over the course of time, a trusted friend, relative or other third party received hints, admissions, etc., concerning those deaths. If the suspect is unaware of a renewed investigation, the third party (under police supervision) may be able to place a tape-recorded phone call to the suspect. If admissions are made, the suspect can be interrogated to secure a full confession. Admissions of criminal culpability on tape are powerful evidence.

AFTER THE ARREST

The police investigation does not end with the arrest of the suspect. Follow up interviews of witnesses, interviewing defense experts, constructing demonstrative exhibits, and background checks of potential jurors and defense experts are pre-trial tasks assigned to the police investigator, especially if there is no investigator working directly for the prosecutor's office.

A review of the case file presents interesting opportunities to present demonstrative evidence. In one case, investigation revealed that a disabled toddler, in presence of witnesses, fell out of a department store shopping cart falling 38 inches, landing head first on a concrete floor and sustaining nothing more than a simple bruise. Several months later the same child, according to the sole adult baby sitter, supposedly (and ironically) fell 38 inches, the distance from crib railing to the padded, carpeted floor, landed on a plastic toy, and sustained massive subdural hematomas, retinal hemorrhage, global brain swelling, and subsequently died! This comparison was part of the evidence to demonstrate the typically benign outcome of the first short fall when contrasted against the catastrophic consequences of the (alleged) second short fall. A black and white photograph of a cold metal shopping cart was contrasted against the victim's crib, decorative sheets, soft mattress, and blanket. This visual comparison helped refute the baby sitter's presenting history.

In another case, a foster father alleged he was holding a 16 month old child at the top of an uncarpeted wooden stairway, whereupon he crouched down and arched backward to pick up a second toddler. The father, demonstrating contortional movements said the 16 month old fell out of his arms, struck his head on a wall, and fell down the stairway. Careful, detailed interviewing when compared to the near fatal outcome (the child lost approximately one third of his brain mass and is severely disabled) revealed an inconsistent history. The same child had evidence of an older healed subdural hematoma and three healed long bone fractures. Exact measurements of the stairway pitch, composition, step size, width, and railing were obtained. The purpose was to reconstruct the stairwell and use a scale model stairwell at trial. Whether or not the defendant takes the witness stand, the investigator can then demonstrate the near absurdity of the defendant's body movements, which, by his own admissions resulted in an approximate three foot short fall. This case is pending as this chapter goes to press.

A final example of demonstrative evidence is an extension of the time line, contrasted by a parallel line. The parallel line uses the same chronology and ratios as the time line, but the parallel line contains only those statements and actions of the defendant. The time line lists witnesses and actions who show the child in an apparent healthy state followed by onset of symptoms, supplemented with medical findings and outcome. The time line is a consistent progression of events by third party witnesses. The parallel line lists the defendant's times and alleged observations and activities and ends with a delay in seeking medical attention. Either the third party witnesses and health care professionals have concocted an elaborate conspiracy or the defendant is lying and is responsible for the trauma.

If a case proceeds to jury trial, all states have some provision for allowing the investigator to assist the prosecution in the courtroom. The investigator sits beside or in immediate proximity to the prosecutors, aptly named "second chair." At this point in the case, the investigator relinquishes control to the prosecutor. The prosecutor decides how to prosecute, and the investigator facilitates this by his/her extensive knowledge of the facts in the case. The investigator, and ultimately the prosecutor, must look at the totality of the investigation and conclusions that can be drawn. There remain some cases that are not prosecutable, and some prosecuted ones that result in not guilty verdicts. This does not mean the abuse did not occur, nor should the detailed information gathered by the investigator go to waste. The investigator should continue to work with social services, child protection workers, guardian ad litems, and civil attorneys. If there is an unidentified perpetrator in a household, the environment remains potentially abusive.

The remaining and potential future children need to be protected. If there is an identified but unconvicted perpetrator, every effort should be made to keep him/her away from children. There is one category of SBS perpetrators that pose the most serious threat to children. That category is the perpetrators who deny they did anything wrong and/or denies the gravity of their actions. This is, purely and simply, anger denied. Anger in denial is anger uncontrolled. Anger uncontrolled is destined to manifest itself in the future. Given the high probability that the perpetrators will parent other children and have access to additional children, there is the high probability an SBS episode will be repeated. Therefore, it is imperative for the investigator to take a proactive stance in tracking these individuals and doing everything within their legal authority to sanction/restrict/deny contact with children. This frequently means the investigation must be kept open, or even expanded, to convict the perpetrator on criminal charges unrelated to the SBS episode. Then the perpetrator can be monitored and somewhat controlled by the state's corrections department. This is a long process, but our efforts must be prioritized to protect society's most vulnerable members.

NOTE

1. Most states allow the admissibility of "other crimes" evidence. For example, in Wisconsin, evidence of other crimes, wrongs, or acts are admissible when offered for the purposes of proof of motive, opportunity, intent, preparation, plan, knowledge, identity, or absence of mistake or accident. 1997-1998 Wisconsin Statutes 904.04(2).

REFERENCES

Adams, S.H. (1996). Statement analysis: What do suspects' words really mean? *FBI Law Enforcement Bulletin*, *65*, 12-20.

Billmire, M.E., & Myers, P.A. (1985). Serious head injuries in infants: Accidents or abuse? *Pediatrics*, *75*, 340-342.

Brodeur, A.E., & Monteleone, J.A. (1994). *Child maltreatment: A clinical guide and reference*. St. Louis, Missouri: G.W. Medical Publishing Co.

Bruce, D.A., & Zimmerman, R.A. (1984). Shaken impact syndrome. *Pediatric Annals*, *18*, 482-494.

Duhaime, A.C., Gennarelli, T.A., Thibault, L.E., Bruce, D.A., Marquiles, S.S., & Wiser, R. (1987). The shaken baby syndrome. A clinical, pathological, and biomechanical study. *Journal of Neurosurgery*, *66*, 409-415.

Estelle v. McGuire, 112 S. Ct. 475,, 116 L. Ed. 2d 385 (1991). See also Annotation, Admissibility of Expert Medical Testimony on Battered Child Syndrome, 98 A. L. R. 3d 306. Supra, 12.

Frankenberg, W.K., Dodds, J., Archer, P., Bresnick, B., Maschka, P., Edelamn, N., Shapiro, H. (1990). *Denver II Screening Manual (DDST-2)*. Denver CO: Denver Developmental Materials, Inc.

Jenny, C., & Hymel, K. (1999). Missed abusive head trauma. *The Journal of the American Medical Association*, *281*, 621-626.

Kempe, C.H., Silverman, F.N., Steele, B.F., Droegemueller, W., & Silver, H.K. (1962). The battered child syndrome. *Journal of the American Medical Association*, *181*, 17-24.

Krauss, J.C., & Warlen, M.S. (1985). The forensic science use of reflective ultraviolet photography. *Journal of Forensic Science*, *30*(1), 262-268.

Michigan Public Health Institute. (1998). *Michigan child death review team protocols*. Okemos, Michigan: MPHI.

Missouri DSS. (1998). *The death scene checklist*. Missouri Department of Social Services, State Technical Assistance Team (STAT), 615 Howerton Court, P.O. Box 88, Jefferson City, MO 65103-0088.

Parrish, R. (1998) The proof is in the details: Investigation and prosecution of shaken baby cases. *National Information Support and Referral Service on Shaken Baby Syndrome*, 4-5.

Perloff, W.H. (1998). Anatomy and physiology of head injuries in children. Symposium presented at the 1998 Wisconsin Conference on Shaken Babies. Madison, Wisconsin.

Showers, J. (1994). What have we learned about victims and perpetrators? *Don't Shake The Baby Campaign News*, *3*(1), 1-2.

Smith, W.L. (1994). Abusive head injury. *The APSAC Advisor*, *7*(4), 16-29.

Walsh, B.(1999). *Interrogation of suspects outline*. Unpublished manuscript. Dallas, Texas Police Department, Investigators Unit, Youth and Family Crimes Division.

Wisconsin Statutes (1998). 904.04(2).

APPENDIX A

This "other crimes" evience comparison was compiled and admitted for jury inspection in a Wisconsin criminal case, State of WI v. William J. Strong, Jr., Marathon County Case 95 CF 300, regarding the reckless homocide of a developmentally disabled child. A jury found the defendant guilty and he received a 40 year prison sentence.

KELLY WITZ	PATRICK COSTIGAN
WILLIAM J. STRONG, boyfriend of legal guardian (MARIE WITZ) acting as sole adult caretaker.	WILLIAM J. STRONG, boyfriend of mother (JEANNE COSTIGAN), acting as sole adult caretaker.
Legal Guardian (MARIE WITZ) at work when severe symptoms exhibited.	Mother (JEANNE COSTIGAN) at work when severe symptoms exhibited.
Victim vomited earlier in the day (prior to nap).	Victim vomited earlier in the day (prior to nap).
History of short fall on 03/16/95.	History of fall down steps on 03/16/83. History of short fall on 03/22/83.
Two minor bruises on left forehead and small cut near right eye.	Minor bruising on right side of forehead.
Put down for nap because of looking tired and cranky.	Put down for nap because of crankiness and vomiting.
Inability to wake child.	Inability to wake child.
Unevenly dilated pupils were observed and reported by WM. STRONG.	Unevenly dilated pupils were observed and reported by WM. STRONG.
Unsuccessful attempt to revive by shaking (multiple incidents).	Unsuccessful attempt to revive by shaking.
WM. STRONG described victim as flexing; and yawning with stiffened, outstretched limbs.	WM. STRONG described victim as having sighing type of breathing.
Legal guardian (MARIE WITZ) telephoned by WM. STRONG; physician's office consulted telephonically; WM. STRONG and legal guardian bring victim to hospital ER in comatose state.	Mother (JEANNE COSTIGAN) telephoned by WM. STRONG; mother meets WM. STRONG and victim at hospital ER, in comatose state.
Victim placed in car seat en route to hospital.	Victim placed in car seat en route to hospital.
Fatal injuries to include bilateral subdural hematoma and retinal hemorrhages.	Fatal injuries to include acute subdural hematoma on right side, multiple areas of bilateral cerebral hemorrhages and retinal hemorrhages.

APPENDIX B

July 02, 1991
Time Line

Appleton, WI - Police Dept. Case #91-0027-579

Mariah C. Belanger 03/18/91

1124 W. Lawrence St. Appleton, WI

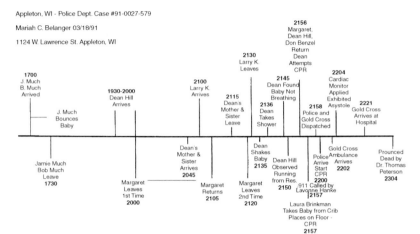

This time line was compiled by the Appleton, WI Police Department, and admitted as evidence in a Wisconsin criminal case, State of WI v. Dean Hill, Outagamie County Case 91 CF 182, regarding the reckless homicide of the 3 1/2 month old child of the defendant's girlfriend. Hill was convicted and received a 20 year prison sentence.

APPENDIX C

PRE-TRIAL INTERVIEW OF EXPERT DEFENSE WITNESSES

- Information to obtain:
    - name
    - other names used
    - date of birth
    - home address
    - work address
    - work phone
    - beeper #
    - fax #
- Request curriculum vitae

- Determine if expert has taught recently; conducted research recently; and has done field/clinical work recently. (This may establish an expert is a full time witness who is not current in area of expertise).

- Ask what information/records were reviewed pertaining to this case:

    - EMT reports
    - hospital records
    - imaging studies
    - medical history
    - autopsy reports
    - did you interview the defendant ?
    - police reports
    - defense attorney's investigative reports
    - hearsay information received
    - any other information (audiotape? videotape? photographs? other observations? etc.)

- Did you arrive at any conclusions to a reasonable degree of medical certainty?

- Will you tell what your conclusions are?

- Did you document your conclusions? Communicate them orally?

- Do you anticipate being called on, under oath, to testify to your conclusions? (If answer is no, ask why defense attorney declined to use this expert.)

- If expert refuses to share his conclusions, ask why there is a refusal.

- If expert has not reviewed all the material you know to exist, ask expert if his findings may be subject to revision if he had access to all information and documentation.

- Has expert ever testified for the defense in other cases? How many times? Where and what cases?

- Have you been called as an expert to review a case, but subsequently not called to testify? Where and what cases?

- What relevant research would you refer me to?

- Who is your supervisor?

- What is your fee schedule? Does this include travel, meals, etc.? What other consideration will you receive?

(If applicable)
- Return to the refusal to share information and findings. Ask the expert to explain why there is a refusal. Advise expert that, as a witness, he will be under jurisdiction of the presiding court. A refusal to share information and findings shows bias.

- NOTE: Timing of the interview is important. If the expert has formulated oral opinions, made notations, recorded impressions, etc., this is defense work product, and is privileged. If the expert writes a formal report, and is intended for use by the defense, the privilege no longer attaches. The investigator should CHECK WITH THE PROSECUTOR before conducting these interviews.

- Run criminal history checks on expert witnesses.

APPENDIX D

BACKGROUND INVESTIGATIONS OF POTENTIAL JURORS

- Run complete criminal history checks.

- Automated local law enforcement agency checks.

- Phone calls to (residence and work) jurisdictions frequented by potential juror.

- Education, job, spouse and family members' jobs may be significant.

- Was there a SIDS death within the potential juror's family?

- Look for ways in which juror may automatically relate to the crime being tried.

APPENDIX E

SOME HINTS FOR INVESTIGATORS AT TRIAL

1. Monitor hall activity and interaction between witnesses. Minimize their contact and comments. Be especially vigilant about complying with witness sequestration orders.

2. Take notes on testimony, both direct and cross-examination. Defense attorneys frequently misquote previous answers, or incorporate erroneous information in structured questions.

3. Pass questions and comments, written on note slips, to prosecutor. It's the prosecutor's decision to:

   a. utilize information on questions
   b. not utilize the information
   c. save information for final argument

4. When inundated with potential expert defense witnesses, excuse yourself and phone the expert's office. Check with expert's secretary/staff, etc., to determine their itinerary, estimated time of arrival, etc. Inform prosecution of results, so they save time and preparation by having advance knowledge of who will arrive, and who cancelled.
5. Provide reports and information to prosecutor to refute defense witnesses and rehabilitate prosecution witnesses.

APPENDIX F

,Background Checks of Expert Defense Witnesses

American Prosecutors Research Institute
National Center for Prosecution of Child Abuse,
Alexandria, VA, (703) 739-0321

- provides news release information concerning what expert said
- can provide a listing of expert's published material
- can provide cases where expert testified, and a summary of testimony–whether it be civil, criminal, board of inquiry, etc.

The Child Abuse Prevention Center, 2995 Harrison Blvd., Suite 102, Ogden, Utah 84403, has developed a reference list of literature on SBS, as well as a list of experts. This agency has frequent and timely contact with defense experts. The contact numbers are 1-888-273-0071, with website: capcenter.org; <e-mail: capcente@ix.netcom.com>.

Contact the Attorney General's offices in those states where the defense expert testified.

Consider contacting the instructors and supervisors of the experts, and possibly hiring them as prosecution experts.

Determine all states where expert is licensed and/or certified. Contact licensing boards to determine any complaints filed against the experts.

Check with child abuse defense organizations, and attempt to obtain presentations made by the defense's expert.

Is the anticipated testimony relevant to the expert's field of expertise?

Chapter Fourteen

Legal Considerations in Shaken Baby Cases

Henry J. Plum

SUMMARY. This article addresses SBS from the perspective of the legal practitioner or prosecutor in both the criminal or juvenile/family court. This analysis includes an examination of the procedural alternatives that the legal practitioners or prosecutor may employ to successfully protect the victim of SBS from further injury and to hold the perpetrator legally accountable. Next there is a discussion of the strategies available for effective case building. Finally, we will examine the methods for gathering and presenting evidence to the court. *[Article copies available for a fee from The Haworth Document Delivery Service: 1-800-342-9678. E-mail address: <getinfo@haworthpressinc.com> Website: <http://www.HaworthPress.com> © 2001 by The Haworth Press, Inc. All rights reserved.]*

KEYWORDS. Legal issues, adjudication, disposition, custody, court-ordered treatment, rules of evidence

The inability of the victim to testify and identify the perpetrator presents a particular difficulty in proving Shaken Baby Syndrome (SBS). Faced with the lack of an eyewitness, the legal practitioner, prosecutor and investigator are

[Haworth co-indexing entry note]: "Legal Considerations in Shaken Baby Cases." Plum, Henry J. Co-published simultaneously in *Journal of Aggression, Maltreatment & Trauma* (The Haworth Maltreatment & Trauma Press, an imprint of The Haworth Press, Inc.) Vol. 5, No. 1(#9), 2001, pp. 263-274; and: *The Shaken Baby Syndrome: A Multidisciplinary Approach* (ed: Stephen Lazoritz, and Vincent J. Palusci) The Haworth Maltreatment & Trauma Press, an imprint of The Haworth Press, Inc., 2001, pp. 263-274. Single or multiple copies of this article are available for a fee from The Haworth Document Delivery Service [1-800-342-9678, 9:00 a.m. - 5:00 p.m. (EST). E-mail address: getinfo@haworthpressinc.com].

frequently challenged to employ other methods for identifying the perpetrator and taking a legally protective approach to battle this form of child abuse.

The diagnosis of SBS requires the legal and medical practitioner to reach the conclusion that a caretaker or someone who is responsible for protecting and nourishing the child has endangered and abused the child. This realization is critical. Once made, case building, evidence gathering and procedural steps taken to protect the child and hold the SBS perpetrator legally accountable are no different from those used in proving any other intentional act of abuse.

This chapter addresses the issue of SBS from the perspective of the legal practitioner or prosecutor. This inquiry includes:

1. An examination of the various procedural alternatives that the legal practitioner/prosecutor may employ to successfully protect the victim of SBS from further injury and to hold the SBS perpetrator legally accountable.
2. A discussion of the strategies available for effective case building in both a Criminal and Family or Juvenile Law context. (In some jurisdictions, "family court" or other nomenclature is used rather than juvenile court. Since these cases are most commonly handled by juvenile courts, that term will be used).
3. Recommendations to help in the gathering and presentation of evidence to the court.

PROCEDURAL ALTERNATIVES

The first critical step in developing an effective approach to SBS cases is understanding that these cases require the practitioner to effectively combine the juvenile system and its protective mechanism with the punitive and deterrent qualities of the criminal system. Since each system has different legal requirements, the basis to proceed in one system will differ from that of proceeding in the other. This may result with the possibility that proceedings initiated in one may not necessarily allow for initiation of proceedings in the other. Consequently, this step requires that the practitioner understand the different outcomes and procedures inherent in each system.

THE JUVENILE JUSTICE SYSTEM

The juvenile system through its focus on protection of the child provides the vehicle through which the following may occur:

Detection and Diagnosis. Detection and diagnosis of intentional acts of child abuse and neglect are authorized under state child abuse reporting laws.

These laws are part of the juvenile system. They provide the authority for the medical practitioner to physically examine a child suspected of being abused or neglected and use diagnostic procedures such as radiographic imaging techniques, photographs, laboratory tests, and other diagnostic steps to detect intentional injuries sustained by the child. Further, child abuse reporting laws provide an exemption from the normal expectations of confidentiality and privilege that apply to medical treatment or medical records and provide immunity from liability for practitioners making reports in good faith.

Placing the Child into Protective Custody. This placement is another option available through the juvenile system. This authority is extended to law enforcement or frequently to the local or state social services agency when there is a belief that a child is suffering from injury, illness or is in immediate danger from its surroundings, and a temporary change in physical custody of the child is necessary to ensure the child's safety. The steps for a protective custody order usually require that the parent or guardian be notified and that judicial review of this protective order be provided in a timely manner (often within 24 to 72 hours) from the point of removal of the child. Medical practitioners may also take protective custody of the child in some jurisdictions pending judicial review.

Removing Custody of the Child from the Caretaker. The caretaker can be a parent, guardian, baby-sitter or other individual who is acting in an "in loco parentis" relationship with the child. Most cases of SBS involve the inability of a caretaker to respond effectively to the needs or the condition of a young, non-verbal child. It is important to note that the abusing caretaker may not always be the primary caretaker. Before the removal of custody alternative is exercised, it is necessary to determine whether the child is safe from further abuse of the abusing or inadequate caretaker. It is noteworthy that since the symptoms of SBS frequently involve serious injuries requiring medical treatment, removal of custody may frequently involve placement in a medical facility for treatment and observation. Depending on the seriousness of the injury and the medical treatment required, this step may require court authorization for medical treatment of the child. The court authorization for treatment may require additional evidence from a medical expert identifying the need for particular medical or surgical procedures. Shunting the child to remove excess fluid from the skull and relieve pressure on the brain is only one example of the type of medical procedures that may be required in these types of cases. Removal of the child from the care of the primary caretaker, and court authorization of medical/surgical procedures for the child is a procedural step available only in the juvenile system.

If a child is removed from the custody or control of the primary caretaker, it will be necessary to file a legal document called a petition. This document will set forth the factual and legal jurisdictional basis for court intervention. The criterion for such a jurisdictional determination of status is set forth in the Children's or Juvenile code for each state. Although terminology may differ from one state to another, the notion of a legal status or condition is uniform among states. The determination by a judge or (in some jurisdictions) by a jury that a child is in a status of being Dependent, Neglected, Abused, In Need of Protection or Services (CHIPS), or a Child in Need of Care (CINC) will result in the court having the authority and control over the child. The terminology for the child's status of being Dependent, Neglected, or In Need of Protection or Services (CHIPS) varies from state to state. Each state will have a specific status definition that addresses those circumstances in which a child has sustained an intentional injury. In some circumstances when the abuser is not the primary caretaker, invoking those sections of the status offense that addresses parental neglect for failure or inability to protect a child from further abuse may be necessary. Since the identity of the abuser may not be ascertainable, it is important that the legal practitioner recognize these differing legal theories that are available to protect the child.

Alternative Dispositions for the Child. Once the court has made a determination or adjudication of Dependency, Neglected, CHIPS, or CINC, alternative dispositions available through a court dispositional order will focus on several issues including the child's medical needs, the need to be safe from further abuse, and the development of a treatment plan for the purpose of the parent or primary caretaker resuming caretaking responsibilities. As part of this treatment plan, the court could require, for example, that the SBS perpetrator undergo treatment or counseling or demonstrate rehabilitation as a precursor to regaining custody of the child. The court would have the option of transferring custody and limiting the nature and frequency of contact between the SBS perpetrator and child while the treatment plan and order remain in effect. In the event the SBS perpetrator is not the primary caretaker, the court would also have authority to prohibit further unsupervised contact with the perpetrator using suspended or supervised visitations. Some jurisdictions provide a statutory basis for the court entering an injunction prohibiting any contact between the child and former caretaker-perpetrator under pain of contempt.

Review of Court-Approved Treatment Plans on a Periodic Basis. This review is required by most state and is required under federal law. If it is determined from the evidence that the SBS perpetrator has achieved the goals of the treatment plan, the juvenile court may authorize reunification with the child. However, if the treatment plan is not achieved in a timely fashion, the court then could consider other alternatives that might include removing permanent custody from the primary caretaker, severance of all parental rights to the child, or other permanent plan for the child.

THE CRIMINAL JUSTICE SYSTEM

The procedural mechanisms and dispositional alternatives discussed above are unique to the juvenile system and may only be accessed through that system. They are not present in the criminal system. Yet the criminal system provides particular deterring qualities not available in the juvenile system. The criminal system should not be ignored but rather be effectively used when it is determined to be appropriate. The criminal system through its emphasis on deterrence, accountability, and punishment provides the vehicle through which the following may occur:

Separation. The SBS perpetrator can be separated from the victim and community through the vehicle of bail and a no-contact order. To set bail, charging the SBS perpetrator with a crime will be necessary. If the evidence is insufficient and charges are not filed, the mechanism of bail is not available. Incarceration of the SBS perpetrator can be achieved through successful criminal prosecution. Depending on the particular criminal charge, the sentence levied could be extensive and could effectively remove the SBS perpetrator from having access to the child, other children and the community for an extended period.

Court-Ordered Treatment. Treatment of the SBS perpetrator is available as a sentencing option. However, if the individual chooses not to participate in treatment once the sentence is served, the perpetrator would not be legally prohibited under the criminal law from having further contact with the SBS victim, community or other children.

COMBINING THE JUVENILE AND CRIMINAL SYSTEMS

The outcomes available through the criminal system are more restrictive than those available through the juvenile system. Criminal proceedings are primarily focused on the accused rather than the victim. Therefore the options available to the juvenile court, such as transferring custody of the child or ordering treatment for the child and other family members, are not available through the criminal court. Since the SBS case is one in which a child sustains an intentionally induced injury at the hands of the child's caretaker (i.e., parent or guardian), using both the juvenile and criminal systems is not only recommended but advocated. It is axiomatic that the immediate and primary focus must be the safety and protection of the child victim rather than the punishment of the perpetrator. The long-term focus might include criminal prosecution or rehabilitation of the perpetrator. Therefore, the decision to intervene should be driven by determinations within the following priority scheme:

1. Obtain sufficient evidence to justify obtaining a protective order from the juvenile court.
2. Gather sufficient evidence to justify filing a petition for Dependency, Abuse, CINC, or CHIPS in juvenile court.
3. Evaluate the sufficiency of evidence to justify initiating proceedings in criminal court.

The protective order obtained through the Juvenile Court will not continue in force if the protective order is not supported by the filing of a Dependency, Abuse, CHIPS, CINC, or other status petition. Therefore, the legal practitioner or prosecutor must be gathering evidence and preparing for the initiation of such proceedings when the condition of the child is learned. Since the identity of the perpetrator is critical to ascertaining whether the child will be safe if returned to the primary caretaker, it will be important that the investigators gather critical evidence immediately.

Frequently in SBS cases, evidence of direct injury or abuse is available. However the identity of the perpetrator may be difficult to learn because there may be multiple caretakers. The legal practitioner or prosecutor must then carefully collect data from several critical areas:

1. Information regarding specific times during which caretaker(s) had direct access and caretaking responsibilities for the child. This includes gathering information that may contradict or corroborate the caretaker's access to the child [United States v. Boise, 916F. 2d 497 (9th Cir. 1990)].
2. Information regarding the methodology or explanation of caretakers' response to the child's needs. For example how the child was held. If the caretaker shook the child, the duration of time and description of the degree of force. It is important to document specific statements.
3. Information regarding how long the child was left alone and which caretaker exercised specific caretaking functions.
4. Information including specific measurements of distance or height if it is alleged the child fell. If the caretaker demonstrates the behavior, document such behavior by videotape or photographs.
5. Information should be obtained as immediately as possible after the incident. If there are subsequent explanations these should be documented as well.
6. Information from the caretaker when symptoms began to manifest.
7. Medical information should be obtained as to the following:

- Nature of the injury
- Cause of the injury
- Degree of force required to cause such injury
- Duration required to cause such injury
  (i.e., amount of time shaking occurred)

- Parameters of time when an injury occurred
- When each symptom of the injury would begin to manifest itself.

Lacking an admission, the legal practitioner or prosecutor must seek and develop circumstantial evidence. This is the process of decision-making by which the judge or jury may reason from circumstances, known or proved; to establish by inference the principal fact (*Black's Law Dictionary, 6th ed.*, St. Paul, MN: West, 1990). Circumstantial evidence is a legitimate method for establishing that a child sustained a non-accidental injury without an admission or eyewitness. The use of the protective order and petition through the juvenile system not only achieves prevention of future injuries to the child but may also support a conclusion of the intentional infliction of injuries by the absence of such recurrence while in protective custody.

STRATEGIES FOR CASE BUILDING

The legal practitioner or prosecutor must recognize that proving the existence of SBS to acquire juvenile court jurisdiction or achieve a criminal conviction is not necessary. Rather, understanding the phenomenon of SBS is critical. The burden of the legal practitioner or prosecutor in the juvenile courts will be to establish that the injuries of the victim were non-accidental. In contrast, the criminal court requires proof that the injuries were caused by the defendant. Using the terminology "Shaken Baby Syndrome" is not critical to the presentation of the case. Proving that the injury or condition of the child was intentionally induced by another individual is the critical element. Evidence of the SBS diagnosis should be introduced through the testimony of an expert witness. Legal practitioners/prosecutors should consider introducing the SBS diagnosis in a manner similar to that for other theories of intentional injury such as the battered child syndrome (Estelle v. McGuire, 502 US 62, 116 L.Ed 2d 385, 112 S.Ct. 475,1991). When introducing SBS, it is recommended that it be used to explain the phenomenon of the injury. Therefore, it is my recommendation that the theory be introduced toward the end of the case presentation.

Even if there is overwhelming direct evidence, the legal practitioner or prosecutor must still be concerned with initiating juvenile proceedings along with criminal proceedings to ensure that the child will receive appropriate care and case planning. A review of alternative options may be very appropriate, ranging from the child's placement in foster care or with relatives, permanent guardianship, or even termination of parental rights with subsequent adoption. As noted, these alternatives would not be available through a criminal prosecution, only through the juvenile court.

Unfortunately, in the vast majority of SBS cases direct evidence such as eye witness testimony of the parent or other caretaker causing the injury to the child is frequently not available. Therefore, a different approach is necessary. Recognizing the importance of establishing an intentional injury caused by an individual at a given point or over a period of time will require proof of several issues:

Evidence That the Condition of the Child Was Not Caused by Accidental Means. This will require a description of each injury, the symptoms of such injuries, and when these symptoms would manifest themselves in the child compared to the approximate time frame when these injuries occurred.

Evidence That the Alleged Perpetrator Had Access, Capacity and Opportunity to Cause the Injuries to the Child. Proving this element might begin with placing the perpetrator with the child during the time during which the injuries occurred. This would include evidence that the perpetrator had exclusive access to the child. This evidence might include information regarding the symptoms observed by the perpetrator and any explanations offered by the perpetrator regarding care provided to the child. Showing that the SBS perpetrator had access to the child would be necessary. Often establishing that the perpetrator had actual and exclusive access to the child is difficult; however, establishing that the perpetrator had the opportunity for exclusive access to the child is important. It is frequently alleged as a defense that an older sibling may have caused the injury to the child. Evidence as to the causation of the injury, including dexterity and force necessary to cause the injury that is physically beyond the capacity of a sibling is an important fact to present. In addition, the statements of the caretaker are frequently useful and can be introduced in evidence under several exceptions to the hearsay rule including medical diagnosis and admissions against interest. Frequently, these statements may serve as an admission to the causation or culpability for the injury.

Establishing the Parameters for the Time Within Which the Injury Occurred. Once the parameters of time have been established, it is easier to prove who had access to the child during the time period and who was providing care to the child. The collection of evidence and statements of the multiple care takers must be obtained as early as possible. Failure to do so may result in an inability to identify the actual perpetrator.

Evidence That the Injuries Occurred During the Time Period the Victim Was in the Exclusive Control of the Perpetrator. The last element will serve as the linchpin in the presentation of the case to the court or jury. It demonstrates that the injury occurred only during the period when the alleged perpetrator had access to the SBS victim. This element does not require an admission since it allows the judge or jury to draw the conclusion that the child could not have inflicted the injury on itself, the only other conclusion left is that the individual having exclusive access to the child caused the injury.

The presentation of any case involving circumstantial evidence presents additional challenges to the prosecutor. Since the function of the prosecutor is to educate and persuade the judge or jury to accept one's theory of the case, one must evaluate how this will be most effectively accomplished. Most cases depend on eyewitness testimony or other forms of direct evidence. In an SBS case, creating the correct atmosphere for teaching the judge or jury is important for the prosecutor. This will require reevaluation of the three critical elements discussed previously but examined here from the perspective of case presentation.

Presenting evidence that demonstrates that the child's condition was not caused by accidental or natural means will, by its very nature, require a detailed examination and explanation of medical diagnostic procedures. This type of evidence can be very confusing and tedious to nonmedical people such as judges and juries. Therefore, use of demonstrative evidence such as audiovisual aids will be critical to this learning process. It is important that the primary witness or witnesses present this data in a clear and understandable manner. The witnesses should be prepared to present their testimony so that they educate the jury or judge in a positive fashion. The prosecutor should consider the use of slides or transparencies containing summaries of critical procedures. Reconstructing the events or cause of the injury can be demonstrated by several methods. Just as an accident reconstruction expert might use audiovisual simulation to reconstruct a car crash in a civil case, the same technique might be used to demonstrate the causation of an intentional injury to a child. The goal of this phase should allow the judge or jury to become familiar with the causation of the injury. If there is evidence of direct injuries, consider transferring and enlarging photographs or X-rays to slides for more effective presentation. This will allow the jury to see and understand the injuries. The only limitation to the use of demonstrative evidence beyond the boundaries of the imagination of the attorney and the evidentiary rule of relevance is whether it will help the judge or jury in reaching a clearer understanding of the evidence and aid their judgment.

The second element of proof addresses the behavior of the alleged SBS perpetrator. An exhaustive review of the records and statements will be required to find the perpetrator's prior inconsistent or suspicious statements regarding the condition of the child. The investigators should interview all of the individuals who had access to the child prior to and during the time period during which the injuries to the child occurred. Often these lay witnesses will recall unusual coincidences and incriminating statements. They may have observed the perpetrator handling the child in a rough manner on previous occasions. There may have been warnings made that the child was being handled too roughly. This type of information will support the conclusion that the behavior of the perpetrator was done in an intentional or reckless manner. An examination will also require a review of the nursing staff's notes to identify inconsistencies in the perpetrator's behavior and discussions made to the medical staff when the child was brought in for medical care. Frequently statements will be made to the nursing staff that could be incriminating when linked with other inconsistent statements made to investigators; therefore, the legal professional or prosecuting attorney needs to conduct a thorough analysis of the records and interview witnesses to detect inconsistent statements of the perpetrator. Often it may be just one statement made to a nurse that will be inconsistent with the explanation offered to the investigator that could determine the culpability of the perpetrator. Once this information is assembled, presenting this evidence in a logical sequence is important. The use of charts or other methods by which the judge or jury can visualize the evidence, such as presenting actual statements of the accused on a slide, can be an effective presentation method. Another example might include presenting comparisons of time and particular events with a Time Line Chart that can be easily explained and understood by the trier of fact.

If the legal practitioner or prosecutor chooses to introduce the SBS theory, careful consideration should be given to method of presentation. A qualified expert will be necessary to present this information. In addition, the expert(s) selected should be familiar with all of the medical evidence. There are several characteristics of SBS that the expert can draw together with the other evidence. The legal practitioner or prosecutor should review these thoroughly with the expert before SBS evidence is presented.

CONCLUSION

There is no fixed rule for presenting a case of Shaken Baby Syndrome. The general principles of logic, common sense and clarity coupled with the goal to teach the judge or jury should serve as the guideline. The SBS case poses a unique challenge for the legal practitioner or prosecutor because it requires an understanding of juvenile and criminal systems and knowledge of how these systems can interact to protect the SBS victim. It also requires a multi-disciplinary approach, bringing together professionals with disparate orientations such as law enforcement (with a primary criminal/investigative focus), social services (with a primary rehabilitation/helping focus), and medicine (with a primary scientific/technological focus). In addition, the legal practitioner or prosecutor should implement particular procedural alternatives to obtain the necessary medical diagnosis evidence to present to the court. The legal practitioner/prosecutor must also become educated as to the causation and explanation of the medical procedures employed to treat and diagnose the child. These cases require coordination, cooperation, and participation on an interdisciplinary level. Recognition of the interdependence between legal and other disciplines and working together as a team are critical ingredients to this interdisciplinary effort. When this occurs, the likelihood of protecting the SBS victim and holding the SBS perpetrator accountable is greatly improved.

Chapter Fifteen

Prosecuting the Shaken Infant Case

Brian K. Holmgren

SUMMARY. This chapter discusses many of the significant legal, investigative and medical issues encountered when Shaken Baby Syndrome cases are prosecuted in court. Heavy emphasis is placed on trial strategies and techniques including theme development and motive evidence, opening and closing statements, lay and expert witness testimony, meeting untrue defenses and cross-examination of defense experts, and effective use of demonstration slides. Emphasis is also placed on the initial preparation of the case including coordination of a multidisciplinary response to the investigation, development of background investigation information to supplement medical findings and discovery of "prior bad acts" evidence, difficulties in making appropriate charging decisions, and pre-trial motion practice. *[Article copies available for a fee from The Haworth Document Delivery Service: 1-800-342-9678. E-mail address: <getinfo@haworthpressinc.com> Website: <http://www.HaworthPress.com> © 2001 by The Haworth Press, Inc. All rights reserved.]*

KEYWORDS. Prosecution, sentencing, criminal, rules of evidence, opening statements, closing statements

---

[Haworth co-indexing entry note]: "Prosecuting the Shaken Infant Case." Holmgren, Brian K. Co-published simultaneously in *Journal of Aggression, Maltreatment & Trauma* (The Haworth Maltreatment & Trauma Press, an imprint of The Haworth Press, Inc.) Vol. 5, No. 1(#9), 2001, pp. 275-339; and: *The Shaken Baby Syndrome: A Multidisciplinary Approach* (ed: Stephen Lazoritz, and Vincent J. Palusci) The Haworth Maltreatment & Trauma Press, an imprint of The Haworth Press, Inc., 2001, pp. 275-339. Single or multiple copies of this article are available for a fee from The Haworth Document Delivery Service [1-800-342-9678, 9:00 a.m. - 5:00 p.m. (EST). E-mail address: getinfo@haworthpressinc.com].

Successful prosecution of shaken infant cases depends on the ability of the prosecutor to assimilate frequently conflicting facts and complex medical science into a legal construct, which is understandable for judges and juries. This is no easy task since most prosecutors and judges and virtually all jurors are unfamiliar with the science underlying these cases, and existing criminal statutes are often poorly suited for this type of conduct.

The discussion, which follows assumes that most prosecutions of shaken infant cases (hereinafter referenced as SBS cases), like most criminal cases in general, will not result in a trial. However, the severity of the potential charges, usually involving homicide or serious felony allegations, and the difficulty of proving SBS cases at trial may result in more SBS cases being litigated than other types of criminal offenses. The suggestions herein should provide direction to prosecutors and other professionals regardless of whether the case results in a plea or a trial. Significant emphasis is placed on trial considerations because of the scant literature on this topic. However, charging considerations and pre-trial preparation of the case are equally if not more important for successful prosecution because of the ability to marshal a compelling case that will discourage contested litigation.

COORDINATING THE INVESTIGATION

Prosecutors must become involved in the SBS case immediately. This necessitates the development of a multi-disciplinary coordinated response when cases are reported to Child Protective Services (CPS) and law enforcement, and a system whereby the prosecutor is available on an on-call basis to assist in the early stages of the investigation. The serious consequences attendant to victims of these violent offenses warrants criminal prosecution on high level felony assault and homicide charges. Accordingly, prosecutors should treat SBS cases as seriously as other high level felony cases from an investigative standpoint prior to charging.

Medical personnel may be more receptive to assisting with criminal investigations when they see the prosecutor's office actively involved at an early point. This may also alleviate concern by medical staff that these cases will not be prosecuted. A coordinated approach between the prosecutor, law enforcement, CPS and medical personnel will permit discussion of strategies on how to approach and interview caretakers. The success of SBS cases depends in large measure on the ability to obtain false and changing histories from caretakers regarding the child's injuries which can be later refuted through expert testimony. This necessitates the ability to interview these caretakers on several occasions.

The initial history provided by the caretaker is false in the vast majority of abuse cases (Brewster et al., 1998; Duhaime, Christian, Rorke, & Zimmerman, 1998; Gilliland, Luckenbach, & Chenier, 1994; Monteleone,1998; O'Neill, Meacham, Giffin, & Sawyers, 1973; Smith, 1994), and frequently evolves or changes over time as the caretaker is confronted with medical findings. A false, discrepant, evolving or absent history is also an important diagnostic component for a medical opinion that the child is a victim of abuse. (Kempe, Silverman, Steele, Droegmueller, & Silver, 1962; Kessler & Hyden, 1991; Lazoritz, Baldwin, & Kini, 1997). The false histories help identify the likely individual who caused the child's injuries by providing compelling evidence of the abuser's "consciousness of guilt" (APRI, 1993; Commonwealth v. Lazarovich, 1989; Kirschner & Wilson, 1994; People v. Evers, 1992; People v. Gordon, 1987; People v. Henson, 1973; People v. Rader, 1995; People v. Wong, 1992; Schleret v. State, 1981; United States v. Bowers, 1981). Equally important is the need to establish a history detailing when the child last appeared well and when symptoms characteristically observed in SBS victims were observed by caretakers (Case, 1998; Levitt, Smith, & Alexander, 1994; Starling, Holden, & Jenny, 1995).

This type of critical information can be jeopardized by inappropriate interviewing procedures, which may prompt caretakers to shut down discussion with professionals or seek out immediate legal representation. The prosecutor who is involved early on will be in a position to offer important strategic advice regarding whether an arrest should be made, whether *Miranda* warnings need be given, etc., so as to maximize the opportunity to develop incriminating statements from the caretaker(s).

Prosecutors are often reluctant to become involved at this stage of the investigation for fear that they will become a witness themselves and be barred from personally handling the case. In most jurisdictions legal precedent suggest this fear is unfounded as long as the prosecutor is not personally interviewing witnesses without an independent witness being present. The prosecutor should also be available to assist law enforcement with securing search warrants for crime scene investigations and may even go along while they are executed so long as she does not personally conduct the search. Such efforts can help ensure that the collection and preservation of evidence will be done within legal parameters that will permit use of the evidence at trial. Prosecutors need to bear in mind, however, that participation in some aspects of the investigative process may afford only qualified immunity (Buckley v. Fitzsimmons, 1993; Burns v. Reed, 1991).

In some instances, the prosecutor may be needed to facilitate agreements, and in rare situations grants of immunity or agreements of non-prosecution, in order to secure the cooperation of reluctant witnesses. Some prosecutors use the grand jury process as an additional means of generating information to aid the investigation, secure the testimony of difficult witnesses, and "lock-in" a vacillating witness' specific version of the facts.

Clearly, the most important reason for early involvement is to ensure that the case will be prosecutable. Important information and evidence may be lost during the critical early stages of the investigation, and the prosecutor is in the best position to advise other professionals of what he or she needs in order to make the case provable in court. Early consultation with medical experts will also potentially help direct the course of the investigation and ensure the prosecution's theory of the case is sound.

In the event that an SBS case results in a fatality, the prosecutor handling the case should attend the autopsy, and coordinate with the medical examiner to meet anticipated and potential defenses that may arise at trial. The benefits to prosecutors of personally viewing the autopsy and obtaining a contemporaneous explanation from the medical examiner of the significance of the medical findings cannot be overemphasized. Prosecutors should have a good familiarity with the medical literature involving both SBS and autopsy procedures before they attend to enable them to effectively participate in this process. Several excellent resources are available in this regard (Case, 1998; Giardino, Christian, & Giardino, 1997; Kirschner & Wilson, 1994; Kleinman, 1998; Levitt et al., 1994; Ludwig & Kornberg, 1992; Lyon, Gilles, & Cory, 1996). Equally important is the prosecutor's participation in multidisciplinary teams that review suspected abuse cases and on child fatality review teams. Frequently prosecutors will identify cases as those involving abuse that may be overlooked by other professionals, or considered not worthy of further investigation or referral for prosecution.

BACKGROUND INVESTIGATION

An important aspect of making the SBS case prosecution ready is securing background information on the victim, family and the suspect. Frequently this information is not immediately available as part of the law enforcement investigative packet submitted to the district attorney's office. The prosecutor must either request further investigation to secure this background information, or seek it through an independent investigation. This information can provide important corroborative evidence solidifying the case, or if not obtained, make the prosecution potentially vulnerable because of the missing facts.

The background investigation on the victim should include securing certified copies of all of the child's past medical records, including the mother's prenatal care records, birth and pediatric records, public health visits and identification of all of the doctors and health care agencies the child has visited. If any testing procedures have been done on the child, the results of these findings must be gathered. Pharmacology records should also be obtained. Birth certificates may also be needed to establish paternity under some child abuse statutes. Similar records should be obtained for any of the defendant's other children, and these children should be examined also for potential abusive injuries (American Academy of Pediatrics, 1993).

These records will help establish a baseline for comparison against the child's current condition, potentially establishing the presence of prior abusive, (Brewster et al., 1998), suspicious or unexplained injuries, symptomology consistent with prior shaking incidents, or the absence of any preexisting medical conditions or abnormalities. They can also help establish the continuum of care or lack thereof, and any potential stressors that might establish a motive for the shaking episode. For example, during prior pediatric visits, the parent may complain that the child is colicky or not sleeping well, thereby suggesting a reason for a later shaking episode (Brewster et al., 1998). Evidence the child has been to multiple physicians might also raise concerns regarding the parent's motivations for the change (e.g., suspicions raised by prior doctor).

The child's developmental history should also be obtained to establish whether the child is capable of rolling over, standing up, crawling, etc. Such information may be available from a variety of sources including the non-offending parent, older siblings, relatives and neighbors, the pediatrician, day care providers and church members. Family photographs and videotapes of the child may also supply important developmental information, as well as documenting the child's physical condition at the time of the recording. This information may be critical in refuting the defendant's explanation for the events or the claims of the defense expert.

The background investigation of the defendant should be conducted with a view toward developing "other crimes" evidence which may be admissible at trial. This necessitates obtaining information on the defendant's past residential and employment history, and military service. Development of this information will facilitate record checks with local law enforcement and CPS agencies for past incidents of family violence. Traffic records should also be checked since these will also suggest local contacts to be followed up on. Local record checks with each agency in the jurisdictions of past residence are necessary to discover complete information, since police investigations that do not result in an arrest will generally not show up on criminal record checks. Similarly, CPS records may not be accessible through a centralized data bank. Welfare and insurance records may also be useful as a source for background information.

If information is developed through these sources, complete copies of the agency records must be obtained, often necessitating a subpoena or court order.

Prior criminal investigations not resulting in an arrest or charge, and "unfounded" CPS referrals may take on new significance in light of the current allegations. These incidents may also be legally admissible despite their prior "unproven" status (Huddleston v. United States, 1988; State v. Driskell, 1983; State v. Landrum, 1995; United States v. Dowling, 1990; Watkins v. Melody, 1996).

Any past history of caretaking of other children, including children from prior relationships should be investigated to see if these children may have been abused or handled inappropriately. Divorce and family court records and interviews of prior spouses and girlfriends can be an important source of information in this regard.

Finally, the prosecutor must ensure that a complete certified copy of the child's medical records for the current injury are obtained. This must include copies of any radiological images, hospital photographs, lab results, hospital social workers and nurses notes, and paramedic and EMT reports which may not routinely be provided. The prosecutor must carefully review these records as soon as possible and consult with medical officials regarding any questions the prosecutor might have. The prosecutor should in any event consult with the doctors who examined the child early on to make sure she understands the significance of the medical findings, and any possible issues that might mitigate the opinions they would offer if called upon to testify.

The doctors can also suggest appropriate medical references to assist the prosecutor in understanding the medical issues involved, or that the doctor might rely upon in support of his opinions. These references can then be filed with the court as "learned treatises" (Federal Rules of Evidence, Rule 803(13)). Hospitals also routinely staff child abuse cases, seeking confirming opinions from other physicians on staff regarding the diagnosis. If the medical records do not indicate this was done, the prosecutor should inquire about this issue, since she will want to know if other doctors share the principal physician's opinion and should also be considered as potential witnesses. Conversely, if there are conflicting opinions the prosecutor can anticipate these doctors will be called as defense witnesses.

Because the medical records may contain only cryptic histories provided by the caretaker, exclusive of elaboration, the prosecutor must ensure these witnesses are thoroughly interviewed for forensic purposes. Additional investigative statements may need to be taken from these medical personnel, establishing the full context of the defendant's statements including the defendant's demeanor at the time, the questions posed by medical personnel and any responses they made to the caretaker's statements or questions. Paramedics, fire and rescue personnel and medical examiner staff also routinely speak with caretakers and should not be overlooked as potential sources for important information regarding the history of the child's injury. Frequently some of the most compelling evidentiary value these statements hold involves the caretaker's affect at the time they are made including a lack of expressed concern or appropriate emotion while discussing the child's grave condition.

Criminal discovery rules in most jurisdictions require the prosecutor disclose to the defense any statements made by the defendant, which the prosecution intends to rely on at trial. Since the defendant's false, discrepant and changing history provides some of the most important evidence of guilt, the prosecutor will most likely seek to introduce all of these statements at trial. Failure to conduct these types of detailed interviews before trial can result in a delay in the proceedings when this information is first discovered during pre-trial preparation, or worse yet, a mistrial when this information is first revealed by the witness during testimony. Defense access to this information at an early stage can also help inform their decision on whether to have a trial.

CHARGING CONSIDERATIONS

The high degree of morbidity and mortality associated with SBS cases suggests that an aggressive posture should be taken toward criminal prosecution. Accordingly, when charges are filed, the nature of the charges should reflect the seriousness of the conduct, both in terms of the degree of violence associated with the assault, and the resulting severity of injury or risk of injury to the child. Unfortunately, past practice has not always reflected this philosophy. (Showers, 1997; Showers & Apolo, 1986). Under most statutory schemes, these charges will be serious felonies. The recidivistic nature of this behavior within families, and the potentially devastating nature of this mechanism of traumatic injury, suggests that criminal prosecution should not be declined when provable cases are presented, regardless of the severity of the child's injuries.

Several key issues must be kept in mind. Most child abuse or criminal assault or homicide statutes require the prosecution to establish the defendant's mental state or mental purpose (*mens rea*) at the time the offense is committed. This *mens rea* is variably described under different jurisdictional statutes by terms such as "intentionally," "recklessly," "negligently," "knowingly," or "purposefully." Still other statutes are written in terms of conduct which "manifests extreme indifference to human life" (APRI, 1994, 1998; Phipps, 1999). One of the most difficult aspects of SBS cases involves translating the defendant's conduct in violently shaking an infant into one of these legal constructs (Rainey & Greer, 1994). The volume of appellate decisions discussing the sufficiency of evidence to support SBS convictions under various state statutes bears testament to this fact.

Although most people who abusively shake children may not specifically intend the child's resultant severe injury or death, this does not suggest that SBS cases are unintentional crimes. The act of picking up a child and violently shaking the infant back and forth dozens of times is a deliberate and purposeful act. The issue becomes how that conduct is considered within the context of the criminal laws of the specific jurisdiction. Does the law require a specific intent to produce the end result, or merely the intent to engage in the act? Does the law require an understanding of the likely consequences of the conduct, or merely an awareness of its abusive nature?

Case law and specific statutory constructions in individual jurisdictions provide varying and often conflicting answers to these questions. Some jurisdictions provide alternative definitions of intent, requiring either the specific intent to produce the resultant injury or death, or alternatively, the awareness that such conduct was practically certain to produce the result. Similarly, a *mens rea* requirement for "knowingly" injuring a child may reflect a subjective standard, i.e., the abuser must appreciate the likely result of his conduct (People v. Rader, 1995), or an objective standard, i.e., the conduct when viewed by another person would suggest that result, or alternatively, the conduct reflects a general standard of abusive conduct such that the perpetrator may be held accountable for all its resultant consequences (People v. District Court, 1990; People v. Roe, 1989; People v. Sargent, 1999).

Two recent decisions have overturned convictions concluding that the evidence did not establish the defendant knew his actions would result in death. (People v. Holmes, 1993; People v. Sargent, 1997). These decisions are poorly reasoned but unfortunately add confusion to these issues as precedent, and may discourage prosecutors from aggressive charging decisions in similar cases. Fortunately, the *Holmes* decision has been criticized in subsequent decisions as improperly decided (People v. Rader, 1995; People v. Ripley, 1997), and *Sargent* was reversed on appeal (People v. Sargent, 1999). These decisions are also inconsistent with medical findings regarding the severity of forces necessary to produce SBS injuries and the caretaker's awareness of the abusive nature of this behavior.

In this context, the statements of recognized experts involving the severity of the forces and assaultive nature of the behavior have particular salience. For example, the American Academy of Pediatrics indicates, that "while caretakers may be unaware of the specific injuries they may cause by shaking, the act of shaking/slamming is so violent that competent individuals observing the shaking would recognize it as dangerous" (American Academy of Pediatrics, 1993, p.872). Similarly others have indicated that "there is no disagreement among professionals in the field that the violent shaking, whether or not it is accompanied by an impact, is not a casual act but rather one that would indicate to a rational observer that severe injury was being inflicted on the child" (Smith, 1994, p. 18).

Not only should the charge reflect this degree of violence, but the expert's testimony at trial must communicate these concepts as well (People v. Nix, 1991; People v. Sargent, 1999; People v. Wong, 1992; State v. Ojeda, 1991). Stated another way, if there were a videotape which captured the event, every rational observer of that tape (e.g., the jurors) would readily appreciate the violent, abusive nature of the conduct and recognize the inherent danger to the child. Unfortunately, the perpetrator is almost never caught on videotape and as will be discussed, in-court demonstrations of this degree of violent shaking using dolls are problematic.

Additional statutory language frequently utilized in SBS cases involve criminal definitions of "recklessness" and "maliciousness." These definitions are well tailored to the type of behavior commonly associated with SBS cases. However, the penalty provisions under criminal statutes utilizing such language are frequently inadequate in comparison to "intentional" crimes. In jurisdictions, which have this shortcoming, prosecutors are well advised to propose legislation for reckless homicide, and reckless causation of great bodily harm with sufficient penalties to reflect the severity of harm and violence associated with SBS cases.

Other jurisdictions have approached the difficult issue of proving intent by adopting "felony murder" or "homicide by abuse" statutes which relieve the state of the requirement of establishing a specific criminal intent to cause the death, or awareness of the risk of death. Instead, if the child dies in the course of the commission of a felony, including child abuse, or where there is a pattern of abuse to the child, first-degree murder charges can be brought. The prosecutor may only be required to show that the defendant intentionally or knowingly engaged in the act(s) of abuse. The intent or *mens rea* element of the child abuse substitutes for the specific intent or *mens rea* normally required to charge murder (APRI, 1993; Parrish, 1998; Phipps, 1999; Rainey & Greer, 1994).

Intent may also be inferred from the severity of the physical injuries. Where there is evidence of impact injury to the head (e.g., skull fracture, subgaleal hemorrhage, caretaker admission), in addition to the evidence of shaking injury, the additional physical findings demonstrate a second mechanism of traumatic injury (i.e., a subsequent or contemporaneous striking of the child's head against a hard object). This additional trauma evidences the deliberate nature of the abusive conduct, and may even support a separate charge. Similarly, evidence of old injury such as a prior subdural hematoma, or old rib or metaphyseal fractures, may likewise demonstrate intent through the repeated nature of the abusive behavior.

Delay in seeking medical attention for the child may also increase the severity of the potential charges. Delay may both increase the severity of the resultant injuries to the child (Bruce & Zimmerman, 1988), and establish a higher level of *mens rea* by demonstrating the caretaker's lack of concern for the child's safety (Loren v. State, 1997; People v. Wong, 1992; State v. Wyatt, 1996). A caretaker's false history to medical personnel when the child is presented for treatment can similarly reflect this mindset and contribute to more serious consequences due to delays in appropriate medical interventions (Bruce & Zimmerman, 1988). Two of the most compelling statements which can be made regarding the caretaker's callous disregard for the child's welfare are the dual arguments that "the caretaker lied about the true cause of the child's injuries to the doctors and nurses who were fighting to save the child's life," and "the caretaker chose not to seek immediate medical intervention that might have rescued the child because of a selfish concern with concealing the abusive conduct."

Delays in seeking appropriate medical intervention and false histories to medical personnel can also support criminal charges for neglect or endangering the welfare of the child. Similar allegations can be made in juvenile court petitions even if criminal charges cannot be brought, or it is unclear who the actual perpetrator of the shaking is. Medical research has demonstrated that when false histories are presented to medical personnel, a proper diagnosis of abuse is often missed, with the resultant consequence that children may be sent back to the abusive caretaker and suffer some additional injury (Jenny, Hymel, Ritzen, Reinert, & Hay, 1999; Lazoritz, 1995).

MULTIPLE PERPETRATORS, NON-PROTECTIVE CARETAKERS AND UNCOOPERATIVE CARETAKERS

Another difficult issue involves the decision of whether the non-shaking or non-abusive parent should be charged. Available research suggests that most shaking takes place in the absence of eyewitnesses other than the perpetrator and child. Where this is not the case and another person with a legal responsibility to care for the child is aware of the shaking and permits it to occur, assists in concealing the abuser's behavior, or fails to seek immediate medical care for the child, then appropriate charges should also be brought against this person. These may involve charges for "neglect," "failure to protect," or "aiding and abetting" the underlying crime (APRI, 1993; Rainey & Greer, 1994).

One of the most difficult prosecutorial decisions involves what to do when the investigation suggests that multiple caretakers could have caused the injuries, and it is unclear who is responsible. This situation occurs with some frequency in SBS cases because of the delayed recognition that a crime has occurred, the difficulty in pinpointing the time when the abusive injuries occurred and the delay in seeking medical attention for the child. The situation can be exacerbated when the caretakers refuse to cooperate with investigators or are advised by attorneys not to do so.

Several factors need to be kept in mind in these circumstances when determining how and against whom to proceed with potential charges. First, false histories are a strong indicator of consciousness of guilt, helping to identify the perpetrator of the offense. Only a person who is in a position to know exactly how the child is injured is in a position to devise a false statement about the cause. One obvious exception to this involves the situation in which the person providing a history for the child's condition is merely repeating the false hearsay explanation offered by the perpetrator.

Second, in fatal and near fatal cases, the onset of symptoms is virtually contemporaneous with the abusive act (Duhaime, 1997; Levitt et al., 1994; Willman, Bank, Senac, & Chadwick, 1997), and the perpetrator may acknowledge these symptoms during questioning (Gilliland, 1997; Starling, Holden, & Jenny, 1995). Accordingly, the prosecutor should be seeking to clarify through the investigation when the child was last well and when the child appeared to evidence some symptoms of an SBS injury, or when an emergency call was placed. This will help define the window of opportunity and narrow down the possible list of suspects who could have caused the fatal or near fatal injuries.

These two factors separately or in combination provide strong evidence of the identity of the person responsible. If the available evidence cannot determine who caused the injuries, one option is to charge the caretaker(s) with failure to protect or endangering safety for the delay in seeking medical attention or failing to intervene to protect the child.

Another option is to charge multiple potential perpetrators jointly (assuming sufficient available evidence to ethically support the charges) and then use the plea negotiation process to help identify the true perpetrator and the relative culpability of each. Prosecutors in these circumstances need to carefully consider the various charging alternatives available, and their theory of the case. In some instances, the charges should be issued under multiple theories of culpability including both active causation of the injuries, co-participation in the offense, and failure to protect. These factual scenarios pose particular difficulties if the case ultimately goes to trial because of the potential for inconsistent verdicts, jury confusion on the precise theory of culpability, and challenges to the sufficiency of the evidence (Berry v. Commonwealth, 1985; Commonwealth v. Lazarovich, 1989; People v. Wong, 1993; State v. Rundle, 1993; State v. Wyatt, 1996).

Charges against multiple potential perpetrators frequently create a situation where one of the charged individuals has a strong incentive to break the wall of silence and seek an agreement for personal benefit. Prosecutors in these circumstances should condition any agreements on receipt of a truthful detailed disclosure and recorded statement from the individual, verified through a polygraph, along with an agreement to provide truthful testimony at the trial of the co-defendant. If the bargained for information includes dismissal or reduction of charges, the prosecutor should delay disposition of the pending charge(s) until after the trial of the co-defendant. This helps ensure the defendant will fulfill the conditions of the agreement to testify truthfully, and helps insulate his or her testimony against the co-defendant's claims that such testimony was already bought and paid for. Failure to follow these precautions can result in trial testimony by an accomplice which is potentially antagonistic to the prosecution's theory of the case, or which leaves prosecutors with little recourse to impeach an accomplice who's testimony is inconsistent with prior statements (State v. Wyatt, 1996).

Additionally the prosecution can convene a grand-jury and compel the testimony of the potential perpetrators under a grant of immunity from the court. This should only be done in jurisdictions where the prosecution can offer grants of "use immunity" rather than "transactional immunity." The prosecutor should attempt to develop the case as thoroughly and completely as possible exclusive of the need for testimony or information from any possible perpetrators. The prosecutor should file a complete copy of the investigative file with the court before any grants of immunity to insulate against claims that investigative leads were developed from the testimony provided under the grant of immunity.

Juries are notoriously skeptical of bargained-for-testimony and may punish the prosecution for making a bargain with a morally if not legally culpable caretaker in order to secure their cooperation. For the same reasons, it may be equally detrimental to the prosecution not to charge a non-protective mother. For example, in the infamous Steinberg case, the jury acquitted Joel Steinberg of the most serious homicide charges in part because of the prosecution's lenient treatment of Hedda Nussbaum who had strong moral culpability as well as legal culpability in the death of her daughter (People v. Steinberg, 1992).

The defense will inevitably attempt to shift blame to the immunized caretaker. Additionally, grants of immunity frequently invite the immunized witness to provide false testimony exculpating the offender. Moreover, in some jurisdictions, a non-protective caretaker or a caretaker granted immunity may be considered an "accomplice" whose testimony must be corroborated in order to support a conviction. In this situation, the prosecution must have sufficient additional evidence corroborating the accomplice's testimony and establishing the defendant's participation in the offense to warrant a finding of guilt. For these reasons, immunity grants and agreements not to prosecute should be pursued only in exceptional circumstances.

THEME DEVELOPMENT

Jurors interpret and process factual information in a trial more effectively when it is centered around a theme–a short memorable phrase which encapsulates a central fact or principle of the case. The theme should be consistent with the facts and theory of the case and the charge issued (Pennington & Hastie, 1991; DerOhannesian, 1998). The theme should be apparent throughout multiple stages of the trial including jury selection, opening statement and closing argument, and during cross-examination. In many instances, multiple themes can be carried through the case as long as they compliment one another and are not inconsistent.

The theme may be oriented to the perspective of the victim, the offender, the jury, the case facts or the law. Themes oriented to the victim's perspective include: "unanswered cries," "betrayal of trust," "innocence lost," and "it shouldn't hurt to be a child." Some additional victim-oriented themes include "throwaway child," "evil is often viewed in the face of a loved one," "silent witness" and "home should be a haven of safety and comfort, not a prison of pain and fear."

Themes oriented toward the offender's perspective include: "violation of trust," "failure to protect," "mom chose the presence of her boyfriend over the safety of her child," "having a child does not make you a mother" and "parents are supposed to cuddle and nurture, not shake and slam." Where the offender tries to shift blame to another caretaker, an effective theme can be "when a man points a finger at someone else he should remember that three fingers point toward himself." When caretakers lie to medical personnel a theme can focus on the "lies told to save oneself rather than truth told to save the child."

Common factual scenarios in SBS cases often involve false histories about how the child came to be injured, thereby inspiring themes such as "the killer couch," "bodyguard of lies," "the defendant's changing stories are but the shifting sands of a guilty conscience," "truth has a ring of its own," or "a lie often contains the seeds of the truth." In severe cases involving repetitive abuse, themes might be "how many times–how many ways," "destined to die," or "the marks on the child bear witness to the fact that he was an object of torture." A theme, which summarizes both of these perspectives is "too many injuries, too many stories, too much indifference."

The theme "acts indicate the intention" can be used where the child's injuries are very severe or where impact injury is also apparent suggesting two distinct mechanisms of trauma. When there has been an obvious delay in seeking medical attention resulting in the child's death or more serious injury an effective theme can be "a hospital is filled with angels of mercy–but they can't save a child they don't see." A theme such as "all things done in the dark come to light" can be used to highlight the secrecy aspects of these generally unwitnessed crimes, and prior shaking incidents, which did not prompt the caretaker to seek out medical intervention.

Defenses are frequently focused on other possible medical explanations for the injuries. A responsive theme might be that "arguments derived from possibilities are idle." Similarly, defense arguments focusing on reasonable doubt, poor investigations, or unusual medical findings can be countered with the theme of "we should not investigate facts by the light of arguments, but examine arguments by the light of facts."

Jurors frequently empathize with the accused in SBS cases, especially where the perpetrator makes a good or sympathetic appearance, evinces some remorse while minimizing their conduct, and the shaking is a one time incident evidencing no past history of abuse. In these instances an aggressive posture toward the defendant may alienate the jury. Similarly, the jury may be reluctant to accept the notion that the parent acted deliberately or violently toward the child. Accordingly, the theme may need to recognize these perspectives and instead emphasize the momentary loss of control common to SBS parents. Themes such as "who has not experienced a loss of control and regretted the consequences later," or "good parents sometimes do bad things" may allow jurors to empathize while still following the law. Additionally, the prosecutor can challenge jurors' tendency to rely on their belief in good natured, caring parents with themes such as "we want the facts to fit the preconceptions, when they don't it's tempting to ignore the facts rather than change the preconceptions," "one knows a person by their actions," "choices reflect our purpose" and "there are no reasons for senseless acts."

Themes which focus on the legal issues in SBS cases include "he who helps the guilty shares the crime," "bond of abuse" or the "callous couple" to deal with co-participant cases, and in failure to protect situations "society permits but one vehicle for parents to escape from their duty to protect and care for their child–adoption." Reasonable doubt can be addressed by themes such as "doubt cannot override a certainty" or "you don't have to see the snake if you hear its rattle."

The theme can also be incorporated into cross-examination strategies. For example, a theme focusing on false statements by the perpetrator to conceal guilt may be incorporated into a series of cross-examination questions, which emphasize all of the different opportunities the perpetrator had to give correct information to aid doctors treating the child. A mother's failure to protect the child can similarly be illustrated by questions establishing all her opportunities to escape the abuser or seek outside intervention, contrasting this against her self-professed helplessness, or her claimed love and concern for the child.

Finally, themes can be drawn from famous quotations. For example, Marcus Tullius Cicero's timeless words "When you have no basis for an argument abuse the plaintiff" are an effective response to the common defense strategy of attacking the sufficiency of the police investigation or the conclusions of medical examiners and physicians. Other powerful quotes include C.K. Chesterton's "For children are innocent and love justice, we are mostly wicked and therefore prefer mercy," or Anna Salter's "Child abuse leaves a footprint on the heart."

EVIDENCE OF MOTIVE

Jurors and judges frequently have a difficult time conceptualizing parents as abusers of their children. They are reluctant to believe that an apparently loving caretaker would purposely injure their child. Many SBS cases do not involve caretakers who deliberately set out to kill or injure the child by violently shaking them. Rather these consequences often result from the caretaker's loss of control and momentary violent behavior directed toward the child. This explanation does not mean that SBS cases are "unintentional" crimes within the legal definition of "intent," or that the offender is less culpable because they did not specifically set out to kill or maim the baby. Shaking a vulnerable infant is still a deliberate act of extreme violence which justifies holding the caretaker accountable for the dire consequences which ensue.

Prosecutors should always explain to jurors that the state is not required to prove a motive in order to support a conviction. Nevertheless, jurors will both want and expect an explanation for why this act occurred. Prosecutors will often not be able to point to a traditional "motive" (e.g., hatred, jealousy, vengeance, greed) to explain the caretaker's conduct. Rather they must reorient jurors to think about motive in a unique context–one that does not reflect a purposeful mental state but instead a risk factor, stressor or catalyst that prompts the caretaker's reactive and abusive conduct. "Motive" in the context of SBS trials is important because it tends to explain why and how the abusive act occurs, although it must be emphasized to jurors that this is not an excuse, justification or mitigation for the conduct. Motive can also help establish the identity of the perpetrator (People v. Avellar, 1993).

The most common motive in SBS cases is anger or frustration resulting from the infant's crying. There may be other motives or stressors that work independent of or in combination with the baby's crying. These include diaper soiling or spitting up food, inability to get the child to sleep, difficulties in feeding the child, or a medical or physical condition of the child which is frustrating for the caretaker. Sometimes a thorough search of the residence can identify physical evidence, which corroborates this motive (e.g., a soiled diaper, medications the child is taking, vomitus, etc.).

Other motives focus more on the adult's situation rather than any specific conduct of the child. These include the caretaker's use of alcohol or drugs, frustration with child care responsibilities, domestic discord, children blamed for interfering with the adult's relationship, lack of experience with caretaking, unemployment or financial difficulties, stress at home or work, exhaustion and post partum depression. Independent corroborative evidence of these factors can often be obtained through investigative methods including scene searches and interviews of the offender and people who know him or her.

However, there are numerous SBS cases, which involve more heinous motives than those identified above. A significant challenge in many of these cases is to look for motive evidence, which elevates the *mens rea* of the offense to one involving malice or a more premeditated type of offense, with shaking being the mechanism by which this motive is carried out. Frequently this requires prosecutors to look beyond the act of shaking itself and the offender's explanation for the offense to the offender's overall attitude toward the child and the past history of caretaking. The presence of prior significant abusive injuries to the child clearly indicates a higher *mens rea* and evidences a motive to deliberately injure or torture the child. Occasionally, life insurance policies taken out on the child may establish a motive to deliberately kill the child. Additionally, the caretakers statements during the commission of the offense and a history of abuse to other family members can establish the violent nature of the crime and the defendant's motive to deliberately inflict injury or death (People v. Holmes, 1993).

Whatever the identified motive(s), the prosecutor must present evidence in support of this during the trial and incorporate the theme and theory of the case to reflect this explanation for the events.

PRE-TRIAL MOTIONS

Pre-trial motions serve a variety of purposes in the prosecution of SBS cases. Although prosecutors are generally less accustomed to motion practice than defense attorneys, pre-trial motions should be viewed as an effective "offensive" weapon in the prosecutor's arsenal which should be aggressively used. Once standard motions are developed, they can be used repeatedly with slight modifications tailored to the specific facts of the case. Effective motion practice is limited only by the creativity of the prosecutor, and the time he or she devotes to the practice. A variety of already prepared motions and supporting briefs are generally available by networking with other prosecutors in the jurisdiction. The American Prosecutors Research Institute's National Center for Prosecution of Child Abuse also maintains a variety of motions and briefs on the topics discussed below from jurisdictions across the country (APRI, 1993).

Effective use of pre-trial motions can serve to (1) educate the trial judge about important aspects of the case through a detailed statement of the facts of the case, (2) make the trial more efficient by obtaining early rulings which narrow the scope of issues that must be litigated at trial, (3) flush out potential defenses and defense theories for the case, (4) limit or exclude potential defenses and the testimony of defense witnesses, (5) secure critical rulings on the admissibility of evidence favorable to the prosecution, and (6) allow the prosecution to appeal potentially adverse rulings by the court which would otherwise not be available once the trial began. The favorable determination of pre-trial motions can also markedly reduce the likelihood that the case will go to trial since the defendant will have a better appreciation of the strength of the prosecution case and the evidence that will be heard by the jury.

Several key areas of pre-trial motion practice should be attended to in every case. These include motions dealing with (1) child witnesses, (2) discovery, (3) expert witness testimony, (4) other acts evidence, (5) general evidentiary issues, and (6) jury instructions.

The complex nature of these cases and the serious stakes involved with trial proceedings necessitate that extra attention be paid to ensuring a fair jury. This is especially true in the wake of media attention to SBS cases and high profile trials, which frequently disseminates potentially inflammatory and incorrect information that can taint prospective jurors. Space does not permit a detailed discussion of jury selection tactics, and the reader is referred to other sources (APRI, 1993; DerOhannesian, 1998; Holmgren, 1999). However, the prosecutor should consider filing pre-trial motions regarding the jury selection process including motions to permit appropriate individual voir dire, use supplemental jury questionnaires, and to expand the length and scope of questioning.

Occasionally, a shaking episode is observed by an older sibling, or that sibling is needed to testify regarding other matters including their own abuse by the caretaker. Child witnesses in physical abuse cases require all the pre-trial preparation that child victims do in sexual abuse cases. To the extent possible, pre-trial motions should be used to facilitate their appearance in court. These may include motions to modify the courtroom environment to allow them to sit in child-appropriate furniture while testifying, to have the presence of a support person, and to limit the length of testimony to accommodate their limited attention span and personal schedule. Motions should also be brought to compel the use of linguistically and developmentally appropriate questions with the child, and to restrict or permit the use of leading questions on direct and cross-examination (Walker, 1999). In limited instances, it may be necessary to have the child's testimony presented via closed circuit television or a videotaped deposition. Motions addressing the need for such procedures must satisfy constitutional standards and generally need to be supported by expert witness testimony (Maryland v. Craig, 1990; People v. Diefenderfer, 1989; State v. Lopez, 1991; State v. Michaels, 1993). The admissibility of the child's prior statements to investigators and lay witnesses pursuant to various "hearsay" exceptions should also be addressed.

Discovery motions are extremely important to ensure the prosecution has adequate notice of the defenses and defense witnesses likely to be called. Many states have reciprocal discovery provisions, requiring disclosure of defense witnesses and experts, and evidence they intend to introduce. Some even permit the right to depose these witnesses, and have access to their reports and any materials they will rely on in their testimony. In jurisdictions which do not provide a statutory right to such information, the prosecutor must file pre-trial motions to compel disclosure of this information. The prosecutor should demand at least the equivalent degree of information she is required to disclose pursuant to defense rights of discovery.

Courts frequently are reticent to agree to such requests in the absence of statutory or case law authority, often reasoning that the defendant is not required to disclose his defense, or that compelling such disclosure may jeopardize his right to a fair trial. The prosecution, however, is also entitled to a fair trial. Several arguments can be advanced in support of this right to discovery. First, such discovery will speed up the trial process by ensuring that delays do not occur in preparation for cross-examination, or in determining the admissibility of proposed defense expert testimony. Judges tend to be quite receptive to arguments designed to maintain an efficient court calendar and to avoid having jurors wait around during trials.

Second, the Federal Rules of Evidence provisions dealing with expert witnesses are premised on the rights of all litigants to have access to information prior to trial so that each side is well prepared to examine and cross-examine the experts (Federal Rules of Evidence, Rule 705, Advisory Committee Notes). The more liberal rules governing admissibility of expert testimony (Federal Rules of Evidence, Rule 702) are to be counterbalanced by the right of each side to challenge the expert's testimony on cross-examination. This can only occur if the parties are well prepared. Additionally, trial courts are now required to act as "gatekeepers" on the admissibility of expert testimony, a job which can only be performed if each side is prepared to identify the strengths and weaknesses in the expert's proposed testimony and scientific methodology (Daubert v. Merrell Dow Pharmaceuticals, Inc., 1993; Kumho Tire Company v. Carmichael, 1999; United States v. Scheffer, 1998).

Pre-trial motions should similarly be brought to limit or exclude inappropriate expert testimony. Recent attention has been brought to the problem of irresponsible medical expert testimony in physical abuse cases (Chadwick & Krous, 1997; Chadwick, Chin, Salerno, Landsverk, & Kitchen, 1998). This problem is fostered by the liberal evidentiary rules facilitating admission of expert testimony, coupled by the prosecutor's frequent lack of familiarity with the medical science and inadequate preparation time for defense experts.

To combat this problem, prosecutors should additionally file pre-trial motions to compel the defense to (1) make an offer of proof regarding the defense expert's proposed testimony, (2) disclose any authority including medical literature that supports this position, and (3) *voir dire* or question the expert before his testimony is heard by the jury to permit the court to determine its admissibility and scope. The prosecutor should also bring a pre-trial motion for use of appropriate "learned treatises" such as medical texts and journal articles (Federal Rules of Evidence, Rule 803(13)). These learned treatises can buttress the testimony of the prosecution's experts while at the same time form a basis for cross-examination of the defense expert.

Some authority exists for excluding expert testimony which is not sufficiently premised on the facts of the case or accepted medical practice (Daubert v. Merrell Dow Pharmaceuticals Inc., 1993; Frye v. United States, 1923; Kumho Tire Company v. Carmichael, 1999; People v. Wernick, 1996; State v. Cressey, 1993). For example, a defense expert seeking to testify that a child's fractures may be caused by osteogenesis imperfecta (OI) should be prohibited from doing so in the absence of additional clinical findings (other than the fractures themselves) supporting the conclusion the child suffers from this disorder. This follows in part from the legal principle of the doctrine of chances and its relation to the relevancy requirements for admission of evidence.

If the statistical frequency of OI is 1 in 15,000-60,000 in the general population of infants (Ablin et al., 1990), then absent some other physical findings suggesting the child suffers from this disorder (e.g., wormian bones, blue sclera, dentinogenesis imperfecta), the mere 1 in 15,000-60,000 possibility the child has this disorder is not sufficient to make this opinion relevant. In fact, other medical commentary has concluded that the probability a child under one year old would have type IV OI in the absence of a family history, while having otherwise normal radiological findings, no wormian bones and normal teeth is between 1 in 1-3 million (Taitz, 1987). Additionally, because retinal hemorrhages, subdural hematomas, and brain injury are not associated with OI, the presence of these additional findings makes any testimony suggesting the presence of OI even less relevant, since the diagnosis of OI cannot explain away the most significant findings associated with a diagnosis of SBS. More recent medical literature critiques the lack of scientific rigor employed in several studies frequently cited by defense experts testifying on this disease, and highlights the importance of a careful differential diagnosis of this disorder before such expert testimony is presented (Lachman, Krakow, & Kleinman, 1998).

Most medical opinions are required to be stated to a reasonable degree of medical certainty or probability. Furthermore, many jury instructions on reasonable doubt exclude doubts premised on mere speculation. These legal principles strongly suggest that expert medical evidence premised on this type of weak "possibility" defense is not something, which the defendant would be constitutionally entitled to present as a matter of due process.

Prosecutors are likely to encounter defense arguments suggesting that these facts all go to the weight of the evidence and the value the jury places on the expert testimony. Indeed, some case law interpreting the liberal relevancy and expert witness provisions of the Federal Rules of Evidence supports these arguments (People v. Jackson, 1971; State v. Sibert, 1994; State v. Stribley, 1995; State v. Warness, 1995). Courts concerned with inhibiting a defendant's right to present a defense and possible reversal on appeal may capitulate to these arguments.

However, it is virtually impossible for the prosecutor or his medical experts to eliminate all the possibilities which might account for the child's medical findings. The test for legal admissibility should be whether these alternatives are both reasonable and likely. Prosecutors should point to other case law discussing the dangers of admitting weak scientific evidence, and the tendency of jurors to place too much weight on expert testimony because of their own lack of knowledge (People v. Beckley, 1990; State v. Bantangan, 1990; State v. Cressey, 1993). Prosecutors can also argue such testimony should be excluded because it will be more prejudicial than probative and is likely to add to jury confusion. Prosecutors should also emphasize the recent trend in appellate decisions requiring trial judges to carefully scrutinize expert testimony before permitting its receipt and the additional requirement that such testimony be "reliable" before admission (Daubert v. Merrell Dow Pharmaceuticals, Inc, 1993; In re Agent Orange Product Liability Litigation, 1985; Kumho Tire Company v. Carmichael, 1999).

Another area for pre-trial exclusion of defense expert testimony is expert testimony designed to show the defendant did not know about the dangers from shaking a child, or did not intend to cause harm to the child. This testimony is generally offered to rebut the specific *mens rea* element the prosecution is required to prove, or to attempt to reduce the degree of offense or the defendant's culpability in the eyes of the jury. Frequently this expert testimony is premised on earlier medical literature suggesting this lack of awareness (Caffey, 1974; Dykes, 1986; Guthkelch, 1971), and on general survey research identifying the degree of public awareness of the dangers of shaking infants.

This testimony and the research on which it is based does not satisfy admissibility standards for expert testimony for several reasons. First and foremost, the law specifically prohibits an opinion on the defendant's state of mind at the time of an offense unless an insanity defense is raised (Federal Rules of Evidence 704(b); United States v. Lewis, 1988). Second, no expert can reasonably claim they know what was going on in the defendant's mind at the time of the offense. Third, the prosecution may not be required to prove subjective awareness of the dangers of shaking as an element of the offense, thereby making this type of expert testimony irrelevant. Although knowledge of such dangers is a factor in aggravation of the conduct because it establishes a higher *mens rea,* ignorance of these dangers is not a mitigator.

Finally, the empirical data upon which this testimony is based is also irrelevant. The issue for the jury is whether an objective person observing the violent shaking would appreciate its abusive nature, and the danger it poses to the child. General public knowledge regarding the dangers of shaking does not inform that jury decision, or say anything about the individual defendant's state of mind. This research was not conducted by having those surveyed watch an actual shaking incident and then asking them whether they thought this conduct is dangerous or abusive. Had the research been conducted in this fashion it might have provided some relevant information for jurors, though it is doubtful the results would have been favorable to the defendant.

Moreover, the suggestion that defendants are unaware of the consequences of shaking infants is simply inconsistent with current medical findings regarding the degree of violence necessary to produce these injuries. As one set of commentators has pointed out, this excuse offered by the defense is the equivalent of saying "I did not know a gun could kill" (Rainey & Greer, 1994). Nevertheless, at least one appellate court has held that it is error to exclude an expert's testimony on the general lack of awareness of the dangers of shaking (United States v. Gaskell, 1993). However, the arguments raised above were not addressed by the court and consequently its value as precedent may be questioned.

Some additional areas for pre-trial motions include motions to admit: (1) autopsy photos, (2) various demonstrative aides, charts or summaries including time lines, (3) novel types of expert testimony, e.g., biomechanics,

(Hymel et al., 1998; Spivak, 1992), (4) the defendant's prior convictions for impeachment and use during cross-examination, and (5) evidence of prior acts of abuse by the defendant or other injuries to the victim, which are discussed in more detail in the next section. Finally, the prosecution may attempt to exclude or limit certain other types of defense evidence. These include motions to exclude (1) any reference to or use of the defendant's self-serving hearsay statements unless the defendant testifies (Brown v. State, 1985; Clemens v. State, 1993), (2) evidence regarding the defendant's character, especially evidence of a "peaceful" or "non-violent" nature, (3) any expert testimony profiling the defendant as someone not likely to abuse children (Byrd v. State, 1992; Hoosier v. State, 1992; People v. Neer, 1987; People v. Wernick, 1996), and (4) expert testimony on battered woman's syndrome as a defense to failure to protect or child endangerment charges involving the non-shaking caretaker (Commonwealth v. Lazarovich, 1989; State v. Mott, 1997; State v. Wyatt, 1996).

Occasionally, an expert attempts to corroborate his opinions by testifying that he has consulted with another non-testifying expert who agreed with his position. Although the rules of evidence permit an expert to rely on facts and data not otherwise admissible "if of a type reasonably relied upon by experts in the particular field" (Federal Rules of Evidence 703), the courts have generally ruled that this provision does not permit such testimony because the opinions of the non-testifying expert are hearsay (O'Kelly v. State, 1980; State v. Towne, 1982; United States v. Grey Bear, 1989). Ironically, the same result can effectively be reached if the defense expert purports to rely on published medical literature which is of questionable validity since the hearsay exception for "learned treatises" specifically permits this type of opinion bootstrapping if the expert self-authenticates the article (Federal Rules of Evidence 803(13)). This is simply one more reason for why the court should permit extensive discovery of the defense expert including voir dire of the expert prior to receipt of his testimony.

Jury instructions can play a critical role in how jurors assess the testimony presented and apply the facts to the legal standards required for conviction. The propriety of these instructions is also a constant source for appellate litigation with erroneous instructions frequently resulting in the reversal of convictions (People v. Sargent, 1999; State v. Wyatt, 1996). The difficulties encountered in translating the medical evidence into appropriate legal constructs through charges under specific statutes are similarly present when the court instructs the jury on the elements of the offense which must be proven by the prosecution. Additionally, cautionary instructions are generally required when certain types of evidence are presented (e.g., other crimes, accomplice testimony, use of autopsy photographs) to reduce the potential for prejudice to a party, and some instructions may place limitations on how evidence may be interpreted (e.g., use of hypotheticals, use of prior inconsistent statement for impeachment or substantive evidence) (DerOhannesian, 1998).

Although prosecutors frequently do not think of addressing such issues during pre-trial motion practice, this setting provides the best opportunity to litigate such matters. There is generally insufficient time during the trial itself to conduct detailed legal research into problematic issues, and trial strategy often cannot be changed to accommodate these concerns. Careful review of the substantive instructions for the charged offense will alert the prosecutor to whether their are subtle nuances in evidentiary requirements that must be attended to at trial, or potentially modified through a motion directed to the court. For example, a prosecutor charging an offense that requires proof of the *mens rea* element of "knowledge" might seek to have the court adopt broader definitions of that term encompassed in case law decisions (People v. District Court, 1990; People v. Sargent, 1999) through a modified jury instruction, rather than the more restrictive definitions typically drawn from the Model Penal Code (American Law Institute, 1962; State v. Wyatt, 1996). Similarly, where alternative theories for legal culpability may be charged, or alternative *mens rea* elements may be alleged, the prosecutor may want to consider a jury instruction on unanimity or a verdict form requiring specific findings to protect against potential post-conviction challenges to the instructions or verdict.

Other Acts by the Defendant and Evidence of the Victim's Prior Injuries

SBS cases frequently involve situations in which there is evidence that the defendant has previously abused the same child, another child, or a spouse (Brewster et al., 1998). Additionally, the victim may evidence prior injuries (old subdural hematoma, healing rib or metaphyseal fractures) suggestive of prior shaking episodes, or other unexplained or abusive injuries (bruises, other findings consistent with a diagnosis of battered child syndrome). The admissibility of such evidence implicates a variety of legal issues, evidentiary rules and case law.

In 1991, the United States Supreme Court decided *Estelle v. McGuire,* an extremely important child homicide case for prosecutors. The child victim in *McGuire* had numerous injuries in different stages of healing, including massive internal injuries that caused her death. Doctors made a medical diagnosis of Battered Child Syndrome (BCS) and ruled the death a homicide. The defendant admitted to police that he was home with the child when the most recent injuries occurred, and suggested these injuries resulted from a fall off the couch. There was no direct evidence the defendant had exclusive custody of the child when several of the older injuries occurred. The trial court permitted introduction of all of the child's injuries nevertheless, and the defense challenged the admission of this evidence on appeal to the Supreme Court.

In issuing its decision, the Court reaffirmed the admissibility of expert medical testimony involving BCS, commenting that every jurisdiction had upheld the admission of this type of evidence. Courts which affirm this type of medical diagnosis also implicitly sanction expert medical testimony commenting on the falsity of the offender's explanation for the injuries, since a discrepant history is part of the differential diagnosis of BCS (Kempe et al., 1962). This represents one of the rare instances in which expert testimony dealing with an offender's credibility is admissible (People v. Gordon, 1987; People v. Montesa, 1995; People v. Stanciel, 1992; Schleret v. State, 1981; State v. Jones, 1990; State v. McKowen, 1989; United States v. Bowers, 1981).

The Supreme Court sanctioned the admission of the child's other injuries, which formed part of the diagnosis of BCS. The Court ruled that evidence of BCS was admissible to prove the offender's intent or *mens rea* (i.e., that the child was deliberately injured or the injuries were the result of abusive acts). The evidence was also admissible to prove the injuries were not the result of an accident or inadvertence. More importantly, the Court ruled the BCS evidence was admissible regardless of whether the defendant claimed the injuries were caused accidentally. As the Court stated, "the prosecution's burden to prove every element of the crime is not relieved by a defendant's tactical decision not to contest an essential element of the offense."

Accordingly, even if a defendant concedes the current injuries are caused by abusive shaking, and only contests that he caused them, evidence of prior injuries supporting a diagnosis of BCS will still be admissible. "Evidence demonstrating battered child syndrome helps to prove that the child died at the hands of another and not by falling off a couch, for example; it also tends to establish that the 'other' whoever it may be, inflicted the injuries intentionally." The import of the Court's holding is not diminished by a charging decision that does not require proof of intent, as for example, where the SBS case is charged under a statute providing for "reckless" or "negligent" injury or death.

In fact, the more times a child is injured, the clearer the evidence of the offender's purpose becomes (Imwinkelried, 1992; Mueller & Kirkpatrick, 1994; Myers, 1997; Wigmore, 1978). Shaking which is severe enough to produce a subdural hematoma will also induce a corresponding central nervous system response, which will be observable to the perpetrator. Although the first shaking episode may not produce symptoms so severe that the offender must seek out immediate medical treatment, this fact does not support an offender's claim that "I shook the baby before and he was all right," nor support the claim the offender was unaware of the potential consequences from shaking an infant (Gilliland, 1997; People v. Evers, 1992). Rather, the failure to seek medical attention in an effort to conceal the shaking episode supports a further inference of the offender's awareness of the dangers inherent in the conduct. Consequently the offender's willingness to shake the baby a second time, in appreciation of the consequences from the first incident, should support a higher level of *mens rea* for a charge involving the second incident.

Even more important was the Supreme Court's holding that evidence of the prior injuries supporting the diagnosis of BCS was relevant even if the prosecution could not establish that the defendant caused the injuries. Following precedent established more than twenty years earlier (People v. Jackson, 1971), the Court stated "proof of battered child syndrome itself narrowed the group of possible perpetrators to the (defendant) and his wife," since "only someone regularly 'caring' for the child has the continuing opportunity to inflict these types of injuries; an isolated contact with a vicious stranger would not result in this pattern of successive injuries stretching through several months" (Estelle v. McGuire, 1991).

Accordingly, BCS evidence helps to prove the identity of the perpetrator, or at least to narrow the class of likely suspects to those with continuing access to the child (People v. Henson, 1973; State v. Moorman, 1996; State v. Phillips, 1991; United States v. Boise, 1990). This can be very important in cases in which the defense attempts to expand the time frame for when the injuries occurred and thereby suggest an alternative perpetrator, or where the defendant specifically seeks to shift blame for any of the child's injuries. The repetitive injuries, make the chances of this defense being true less likely.

The key to admission of this evidence lies in establishing the defendant had the opportunity to cause the prior injuries (State v. Moorman, 1996). Where evidence of prior injuries exists, it is extremely important for investigators to expand the time line for the offense to include the time period during which the earlier injuries were produced. Every effort should be made to show the defendant's continuing access to the child during this period. The reasoning of the Court in *McGuire* may not apply where the prosecution cannot establish the defendant could have caused the injuries. In this circumstance, the injuries which do not fall within the time period where the defendant had access to the child may be considered irrelevant and inadmissible. For the same reason, the expert may be precluded from considering such injuries in forming his opinion on whether the child's current injuries are the result of abuse.

When there is direct evidence that the defendant caused the prior injuries, the prosecutor should consider charging the defendant with these injuries as well. If the defendant did not directly cause the injuries but was aware of their existence, an additional criminal charge for neglect or failure to protect can be brought. The additional charges should be issued on the same complaint or information to avoid the need to file a subsequent motion for joinder of the separate counts for trial. Charging additional counts for the other injuries may obviate the need to file a separate pre-trial motion for use of the other acts evidence, and may compel the defense to reveal their trial strategy should they object to the use of such evidence or the joinder of the different counts at trial.

Other acts of abuse to the child or prior injuries are admissible even if they are not the same type as the current injuries or produced by a similar mechanism (Myers, 1997; People v. Robbins, 1988; Wigmore, 1978;Wright & Graham, 1990). The injuries in the *McGuire* case were produced by different mechanisms and many of the types of injuries encompassed by the diagnosis of BCS can be produced by a variety of abusive acts. Similarly, abusive acts involving other child victims are generally admissible, even if the acts are of a different type. The rationale of the *McGuire* decision is equally applicable in these instances and abundant case law supports the admission of these prior acts (APRI, 1993; Myers, 1997).

Pre-trial motions to admit other act evidence should be brought well in advance of the anticipated trial date, and should be supported with appropriate legal authority set forth in a trial brief. Sample briefs on this topic are generally available from other prosecutors within the state, from the state attorney general's office, and through the National Center for Prosecution of Child Abuse. The prosecutor should set forth as many arguments in support of admission as possible, since this will afford the court the greatest discretion in admitting the evidence. Additionally, if the court admits the evidence under multiple theories, the admission may be upheld on appeal under an alternative theory even if one of the grounds for admission is determined to be improper on post-conviction appellate review. The trial court's pre-trial exclusion of other acts evidence may also be reviewable through interlocutory appeal by the prosecution under case law and statutory authority in some jurisdictions.

LAY WITNESSES

Effective use of lay witness testimony is an integral part of any successful trial effort in SBS cases. Every witness who has had caretaking responsibilities with the child during the relevant time period when the abusive injuries occurred must be called to testify to establish they handled the infant in an appropriate manner. This should include calling the EMTs who responded to the scene and transported the child to the hospital to establish their care in handling and treating the child . The absence of any of these caretakers will invite the defense suggestion that they, not the defendant, may have caused the injuries, with their absence at trial attributed to an attempt to conceal their own improper conduct.

Lay witnesses should also be utilized to provide important foundational support for the expert's testimony. Others having contact with the child can establish the time line during which the baby is well and potentially when the baby becomes symptomatic. They may also establish the infant's developmental capabilities to rebut specific defenses such as the child "rolled off the changing table."

The child's pediatrician or family doctor is often an important non-expert witness, establishing the infant's overall health and development and findings from prior well-baby checkups. Testimony regarding missed appointments may suggest the caretaker was trying to conceal prior injuries. Some pediatricians provide specific instructions on appropriate caretaking. These may include the importance of always supporting the child's head, or warnings regarding inappropriate behavior, such as don't shake, bounce or toss the baby. Pediatricians may also provide take-home literature on these topics and note this protocol in the child's medical record. The presentation of such information to the caretaker can establish the defendant's "knowledge" regarding the risks of this type of abusive conduct. While the absence of such knowledge is not a factor in mitigation, its presence may be an important consideration in aggravation.

Not uncommonly, pediatricians and other physicians have failed to diagnose symptoms associated with SBS injuries on occasions prior to the charged event (American Academy of Pediatrics, 1993; Billmire & Myers, 1985; Jenny et al., 1999; Lazoritz, 1995). Frequently this results from the abusive caretaker presenting the child and offering a false history to conceal the etiology of the symptoms, or where a non-abusive caretaker presents the child and is unaware of the abusive conduct precipitating the child's condition. The pediatrician's testimony involving these events and their prior medical diagnosis may be tricky, especially when there is a suggestion that the doctor misdiagnosed the child's condition. In this situation, the prosecutor must first seek to have the doctor acknowledge his mistaken diagnosis, and then emphasize that this misdiagnosis was the direct result of the perpetrator's failure to disclose how the child came to be symptomatic.

Any witness to whom the defendant has provided an explanation for the child's injuries should be called, preferably in chronological order to demonstrate the evolving or changing histories that are common in SBS cases. An effective piece of demonstrative evidence during trial is a chart showing all the defendant's statements about the child's condition and the events, when these statements were made, and to whom. The foundational requirements for introduction of this exhibit can only be met by calling each of these people to testify to the defendant's admissions (Federal Rules of Evidence, Rule 801(d)(2)(A)). This will encompass any medical personnel having contact with the defendant including nurses and paramedics. Personnel monitoring 911 or emergency calls, and any other people who the defendant may telephone immediately following the abuse should also be presented. Frequently the identity of these individuals can be obtained through subpoenas for telephone records of incoming and outgoing calls, and admissions by the defendant during questioning.

The defendant's inappropriate affect or conduct in the presence of these witnesses should also be presented. For example, EMT and medical personnel frequently observe that the defendant appears to show little concern about the child's grave condition. They can testify that the normal response of parents toward their injured children is to immediately seek out medical assistance, question the status of their child's condition and seek reassurance from medical personnel that their child will be all right. This type of testimony can be combined with evidence of the defendant's false histories for the event to show that while medical personnel were showing appropriate concern for the child's condition and treatment, the defendant was not.

Lay witnesses can also provide important background information on the caretaking habits of the defendant. Although these witnesses may rarely witness the defendant shaking the child on prior occasions, they may have observed instances in which the defendant acted inappropriately toward the child, lost his or her temper with the child, or observed violent behavior by the defendant directed toward others including a spouse, sibling or the victim. Neighbors frequently witness these inappropriate behaviors and should be interviewed by the prosecutor if the investigator has not already done so. Former spouses and boyfriends/girlfriends may also have important information regarding the defendant's conduct toward them, the victim and other children.

The prosecutor should seek a pre-trial ruling on the admissibility of such prior conduct evidence. In some instances, lay testimony establishing an inappropriate caretaking history has supported an expert's opinion the child suffered from Battered Child Syndrome (State v. Jurgens, 1988; State v. Ostlund, 1987; State v. Phillips, 1991; State v. Toennis, 1988). In other cases lay witnesses have been permitted to identify injuries observed on other children who were entrusted to the defendant's care (Davis v. State, 1996; People v. Wong, 1992).

Conversely, evidence of the defendant's appropriate caretaking of other children can help establish the defendant had experience in dealing with the stresses of caring for children and, therefore, knew how to respond appropriately when the child would not stop crying. Such testimony can go a long way toward demonstrating that the defendant's conduct in this instance was not an unfortunate momentary response to a difficult and stressful situation, but rather a deliberate choice by someone who knew better.

EXPERT TESTIMONY

The key to any successful prosecution are high quality expert medical opinions diagnosing the child's injuries as a consequence of SBS. The expert may never have occasion to testify about these opinions in court, but these opinions may nevertheless be critical to curtailing the potential for defense challenges during any stage of the criminal process. Solid medical opinions create a disincentive for defendants to go to trial and help ensure appropriate charging decisions and plea negotiations.

Unfortunately, there is no shortage of experts willing to offer opinions challenging the medical findings typically seen in these cases. Irresponsible expert medical testimony continues to confound the truth finding process (Chadwick, Kirschner, Reece, & Ricci, 1998; Chadwick & Krous, 1997), and there is little likelihood this trend will abate in the near future. In fact, exactly the opposite is likely to result from the high profile given these cases recently in the media, and the willingness of many defense experts to advertise their services through public statements challenging well established medical science.

It is incumbent on prosecutors to confront this challenge in several ways. First, prosecutors must have a thorough understanding of the medical issues. Prosecutors should try to find a trusted "medical mentor" within their community to aid them with this process. The medical mentor can provide an orientation to basic anatomy and physiology and help explain the more complicated aspects of SBS. This physician can also provide access to medical texts, help with securing current literature on the topic, and provide answers to questions that may arise when reading the medical literature. If the physician attends conferences that deal with child abuse topics he or she can provide a ready source for the most current developments and literature in the field. Most importantly, the medical mentor can act as a sounding board for bouncing ideas off of and serve as a potential informal consultant when issues involving cases arise. Good sources for a medical mentor include local physicians who belong to the American Academy of Pediatrics (AAP) and/or to the American Professional Society on the Abuse of Children (APSAC).

Second, they must ensure that the experts they use offer solid medical opinion testimony well supported by appropriate medical research. To effect this, it is suggested that prosecutors be conservative with expert testimony in court. There is still a lot that is not well understood about the science of SBS, and reasonable experts debate a number of principles involved with the mechanism of injury in specific types of cases. Third, prosecutors must strenuously challenge irresponsible expert testimony at every stage of the proceeding. Elliot (1987) states, "the law extends equal dignity to the opinions of charlatans and Nobel

Consideration of Other Procedural and Dispositional Options. Mechanisms and Procedural Options available through juvenile court proceedings include:

- Court-ordered physical examination of the child.
- Court-ordered treatment of the child.
- Court-ordered psychological examination of the parent/primary caretaker.
- Court-ordered treatment of the parent as a condition of reunification with the child.
- Court-appointed legal advocate (adversary counsel or guardian ad litem) for the child.
- Court-appointed legal counsel for the parent.
- Court-ordered agency services for both the child and parent.
- Court-ordered no-contact provisions for parents or other individuals related to the child.

In juvenile proceedings involving abuse or neglect of a child, a lower burden of proof than that required in the criminal system is statutorily mandated. State statutes provide that the amount of evidence required to establish the status of Dependency, Neglect, CINC, or CHIPS is either a "preponderance" or "clear and convincing" evidence depending on the jurisdiction. Either burden of proof is less than the criminal burden of proof that is "beyond a reasonable doubt."

The civil rules of evidence prevail in most jurisdictions. Rights of confrontation and rights against self-incrimination are handled differently. In a criminal proceeding, the failure or refusal of a defendant to testify prohibits any negative inference regarding the defendant's guilt. However, in a civil proceeding a parent's refusal or failure to testify does allow the judge or jury to draw a negative inference regarding the parent's culpability. In addition, the rules of discovering information through such vehicles as depositions or written interrogatories are available to the legal practitioner/prosecutor in juvenile proceedings.

It is important that legal practitioner or prosecutor understand and communicate clearly the status of the case and the overall goals and end result of the juvenile proceedings to nonlegal professionals. Such communication at each step is important to achieve and maintain a unified interdisciplinary approach. Health care professionals need to understand that the juvenile court is not the vehicle through which parents can be punished and that there are differences between juvenile court and criminal courts concerning case outcomes and evidentiary requirements.

Prize winners." It is up to prosecutors to distinguish these two brands of expert witnesses in the courtroom.

There are a number of things prosecutors can do to satisfy this task. Prosecutors can consult multiple experts in connection with any given case (APRI, 1993; Stern, 1997). There is strength in numbers, at least insofar as the prosecutor's confidence level in the experts' opinions he is relying on. The danger to this, of course, is that experts may often have slightly different opinions on some issues, which may not be central to the diagnosis of SBS. Nevertheless, these differences may operate to create arguably "exculpatory" information which must be ethically disclosed to the defense, or raise the possibility of jury confusion and reasonable doubt.

Most SBS cases necessitate the use of multiple experts regardless of the prosecutor's desire to seek outside opinions. The highly specialized nature of the medical investigation frequently results in multiple experts being involved with any given case, including emergency room physicians, pediatric specialists, ophthalmologists, radiologists, surgeons, pediatric neurologists and pathologists. It therefore becomes extremely important that the prosecutor coordinate with all of the medical experts who may be needed to testify to ensure the testimony offered is consistent and conclusive (APRI, 1993). All of the experts need to have access to the investigative facts, and be thoroughly familiar with the entire medical record and the findings and opinions of the other experts in the case. If the experts do have differing opinions they should be encouraged to talk with each other to see if they can resolve their differences or limit their disagreements to minor points.

Many of the difficulties encountered with the presentation of expert testimony in SBS cases can be eased by referencing the medical literature. Several child abuse medical references provide excellent discussion of the medical literature and contain extensive reference bibliographies (Ludwig & Kornberg, 1992; Giardino et al., 1997; Monteleone, 1998; Reece, 1994). Additional references abstract this literature and provide a means of keeping current with ongoing research (Jenny, Taylor, & Cooper, 1996; The Institute for Professional Education, 1998). Prosecutorial offices should have one or more of these texts in their libraries, or have ready access to them through other professionals in the community.

This literature can be used to either buttress the expert's opinion, or to demonstrate that even well respected medical experts in the field of SBS sometimes disagree or engage in professional debate through the literature. Such debate does not invalidate the core science of SBS, and the central findings of the syndrome, but it does counsel a more reserved approach to issues which are less well settled. As one set of commentators has noted:

Better understanding of the facts behind physicians' judgments has the paradoxical effect of both increasing and decreasing one's confidence in those judgments. On the one hand, one appreciates the fact that the physician's opinion is based on both an understanding of the mechanisms by which injuries occur and an awareness of the probabilities of various causes drawn from research. On the other hand, one's confidence may be decreased when one recognizes the margin of error within which physicians operate, making it impossible to always state with certainty that abuse occurred. (Lyon et al., 1996, p. 167)

Additionally, both prosecutors and experts must be ever mindful that science is an ongoing process and medical research can quickly become dated. Resort to old research or summaries of research and the conclusions drawn therefrom can be problematic if one is not familiar with the current state of affairs. The prosecutor may joke that he became a lawyer so he wouldn't have to read the science, but he will be the subject of jokes regarding his courtroom performance if he chooses to remain unfamiliar with this necessary area of practice. Without a full understanding of the medical research that underlies an expert's opinion, the prosecutor can neither make full use of the physician's expertise, nor adequately cross-examine the opposing expert (Lyon et al., 1996).

Two examples illustrate this point. First, in 1995, a review of the medical literature on the time interval between lethal infant shaking and the onset of symptoms suggested there was insufficient medical literature to confer scientific legitimacy to any authoritative discussions of this issue. (Nashelsky & Dix, 1995). This time interval is frequently a critical issue in defenses attempting to suggest a so-called "lucid interval" period during which other caretakers may have abused the child. Accordingly, a defense expert might resort to this study in challenging the prosecution's expert testimony that in fatal or very severe SBS cases, the child would have become immediately symptomatic. Regardless of the accuracy of this earlier position, current research and professional consensus within the medical literature clearly supports the conclusion that CNS damage, which is severe or fatal is immediately apparent and there is no lucid interval (Case, 1998; Duhaime, 1997; Duhaime et al., 1998; Lyon et al., 1996; Willman et al.,1997).

Second, an expert witness frequently called by the defense in SBS cases commonly testifies that short falls can produce subdural hematomas. In support of this position, the expert references a recent medical article published in England (Howard, Bell, & Utley, 1993). A careful review of this relatively obscure article, however, reveals a small number of children studied (N = 28). More troubling are the authors' conclusions noting a race-dependent pattern of subdural hematoma pathophysiology with non-Caucasian infants being more prone to subdural hematomas than Caucasians and being more likely to suffer these hematomas after trivial trauma. A prosecutor familiar with this bizarre finding would relish the opportunity to challenge the expert's willingness to rely on data that suggest there's something physically different between Caucasian and non-Caucasian brains.

Expert testimony involving a diagnosis of SBS is well recognized and does not need to satisfy the *Daubert* or *Frye* standards governing the admissibility of expert testimony or novel scientific evidence (Myers, 1997; State v. Lopez, 1991; State v. McClary, 1988). SBS represents a constellation of potential findings, not all of which need be present before the diagnosis can be made or testified to in court (Duhaime et al., 1998; Lazoritz et al., 1997; Levitt et al., 1994). However, the absence of certain types of findings (e.g., retinal hemorrhages, fractures of the head, ribs or long bones) will invariably be brought out as a challenge to the expert's diagnosis. This will not preclude the expert's courtroom opinion the child suffered from SBS, but will instead go to the weight the jury accords the diagnosis.

The expert should emphasize any highly specific findings which permit conclusive or near conclusive diagnosis of SBS or abuse. For example, the presence of metaphyseal fractures is recognized as virtually pathognomonic of abuse and this finding is also very consistent with shaking as a mechanism. Similarly, retinal hemorrhages, bilateral subdural hematoma, and diffuse axonal injury are highly specific for SBS as a mechanism.

Not only must the expert testify regarding the significance of specific medical findings, he must also explain for the jury how it is that the child may suffer grave internal injuries without evidencing any external signs of trauma to the head (Case, 1998). Jurors who are unable to understand this apparent dichotomy may conclude that significant forces could not have been applied to the head, in the absence of physical markers such as significant bruises, lacerations or skull fracture. As one author has commented:

> Sufficiently important to justify repetition is the generalization that absence of external traumata does not preclude the presence of grave internal injuries. The most common form of 'concealed' fatal trauma, whether it involves the head, neck, chest or abdomen, is that caused by blunt force . . . the pathologist must be aware of the frequently encountered combination of minor or absent external injuries associated with internal traumata of sufficient gravity to be fatal. (Adelson, 1974, p. 381)

The expert must also describe, and if possible illustrate with demonstrative aides (discussed *infra*), how many of the serious injuries sustained by the child consist of very tiny or microscopic findings, e.g., tears of bridging veins and diffuse axonal injury.

Similarly, the expert should explain the mechanism for how these injuries are manifested. Here also medical illustrations and other demonstrative aides are important in simplifying the medical science. Equally important is an explanation of how impact against a soft object such as a bed mattress or sofa cushion can magnify the shearing forces to the infant's brain, yet leave no telltale evidence on the skin or head. The mechanisms for brain swelling and disruption of respiratory centers in the brain caused by SBS trauma must also be explained. Emphasis should be placed on explaining how and why hypoxia, edema, diffuse axonal or other significant brain injury is the critical finding in understanding the child's death or injury, and correspondingly how the subdural hematoma is a marker for this type of mechanism of trauma and the magnitude of forces involved, rather than the cause of death itself.

These facts can also be used to explain why there is a rapid onset of symptomology in severe cases to refute defense efforts to expand the time frame for the child's injury or suggest a "lucid interval" defense. For example, the expert can explain that if the child suffers diffuse axonal injury during the shaking, the wiring system in the child's brain is immediately disrupted. The wiring system doesn't function appropriately for a period of time with the child appearing normal and then suddenly collapsing. Rather the child suffers devastating neurological impairment, which is immediately apparent. The expert can analogize this scenario to having all the household appliances plugged in and working in the home, and then cutting the electrical wires on several of the appliances. The appliances won't continue to work for a while and then shut off. Instead, the homeowner will immediately notice that the appliances aren't functioning.

A key component of any expert testimony on SBS involves translating the mechanism of trauma into constructs jurors can readily understand and which adequately reflect the *mens rea* requirements for the charge. This can be done in a variety of ways. First, experts can provide analogies for the degree of violence associated with this conduct. For example, the expert can testify that the forces the child experiences are the equivalent of a 50-60 m.p.h. unrestrained motor vehicle accident, or a fall from 3-4 stories onto a hard surface (Commonwealth v. Merola, 1989; Jones v. State, 1994; People v. Evers, 1992; State v. Ojeda, 1991; United States v. Merriweather, 1986). Another explanation relates the gravitational or "G" forces minimally necessary to produce some of these injuries (greater than 10 G's) to experiences jurors may have had, e.g., a roller coaster ride (1-2 G's). Dr. Randell Alexander (personal communication) provides another helpful analogy, comparing the difference in size and strength between the adult perpetrator and the child as the equivalent of a 200 pound man being shaken by a 2,000 pound gorilla.

Second, the expert can use a variety of adjectives to describe the force involved in the shaking. Commonly this involves testimony that the shaking had to be "severe" and "repeated," "violent" and involving "very substantial force creating a substantial risk of death" (People v. Nix, 1991; People v. Rader, 1995; People v. Wong, 1992). The expert may describe that the shaking must be "sustained," lasting for several seconds and generally involving more than 10 oscillations where the child's head moves back and forth impacting the chin against the chest and the back of the head against the back. Frequently the expert will explain that shaking forces involve the adult shaking the child as hard as they can until the adult becomes tired and stops.

Third, the expert can remind jurors of their own knowledge and experience in delicately handling children and the importance of supporting infant's heads at all times, thereby providing a pointed contrast with the defendant's conduct and that of an appropriate caretaker. An expert who testifies that the person doing the shaking would themselves witness the child's head "bouncing back and forth on top of the infant's body as the shaking is happening" will create a visual image of conduct which is certain to be recognized by jurors as both abusive and potentially lethal, while at the same time emphasizing the purposeful or knowing conduct of the perpetrator.

Experts can also indicate that if shaking deaths could be inflicted by trivial forces or common events, then we would expect to see a lot more child fatalities since infants are often subjected to accidents or falls, playful tossing or bouncing, or rapid deceleration in braking automobiles, but these events generally don't produce severe or fatal injuries (People v. Wong, 1992). The expert should always emphasize that the amount of violence involved with the shaking is such that any competent individual would recognize that it was dangerous and the child was being injured (American Academy of Pediatrics, 1993; People v. Rader, 1995; People v. Sargent, 1999; Smith, 1994; State v. Ojeda, 1991). Some literature additionally supports the position that the severity of injury experienced by the child is representative of the severity of forces visited upon them (Green, Lieberman, Milroy, & Parsons, 1996).

When there is evidence of multiple non-accidental injuries to the child of different ages the expert will likely diagnose the infant as suffering from battered child syndrome (BCS) as well as SBS. During testimony, the expert should explain the factors, which make up the differential diagnosis of BCS, emphasizing that not all of the factors need be present to make the diagnosis (People v. Henson, 1973; Schleret v. State, 1981; State v. Holland, 1984). For example, the absence of neglect findings does not rule out a diagnosis of BCS when the child has multiple long bone fractures and a subdural hematoma.

Most importantly, the expert must comment upon the caretaker's false or discrepant history as an important part of the differential diagnosis, emphasizing that use of these false histories is a well recognized and widely utilized medical diagnostic principle in determining whether injuries are abusive (Gideon v. State, 1986; People v. Gordon, 1987; People v. Montesa, 1995; State v. Jones, 1990). This represents one of the rare instances in which prosecutors can call an expert witness to offer an opinion on credibility, in effect testifying that the defendant has lied (or is lying at trial if he repeats the false history through testimony), and why that fact leads to a conclusion that the child was abused or the death is a homicide. The expert should also emphasize that the constellation of the child's injuries must be considered, not simply isolated injuries, which might have a plausible benign explanation to account for their presence.

The expert's testimony should establish that he considered and ruled out alternative causes for the child's medical findings before making the diagnosis of abuse or homicide. This represents an opportune time to preempt the testimony of the defense expert by addressing the "alternative theories" the defense expert is proposing. The state's expert can indicate he considered these alternative theories and explain why he rejected them. When jurors later hear the defense expert offers these theories, they are less likely to be accepting of them, having been already told why these theories don't make sense.

The key to establishing the timing of injuries in less serious SBS cases is to focus on establishing when the baby last appeared well and without symptoms, and correspondingly when the symptoms typically accompanying SBS injuries will manifest (Case, 1998; Levitt et al., 1994). This may be problematic where the symptomology is more subtle, there is a significant delay in the child being seen for treatment, or there are multiple incidents of trauma with overlying symptoms associated with each. Additionally, the symptomology can be both the result of the abuse, or a stress factor leading to its cause, potentially confounding this timing (Duhaime, 1997; Lazoritz, 1995). For example, the child's irritability can be both the trigger for abuse and a response to pain associated with a past incident of shaking. Where multiple incidents of trauma occur, this scenario may become very difficult to sort out. Shaking may be repeated precisely because it does temporarily quiet children (Levitt et al., 1994; Spaide, Swengel, Scharre, & Mein, 1990), with the conduct reoccurring until the child's symptoms become serious enough to necessitate medical treatment.

The expert witness should identify the clinical symptoms commonly associated with SBS and the symptoms they would expect to see based on the type of injuries present in the child. This can then be correlated with the defendant's admissions regarding the presence of these symptoms and lay witness testimony regarding the absence of these symptoms prior to the time the defendant assumed care of the child.

Finally, the prosecutor must take full advantage of the fact that medical examiners and forensic pathologists are entitled to offer expert opinions dealing with both the "cause" of death, and the "manner" of death, i.e., accident or homicide. Forensic pathologists undergo additional medical training and practical experience in the field enabling them to render this specialized medical-forensic type of diagnosis. A defense expert who does not share these qualifications is arguably not capable of providing an expert medical opinion on the "manner" of death, although they may be able to offer a non-abusive explanation for the "cause" of the medical findings. This contrast in relative expertise should be emphasized in cross-examination of the opposing expert and during the closing argument.

A lengthy discussion of other considerations in the presentation of expert witness testimony is beyond the scope of this discussion. Several additional resources provide excellent practical suggestions and prosecutors should consult these in preparation for trial (APRI, 1993; DerOhannesian, 1998; Stern, 1997).

IN-COURT DEMONSTRATIONS BY THE EXPERT

Prosecutors frequently want to have their expert provide an in-court demonstration of the amount of force necessary to cause the victim's injuries. In *United States v. Gaskell,* a conviction for SBS was reversed based on the court's determination that the expert witness should not have been permitted to give such a demonstration with a rubber mannequin to the jury. The expert conceded he did not know how long the shaking lasted, or how many oscillations of the child's head were necessary to produce the injuries. Additionally, the mannequin was not similar to the victim in size, weight and neck rigidity, thereby requiring more force to produce the head movement on the doll than would have been needed with the child. Consequently, the court held that the conditions of the demonstration were not sufficiently similar to the alleged actions of the accused to allow the jury to make a fair comparison, and the expert's demonstration was without sufficient foundation (United States v. Gaskell, 1993).

The *Gaskell* decision is well reasoned and illustrates several problems inherent with this type of demonstrative evidence in SBS cases. Medical studies suggest that the rotational components of the shaking, and/or a sudden deceleration produced by shaking and impact may greatly increase the shearing forces on the blood vessels and brain tissue, as compared with simply shaking a child with no impact. Stated another way, a demonstration of the amount of force and/or length of time necessary to produce the injuries might be greater in a "pure shaking" or no-impact scenario, as compared to a situation in which the child is shaken and thrown down on a soft mattress. Additionally, many experts disagree on whether impact is necessary to produce certain types of severe injury (Alexander, Sato, Smith, & Bennett, 1990; Bruce & Zimmerman, 1988; Duhaime et al., 1992; Duhaime et al., 1987; Gilliland & Folberg, 1996; Hadley, Sonntag, Rekate, & Murphy, 1989). Consequently, in the absence of an accurate and complete history by the abuser of the act producing the trauma, which is almost never provided, an expert arguably may not have sufficient foundational information to perform an in-court demonstration, at least to the required level of certainty now expected of expert testimony (Daubert v. Merrell Dow Pharmaceuticals, Inc., 1993; Kumho Tire Co. v. Carmichael, 1999). Additionally, prosecutors can anticipate that a defense expert will likely testify there is not sufficient scientific consensus to permit such demonstrations to be made with any degree of accuracy, thereby affording another basis for appellate scrutiny.

These factors may be further complicated by the size and strength of the perpetrator (relative amount of force generated), the method used to shake the child, the degree of angular movement of the head during the shaking, and the unique differences in the child's physical condition at the time of the shaking (degree of myelination of the brain, elasticity of the skull).

At the present time, a conservative approach toward expert witness testimony in this area is suggested. Several subsequent cases have distinguished the *Gaskell* holding (State v. Powell, 1997; United States v. White, 1996), but these decisions are less well reasoned. In a decision pre-dating *Gaskell,* an expert demonstrated the amount of force utilizing a mannequin commonly used for CPR (United States v. Winter, 1991). During the demonstration the head flew off the mannequin and the defendant argued on appeal that this was prejudicial. The conviction was not reversed since the demonstration occurred in a bench trial rather than before a jury. Although the appellate court ruled the demonstration assisted the trier of fact to understand the expert's testimony on the amount of force needed to produce the injury, no foundational challenges to the demonstration were made along the lines brought by the defense in *Gaskell.*

These cases illustrate the importance of having investigators obtain a videotaped demonstration by the offender of the mechanism and force used to shake the child, and the importance of careful questioning to determine if any form of impact was involved. In a recent case, a detective was permitted to recreate for the jury the defendant's non-videotaped demonstration of the shaking mechanism (People v. Kendall, 1998).

The holding in *Gaskell* does not prohibit an expert from reviewing a videotape or recreation of the defendant's demonstration, and offering an opinion on whether the defendant's demonstration and explanation offered are sufficient to produce the degree of injury the child sustained. As noted earlier, this is one of the rare instances in which an expert can comment on the defendant's credibility. Additionally, the *Gaskell* decision does not preclude a demonstration of the mechanism of injury so long as that demonstration does not represent the amount of force or length of shaking involved in the case at hand (People v. Kendall, 1998; People v. Shatell, 1992). Similarly, the expert should be able to demonstrate that bouncing the child up and down on the knee, tossing the baby in the air, and rocking the baby up and down while cradled in an adult's arms are not the types of conduct which generate sufficient forces to produce this type of injury.

If a demonstration is permitted by local practice to illustrate the amount of force involved in a shaking incident, several steps should be followed to protect the record. First, the expert should be expected to state that in their opinion an in-court demonstration, rather than simply verbal descriptions, is necessary to communicate the amount of force involved so that jurors have a sufficient appreciation of the violence associated with this form of traumatic injury (Levitt et al., 1994). This may be even more critical where the defendant has previously offered an explanation that minimizes the degree of force involved or claims a lack of awareness for the dangerousness of the conduct. Second, the expert should articulate that the demonstration does not represent their opinion of what the defendant actually did, either in terms of the exact mechanism for shaking the child, or the length of time or number of shakes-oscillations involved. Instead, the expert should indicate that the demonstration merely represents or illustrates the type of force needed to produce this type of injury to a child.

Another consideration is whether the expert should use a doll or stuffed animal for the demonstration. On the one hand, the doll is more lifelike in appearance, although defendants will argue this adds to the prejudice of the demonstration. Additionally, the doll cannot approximate the physical conditions of the child (e.g., head and body weight, neck rigidity, etc.). A stuffed animal is less prejudicial but, similarly, cannot approximate the child's physical stature. The expert should clearly articulate that these conditions cannot be duplicated for purposes of the demonstration regardless of whether a doll or stuffed animal is chosen. Finally, the expert should qualify the demonstration by indicating that the duration of the shaking incident, the strength of the individual, the number of oscillations, the angular or rotational forces generated during the shaking, and whether impact was involved are all variables which affect the forces injuring the child.

MEETING UNTRUE DEFENSES AND CROSS-EXAMINATION OF DEFENSE EXPERTS

Defenses to SBS cases have become increasingly sophisticated in recent years with the advent of several defense experts who routinely appear in court.

Several of these experts promote their services through contacts with the media and the legal community. One need only review media accounts on the topic of SBS or high profile cases to discern the identity of these experts, and it is likely that their presence in courtrooms will continue to spread as they gain this exposure. Unfortunately, the irresponsible representations made by these experts regarding the science of SBS, which are publicized in the media also tend to influence the pool of prospective jurors exposed to these accounts, and the attitudes of judges who preside over SBS cases. These practices have justifiably prompted public and professional critique (Ablin & Sane, 1997; Chadwick et al., 1998; Chadwick & Krouse, 1997; Higgins, 1998). As Dr. Carolyn Levitt has commented, "medicine knows some things, lawyers interpret it, and something gets lost in the translation" (as cited in Thayer, 1997, p. 20).

A caretaker's explanation for the event and the child's injuries may or may not dictate the defense strategy at trial. Since many of these explanations are readily defeated (e.g., accidental fall), the defense focus at trial may be in different areas. The rule of thumb in approaching these cases should be that there is always a defense, and usually someone who will support it. As one court aptly noted, "there is hardly anything not palpably absurd on its face that cannot now be proved by some so-called expert" (Chaulk v. Volkswagen of Am. Inc., 1986). And another has stated,

> the problem that arises . . . in this age where the 'forensic expert' populates the judicial landscape in ever increasing numbers, is that there is a plethora of experts who look good on paper and do not reveal their shortcomings until they start testifying. Although we would hope that the adversary system would be a safeguard against misinformation, such is not always the case. (Rocha v. Great American Insurance Co., 1988)

However, responsible experts will sometimes take issue with medical findings and conclusions in these cases and support the defense. When they do, their opinions should be strongly considered by prosecutors in evaluating the case, providing such opinions comport with the accepted medical research. Other experts are simply poorly informed on the science, and offer opinions consistent with their lack of expertise. The bottom line is that prosecutors must take these defenses seriously, no matter how absurd or irresponsible. Since jurors will generally have little knowledge regarding the science of SBS, there is always a danger they will accept unscientific representations cloaked in the guise of expertise. Defense attorneys appreciate the common response of many jurors to conflicting medical experts–"if the doctors can't agree, how can we?" Consequently, there is always tremendous incentive to put forward an opposing expert in an effort to create reasonable doubt.

In general, the strategy of defense experts takes one or more of the following courses: (1) to establish "other" possibilities for the child's medical findings, including medical causes that were not ruled out by the doctors or medical examiner; (2) to support an accidental fall or injury as the mechanism for the head trauma; (3) to substantiate the defendant's explanation that the shaking was done to revive or awaken an unresponsive child or because the child was choking; (4) to expand the time frame or window of opportunity for the injuries to create additional suspects; (5) to support the defendant's claim that he didn't mean to hurt the child or didn't realize the danger involved with shaking; and (6) to suggest that the case does not meet the parameters for a diagnosis of SBS because there were no retinal hemorrhages, long bone fractures, or evidence of impact trauma.

There is a veritable laundry list of alternative medical possibilities that are commonly proffered to account for some of the child's medical findings or symptoms. These include but are certainly not limited to Osteogenesis Imperfecta (OI), glutaric aciduria, Alagille syndrome, DPT vaccinations, meningitis, and bleeding and seizure disorders. Additionally, experts often postulate other events as a cause for the symptoms including CPR and birthing to explain retinal hemorrhages and fractures, and accidental falls.

Several responses can be made to the "alternative medical possibilities" type of defense. First, this strategy generally attempts to account for one of the child's physical findings but invariably cannot account for multiple findings. For example, OI may be offered to account for the child's broken ribs but cannot explain retinal hemorrhages or subdural hematomas. Similarly, subdural collections may be seen with glutaric aciduria, but retinal hemorrhages and fractures have not been described as part of the disease (Duhaime et al., 1998). The prosecutor can challenge the defense expert that no other mechanism besides SBS can account for all of the features commonly seen in SBS cases (Duhaime et al., 1998).

Second, the prosecutor can gather relevant medical articles dealing with the proffered defense theory or condition, and file these as learned treatises. The articles can then be used to cross-examine the expert pointing out inconsistencies between the expert's position or diagnosis and the accepted medical literature.

For example, some experts still maintain that based on their experience short falls can produce life-threatening injuries. The expert who offers this opinion exposes himself to the rejoinder that his experience must be from a different gravitational field because it is certainly not based on scientific data. There are dozens of studies examining injuries from falls by children. These studies provide ready ammunition for impeaching this defense, establishing conclusively that children do not sustain life threatening head injuries from short falls (Chadwick, Chin, Salerno, Landsverk, & Kitchen, 1991; Helfer, Slovis, & Black, 1977; Kravitz, Dreissan, Gomberg, & Korach, 1969; Lyons & Oates, 1993; Reiber, 1993; Rivara, Alexander, Johnston, & Soderberg, 1993; Williams, 1991). Similar techniques can be applied to claims that CPR produced the retinal hemorrhages or rib fractures (Gilliland & Luckenbach, 1993; Gilliland et al., 1994; Kanter, 1986; Odom et al., 1997). Synthesis of data from multiple studies with large numbers of children makes for a powerful statistical challenge to the defense expert.

Third, the expert can be challenged on whether there are any medical findings, other than the injuries themselves, which support the alternative hypothesis. Usually, these alternative medical conditions have associated symptomology that will be present in the child. If the expert cannot point to their presence, then the suggestion the child may have this condition is simply speculative, and the expert's opinion should not be permitted (Daubert v. Merrell Dow Pharmaceuticals Inc., 1993; People v. Wernick, 1966; State v. Cressey, 1993).

A common response to this challenge is to suggest that the doctors or medical examiner did not test for this condition, and therefore its presence cannot be ruled out. Here again, the relevance of the defense expert's speculation is conditioned on the frequency or likelihood that the child may suffer from this condition based on population data. If the court does not exclude the expert's opinion, then the prosecutor should cross-examine the expert on the frequency data, letting the jury know the expert is guessing that the child might have this condition, and that there is only a "one-in-(x) thousand" chance the child does.

For these same reasons, opinions which are couched in terms such as "possibilities" rather than "to a reasonable degree of medical certainty" should be challenged. Some courts will exclude opinions which are not offered in terms of this degree of certainty, although other authority suggests these qualifications go to the weight to be given the expert's opinions, not their admissibility (People v. Brown, 1986; People v. Jackson, 1971; State v. Sibert, 1994; State v. Stribley, 1995; State v. Warness, 1995). Irresponsible experts frequently exploit the lack of definitiveness implicit in the terms "reasonable degree of medical certainty" or "probability" assigning their own sliding scale or definitional constructs in this regard to support their opinions. The prosecutor can always point out to the jury that the state's expert offered his opinions to a much higher degree of professional certainty. Similarly, the prosecutor should argue that while "anything is possible," "possibilities" do not constitute "reasonable doubt."

Finally, a rebuttal expert can be called by the state to contradict the opinions offered by the defense expert. The rebuttal expert can also incorporate the relevant medical literature in support of his or her opinions, so that the rebuttal testimony has even greater force.

When the defense expert is called to support the defendant's claim that he shook the child to revive or awaken him, several other options present themselves. This defense is generally only present because the defendant has admitted shaking the child and there is no evidence of prior injury. The expert's testimony, therefore, is premised on acceptance of the caretaker's false account which reverses the true sequence of the events, i.e., the child became non-responsive because he was shaken.

The expert should acknowledge he is relying on the accuracy of the defendant's account, and that if the defendant is lying this would alter his opinion. The expert should also concede that the medical findings support the alternative hypothesis, that the child became unresponsive because he was shaken. If the defendant has given other false information, the expert can be reminded of these false statements, suggesting there is good reason to doubt the version the defendant is now offering. The expert can also be questioned about the cause for the child's initial unresponsive condition. Usually the defendant has offered no explanation for this fact. Finally, the expert must be challenged on the fact that the defendant's account of how hard he shook the child to revive him is grossly inconsistent with medical knowledge about the amount of force necessary to produce these injuries. Medical consensus is clear that mild shaking does not produce severe trauma.

The expert who is called to expand the time frame for the injuries is also vulnerable in several key areas. Both research findings and clinical experience support the position that children who suffer severe and fatal injuries are immediately affected. Clinical and pathologic findings of massive edema and significant traumatic injury to the brain tissue itself are simply inconsistent with a period of normal activity followed by a rapid onset of symptoms which suddenly disable the child. Experts who proffer such positions not only have no science to back up their theories, but will appear to be out in left field to most jurors.

The so-called lucid interval and "rebleed" theory has become popular amongst several defense experts in an effort to expand the time frame for the alleged traumatic injury to the child. This theory postulates that children may experience a trivial trauma, which aggravates a preexisting brain injury or subdural collection causing new injury that results in a sudden collapse of the child. The expert generally postulates that the child appears symptom free up until the secondary trauma and then suffers a sudden collapse.

This theory should be attacked on several grounds. First, there is no scientific research which supports the rebleed theory of causation in very young children. The only documented instances of this occurring are with adults and older children. Accordingly, the application of this theory to infants should be challenged on *Frye* and *Daubert* grounds before it is admitted before the jury.

Second, this theory necessitates a second trauma to the child to support the expert's hypothesis. Not only is this secondary trauma frequently undocumented in the initial histories provided by the caretaker, but such trauma is inconsistent with the developmental stage of the pre-mobile infant who should not be subjected to any form of trauma, whether trivial or more severe, on one let alone two separate occasions.

Finally, the theory is premised on the idea that the bleeding itself is what causes injury to the child. The fact is that in most SBS cases the subdural collection is generally quite small, serving as a marker for a rotational shaking-type injury mechanism, but rarely becoming massive enough to cause injury to the brain itself. Where there is evidence of massive underlying brain injury, such findings are not only inconsistent with a symptom-free lucid interval, but the secondary trauma, if truly trivial, cannot be used as the causative agent for its presence.

The expert may be on firm ground in stating that injuries such as bruises, subdural hematomas and fractures cannot be precisely dated, but the expert should concede that there are generally recognized time frames for dating these injuries. The expert should also concede the various types of clinical symptomology generally seen in SBS cases, and their importance as indicators of when the injury occurred. The defendant's acknowledgment of the presence of any of these symptoms can then be used to narrow the expert's attempts to expand the time frame for the injury. The expert can also be asked to concede that a responsible adult would seek out prompt medical attention in response to observing these symptoms, and that delay in doing so jeopardized the child's welfare.

Defense experts may also attempt to suggest that the absence of certain physical findings such as bilateral retinal hemorrhages, or impact injury to the head suggests the child was not shaken. The response to this untrue defense requires the state's expert to point out that retinal hemorrhages are not present in every case. The expert should identify the many research studies that establish this point and the frequency of this type of injury marker (American Academy of Pediatrics, 1993; Billmire & Myers, 1985; Duhaime et al., 1998; Duhaime et al. 1987; Levin, 1990; Ludwig & Warman, 1984; Starling et al., 1995). Conversely, where retinal hemorrhages are present, the expert should be confronted with medical literature indicating the highly specific nature of this finding for diagnosing SBS (Billmire & Myers, 1985; Buys et al., 1992; Duhaime et al., 1992; Elner et al, 1990; Johnson, Braun, & Friendly, 1993; Levin, 1990, 1991; Massicotte et al., 1991; Munger et al., 1993).

Similarly, the defense expert may suggest that, according to the research of several experts on SBS, serious injuries cannot occur in the absence of impact. Consequently, if there is no direct evidence of impact injury, this non-finding suggests a mechanism other than SBS as a cause for the medical findings. The prosecution must point out that even the research findings relied on by the defense expert note there are frequently no observable signs of trauma even when impact occurs. The prosecution's expert can explain the biomechanics that account for this fact, noting that impact against a soft object or a broad flat surface can distribute forces in a manner that does not result in bruises or fractures to the head, yet still produce significant deceleration forces that are traumatic to the brain (Ludwig & Kornberg, 1992). Here again an analogy may prove helpful. For example, the expert can explain that "a boxer may be knocked unconscious with injury to the brain after impact from a gloved hand yet suffer no facial bruising" (Monteleone & Brodeur, 1998, p. 14).

Some additional guidelines should be considered when cross-examining the defense expert. First, the expert will frequently agree with many of the points made by your expert. This is less likely to happen once a confrontational approach is taken during cross. Accordingly, the cross-examination should begin by seeking the areas of agreement, before attempts are made to challenge the defense expert's position. This also serves to narrow the issues in "dispute" for the jury. Conversely, where the defense calls multiple expert witnesses, any areas of disagreement in their respective opinions should be clearly identified on cross-examination.

One important area of agreement that can be sought in most cases is the importance of the attending physicians receiving accurate information in order to properly treat the child. It can be devastating to the defense to have their own expert acknowledge that a false or discrepant history compromised the child's condition. Similarly, most responsible experts will concede that a false or discrepant history is an important criteria for determining whether injuries are the result of abuse.

Second, the expert should be forced to acknowledge that he did not have an opportunity to personally examine the victim, and therefore, is not in as good a position as the doctors who did see the child to comment on the injuries or the child's overall condition. Third, the expert's expertise and experience should be challenged when appropriate. Many experts appearing in court are not pediatric or forensic specialists, lack practical experience in dealing with children, or have never conducted any research in the field.

The expert's access to information on the case should also be explored. If they have not been provided with all of the facts, this can be brought out. This scenario reflects negatively on both the defense attorney who may be viewed as hiding things, and the expert who is willing to offer opinions without access to all the facts. If the expert does not alter his position when confronted with the new facts, he will appear dogmatic and not objective. Along these same lines, the defense expert on direct examination should be forced to identify the facts, experience or literature he is relying on in forming his opinions before those opinions can be expressed before the jury. This will help ensure there is an adequate foundation for the opinion and allow the prosecutor to analyze the potential weaknesses in this foundation which can be explored on cross-examination.

Another effective strategy is to send a letter to the defense expert requesting the expert provide before trial a copy of all of his notes, reports, test data and other materials he prepared or relied on in forming his opinions. Alternatively, the prosecutor can request the expert bring these materials with him to court when testifying. If the expert provides these items the prosecutor will have an opportunity to review them before cross-examining the expert. If the expert does not, the prosecutor's letter can be marked as an exhibit and used to question the expert regarding why the materials were not produced.

Finally, the expert cannot be permitted to confine his opinions to attacking isolated facts or medical findings. The expert must be confronted with the full spectrum of injuries and asked his opinion about whether the totality of injuries is consistent with abusive trauma, and SBS. The expert who acknowledges the classic findings of SBS include subdural hematoma, retinal hemorrhage and edema, but chooses to ignore this constellation of findings in favor of an alternative hypothesis will appear foolish.

A detailed discussion of cross-examination strategies is not possible herein, and the reader should consult several other excellent resources on this topic (APRI, 1993; DerOhannesian, 1998; Stern, 1997). Additionally, APRI's National Center for Prosecution of Child Abuse maintains files on expert witnesses including copies of their curriculum vitae, transcripts of prior testimony and listings of prosecutors who have had contact with the expert, articles written by them, and case decisions involving the expert. Prosecutors can obtain these items by calling the National Center. Similar materials are frequently available from other prosecutors in the region where the expert resides, and these prosecutors should also be consulted. They can often be a better source for information on how the expert comes across as a witness, and advise on the strategies for dealing with the particular expert.

DEMONSTRATIVE AIDS

It has long been said that a picture paints a thousand words. This is nowhere more true than in the use of demonstrative aids in the courtroom. Trial research consistently reveals that jurors better comprehend and retain more information from expert witnesses when the expert's verbal testimony is augmented by visual aids. (DerOhannesian, 1998). Demonstrative aids also convey a message of preparedness and importance surrounding the expert's testimony, thereby elevating the credibility of the expert in the eyes of jurors. However, the use of visual aids need not be confined to expert witnesses. The complex medical and lay testimony present in SBS cases necessitates the use of effective demonstrative aids to assist jurors in finding the truth.

These aids can run from simple use of medical illustrations (Kessler & Hyden, 1991), to computer generated simulations of the mechanism of shaking and brain injury. Medical models, medical illustrations and photographs are an easy source for demonstrative aids. Several series of illustrations and photographs are commercially available (American Academy of Pediatrics, 1994; CIBA-GEIGY), or can be produced by photographing, photocopying, or scanning images from medical texts (Monteleone, 1998; Reece, 1994). These texts contain representations of retinal hemorrhages and subdural hematomas, as well as metaphyseal and rib fractures, and frequently contain depictions for the mechanism of these traumatic injuries.

Additionally, prosecutors routinely have medical illustrators diagram the child's specific injuries from photographs and autopsy findings. The use of medical illustrations in lieu of autopsy photographs can avoid defense objections arguing such photographs are "inflammatory" or "prejudicial." These illustrations may also be easier for jurors to view and permit the use of overlays to highlight injuries. Similarly, injuries may be drawn in on mannequins or dolls to illustrate the location or extent of the injuries. The use of mannequins or dolls may permit some manipulation of the demonstrative aid before the jury to demonstrate how the injury was produced.

Nevertheless, some autopsy photographs may be needed and case law supports their use despite their graphic nature (Bridges v. State, 1998; DerOhannesian, 1998; State v. Altum, 1997; State v. Morrison, 1989; State v. Prouse, 1989; United States v. Bowers, 1981; Watson v. State, 1986). Autopsy photographs should nevertheless be identified and admitted into evidence through the pathologist, even if they are not intended to be published to the jury. The photographs will then become part of the court record, and can be used during cross-examination of any defense experts.

The use of 35mm slides rather than photographs is preferable for courtroom purposes (Jenny et al., 1996). Slides permit jurors to contemporaneously view the subject matter the expert is testifying to, rather than having the expert identify a photograph, describe it and then publish it to the jury. If slides are used, photographic copies of the slides, preferably in an 8 × 10 or larger size should also be admitted so the jury can have a hard copy for use in deliberations. Enlargements of photographs to poster size are an alternative but are more expensive. Law enforcement and medical personnel who routinely photograph injuries in SBS cases should consider these facts in determining the appropriate method to record these findings. Radiographic findings from x-rays, MRI and CT scans are also routinely utilized to support expert testimony. These necessitate at a minimum a high quality light box for in court use. Preferably, alternative methods such as slide reproductions of radiographs or the use of an Elmo to project larger images should be used.

Overhead transparencies of witness statements, especially the offender's statements can be effective for impeachment purposes if the witness changes his story. If the defendant has given an audiotaped or videotaped statement which will be played in court, the statement should be carefully transcribed and individual copies distributed to jurors as an aid to them in following along with the recorded statement.

Transparencies of important portions of the medical records can also be used with experts as well as other medical personnel. Alternatively, these items can be blown up to poster size by a photocopying service and mounted on foamboard. Similar use can be made of relevant excerpts from medical articles (e.g., data from fall studies, quotes from highly respected authorities, etc.).

When injuries are attributed to falls from household furniture, the so-called "killer couch" defense, it is often beneficial to bring the actual item into court, not just a photograph to illustrate the ridiculous nature of the defense. Crime scene diagrams, scene photographs and videotapes can also be useful in challenging the defendant's account of the events. The relative height and position of various household items should be clearly depicted through these visual aides. At least one court decision has upheld the prosecutor's right to inspect and photograph the defendant's home under the state's criminal procedural rules finding that in any homicide the scene of the crime is both relevant and material (Eslava v. State, 1985; Rule 18.2, Alabama Rules of Criminal Procedure; Rule 16(b), Federal Rules of Criminal Procedure). Similarly, a jury view of the scene may be appropriate and the best demonstrative evidence available to assist the jury's understanding of the facts.

Timelines are also an important demonstrative aide in SBS cases. Frequently these time lines can be quite complex, especially where there are multiple victims and witnesses involved, and the perpetrator has given evolving histories of the events to multiple people. Careful thought should be given as to how best to present this evidence through visual methods. This may require the use of multiple time line charts with one chart used to present the defendant's explanations and another used to present the victim's condition, injuries and symptomology.

Videotapes and photographs of the child are also helpful pieces of demonstrative evidence establishing the child's developmental capabilities, as well as the relative size and vulnerability of the child. The prosecution may also be required to establish the severity of the child's injuries or their permanency under specific aggravated battery statutes. Videotaped depictions of the child's current physical and mental condition can be a powerful means of communicating this proof in addition to expert medical testimony. These videotapes can also be used at the time of sentencing to impress on the judge or jury the extent of harm caused by the defendant's acts.

Audiotapes of 911 calls are frequently one of the most dramatic pieces of demonstrative evidence, which can be produced during the trial. Transcripts of the actual dialogue should be made and provided to the jury to aid them in understanding and remembering what was said. The prosecutor should pay careful attention to any background noises on the tape, and when necessary, use the services of the FBI or a crime laboratory to enhance the clarity of the recording.

OPENING STATEMENTS AND CLOSING ARGUMENTS

Opening statements and closing arguments in SBS represent a unique opportunity for the prosecutor to communicate the essence of the case to jurors in an uncomplicated fashion, removed from the technical aspects of the medical testimony and the legal instructions they receive from the court. The prosecutor must make good use of this opportunity to simplify the complex medical evidence and confusing language of the charges and instructions in a fashion the jury can understand. It is also a time to dramatically emphasize the devastating nature of the infant's victimization, and the violent nature of the defendant's conduct in producing it.

Both the opening and closing should tell a story, painting vivid word pictures for the jurors. The story should repeatedly emphasize the theme(s) of the case with narration of facts organized around the themes. Highly descriptive language should be used to characterize the victim's injuries and the defendant's actions.

Organizational structure can vary for dramatic effect. For example, while many prosecutors prefer a straightforward chronological approach to reciting the facts, an effective opening can start with the 911 call, or the doctors' efforts in the emergency room and then jump backwards to describe the events leading up to how the infant came to be injured or taken to the hospital. The opening can then continue forward describing the valiant efforts of the medical staff to save the child, their findings of the cause for the child's condition, and the caretaker's explanations for the events.

Similarly, the closing argument can be organized to address the elements of the crime at the start, the end or throughout the body of the presentation. One effective method is to identify the legal elements of the crime through a chart, paraphrase those elements for the jury, and then list all of the facts which establish these elements. Another organizational strategy might utilize the definition of reasonable doubt, often phrased in jury instructions as "a reasonable hypothesis consistent with the defendant's innocence" or "a doubt based upon reason and common sense." The prosecutor can then take the defendant's representations of the facts or the defense expert's theories and ask the rhetorical question, "is this a reasonable hypothesis consistent with the defendant's innocence?" or "does this make sense to you?" This is followed by identifying the facts which are inconsistent with this theory and the prosecutor's arguments for why the jury should reject it. This technique is particularly effective for rebuttal argument since the defendant will not have an opportunity for rejoinder.

Rhetorical questions followed by dramatic pauses are an effective tool for closing argument. This technique works well when emphasizing a contrast between the defendant's conduct, and the expectations jurors have for appropriate parental behavior. For example, "What does a mother do when she hears her child's cries?" "How were this child's cries answered?" "What would a mother do if she saw her baby being hurt?" "What did this person who calls herself a mother do?" After giving the jury a moment to think about these questions, the prosecutor can describe the defendant's illegal or inappropriate conduct.

The prosecutor must use reason and common sense when attacking the unreasonableness of the defense, and not simply ridicule the testimony of the defense expert. The defense expert's testimony may be worthy of contempt, but a cynical attitude toward this testimony communicated through closing argument is not likely to be effective, and may alienate jurors if they liked or believed even part of the testimony. Instead the prosecutor must explain why the expert's opinions are not worthy of acceptance. Jurors should be reminded that doctors are not always right, alerting jurors to their own common experience in seeking out more than one medical opinion for precisely this reason.

The legal propriety of various arguments will of necessity vary according to the case law within different jurisdictions. Subtle differences in semantics may have profound implications for the appropriateness of the rhetoric used during closing summations. For example, a prosecutor in one jurisdiction may not be able to call the defendant a liar, but may be able to tell the jury that he lies. Another may permissibly remind jurors that "one of the ten commandments is Thou Shalt Not Kill" while this same reference in a neighboring state may constitute a prosecutorial sin. Nuances such as these must be thoroughly researched by prosecutors before they wax eloquent before the jury, lest they find themselves reaching out to recapture misspoken words which have escaped their lips just as the defense attorney parts his lips to ask for a mistrial. With these principles in mind, I offer some of my own thoughts, and those of several learned colleagues, as but one example of how we might sum up our proof.

A SAMPLE CLOSING

There is a grace bestowed on all parents by God upon the birth of a child. It is a gift that opens our hearts to all the wonders and possibilities of life itself. And in return for this gift there is a covenant as old as time itself that we shall love, nurture and protect that child, for that child's life and spirit are entrusted to our care. But we are given two more gifts to aid us in maintaining that covenant–the gifts of reason and compassion. Reason to help us work through the difficulties that all parents face in caring for their children. Compassion to bring forth our love to those precious beings even during the times when they are most trying.

Bobby's injuries bear witness to the fact that the defendant ignored these gifts of reason and compassion. The defendant chose instead to be a parent who allowed his rage to overcome reason, to be a person whose own instincts for self preservation replaced his duty of protection toward his son. The defendant chose to betray this sacred covenant with his son, and in return Bobby's life became the ultimate sacrifice.

The defendant is charged with First Degree Intentional Homicide. The law provides that in order for you to find him guilty of this crime, you must be satisfied of two things. First, that he caused the death of his son Bobby, and second that he did so intentionally. The law defines that intent as the mental purpose to cause the death of another, or the awareness that one's conduct is practically certain to cause that result. The evidence in this case establishes overwhelmingly that the defendant's conduct in violently shaking and throwing Bobby into the crib satisfies these elements. This evidence comes from the perverted lies and half truths this defendant offered to conceal his own guilt, and from the broken and battered body of little Bobby–spoken through the words of the doctors who bore witness to his anguished testimonial in death.

First, we know that Bobby was an abused child. His body bore evidence of healing broken bones, and of prior bleeding on his brain. The doctors told you that Bobby had previously been shaken, that this was not the first time he had been seriously injured by an adult violently shaking him. The healing fractures of his ribs and the metaphyseal or corner fractures on the ends of his leg bones were the types of injuries commonly seen from this type of abuse. The evidence of a prior subdural hematoma, old bleeding on his brain, is also a marker for this type of abuse. And you heard the doctors tell you that the constellation of these old injuries and the new injuries that caused Bobby's death lead to a medical diagnosis of Battered Child Syndrome, a medical diagnosis defining this child as a victim of child abuse on multiple occasions.

Second, these doctors told you that the diagnosis of Battered Child Syndrome refutes the explanations offered by the defendant that Bobby's fatal injuries are the result of an accidental fall from his arms that day. The doctors tell us that none of Bobby's injuries can be accounted for by this story of being dropped from his father's arms onto a hard floor. The doctors tell us that dozens of studies have examined accidental falls involving thousands of children, and that the children in these studies did not get the type of fatal injuries that Bobby received. It just couldn't happen the way the defendant says—not unless the laws of physics and gravity are different in the defendant's house. These doctors tell us that the defendant is a liar.

Which brings us to the third factor that conclusively establishes the defendant's guilt for murder in the first degree. A defendant who lies to protect himself points the finger of guilt upon himself. It is a law of human experience as old as the laws of nature demanding protection of one's children. When a man lies to conceal wrongdoing, the words spoken echo his consciousness of guilt. When the light of truth is cast upon those lies, it reveals the liar crouching in the shadows. That light radiates in this courtroom today.

But even as you sit here convinced that this man is responsible for causing these fatal injuries in little Bobby, you may still ask "how is it that we know the defendant's intent for this crime?" "How are we to find him guilty of intentional homicide?" "Can we believe the defendant set out to kill Bobby?" "Would any parent purposely kill their own child?" It is, I'm sure, difficult for you all to conceive how a parent can deliberately kill a tiny four- month-old infant.

These questions and concerns reflect the degree of reason and compassion we all have as parents of children and as human beings. If the defendant had shown similar reason and compassion he would not be on trial here today. But the law you are to consider asks a different question. The law asks instead whether the defendant's acts reflect the mental purpose to cause death or an awareness that his conduct was practically certain to cause that result. The evidence leaves no doubt that the answer to this question in this case is yes.

That evidence tells us that the amount of force visited on little Bobby was the equivalent of a fall from several stories onto a hard surface, or an unrestrained motor vehicle collision at a speed of 50-60 m.p.h. Many of you I'm sure have ridden roller coasters at amusement parks. You know the feeling of force on your head and body at the bottom of a steep drop or curve. Those forces are known as G-Forces or gravitational forces. On the roller coaster you felt one or two G's of force. When Bobby was shaken his brain experienced at least ten times that amount.

These are tremendous forces which should never be brought to a baby. These are tremendous forces which leave no doubt as to the intent of the person who causes them. I ask you to draw on your own common experiences in handling infants. Remember how concerned we have all been in picking up that little bundle, the care we took to support their head and neck at all times, the sense that their tiny bodies were so fragile. And although we learned that babies are really not that fragile, the idea of grabbing a baby around the chest and violently shaking the child is something everyone knows is extremely dangerous. As the doctors told you, the violence involved in shaking children is something that any reasonable person observing the conduct would clearly recognize as dangerous to the child–would clearly recognize as an act of child abuse.

And this violence lasted for a period of time on both occasions. To sustain the type of injuries Bobby received during these episodes of shaking, Bobby had to be shaken violently for a minimum of several seconds. His tiny head had to whiplash back and forth uncontrollably dozens of times during that period. The defendant had time to stop. He didn't until his arms were tired.

The defendant made several more choices that demonstrate his intent. When he tired from shaking Bobby, he threw him back into his crib. That second deliberate act caused Bobby's head to impact against the mattress causing a rapid deceleration in the movement of his brain inside his skull and magnifying by several times the forces injuring his brain, forces that would ultimately take his life. In an act reflecting how the defendant had thrown away all love for his son, the defendant threw his son out of his arms, and threw away Bobby's life as well.

As if the repeated acts of physical abuse were not enough of a betrayal of this covenant to love and protect his son, his conduct in the hours that followed these acts consigned Bobby to a certain death.

As Bobby lay in his crib, his crying silenced by the defendant's act of shaking and throwing him down, already his tiny fragile brain was beginning to bleed, to swell, to die. But the defendant chose to betray his son several times again. Eventually, the defendant would admit to detectives that he left Bobby alone for an hour before he returned to Bobby's room to check on him. But as Bobby's imperiled health began to reveal itself to the defendant, first through the seizures in Bobby's arms and legs, and then through his erratic breathing, the defendant betrayed his son again. He chose not to summon medical help that might have saved Bobby's life, but instead to call his wife at work and tell her that something was wrong and she needed to come home. When she returned, she recognized immediately that Bobby was in peril and called for help and Bobby was taken by paramedics to the hospital.

Then as the doctors worked valiantly to save Bobby's life, the defendant would betray his son yet again. Doctors would question the defendant about how Bobby came to be in this condition so that they could perform appropriate medical intervention. But in an act of cowardice designed to conceal his own guilt rather than help his son, the defendant would choose to lie to those doctors and claim that he had accidentally dropped Bobby while lifting him out of the crib. Only after being confronted by doctors and police investigators after Bobby had passed away would the defendant change his story and acknowledge that he had shaken his son. Even then, however, he would try to claim he had shaken Bobby to get the child to start breathing, inverting the true order of events that Bobby stopped breathing because the defendant had shaken him.

During the hours between the time when the defendant violently shook Bobby, and Bobby ultimately died, a time period when prompt medical attention might have intervened to stop the swelling of Bobby's brain that caused him to die, the defendant chose instead to deny that opportunity for treatment, to conceal his son's injuries, and to lie about his hand in producing them. He betrayed his son time and time again that day, conduct that reflects not only on his intent in this crime, but on his instincts as a parent and his character as a human being as well.

Bobby should have known the safety of a baby's crib–that crib became a scene of violence and death. Bobby should have known the warmth of a comforting hug–he found instead hands that gripped his chest, and broke his ribs; hands that shook the cries from Bobby's voice at the same time those hands shook the life out of this beautiful baby boy. Bobby will never have bruises on his knees from falls on playgrounds, the bruises on his brain erased all chance of that. Bobby's mother and grandparents will never know the joy of buying birthday presents and gifts at Christmas–Bobby never grew big enough to hold his first toy.

Bobby deserved far better from this defendant in life, but your verdict can bring justice for his death. This father ignored the most basic human instincts of love and compassion for his son. He violated his covenant with his son just as surely as he violated the laws of man you enforce here today. The defendant's repeated acts of abuse destroyed the gift of life that beautiful child represented. The defendant chose to betray Bobby, and you must evaluate that choice by one of your own. I'm confident that the verdict you choose for this defendant today will tell the defendant he made the wrong choices. While Bobby's cries could be silenced by his father's shaking, what cannot be silenced is his father's guilt.

SENTENCING

Historically, sentences have not reflected the severity of SBS offenses. (Showers, 1997). This is likely due to a number of factors: (1) judicial reluctance to judge caretakers harshly; (2) reluctance to believe there was any intent to harm the child; (3) convictions on less serious offenses than the conduct warrants; (4) inappropriate maximum sentence ranges for offenses defendants are typically convicted under for SBS crimes; (5) bad plea bargains by prosecutors; and (6) ineffective sentencing arguments and recommendations by prosecutors. The significant morbidity and mortality associated with SBS crimes suggests that much more severe consequences should follow to those convicted of visiting these dire consequences on tiny infants. Future research is desperately needed to review the sentencing practices of courts, and the outcomes of SBS cases in general.

Some research is now being published on the significant medical, social and victim impact costs associated with this form of abuse (Miller, Cohen, & Wiersma, 1996; U.S. Advisory Board, 1995). The National Research Council indicates that the future lost productivity of severely abused children is between $658 million and $1.3 billion if their impairments limit their earnings by only five to ten percent (National Research Council, 1993). Victims of SBS frequently have much greater disabilities and their financial impairments include not only lost productivity, but extremely high medical and rehabilitative costs, and a significantly reduced quality of life.

The sentence is the ultimate objective of filing the criminal charge. The prosecutor must make sure that the sentencing process is not anticlimactic by preparing for and advocating at this hearing as thoroughly as during other aspects of the case. A good rule of practice is to treat the sentencing remarks as though they were a closing argument at trial. Paint a picture for the court and humanize the tragedy for the victim and family. The theme at this stage should be protection of children and retribution for an extremely violent crime committed against a helpless infant.

The sentencing hearing represents an opportunity to educate the court and the public regarding the myths and realities of SBS for the case at hand and future cases. The prosecutor should not assume the court will be familiar with this topic or the seriousness of SBS cases, even if the court has had prior SBS cases. Sentencing memoranda filed well before the sentencing hearing, are an excellent way to accomplish this task, and can be used over again from case to case. The memoranda and sentencing arguments should provide the court with some of the statistical data listed above and highlighted throughout this book, to give the court a broader perspective on the seriousness of this problem. Medical research and public reports (Showers, 1997; U.S. Advisory Board, 1995) are another excellent source of information in support of these arguments.

At a minimum, the court should be advised that there are annually about 2,000 child homicides, a substantial percentage of which involve abusive head trauma resulting from SBS (U.S. Advisory Board, 1995). The court should also be advised that abusive head trauma is the leading cause of morbidity and mortality in child abuse cases, that twelve percent of children diagnosed with abusive head trauma die, and that most survivors suffer lifetime disabilities (American Academy of Pediatrics, 1993; Smith, 1994). Additionally, 18,000 children annually suffer serious injury or are permanently disabled from physical abuse (U.S. Advisory Board, 1995), with again a substantial percentage of these children being victims of SBS. These statistics are important to communicate the seriousness of this form of child abuse and the need for the court's sentence to reflect this fact, to protect the community and to deter others from engaging in this conduct.

Victim participation should be encouraged through representation by other family members, including presence at the sentencing hearing and an opportunity to address the court. Most courts and many statutes permit the use of victim impact statements, and victim input is also generally included in the pre-sentence report. Impact statements from the child's siblings, grandparents and extended family members, in addition to the parents, can be very powerful in communicating the far-reaching emotional devastation brought to the family. The victim's family may take a different position regarding sentencing than the prosecutor, often preferring a more lenient disposition, especially when the defendant is the child's parent. If this issue has not already been discussed with family members as part of the plea negotiation process, it should be discussed in preparation for sentencing to avoid potential conflicts at the hearing. The prosecutor should advise the family of the reasons for his or her recommendation, and supportively acknowledge their right to take a different position.

Prosecutors should not bind the hands of the sentencing court by making lenient recommendations the court may feel obligated to follow. Substantial incarceration should be the recommendation in most cases involving serious injury, and all homicide cases. Sentencing arguments need to emphasize the violence associated with this crime, the special vulnerability of this class of victims, and the severe consequences resulting from these types of traumatic brain injury.

It may not always be possible to assess the full extent of trauma or the potential developmental consequences by the time of sentencing on the criminal charges. Some recent research, however, suggests that the long-term prognosis for many if not most of these children is poor, even if there appears to be a symptom free interval in the short term (Bonnier, Nassogne, & Evard, 1995). Courts need to be advised of this potential.

Additionally, courts must be told that what separates children who die, from those who suffer lifetime disabling injuries or less severe consequences is realistically a matter of God's grace, and nothing more. Certainly there is nothing the defendants are consciously doing during their violent shaking episodes that mitigates the resultant consequences for the victim. The fact is that some children are simply more fortunate than others, but every shaking episode is a *life threatening event* for the child.

The prosecutor must correct any misstatements made by the defense attorney or defendant regarding the facts of the case or SBS generally. As with trial, prosecutors should anticipate the defense arguments that will be raised and prepare responses to them. Defendants almost universally argue for mitigation of sentence based on claims they did not mean to harm the child or were not aware of the dangers of their conduct. These representations must be countered in several ways.

First, these claims may be inconsistent with the findings made by the jury. If the defendant made these same representations during his testimony at trial and was convicted nonetheless, the jury's verdict can be said to be a rejection of this claim. Second, these representations are inconsistent with medical knowledge regarding the severe forces needed to produce these injuries. These representations do not gain more validity because they are made at sentencing in an effort to garner a sympathetic disposition from the court. Many court decisions similarly reject these claims (People v. Rader, 1995; People v. Ripley, 1997; People v. Sargent, 1999). Third, the defendant's other behavior in delaying calls for assistance or concealing the nature of his conduct are inconsistent with the validity of this claim The court should be reminded that medical research and clinical experience repeatedly indicate that even when defendants admit the shaking, they rarely acknowledge the full extent of their conduct, opting instead to minimize its severity or their culpability.

At the present time, there is no per se "treatment" option for SBS defendants. Accordingly, the court's traditional consideration of rehabilitation as one aspect of the sentencing process is less significant in SBS cases. At most, efforts at treatment may be directed toward reducing some of the stressing factors that prompted the violent episode. Intervention strategies by social service and parenting agencies should offer little in the way of mitigation toward sentencing in this type of case.

As in all areas of child abuse, the defendant's truthful acknowledgment of responsibility weighs in mitigation of sentence. However, this fact should be qualified somewhat in SBS cases. Unlike other abuse crimes where such acknowledgment is a necessary component of treatment efficacy (e.g., sexual abuse), such is not the case with SBS offenders. The acknowledgment here serves as a mitigation factor because it demonstrates remorse. Additionally, the acknowledgment must be carefully considered to determine if it is a complete and truthful admission regarding the severity of the conduct. Additional mitigating factors include a lack of prior criminal history and those factors identified by statute or sentencing guidelines. By contrast, a prior history of family violence should be a strong factor in aggravation of sentence, since both prior incidents of domestic violence and physical abuse are strongly associated with repeat violence and child homicide (U.S. Advisory Board, 1995).

CONCLUSION

In the nine short months of her life, little Mina had endured at least three separate incidents of shaking. The doctors who examined her at the children's hospital discovered both an acute and an old subdural hematoma. She had more than thirty fractures in various stages of healing involving virtually every major bone in her tiny body. The doctor who examined her, a veteran of thousands of child abuse cases, testified at the trial of her mother's live-in boyfriend that it was the worst constellation of injuries he'd seen in a child who lived. The judge echoed those sentiments in imposing a sentence of twenty-five years in prison.

But despite her injuries, Mina would be one of the lucky victims of shaken baby syndrome. Today she is a bright, active and happy child who so far bears no outward signs of the terrible damage that was visited upon her as an infant. She has since been adopted by her foster mother, a pediatric nurse who helped her for several years to recover the use of her arms and legs, and her spirit.

When the trial of Mina's abuser was concluded, her foster mother addressed a letter to the prosecutor on behalf of Mina.

> Dear Mr. Prosecutor: I just want to thank you for working so hard on my behalf. I am only a small child with a small voice–unable to be heard. I am thankful for persons like you who use their voices to protect myself and other children in similar situations as mine. I am doing very well. My foster family loves me very much. I am working hard in therapy and I am very determined to get my wrists and arms strengthened. God bless you. Please continue your service of making a difference in children's lives. Mina

There are happy endings. For those whose voice will never be heard–can never be heard–we must speak for them, and forever remember their spirit to fortify our own. We must also remember that for the children whose lives we are entrusted to protect, we do make a difference. May we go forward with all the skill and dedication that we can in that effort.

AUTHOR NOTE

The author wishes to acknowledge the thoughtful input of prosecutors Cindi Nanetti, Victor Vieth, Dyanne Greer, Rob Parrish, Judy Johnston Paul DerOhannesian, Jill-Ellyn Strauss, Cathy Stephenson and Sandy Sylvester, APRI staff attorneys Erin O'Keefe and Susan Smith-Newell, and Dr. Randell Alexander whose research, discussion, outlines and training materials on this topic significantly contributed to the ideas expressed herein, and whose insightful review and editing of the manuscript improved the final product immeasurably.

REFERENCES

Ablin, D.S., Greenspan, A., & Reihart, M.A. (1990). Differentiation of child abuse from osteogenisis imperfecta. *American Journal of Roentgen, 154,* 1035-1046.

Ablin, D.S., & Sane, S.M., (1997). Non-accidental injury: Confusion with temporary brittle bone disease and mild osteogenesis imperfecta. *Pediatric Radiology, 27,* 111-113.

Adelson, L. (1974). *The pathology of homicide.* Springfield, IL: Charles C. Thomas Publishing Co.

Alabama Rules of Criminal Procedure, Michie's Alabama Code, Title 15.

Alexander, R., Sato, Y., Smith, W., & Bennett, T. (1990). Incidence of impact trauma with cranial injuries ascribed to shaking. *American Journal of Diseases in Children, 144,* 724-726.

American Academy of Pediatrics and the C. Henry Kempe National Center for the Prevention and Treatment of Child Abuse and Neglect. (1994). *The visual diagnosis of child physical abuse.* Elk Grove Village, IL: American Academy of Pediatrics.

American Academy of Pediatrics, Committee on Child Abuse and Neglect. (1993). Shaken baby syndrome: Inflicted cerebral trauma. *Pediatrics, 92,* 872-875.

American Law Institute, *Model Penal Code,* Official Draft (1962).

American Prosecutors Research Institute (APRI), National Center for Prosecution of Child Abuse. (1993). *Investigation and prosecution of child abuse* (2nd ed.). Alexandria, VA: American Prosecutors Research Institute.

American Prosecutors Research Institute (APRI), National Center for Prosecution of Child Abuse. (1994). *Selected case law: Child homicide, physical abuse, and criminal neglect.*

American Prosecutors Research Institute (APRI), National Center for Prosecution of Child Abuse. (1998). *Selected case law: Child homicide and physical abuse–1998 supplement.*

Berry v. Commonwealth, 473 N.E.2d 1115 (Mass. 1985).

Billmire, M.E., & Myers, P.A. (1985). Serious head injury in infants: Accident or abuse? *Pediatrics, 75,* 340-342.

Bonnier, C., Nassogne, M.C., & Evard, P. (1995). Outcome and prognosis of whiplash shaken infant syndrome: Late consequences after a symptom-free interval. *Developmental Medicine and Child Neurology, 37,* 943-956.

Brewster, A.L., Nelson, J.P., Hymel, K.P., Colby, D.R., Lucas, D.R., McCanne, T.R., & Milner, J.S. (1998).Victim, perpetrator, family, and incident characteristics of 32 infant maltreatment deaths in the United States Air Force. *Child Abuse & Neglect, 22(2),* 91-101.

Bridges v. State, 706 A.2d 489 (Del. 1998).

Brown v. State, 485 N.E.2d 108 (Ind. 1985).

Bruce, D.A., & Zimmerman, R.A..(1988). Shaken impact syndrome. *Pediatric Annals*, *18*, 482-494.

Buckley v. Fitzsimmons, 509 U.S. 259, 113 S.Ct. 2606, 125 L.Ed.2d 209 (1993), *cert denied* 513 U.S.1085 (1995).

Burns v. Reed, 500 U.S. 478, 111 S.Ct. 1934, 114 L.Ed.2d 547 (1991).

Buys, Y.M., Levin, A.V., Enzenauer, R.W., Elder, J.E., Letourneau, M.A., Humphreys, R.P., Mian, M., & Morin, J.D. (1992). Retinal findings after head trauma in infants and young children. *Ophthalmology, 99,* 1718-1723.

Byrd v. State, 593 N.E.2d 1187 (Ind. 1992).

Caffey, J. (1974). The whiplash shaken infant syndrome: Manual shaking by the extremities with whiplash-induced intracranial and intraocular bleedings, linked with residual permanent brain damage and mental retardation. *Pediatrics, 54(4),* 396-403.

Case, M.E.S. (1998). Head injury in child abuse. In J.A. Monteleone (Ed.), *Child maltreatment: A clinical guide and reference* (2nd ed.) (pp. 87-103). St. Louis, MO: G. W. Medical Publishing, Inc.

Chadwick, D., Chin, S., Salerno, C., Landsverk, S., & Kitchen, L. (1991). Deaths from falls in children: How far is fatal? *Journal of Trauma, 31*(10), 1353-1355.

Chadwick, D., Kirschner, R., Reece, R.M., & Ricci, L.R. (1998). Shaken baby syndrome–A forensic pediatric response. *Pediatrics, 101*(2), 321-323.

Chadwick, D., & Krous, H.F. (1997). Irresponsible medical testimony by medical experts in cases involving the physical abuse and neglect of children. *Child Maltreatment, 2(4),* 313-321.

Chaulk v. Volkswagen of Am. Inc., 808 F.2d 639, 644 (7th Cir. 1986).

CIBA-GEIGY, *The CIBA Collection of Medical Illustrations* and *Clinical Symposia*, Newark, NJ: CIBA-GEIGY Corp, 1982.

Clemens v. State, 610 N.E.2d 236 (Ind. 1993).

Commonwealth v. Lazarovich, 547 N.E.2d 940 (Mass. Ct. App. 1989).

Commonwealth v. Merola, 542 N.E.2d 249 (Mass.1989).

Davis v. State, 925 S.W.2d 768 (Ark. 1996).

Daubert v. Merrell Dow Pharmaceuticals, Inc., 509 U.S. 579, 113 S.Ct. 2786, 125 L.Ed.2d 469 (1993).

DerOhannesian, P. (1998). *Sexual assault trials* (2nd ed.). Charlottesville, VA: The Michie Co.

Duhaime, A.C. (1997). Head trauma. In A.P. Giardino, C.W. Christian, & E.R. Giardino (Eds.), *A practical guide to the evaluation of child physical abuse and neglect* (pp. 147-168). Thousand Oaks, CA: Sage.

Duhaime, A.C., Alario, A.J., Lewander, W.J., Schut, L., Sutton, L.N., Seidl, T., Nudelman, S., Budenz, D., Hertle, R., Tsiaras, W., & Loporchio, S. (1992). Head injury in very young children: Mechanisms, injury types, and ophthalmologic findings in 100 hospitalized patients younger than 2 years of age. *Pediatrics, 90,* 179-185.

Duhaime, A.C., Christian, C.W., Rorke, L.B., & Zimmerman, R.A. (1998). Nonaccidental head injury in infants–The "Shaken-Baby Syndrome." *New England Journal of Medicine, 338,* 1822-1829.

Duhaime, A.C., Gennarelli, T.G., Thibault, L.E., Bruce, D.A., Margulies, S.S., & Wiser, R. (1987). The shaken baby syndrome: A clinical, pathological, and biomechanical study. *Journal of Neurosurgery, 66,* 409-415.

Dykes, L.J. (1986). The whiplash shaken infant syndrome: What has been learned? *Child Abuse & Neglect, 10,* 211-221.

Elliott, D. (1987). Science panels in toxic tort litigation: Why we don't use them. In ICET Symposium III Immunotoxicology: *From Lab to Lab 115,* 117 (Ithaca, NY: Institute for Comparative and Environmental Toxicology, Cornell University, 1987).

Elner, S.G. et al. (1990). Ocular and associated systematic findings in suspected child abuse. A necropsy study. *Archives in Opthalmology, 108*(8), 1094-1101.

Eslava v. State, 473 So.2d 1143 (Ala. Crim. App. 1985).

Estelle v. McGuire, 502 U.S. 62, 112 S.Ct. 475, 116 L.Ed.2d 385 (1991).

Federal Rules of Criminal Procedure.

Federal rules of evidence, with advisory committee notes and legislative history. (1996). Mueller, C.B., & Kirkpatrick, L.C. (Eds.). Boston, MA: Little, Brown & Co.

Frye v. United States, 54 App. D.C. 46, 293 F. 1013 (1923).

Giardino, A.P., Christian, C.W., & Giardino, E.R. (1997). *A practical guide to the evaluation of child physical abuse and neglect.* Thousand Oaks, CA: Sage.

Gideon v. State, 721 P.2d 1336 (Okla. Crim. App. 1986).

Gilliland, M.G.F. (1997). Interval duration between injury and severe symptoms in non-accidental head trauma in infants and young children. *Journal of Forensic Sciences, 43(3),* 723-725.

Gilliland, M.G.F., & Folberg, R. (1996). Shaken babies–Some have no impact injuries. *Journal of Forensic Sciences, 41,* 114-116.

Gilliland, M.G.F., & Luckenbach, M.W. (1993). Are retinal hemorrhages found after resuscitation attempts? A study of the eyes of 169 Children. *American Journal of Forensic Medicine and Pathology, 14* 187-192.

Gilliland, M.G.F., Luckenbach, M.W., & Chenier, T.C. (1994). Systemic and ocular findings in 169 prospectively studied deaths: Retinal hemorrhages usually mean child abuse. *Forensic Science International, 68,* 117-132.

Green, M.A., Lieberman, G., Milroy, C.M., & Parsons, M.A. (1996). Ocular and Cerebral trauma in non-accidental injury in infancy: Underlying mechanisms and implications for pediatric practice. *British Journal of Ophthalmology, 80,* 282-287.

Guthkelch, A.N. (1971). Infantile subdural hematoma and its relationship to whiplash injuries. *British Medical Journal, 2,* 430-431.

Hadley, M.N., Sonntag, V.K.H., Rekate, H.L., & Murphy, A. (1989). The infant whiplash-shake injury syndrome: A clinical and pathological study. *Neurosurgery, 24,* 536-540.

Helfer, R.E., Slovis, T.L., & Black, M. (1977). Injuries resulting when small children fall out of bed. *Pediatrics, 60*(4), 533-535.

Higgins, M. (1998). Docking doctors? AMA eyes discipline for physicians giving false testimony. *American Bar Association Journal, 84,* 20.

Holmgren, B. (1999). Juror selection in child abuse cases. (Available through the American Prosecutors Research Institute, National Center for Prosecution of Child Abuse and the author).

Hoosier v. State, 612 So.2d 1352 (Ala. Crim. App. 1992).

Howard, M.A., Bell, B.A., & Utley, D. (1993). The pathophysiology of infant subdural hematoma. *British Journal of Neurosurgery, 7*, 355-365.

Huddleston v. United States, 485 U.S. 681, 99 L. Ed. 2d 771, 108 S. Ct. 1496 (1988).

Hymel, K.P., et al. (1998). Abusive head trauma? A biomechanics-based approach. *Child Maltreatment, 3*(2),116-128.

Imwinkelried, E.J. (1992). *Uncharged misconduct evidence*. Deerfield, IL: Clark, Boardman Callaghan.

In re Agent Orange Product Liability Litigation, 611 F. Supp. 1223 (E.D.N.Y. 1985).

The Institute for Professional Education. (1998). Massachusetts Society for the Prevention of Cruelty to Children. *The Quarterly Child Abuse Medical Update*. Boston, MA: The Institute for Professional Education.

Jenny, C., Hymel, K.P., Ritzen, A., Reinert, S.E., & Hay, T.C. (1999). Analysis of missed cases of abusive head trauma. *Journal of the American Medical Association, 281*, 621-626.

Jenny, C., Taylor, R.J., & Cooper, M. (1996). *Diagnostic imaging and child abuse: Technologies, practices and guidelines*. Washington, DC: Medical Technologies and Practice Patterns Institute.

Johnson D.L., Braun, D., & Friendly, D. (1993). Accidental trauma and retinal hemorrhage. *Neurosurgery, 33*, 231-235.

Jones v. State, 439 S.E.2d 645 (Ga. 1994).

Kanter, R. (1986). Retinal hemorrhages after cardiopulmonary resuscitation or child abuse. *Journal of Pediatrics, 108*, 430-432.

Kempe, R.S., Silverman, F.N., Steele, B.F., Droegmueller, W., & Silver, H.K. (1962). The battered child syndrome. *Journal of the American Medical Association, 181*, 105-112.

Kessler, D.B., & Hyden, P. (1991). *Clinical symposia: Physical, sexual and emotional abuse of children*. Vol. 43, No. 1, Summit, NJ: CIBA-GEIGY Corp.

Kirschner, R.H. & Wilson, H.L. (1994). Fatal child abuse: The pathologist's perspective. In R. Reece (Ed.), *Child abuse: Medical diagnosis and management* (pp. 325-357). Philadelphia, PA: Lea & Febiger.

Kleinman, P.K. (1998). *Diagnostic imaging of child abuse* (2nd ed.). St. Louis, MO: Mosby.

Kravitz, H., Dreissan, G., Gomberg, R., & Korach, A. (1969). Accidental falls from elevated surfaces in infants from birth to one year of age. *Pediatrics, 44*, 869-876.

Kumho Tire Company, Ltd. et al. v. Carmichael, etc. et al., 119 S.Ct 1167 (1999).

Lachman, R.S., Krakow, D., & Kleinman, P.K. (1998). Differential diagnosis II: Osteogenesis imperfecta. In P.K. Kleinman (Ed.), *Diagnostic imaging of child abuse* (2nd ed.). St. Louis, MO: Mosby.

Lazoritz, S. (1995). *The "shaken" infant: Historical aspects and characteristics*. Paper presented at the First National Conference on Shaken Baby Syndrome, October 1995, Salt Lake City, Utah.

Lazoritz, S., Baldwin, S., & Kini, N. (1997). The whiplash shaken infant syndrome: Has Caffey's Syndrome changed or have we changed his syndrome? *Child Abuse & Neglect, 21*(10), 1009-1014.

Levin, A. (1990). Ocular manifestations of child abuse. *Journal of Ophthalmology Clinics of North America, 3*, 249-264.

Levin, A. (1991). Ophthalmologic manifestations. In S. Ludwig (Ed.), *Child abuse: A medical reference* (pp. 191-212). New York: Churchill Livingstone.

Levitt, C.J., Smith, W.L., & Alexander, R.C. (1994) Abusive head trauma. In R. Reece (Ed.), *Child abuse: Medical diagnosis and management* (pp. 1-22). Philadelphia, PA: Lea & Febiger.

Loren v. State, 493 S.E.2d 175 (Ga. 1997).

Ludwig, S., & Kornberg, A.E. (Eds.). (1992). *Child abuse: A medical reference* (2nd ed.). New York: Churchill Livingstone.

Ludwig, S., & Warman, M. (1984). Shaken baby syndrome: A review of 20 cases. *Annals of Emergency Medicine, 13*, 104-107.

Lyon, T.D., Gilles, E.E., & Cory, L. (1996). Medical evidence of physical abuse in infants and young children. *Pacific Law Journal, 28*, 93-167.

Lyons, T.J., & Oates, R.K. (1993). Falling out of bed: A relatively benign occurrence. *Pediatrics, 92(1)*, 125-127.

Maryland v. Craig, 497 U.S. 836, 110 S.Ct. 3157, 111 L.Ed. 2d 666 (1990).

Massicotte, S.J., Folberg, R., Torczynski, E., Gilliland, M.G.F., & Luckenbach, M.W. (1991). Vitreoretinal traction and perimacular retinal folds in the eyes of deliberately traumatized children. *Ophthalmology, 98*, 1124-1127.

Miller, T., Cohen, M.A., & Wiersma, B. (1996). *Victim costs and consequences: A new look*. Washington, DC: United States Department of Justice.

Monteleone, J.A. (Ed.). (1998). *Child maltreatment: A clinical guide and reference* (2nd ed.). St. Louis, MO: G. W. Medical Publishing, Inc.

Mueller, C.B., & Kirkpatrick, L.C. (1994). *Federal evidence* (2nd ed.). New York: Lawyers Cooperative.

Munger, C.E., Peiffer, R.L., Bouldin, T.W., Kylstra, J.A., & Thompson, R.L. (1993). Ocular and associated neuropathologic observations in suspected whiplash shaken infant syndrome. *The American Journal of Forensic Medicine and Pathology, 14(3)*, 193-200.

Myers, J.E.B. (1997). *Evidence in child abuse and neglect cases* (3rd ed.). Somerset, NJ: John Wiley & Sons.

Nashelsky, M.B., & Dix, J.D. (1995). The time interval between lethal infant shaking and onset of symptoms: A review of the shaken baby literature. *The American Journal of Forensic Medicine and Pathology, 16(2)*, 154-157.

National Research Council. (1993). *Understanding child abuse and neglect*. Washington, DC: National Academy of Sciences 40.

Odom, A., Christ, E., Kerr, N., Byrd, K., Cochran, J., Barr, F., Bugnitz, M., Ring, J., Storgion, S., Walling, R., Stidham, G., & Quasney, M.W. (1997). Prevalence of retinal hemorrhages in pediatric patients after in-hospital cardiopulmonary resuscitation: A prospective study. *Pediatrics, 99*, e3.

O'Kelly v. State, 607 P.2d 612 (N.M. 1980).

O'Neill, J.A., Meacham, W.F., Griffin, P.P., & Sawyers, J.L. (1973). Patterns of injury in the battered child syndrome. *Journal of Trauma, 13*, 332-339.

Parrish, R. (1998). The proof is in the details: Investigation and prosecution of shaken baby cases, national information, support and referral service on shaken baby syndrome. *Child Abuse Prevention Center of Utah, Winter*, 4-5.

Pennington, N., & Hastie, R. (1991). A cognitive theory of juror decision making: The story model. *Cardozo Law Review, 13*, 519-557.

People v. Avellar, 622 N.E.2d 635 (Mass.1993).

People v. Beckley, 456 N.W.2d 391 (Mich.1990).

People v. Brown, 496 N.E.2d 663 (N.Y. App.1986).

People v. Diefenderfer, 784 P.2d 741 (Colo. 1989).

People v. District Court, 803 P.2d 193 (Colo. 1990).

People v. Evers, 10 Cal. App. 4th 588, 12 Cal. Rptr. 637 (1992).

People v. Gordon, 738 P.2d 404 (Colo. Ct. App. 1987).

People v. Henson, 349 N.Y.S.2d 657, 304 N.E.2d 358 (1973).

People v. Holmes, 616 N.E.2d 1000 (Ill. App. 3d 1993).

People v. Jackson, 18 Cal. App. 3d 504, 95 Cal. Rptr. 919 (1971).

People v. Kendall, 678 N.Y.S.2d 182 (N.Y. App. Div.1998).

People v. Montesa, 621 N.Y.S.2d 359 (App. Div.1995).

People v. Neer, 512 N.E.2d 571 (N.Y. 1987).

People v. Nix, 569 N.Y.S.2d 677 (App. Div. 1991).

People v. Rader, 651 N.E.2d 258 (Ill. App. 4th 1995).

People v. Ripley, 685 N.E.2d 362 (Ill. App. 3d 1997).

People v. Robbins, 755 P.2d 355 (Cal. 1988).

People v. Roe, 542 N.E.2d 610 (N.Y. 1989)

People v. Sargent, 70 Cal. Rptr. 2d 203 (Ct. App. 1997), *review granted*, 1998 Cal. LEXIS 1826.

People v. Sargent, 970 P.2d 409 (Cal. 1999).

People v. Shatell, 578 N.Y.S.2d 694 (App. Div. 1992).

People v. Stanciel, 606 N.E.2d 1201 (Ill. App. 2d 1992).

People v. Steinberg, 584 N.Y.S.2d 770 (N.Y. 1992).

People v. Wernick, 674 N.E.2d 322 (N.Y. 1996).

People v. Wong, 588 N.Y.S.2d 98 (App. Div. 1992), *reversed on other grounds* 81 N.Y.2d 600, 619 N.E.2d 377 (1993).

Phipps, C.A. (1999). Responding to child homicide: A statutory proposal. *Journal of Criminal Law & Criminology, 89(2)*, 535-613.

Rainey, R.H., & Greer, D.C. (1994). Prosecuting child fatality cases. *APSAC Advisor, 7(4)*, 28-30.

Reece, R. (Ed.). (1994). *Child abuse: Medical diagnosis and management.* Philadelphia, PA: Lea & Febiger.

Reiber, G.D. (1993). Fatal falls in childhood: How far must children fall to sustain fatal head injury? Report of cases and review of the literature. *The American Journal of Forensic Medicine and Pathology, 14(3)*, 201-207.

Rivara, F.P., Alexander, B., Johnston, B., & Soderberg, R. (1993). Population-based study of fall injuries in children and adolescents resulting in hospitalization or death. *Pediatrics, 92*, 61-63.

Rocha v. Great American Insurance Co., 850 F.2d 1095 (6th Cir. 1988).

Schleret v. State, 311 N.W.2d 843 (Minn. 1981).

Showers, J. (1997). *The national conference on shaken baby syndrome. A medical, legal & prevention challenge: Executive summary.* Alexandria, VA: National Association of Children's Hospitals and Related Institutions.

Showers, J., & Apolo, J. (1986). Criminal disposition of persons involved in 72 cases of fatal child abuse. *Medical Science and Law, 26(3),* 243-247.

Smith, W.L. (1994). Abusive head injury. *APSAC Advisor, 7(4),* 16-19.

Spaide, R.F., Swengel, R.M., Scharre, D.W., & Mein, C.E. (1990). Shaken baby syndrome. *American Family Physicians, 41*(4), 1145-1152.

Spivak, B.S. (1992). Biomechanics of nonaccidental trauma. In S. Ludwig & A.E. Kornberg (Eds.), *Child abuse: A medical reference (2nd ed.)* (pp. 61-78). New York: Churchill Livingstone.

Starling, S.P., Holden, J.R., & Jenny, C., (1995). Abusive head trauma: The relationship of perpetrators to their victims. *Pediatrics, 95,* 259-262.

State v. Altum, 941 P.2d 1348 (Kan.1997).

State v. Bantangan, 799 P.2d 48 (Hawaii 1990).

State v. Cressey, 628 A.2d 696 (N.H. 1993).

State v. Driskell, 659 P.2d 343, 349 (Okla. Crim. App. 1983).

State v. Holland, 346 N.W.2d 302 (S.D. 1984).

State v. Jones, 801 P.2d 263 (Wash App.1990).

State v. Jurgens, 424 N.W.2d 546 (Minn. Ct. App. 1988).

State v. Landrum, 528 N.W.2d 36 (Wis. Ct. App. 1995).

State v. Lopez, 412 S.E.2d 390 (S.C. 1991).

State v. McClary, 541 A.2d 96 (Conn. 1988).

State v. McKowen, 447 N.W.2d 546 (Iowa App.1989).

State v. Michaels, 625 A.2d 489 (N.J. Super 1993).

State v. Moorman, 670 A.2d 81 (N.J. Super.1996).

State v. Morrison, 437 N.W.2d 422 (Minn. Ct. App. 1989).

State v. Mott, 931 P.2d 1046 (Ariz. 1997).

State v. Ojeda, 810 P.2d 1148 (Idaho App. Ct. 1991).

State v. Ostlund, 416 N.W.2d 755 (Minn. Ct. App. 1987).

State v. Phillips, 399 S.E.2d 293 (N.C. 1991).

State v. Powell, 487 S.E.2d 424 (Ga. App. 1997).

State v. Prouse, 767 P.2d 1308 (Kan. 1989).

State v. Rundle, 500 N.W.2d 916 (Wis. 1993).

State v. Sibert, 648 N.E.2d 861 (Ohio App.1994).

State v. Stribley, 532 N.W.2d 170 (Iowa Ct. App. 1995).

State v. Toennis, 758 P.2d 539 (Wash Ct. App. 1988).

State v. Towne, 453 A.2d 1133 (Vt.1982).

State v. Warness, 893 P.2d 665 (Wash. App. 1995).

State v. Wyatt, 482 S.E.2d 147 (W.V. 1996).

Stern, P. (1997). *Preparing and presenting expert testimony in child abuse litigation: A guide for expert witnesses and attorneys.* Thousand Oaks, CA: Sage.

Taitz, L.S. (1987). Child abuse and osteogenesis imperfecta. *British Medical Journal, 295,* 1082-1083.

Thayer, J.T. (1997). The latest evidence for shaken baby syndrome – What defense lawyers and prosecutors need to know. *Criminal Justice, Summer*, 14-22.

United States Advisory Board on Child Abuse and Neglect. (1995). *A nation's shame: Fatal child abuse and neglect in the United States*. Washington, DC: U.S. Advisory Board on Child Abuse and Neglect.

United States v. Boise, 916 F.2d 497 (9th Cir. 1990).

United States v. Bowers, 660 F.2d 527 (5th Cir.1981).

United States v. Dowling, 493 U.S. 342, 110 S. Ct. 668, 107 L. Ed. 2d 708 (1990).

United States v. Gaskell, 985 F.2d 1056 (11th Cir. 1993).

United States v. Grey Bear, 883 F.2d 1382 (8th Cir.1989), *cert. denied*, 993 U.S. 1047 (1990).

United States v. Lewis, 837 F.2d 415 (9th Cir. 1988).

United States v. Merriweather, 22 M.J. 657 (A.C.M.R. 1986).

United States v. Powers, 59 F.3d 1460 (4th Cir. 1995).

United States v. Scheffer, 118 S. Ct. 1261, 140 L. Ed. 2d 413 (1998).

United States v. Tsinnijinnie, 91 F.3d 1282 (9th Cir. 1996).

United States v. White, 1996 W.L. 399973 (A.F.C.M.R. 1996).

United States v. Winter, 32 M.J. 901 (A.F.C.M.R. 1991).

Walker, A.G. (1999). *Handbook on questioning children: A linguistic perspective* (2nd ed.). Washington, D.C.: American Bar Association.

Watkins v. Melody, 95 F.3d 4 (7th Cir. 1996).

Watson v. State, 720 S.W.2d 310 (1986)

Wigmore, J.H. (1978). *Evidence in trials at common law*. Chadbourne rev. ed. Boston, MA: Little, Brown & Co.

Williams, R.A. (1991). Injuries in infants and small children resulting from witnessed and corroborated free falls. *Journal of Trauma, 31(10)*, 1350-1352.

Willman, K.Y., Bank, D.E., Senac, M., & Chadwick, D.L. (1997). Restricting the time of injury in fatal inflicted head injuries. *Child Abuse & Neglect, 21*(10), 929-940.

Wright, C.A., & Graham, K.W. (1990). *Federal practice and procedure*. St. Paul, MN: West Publishing Co.

Chapter Sixteen

Ethical Challenges in the Care of the Shaken Baby

Steven R. Leuthner

SUMMARY. The Shaken Baby Syndrome can result in severe neurologic injury that leads to ethical challenges in medical care. This article addresses the perceived distinctions between withholding and withdrawing life-sustaining medical treatment, demonstrating that in a severely injured child the burdens of therapy may be disproportionate to the benefits. In this case, withdrawal of support could be in the child's best interest. The article then addresses the issue of who can participate in that best interest decision. While parents must be allowed to participate, there may be circumstances of conflicts of interest for a parent in the Shaken Baby Syndrome that don't allow the parent to make a choice in their child's best interest. In these situations, the health care team and the state services must use their *parens patriae* to act in the best interest of a child which could include withdrawal of support of life-sustaining therapy. *[Article copies available for a fee from The Haworth Document Delivery Service: 1-800-342-9678. E-mail address: <getinfo@haworthpressinc.com> Website: <http://www.HaworthPress.com> © 2001 by The Haworth Press, Inc. All rights reserved.]*

KEYWORDS. Withdrawing life support, self-realization, parens patriae, best interest

[Haworth co-indexing entry note]: "Ethical Challenges in the Care of the Shaken Baby." Leuthner, Steven R. Co-published simultaneously in *Journal of Aggression, Maltreatment & Trauma* (The Haworth Maltreatment & Trauma Press, an imprint of The Haworth Press, Inc.) Vol. 5, No. 1(#9), 2001, pp. 341-347; and: *The Shaken Baby Syndrome: A Multidisciplinary Approach* (ed: Stephen Lazoritz, and Vincent J. Palusci) The Haworth Maltreatment & Trauma Press, an imprint of The Haworth Press, Inc., 2001, pp. 341-347. Single or multiple copies of this article are available for a fee from The Haworth Document Delivery Service [1-800-342-9678, 9:00 a.m. - 5:00 p.m. (EST). E-mail address: getinfo@haworthpressinc.com].

The American Academy of Pediatrics Policy Statement on Shaken Baby Syndrome reports that SBS is the leading cause of serious head injury in infants and has as high as a 60% severe morbidity or mortality rate (AAP, 1993). Although there are dramatized cases where the diagnosis of Shaken Baby Syndrome may be called into question, the great majority of these cases are easily diagnosed as child abuse. The simple presence of this form of child abuse challenges our ethical concepts of family, societal or community obligations and physician responsibilities. While it is beyond the scope of this chapter to review all ethical issues involving child abuse and neglect, there are two issues that are often mentioned which are pertinent to severely injured children from this syndrome. One is the issue of withholding and withdrawing support, and the other is who should be involved in making that decision.

WITHHOLDING/WITHDRAWING
LIFE-SUSTAINING MEDICAL TREATMENT

The first step is to examine the perceived distinction between withholding and withdrawing therapy. Despite most philosophical and legal commentators agreeing that there is no ethical distinction between withholding (not starting) therapy and withdrawing (stopping) therapy after it has been initiated, there continues to be studies showing that at least psychologically this distinction exists (Ashwal, 1992; Caralis & Hammond, 1992; Rubenstein, Yanoff, & Albert, 1968; Solomon et al., 1993). For some, the distinction is seen as a moral difference between an act versus an omission. For others, it seems emotionally easier to not start than to stop. Perhaps it is easier to walk away from something when the professional time investment has not been made. Many philosophers feel that this is not morally relevant because, when analyzed, the responsibility of participating in a decision is still there, no matter what the choice. From a legal perspective, the courts also have consistently ruled against any distinction (Meisel, 1991). The President's Commission for the Study of Ethical Problems in Medicine and Biomedical and Behavioral Research (1983) noted a danger in a philosophy of not starting therapy because of fear that one can't stop, because one might avoid a therapy that could have otherwise been helpful. If a therapy was begun, and it is not thought to be beneficial after starting, there is more justification in stopping than was present when therapy had not been started. One has now completed a "time-limited trial" (Junkerman & Scheidermayer, 1998). In fact, this occurs day-to-day in practice where in a pediatric intensive care unit the most common mode of death was withdrawal of support (Vernon, Dean, Timmons, Banner, & Allen-Webb, 1993).

The American Academy of Pediatric Committee on Bioethics defines Life-Sustaining Medical Treatment as transplantation, respirators, kidney dialysis machines, vasoactive drugs, antibiotics, insulin, chemotherapy, and nutrition and hydration provided intravenously or by tube (AAP, 1994). An infant who has suffered significant injury from shaken baby syndrome may require many of these therapies including respirator, antibiotics, and artificial means of providing nutrition and hydration. If one is to follow the above argument, it is clear that for the suspected shaken baby, it is ethically appropriate and required that life-sustaining treatment is initiated because the diagnosis is unknown, outcome is uncertain, and some of these children may recover. But what happens when the predicted outcome is not a return to baseline normalcy, but to severe neurological injury?

The first question to address is when can one consider withdrawing life-sustaining support in any neurologically-damaged baby. The simple answer is that life support should be withdrawn when it is not in the child's best interest to continue it. Determining best interest is the difficult part of the decision making process. It has been argued that there are two situations that withdrawal of support ought to be considered (Nelson & Nelson, 1992). The first is when treatment is considered physiologically futile, meaning that with reasonable medical certainty the treatment will not preserve some physiologic function. The other is when the therapy provides a "disproportionate burden," meaning that the therapy either causes pain and suffering or does not return the patient to an acceptable quality of life. The authors argue the first case is strictly a medical decision that could be applied unilaterally, while the second situation involves decisions based on value judgments regarding treatment burdens. It is this second situation where one tends to find the victims of SBS. An infant's control of respiration could be damaged, yet a ventilator can provide physiologic support. This leads to the decision about tracheotomy and chronic ventilation. Or there can be the child in a persistent vegetative state where a decision to place a gastric tube to provide nutrition is needed despite no hope of return to normal function. These cases lead to ethically appropriate questions of disproportionate burden.

Ethical theory and legal practice argue that benefits and burdens of treatment for the patient should provide reasons to start or stop treatments (Nelson et al., 1995; Wanzer et al., 1989). This should be no different for the shaken baby than any other severely neurologically-injured child. The next question of course is who determines the values for deciding whether there is disproportionate burden when there is known child abuse.

WHO DECIDES IF AND WHEN LIFE-SUSTAINING TREATMENT CAN BE WITHDRAWN?

Decisions to withhold or withdraw Life-Sustaining Medical Treatment in the pediatric patient population are more complex than in adult medicine. Since children are generally unable to participate in these decisions, the physician has the responsibility to provide for the parent the adequate information about diagnostic and therapeutic interventions and the prognosis. Then parents are given considerable discretion in making medical choices for their children. Nowhere should the fundamental value of parental decision-making be upheld more than with a decision to stop life-sustaining therapy. A pluralistic society tolerates multiple forms of parenting behavior whether they are decisions regarding education, extra-curricular activities, discipline or medicine. Much of this is based on the libertarian notion of family autonomy and privacy. This value is based on the assumption that parents, like everyone else making medical decisions for children, are obligated and will act responsibly according to their child's best interest. There is an expected commitment to the best interests of the child. The AAP Committee on Bioethics recommends that the physician should work with the family to help them overcome any lack of capacity to be a decision-maker, if possible. This includes disclosing all information and working as a partner with them. The ethical and legal presumption of parental capacity to make a decision for their child should govern unless countervailing evidence arises to recall the presumption into question (AAP, 1994). Just as the political environment is important in defining family autonomy, the state has a threshold for intervention that warrants breaching family autonomy and privacy. The state's *parens patriae* power is based on its legitimate interest in the welfare of children as current human beings and future citizens (Sorentino, 1976). It assumes a public role in protecting children through political-judicial intervention with the aid of others such as teachers, social workers and healthcare providers. This threshold for intervention is not really a threshold for best interest in the sense of what is "best" but in the sense of protecting from harm (Fost, 1986). In medicine, this power has been used by the state to allow physicians to treat children when the parents, based on religious principles or other values, do not want medical treatment for their children. An example is when a child of a Jehovah's Witness needs a blood transfusion. More recently, this concept of protecting a child from harm was used when a parent wanted to continue treatment that was felt to be burdensome and without benefit (Fleming, 1998). It was argued that just as adults are allowed to make decisions to refuse unwanted medical treatment, children do not lose this right because they are incompetent. Instead, they ought to be protected from the harm of overtreatment.

Parens patriae then puts the pediatrician in a difficult position of family confidant and agent of the state. So how is a decision made on whether continuation or withdrawal of treatment is in the child's best interest? In general, the health care team and the parents should enter open and compassionate discussions regarding the values, goals of therapy, and reasons for potential conflict. In the case of SBS (despite the issue of child abuse) the parent likely retains guardianship to be the decision-maker for the child and should be treated as such.

To not victimize the non-offending parent is clinically challenging (D'Lugoff & Baker, 1998). The difference in the health care team's role for SBS is evaluating the potential conflicts of interest of the parent participating in these decisions. In a typical scenario, it is the mother's boyfriend or husband who has committed the abuse. She now may have a number of interests in mind and could make one of three possible decisions: (1) protect the spouse or significant other who is jailed; (2) want to get revenge or cause harm to the significant other through allowing the child to die; or (3) separate herself from that partner and only address the child's health status. Only in the third scenario can one accept her decisions as truly in the interest of her child.

Another scenario occurs when the mother herself is the perpetrator. While she will immediately lose custody of her child while she is jailed for criminal child abuse, she maintains guardianship for decision making. A case fitting these circumstances has recently been reported where there was a conflict of interest or a situation of "Double Jeopardy" (Fleming, 1998). If the perpetrating mother allowed the withdrawal of support and subsequent death of her severely neurological impaired child, she could then be prosecuted for murder instead of criminal child abuse. It was a choice of her own life in prison versus her daughter's life. Can a woman or man in jail for criminal child abuse actually have that child's best interest in mind if the criminal charges will change based on their decision to withdraw life support? These potential conflicts of interest require the health care team to thoroughly evaluate the parental input into best interest decision regarding withdrawal of support.

EVALUATION AND RESOLUTION

In Shaken Baby Syndrome it is recommended that the issues of strict futility and disproportionate burden should first be addressed from a medical standpoint to determine whether withdrawal of support is even an option one should consider. Discussions with the parents ought to include these medical opinions, be open to parental values, and evaluate conflicts of interests. The health care team should work together with child protective services and other social agencies. If consensus among the health care team and parent are met, and the evaluation of the parent's decision indicates that they are acting in the best interest of their child, support may be withdrawn with provision of appropriate palliative care. If there is disagreement between the health care team and parent, it is important to maintain open communication by addressing values, helping the family explore reasons for their decision. Additional ethical input from an ethics consultation process may be helpful. If in the end there is an unresolvable conflict between the parental right to decide and the physician's duty to not inflict burdensome treatment, the physician has four options available: (1) transfer care to another physician or hospital that would be willing to continue treatment; (2) continue to treat the child and ignore one's ethical concerns; (3) seek a court order to stop treatment; or (4) refuse to continue treatment and force the family to pursue a legal challenge (Nelson & Nelson, 1992).

In the case of a shaken baby where a conflict of interest extinguishes the parent's ability to act in the best interest of their child, the conflict between the parental right to decide and the physician's duty no longer exists. Because there is no parent that can be trusted in the decision, the physician must pursue other avenues. Although the four options above may still be available, transferring care or continuing treatment are more difficult to justify when the parental decision is so clearly without concern for the child. In this situation, the fourth option seems more justified if the burdens are truly disproportionate. An ethics consultation may be helpful in evaluating whether withdrawal of support is in the child's best interest, so as not to make a unilateral move appear unsupported. Yet, because of the complexities of the legal situation and because the decision has legal consequences for the perpetrator, one must consider a court order to remove guardianship and withdraw support.

CONCLUSION

The decision to withdraw life-sustaining support for a victim of SBS challenges the intellectual and emotional capabilities of all involved. As professionals, we must maintain our focus on the balance between the best interest of the child and the value of parental autonomy. As child abuse awareness grows in our country, from medical diagnostic abilities to social justice programs, it is critical to be aware of the general ethical principles in pediatric medicine and what responsibilities the pediatrician and health care team must maintain.

REFERENCES

American Academy of Pediatrics, Committee on Bioethics. (1994). Guidelines on forgoing life-sustaining medical treatment. *Pediatrics, 93,* 532-536.

American Academy of Pediatrics, Committee on Child Abuse and Neglect. (1993). Shaken baby syndrome: Inflicted cerebral trauma. *Pediatrics, 92,* 872-875.

Ashwal, S. (1992). The persistent vegetative state in children: Report of the Child Neurology Society Ethics Committee. *Annals of Neurology, 32,* 570-576.

Caralis, P.V., & Hammond, J.S. (1992). Attitudes of medical students, housestaff, and faculty physicians toward euthanasia and termination of life-sustaining treatment. *Critical Care Medicine, 20,* 683-690.

D'Lugoff, M.I., & Baker, D.J. (1998). Case study: Shaken baby syndrome–One disorder with two victims. *Public Health Nursing, 15,* 243-249.

Fleming, M.S. (1998). A case study of child abuse and a parent's refusal to withdraw life-sustaining treatment. *Human Rights, 26,* 12-14.

Fost, N. (1986). Parents as decision makers for children. *Primary Care, 13,* 285-293.

Junkerman, C., & Scheidermayer, D. (1998). *Practical ethics for students, interns, and residents.*

Meisel, A. (1991). Legal myths about terminating life support. *Archives of Internal Medicine, 1551,* 1497-1502.

Nelson, L.J., & Nelson, R.M. (1992). Ethics and the provision of futile, harmful, or burdensome treatment to children. *Critical Care Medicine, 20,* 427-433.

Nelson, L.J., Rushton, C.H., Cranford, R.E., Nelson, R.M., Glover, J.J., & Truog, R.D. (1995). Forgoing medically provided nutrition and hydration in pediatric patients. *Journal of Law, Medicine and Ethics, 23,* 33-46.

President's Commission for the Study of Ethical Problems in Medicine and Biomedical and Behavioral Research. (1983). *Deciding to forego life-sustaining treatment: Ethical, medical and legal issues in treatment decisions.* Washington, DC: US Government Printing Office.

Rubenstein, R.A., Yanoff, M., & Albert, D.M. (1968). Thrombocytopenia, anemia, and retinal hemorrhage. *American Journal of Ophthalmology, 65,* 435-439.

Solomon, M.Z., O'Donnell, L.O., Jennings, B., Guilfoy, V., Wolf, S.M., Nolan, K., Jackson, R., Koch-Weser, D., & Donnelley, S. (1993). Decisions near the end of life: Professional views on life-sustaining treatments. *American Journal of Public Health, 83,* 14-23.

Sorentino v. Family and Children's Soc. of Elizabeth, 367 A.2d 1168 (New Jersey 1976).

Vernon, D.D., Dean, J.M., Timmons, O.T., Banner, W., & Allen-Webb, E.M. (1993). Modes of death in the pediatric intensive care unit: Withdrawal and limitation of supportive care. *Critical Care Medicine, 21,* 1798-1802.

Wanzer, S.H., Federman, D.D., Adelstein, S.J., Cassel, C.K., Cassem, E.H., Cranford, R.E., Hook, E.W., Lo, B., Moertel, C.G., Safar, P. (1989). The physician's responsibility toward hopelessly ill patients: A second look. *New England Journal of Medicine, 320,* 844-849.

Chapter Seventeen

Preventing Shaken Baby Syndrome

Jacy Showers

SUMMARY. Although the prevention of shaken baby syndrome is questioned by some professionals, there is no doubt that prevention is the ideal goal. Education about the dangers of shaking babies is paramount, especially in light of the fact that messages have historically been distributed that shaking is an acceptable practice. Such messages have included instructions regarding apnea as well as infant cardiopulmonary resuscitation. While it can be argued that the amount of shaking advised in these instances does not correlate with the amount of shaking needed to cause SBS, the important prevention message is that babies and children should never be shaken for any reason. This dictum, along with information about the specific injuries caused by shaking should be provided to everyone, from youngsters to senior citizens. Common approaches to educating the public are discussed and evaluation of these efforts will also be reviewed. Other programs in schools, hospital maternity units and through child care licensing are also being implemented. The responsibility for SBS prevention belongs to every professional who works with children and families and to each individual who cares for a baby or young child. *[Article copies available for a fee from The Haworth Document Delivery Service: 1-800-342-9678. E-mail address: <getinfo@haworthpressinc.com> Website: <http://www.HaworthPress.com> © 2001 by The Haworth Press, Inc. All rights reserved.]*

[Haworth co-indexing entry note]: "Preventing Shaken Baby Syndrome." Showers, Jacy. Co-published simultaneously in *Journal of Aggression, Maltreatment & Trauma* (The Haworth Maltreatment & Trauma Press, an imprint of The Haworth Press, Inc.) Vol. 5, No. 1(#9), 2001, pp. 349-365; and: *The Shaken Baby Syndrome: A Multidisciplinary Approach* (ed: Stephen Lazoritz, and Vincent J. Palusci) The Haworth Maltreatment & Trauma Press, an imprint of The Haworth Press, Inc., 2001, pp. 349-365. Single or multiple copies of this article are available for a fee from The Haworth Document Delivery Service [1-800-342-9678, 9:00 a.m. - 5:00 p.m. (EST). E-mail address: getinfo@haworthpressinc.com].

KEYWORDS. Prevention programs, triggers, public health implications, public knowledge, intervention

BACKGROUND

In describing shaken baby syndrome (SBS), Caffey (1972) concluded that, "The wide practice of habitual whiplash-shaking . . . warrants a massive nationwide educational campaign to alert everyone responsible for the welfare of infants on its potential and actual pathogenicity" (p. 163). Yet, for nearly 15 years, very little was done in the way of prevention (Dykes, 1986), although numerous physicians and researchers supported the recommendation (Caffey, 1974; Curran, 1984; Eagan, Whelan-Williams, & Brooks, 1985; Ludwig & Warman, 1984; Showers & Apolo, 1986; Showers, Apolo, Thomas, & Beavers, 1985). While isolated local efforts to prevent SBS were initiated in the mid-1980's, an effort to begin or expand shaken baby syndrome prevention programming throughout the United States was not begun until 1992. Reasons for this rest primarily with issues of denial and a historical predilection in the United States toward intervention over prevention as it relates to child abuse.

PREVENTABILITY OF SBS

The preventability of SBS is still in question, in large part because there is no epidemiologic data about the actual incidence and prevalence of SBS against which to measure prevention efforts. It will not be possible to gauge whether prevention initiatives have had any impact on the number of SBS cases until death certificates and child abuse reporting systems accurately identify victims of SBS. However, even the suggestion of a need for prevention has met resistance by some professionals (Thayer, 1996). The root of the resistance is denial, and to deny the potential benefit of education about the dangers of shaking babies is to oversimplify the issue and minimize the lifelong trauma experienced by families who live with the aftermath of SBS. These families often wonder if prevention might have made a difference in even one case.

Denial regarding SBS as a medical entity and as a phenomenon, which should be known to the public has been pervasive. Not until 1993 was a position paper on SBS issued by the American Academy of Pediatrics regarding the under-recognition of this form of child abuse and the possible need for prevention efforts (American Academy of Pediatrics Committee on Child Abuse and Neglect, 1993). There is still current reluctance among a few medical professionals to admit that SBS exists or is a significant problem. Such resistance correlates with a philosophy that prevention is not needed for such a rare or non-occurring medical condition. Even when shaking is acknowledged as a significant health threat, the opinion has been expressed that prevention efforts specifically about SBS are not needed (Thayer, 1996). This opinion is based on the concept that everyone "knows" shaking a baby hard is dangerous. The flaw underlying this premise is that no one knows the exact threshold of shaking before injury occurs for any given child. Therefore, everyone should be educated not to shake babies or children for any reason. The overall goals should include 100% public education, zero tolerance for shaking practices, and prosecution of shaking to the fullest extent of the law as a crime against children. To achieve this, a generation of educational efforts should become public policy, with appropriate funding to achieve this goal.

Two dichotomous views of prevention have also inhibited initiatives to educate the public about SBS. At one end of the continuum is the bias that all cases of SBS are preventable through educational efforts. Although a laudable goal, the fact is that not all cases of SBS are preventable by conventional means. The reaction of some professionals to this view is to distance themselves from prevention efforts because they do not wish to be associated with the position that all SBS cases are preventable. In fact, there are case examples in which there was clear documentation that shakers knew the potential harm of their actions and shook babies anyway. In a few cases, perpetrators had been charged or convicted of shaking other children on prior occasions (Alexander, Crabe, Sato, Smith, & Bennett, 1990). At the opposite end of the spectrum is the tenet that SBS prevention will never be effective because all shakers are sociopaths and that no amount of education will change their behavior. In fact, some shakers do have histories of sociopathic behavior, but many have no history of prior interpersonal violence against babies, children, or adults. This view disputes the fact that there is a relationship between knowledge and behavior, and negates the fact that thousands of Americans who have been educated about the dangers of shaking babies subscribe to the belief that such education will reduce the potential incidence of shaking episodes (Showers, 1992a, 1992b, 1997).

Case examples in recent years illustrate the need to acknowledge the range of preventability in SBS cases. In one case, a seven-week-old girl was jabbed, bitten, beaten and sexually molested before being shaken to death. The facts of this case indicate that it was clearly perpetrated by an individual who had no regard for human life and who would not have been influenced by education about SBS. In another case, a two-month-old boy was shaken by his 13-year-old brother on two consecutive evenings. The teenager was trying to console the baby and stop his crying on both occasions. When the baby quieted on the first evening, the teen thought he had used an effective means of controlling the baby's crying. Unfortunately, the second time he shook the baby for the same purpose, the baby died. The teenager readily admitted to shaking, was very remorseful, and indicated that he would never have shaken the baby if he had known it was dangerous. Whether education would truly have prevented the latter case will never be known. What cannot be disputed is that education would not have done any harm, and it may have saved a life.

Historically, the legal burden of proof for shaking as a crime rested with whether the act was committed willfully, recklessly, intentionally, and/or knowingly. An increase in the knowledge about SBS may not only prevent incidents of shaking, but can be used in an investigation or prosecution of a case to prove that shakers knew or should have known shaking could be harmful to a child's well-being.

COMBATING MESSAGES THAT SHAKING IS OKAY

One of the reasons SBS prevention is imperative is to combat messages that indicate shaking of children is okay or even advisable as a response to apnea or for resuscitation purposes. For many years parents were instructed to shake babies for apnea (Chadwick, 1988). In some cases, written instructions with the imprint of hospitals or individual physicians were given to parents telling them to shake their infant if the child stopped breathing. Although some instructions said to "shake the baby gently," others stated, "shake gently, then vigorously" (Chadwick, 1988). In the past decade, the use of these instructions has reduced, but advice to parents to shake babies for apneic episodes has still been reported.

Historically, it was also standard for instructions regarding cardiopulmonary resuscitation (CPR) instructions to begin with the words "shake and shout." In some CPR courses, the first instruction for infant and child CPR is still "shake." Although many professionals suggest that the amount of force used in shaking for CPR or in response to an apneic episode is much less than that used in shaking which results in SBS, the message to the public is still contradictory. Either shaking is okay, or it isn't. Since there has been no scientifically established threshold of shaking which an individual child can stand without harm, there should be zero tolerance for shaking. All instructions, which indicate that shaking is acceptable, should be abolished (Chadwick, 1988). It would have been unthinkable for recommendations to be made to parents to "burn" children or to "slap" children in response to apnea and CPR. Professionals would not have made these recommendations even with the stipulation to do it gently. Yet shaking can cause as much or more damage than these forms of child abuse. In light of this, the need for specific education about the dangers of shaking babies should be perceived as a high priority.

The toy industry is a third and perhaps more controversial arena in which instructions have been distributed that it is acceptable to shake babies. In recent years, several toy "dolls" have been marketed with specific instructions to "grab my neck and shake my head," or "shake {me} vigorously in all directions." Such toys, while they may or may not result in SBS cases, clearly give consumers the idea that shaking a baby-like toy is a fun or advisable thing to do. Children need to learn the opposite message early and often.

MINIMIZING THE POTENTIAL HARM OF SHAKING VS. OTHER CHILD "DISCIPLINE"

One of the themes that has repeatedly appeared in the literature is that caretakers of children "may be unaware of the specific injuries they may cause by shaking" (American Academy of Pediatrics Committee on Child Abuse and Neglect, 1993) and may perceive shaking as less abusive or less culpable than other forms of child "discipline" (California Medical Association, 1990; Curran, 1984; Spaide, Swengel, Schane, & Mein, 1990). The opinion has been expressed by some SBS experts that people may not actually be aware of how seriously shaking can hurt a child (Showers, 1997). Prevention efforts can help eliminate the notion that shaking may not be as harmful as spanking, punching, or otherwise hitting children. Furthermore, although there is controversy about whether shakers actually intend to seriously hurt or kill babies or children (Bruce & Zimmerman, 1989), there has been some speculation that subservience to an adult's wishes is a more primary goal than injury to the child (Spaide et al., 1990). In this regard, anticipatory guidance for parents and other child caregivers about child behaviors which may trigger an adult's anger or frustration may be the most effective prevention approach for SBS.

The potential harm, which can be caused by shaking will not be reduced by allowing the attitude to prevail that shaking is not as dangerous as other forms of "discipline." The notion that shaking is innocuous or preferable to other approaches to gain behavioral compliance by babies or children must be combated proactively. It has now been well established that shaking can cause a myriad of sequelae including brain damage or death. That message must be communicated systematically and comprehensively to the public at large, and prevention programs should be put in place to educate people about what to do when they are frustrated and angry about a child's behavior or about stressors in their own lives.

"TRIGGERS" FOR SBS AND IMPLICATIONS FOR PREVENTION

The core message in SBS prevention is, "Never shake a baby or young child for any reason." To restrict education to this is shortsighted. While they can leave a lasting impression, negative messages do not address the broader agenda of training parents and care-givers for their roles. Therefore, it is important to address the issues that precipitate shaking and to educate people about how to approach these events.

In many shaking cases, the primary precipitating factor is an adult's anger or frustration caused by stressors in his or her own life in combination with the behavior of a baby or child. Frequently, this child behavior is crying (American Academy of Pediatrics Committee on Child Abuse and Neglect, 1993; Caffey, 1974; Curran, 1984; Frank, Zimmerman & Leeds, 1985; Krugman, 1985; Ludwig & Warman, 1984; Showers, 1998). As primary prevention for SBS, parents and care givers should have an "anger plan" before they take care of children. Anger management should emanate not from a reactive position but from a proactive philosophy. Regardless of the exact internalization or articulation of this philosophy, an underlying tenet must be to err in the direction of the safety of a child when coping with frustration or anger.

Before teenagers and adults undertake the responsibilities of childcare or child-rearing, they should be cautioned that they may become angry either as a result of their own stressors or fatigue or as a reaction to a child's behavior. They need to be educated to identify risk factors in their own lives, which may leave them less capable or unable to safely care for children. They should have an advance plan for what they will do when they feel exasperated, whether it is asking for help from someone they trust, removing themselves from the situation, calling an emergency number or some other approach. Professionals who work with families can ask them periodically "What will you do when you've had all you can take with this child?" as a way to help them anticipate problem times and plan safe solutions. The important thing is that every child caregiver understands that the responsibility of taking care of babies and children is stressful, that frustration is normal, and that child safety is the highest priority.

Perhaps the most valuable tenet that can be taught in order to prevent shaking and other forms of child abuse is "Never touch a child in anger." People need to be coached that, if they are holding a baby or child and feel themselves becoming frustrated or angry, they should put the child in a safe place and take a "timeout." They need to know ahead of time that if they are watching or listening to a child and begin to feel angry or frustrated they should not touch the child as long as the child is safe.

Although crying is the most commonly reported precipitating event for shaking, other child behaviors are sometimes associated with shaking episodes. These include toilet training problems, feeding difficulties, and children interrupting adults (Krugman, 1985; Showers, 1998). A number of cases have been reported in which infants and toddlers have been shaken as a result of interrupting an adult's viewing of a television show, most specifically a sporting event. In creating a proactive approach to child care-giving, it is important for adults to include recognition of when children are best served by not being in their care. Sometimes, this includes scheduling other caregivers when an adult is very interested in watching an event or following the story line in a television program. Anticipatory guidance about routine daily activities such as eating, toileting, and sleeping are also an important component of SBS prevention programming. Studies indicate that reading materials about child development and nonviolent child behavior management significantly improves knowledge (Showers, 1989, 1991, 1993). In many cases parents report that such information results in changes in their approaches to child behavior management (Showers, 1989).

There are less common reasons for shaking that merit attention and education. These include using shaking as a method to adjust a child's sleep schedule to coincide with an adult's and shaking children during the course of violence against another adult. Because the range of precipitating events is so broad, the message not to shake children for any reason is paramount.

DOCUMENTATION OF LACK OF KNOWLEDGE

In the past decade, several studies documented lack of knowledge among young people in particular about the dangers of shaking babies (Showers, 1991; Showers & Johnson, 1984, 1985). In one study of high school students, only 50% of respondents knew that it was dangerous to shake a baby (Showers & Johnson, 1985). College students scored only slightly higher (Showers & Johnson, 1984). The combination of inadequate knowledge about the dangers of shaking babies, the discovery that people were being given messages that shaking was advisable, and the growing recognition of shaken baby syndrome led to early prevention efforts.

Data collected nationally between 1993-1996 from people receiving information regarding the dangers of shaking babies revealed that for 37% it was the first time they had received such information (Showers, 1996). Even as the turn of the century arrives, millions of Americans are not aware of the specific harm that can be caused by shaking a baby or child.

EVALUATION OF EARLY PREVENTION EFFORTS

Beginning in 1987, several projects conducted in Ohio involved providing information to people about the dangers of shaking babies and how to cope with crying infants and evaluated the response of the target audiences. A comparison of pre- and post-test results on knowledge about the dangers of shaking babies revealed statistically significant improvements among three populations studied (Showers, 1992a). While pre-test average correct scores ranged from 67-74%, post-test average correct scores increased to 93-97%. These increases in knowledge occurred after respondents read a brief card entitled, "Crying . . . What Should I Do?" which included the warning that shaking a baby can be dangerous.

Because the results of these studies showed promising increases in knowledge, an expansion of the project known as "Don't Shake The Baby" was made to include all parents of newborns in one Ohio county for a twelve-month period, beginning in August 1989. This project included all six medical facilities, which had licensed maternity units and reached parents of 15,708 newborns with print material on how to cope with crying infants and the dangers of shaking babies. Evaluation data returned by 21% of the parents ranging in age from 14-44 years indicated that the material was perceived as helpful by the vast majority of parents; 91% indicated that it should be given to other people (Showers, 1992a). Due to its success, the project was expanded to hospitals in four other states (Delaware, New Jersey, Illinois, Utah) from 1990-1992 where evaluation data from thousands of parents revealed similar results (Showers, 1992b). Perhaps the most poignant finding from the combined five-state project was that fifty-one (51%) percent of respondents indicated that they were less likely to shake babies as a result of reading the "Crying . . . What Should I Do?" card.

EVOLUTION AND SCOPE OF PREVENTION APPROACHES

As the "Don't Shake the Baby" project was conceived, piloted and expanded, the *NEVER SHAKE A BABY* theme was featured on other products in order to reach a broader population. Posters and public service announcements (PSAs) were produced and published in news magazines such as *Time* and *Sports Illustrated* and on television and radio. It was not possible to systematically evaluate the impact of these approaches, but anecdotal feedback indicated that they were promising ways to reach the public. In 1987, The Children's Trust Fund of Texas issued a brochure and a PSA based on the concept of petals falling off a flower as an analogy to shaking a child. Shortly thereafter, other themes were developed by concerned agencies to bring attention to SBS and its prevention. In addition to the *NEVER SHAKE A BABY* warning, two themes have commonly been adopted by other agencies around the country. *BABIES ARE FRAGILE. PLEASE DON'T SHAKE A CHILD* with an illustration of babies in an egg carton was created jointly by Children's Hospital and Medical Center of Seattle and the Washington Council for Prevention of Child Abuse and Neglect. *SHAKE THIS [A RATTLE] NOT A BABY* was, developed by The Junior League of St. Paul, Inc. and Midwest Children's Resource Center at Children's Hospital of St. Paul in Minnesota and has also been widely used. These themes have often appeared in print materials, brochures, posters, billboards and on other prevention materials. In the past several years, the variety of print materials has increased at local and state levels.

In addition to print products and public media materials, a number of professionally produced videotapes designed for SBS prevention became available in the 1990's. These include the videos "Crying . . . What Can I Do? (Never Shake a Baby)" and "Portrait of Promise: Preventing Shaken Baby Syndrome" which were reviewed and approved by the American Academy of Pediatrics (AAP) when they were released in 1992 and 1995, respectively. A number of videotapes have been used in prevention efforts and tend to be perceived by the public as very effective in conveying messages about the dangers and potentially harmful consequences of shaking children (Showers, 1996).

The way in which SBS prevention messages are displayed has proliferated. Themes warning people about the dangers of shaking babies now appear on bumper stickers, billboards, bus signs, metro signs, bookmarks, notepads, T-shirts, bibs, burp rags, blankets, door hangers, calendars, athletic schedules, milk cartons, grocery bags, utility company mailing inserts, magnets, stickers, buttons, and pencils. The continuing evolution of approaches to SBS prevention is limited only by our imagination.

A more formalized method of education, which began in 1993, was the development of curricula specifically for school-aged children and teenagers. A comprehensive curriculum was created by The Junior League of St. Paul, Inc. and the Midwest Children's Resource Center at Children's Hospital of St. Paul, Minnesota. *"FRAGILE: Handle With Care: Shaken Baby Syndrome"* was specifically designed to teach sixth-graders not only that it is never okay to shake a baby but that baby-sitting and parenting are difficult undertakings (Couser, 1993). The model includes classroom discussion, activities and an interactive videotape. Comprehensive in scope, this curriculum began as four weekly, 50-minute classroom sessions and has now been abridged so that shorter versions can be provided if there are time constraints. Other lesson plan models have been developed by other agencies for children of different ages for presentation in the schools or through community programs such as the Boy Scouts or Girl Scouts.

There has been a trend over recent years for families of SBS victims to become involved in SBS educational efforts. The Shaken Baby Alliance, a support and networking nonprofit organization for SBS families, began in 1998 and is rapidly expanding its efforts to raise public awareness both about the need for prevention and the devastating consequences to families. The voice of SBS families is crucial in prevention efforts because it brings real stories and faces to the problem and often has the most enduring impact on audiences attending prevention programs.

NATIONAL SBS PREVENTION

In 1992, the National Center on Child Abuse and Neglect (NCCAN) funded a three-year project called "Don't Shake the Baby: Replication of a Successful Model" with the goal of assisting all 50 states, Washington, D.C. and Puerto Rico to begin or expand efforts to prevent SBS. A lead agency was identified in each state and was the primary determinant of how resources provided by the grant would be used. Each lead agency was given technical assistance and an allocation of SBS materials based upon the number of annual births in their state. Products selected included educational manuals, videotapes, posters, print packets, bumper stickers, pencils, bookmarks and public service announcements with the *NEVER SHAKE A BABY* message.

Although estimates from lead agencies indicated that more than 500,000 people were reached during the three years, resources were by no means sufficient to achieve statewide outreach in any state. While this effort constituted a landmark event in raising awareness about SBS and the need for prevention, two follow-up findings were concerning. First, continued funding for SBS prevention is a major problem. For a number of states, when the grant ended, so did systematic efforts to prevent SBS. Second, during the course of the three-year project, the contact person changed in 42% of the states, highlighting a problem in maintaining continuity in both direction and momentum for SBS prevention. On the other hand, the NCCAN-funded project represented a solid beginning for some states, and lead agencies have built upon this by expanding initial efforts and creating new programs. In some cases, they have also sponsored local, state, or regional training to better educate multidisciplinary professionals and to build a cadre of trainers to continue prevention efforts.

Significant outcomes from the national project were that it gave birth to many SBS prevention efforts and that it served as a springboard for the first National Conference on Shaken Baby Syndrome in 1996. This conference was a significant step toward helping professionals from all disciplines to network with each other, as well as with SBS families. It was a much needed catalyst for highlighting the need for prevention of SBS, and for providing state-of-the-art information about medical, investigative, and legal issues.

An important outcome of the national effort was the evaluation feedback from people across the country who either received the print card or viewed the videotape provided through the grant (Showers, 1996). Table 1 shows the aggregate data collected. The project was viewed as valuable to those responding to the program and revealed that for more than one-third of those providing feedback, this program was the first time they had been informed about the dangers of shaking babies. Men were less likely to have been informed than women, and people of minority races were less likely to have been previously educated about SBS than Caucasians.

OPTIMUM OPPORTUNITIES FOR PREVENTION

SBS prevention efforts should begin with children as young as three years of age and continue through the grandparenting years. Experience shows that the best way to systematically reach both young males and females is through SBS prevention programs at the middle school level. Students at this age are more receptive to the information than are high schoolers. It is possible and advisable to reach both boys and girls, since many of them have younger brothers

TABLE 1. National Video Evaluation, Summary 1993-1996*

Title: "Crying. . . What Can I Do? (Never Shake a Baby)"

Responses: 8,353 from 38 states and Puerto Rico

- I found the video helpful 91%
- I learned more about the dangers of shaking a baby. 85%
- I think parents who see this video will be less likely to shake their babies 86%
- This is the first information I have been given about the dangers of shaking babies. . 38%
- This is the first time I've been taught what to do if a baby cries a lot. 23%
- I think other parents should see this video 94%

Title: "Crying. . . What Should I Do?" (Crying Card Evaluation)

Responses: 8,110 from 39 states, Washington D.C. and Puerto Rico

- I found the "Crying. . . What Should I Do?" card helpful 80%
- I learned more about the dangers of shaking a baby. 61%
- I think parents who read this card will be less likely to shake their babies 82%
- This is the first information I have been given about the dangers of shaking babies. . 37%
- This is the first time I've been taught what to do if a baby cries a lot. 23%
- I think other parents should read this card 90%

and sisters and are beginning to formally baby-sit. It is also a very opportune time because some of these youngsters will drop out of school as teenagers. In addition, unfortunately, some students will become parents in their preteen or teen years and need to know early on about how to take care of babies and the potential dangers of shaking them.

Repetition of warnings about the dangers of shaking children and how to cope with adult anger and frustration is warranted. Programming to this end should be repeated at the high school and post-high school levels, including prenatal classes, offices of obstetricians and gynecologists, birthing units, and during post-natal visits and parenting classes. Ideally, new parents should not be allowed to take a newborn home from the hospital until they have viewed a videotape about how to cope with crying and the dangers of shaking, received written material to this effect, created an anger plan, and signed a statement that they understand babies should never be shaken for any reason. Such protocols might reduce the risk of shaking episodes and would provide valuable documentation for the prosecution of cases should shaking occur.

Other ideal times for SBS prevention include the first visit to the pediatrician, any encounter with a professional during which a family member reports that a baby is colicky, and at the time of vaccinations. Parents are often told to expect that their child will be fussy after a shot; they need to be advised or reminded at the same time that shaking is never okay. The recommended vaccination at two months of age is an especially important time to reinforce this warning, as the most common age for shaking babies is two months (Showers, 1998). Warnings about shaking should also be reiterated when a baby is reported as fussy because of teething, diaper rash, or other reasons. Nurses can play a crucial role in educating parents and other child care givers about the dangers of shaking babies during these and other times (Chiocca, 1995; Coody, Brown, Montgomery, Flynn, & Yetman, 1994).

Finally, one of the most opportune times to emphasize information about the dangers of shaking a baby and early signs and symptoms of SBS is when a parent is changing child care. Whether the change in care is shifted to a spouse, significant other, family member, or child care provider, parents should be advised to keep this information in mind and to share it with other people who will be caring for their children. The recognition of early signs and symptoms such as poor feeding, irritability and vomiting can result in the termination of access of a shaker to a child, preventing a subsequent episode that may be more devastating or deadly.

TARGETING SPECIAL POPULATIONS

The trend in the mid to late 1990s has been to make special efforts to reach males. This was, in part a response to growing awareness that males constitute the majority of identified perpetrators in SBS cases (Showers, 1994, 1997; Starling, Holden, & Jenny, 1995). Although such efforts are important, it is critical to reach both males and females of all ages as perpetrators come from all socioeconomic, ethnic, and age groups, and both genders. Their relationship to the children shaken varies greatly, and includes siblings, parents, stepparents, adoptive parents, foster parents, grandparents, aunts, uncles, boyfriends of mothers, girlfriends of fathers, other relatives, nannies, au pairs, licensed child care providers, unlicensed child care providers, friends, and neighbors (Showers, 1998). The need for education and prevention is everywhere.

In addition to including males in SBS prevention programs in schools, getting the information to males to never shake a baby has been done by targeting venues such as scouting programs, sporting events, athletic facilities, and even male dominated businesses or institutions. One such initiative, funded by the Colorado Children's Trust Fund, provided *NEVER SHAKE A BABY* story cards to people buying fishing and hunting licenses, the majority of whom were male. Some agencies have created public service announcements by well-known sports figures emphasizing that, while sports can be rough, men need to be gentle with babies. A recent program in Ann Arbor, Michigan exemplified this approach using University of Michigan varsity athletes. Information about SBS has also been incorporated into programming for incarcerated juveniles and adults. This approach is important because many of these men and women will care for children after they are released, and some have histories of anger management problems and interpersonal violence.

Because data also indicate that female child care providers and licensed day care providers also constitute a significant group of perpetrators (Starling et al., 1995), more efforts are being directed toward better screening and training of this population. All child licensing requirements should mandate education about the dangers of shaking babies, as should baby-sitting classes specifically designed for preteens and teenagers. Information about SBS and visible warnings about the dangers of shaking should also be displayed in early child development facilities such as Early Head Start and Head Start, as well as churches, malls, recreation centers and other facilities that provide drop-in child care.

An additional group that has been identified as an appropriate special population for SBS prevention is military personnel (Gessner & Runyon,

1995). Many of the Family Advocacy Programs in the Armed Forces have included SBS information in their programs. This is a laudable initiative that should be standard for all military personnel who are current or expectant parents.

Since previous messages have been given to the public that shaking a baby is okay or advisable for apnea and CPR, families who report a history of apnea in any child and all persons trained in CPR should be strongly warned against shaking children for any reason. One method of increasing awareness is to dress infant and child CPR mannequins in T-shirts that convey the message that it is never okay to shake a baby or child.

Families with twins or multiple births should also be cautioned about the added stress that can occur as a result of multiple babies crying, and they should be given information about how to cope when they feel tired and frustrated. Although more research is needed about the relationship of SBS and twin status, this correlation has been suggested as a possibility (Becker, Liersch, Tautz, Schlyeter, & Andler, 1998).

Professional groups are also special target populations for training regarding the medical, investigative, legal, protective, therapeutic, and prevention aspects of SBS. Prevention specialists have played an important role in planning special training and conferences that include prevention information but also address the training needs of professionals responsible for recognition, intervention, and adjudication issues. These efforts should also be expanded through multidisciplinary efforts.

WHO IS RESPONSIBLE FOR SBS PREVENTION?

The responsibility for SBS prevention belongs to every professional who provides medical care for, or education to parents and prospective parents, baby-sitters and child care providers. School teachers, childbirth educators, nurses, pediatricians, and other primary care physicians (Curran, 1984) are in unique positions to educate people at teachable times.

Although school systems often resist adding one more educational module to their curriculum, this information is essential for school-age children as it could save a baby's life. It can be taught in as little as half an hour and may be the only time a potential child care giver is accessible. Childbirth educators often are able to reach prospective parents, especially first time parents, when they are most receptive to information about child care. Since physicians tend to be relied on by parents as their best source of information about child health, safety and care, they have special opportunities to educate families about SBS. This can be done through messages displayed in their offices and examination rooms and through specific anticipatory guidance regarding common child behaviors. In addition, physicians can help by probing parents about their actions when they feel exasperated with children and helping them create a plan to cope with difficult parent-child interactions. All such efforts should be documented.

In addition, as parents themselves become educated about SBS, they share the responsibility of informing anyone in whose care their children are placed that their children should never be shaken. Unfortunately for many SBS families, the first time they learned about the dangers of shaking was when they were informed that their child was a victim. Although shaking which occurs at the hands of others, SBS family members have consistently expressed the wish that they had known earlier about the potential dangers of shaking and the early signs and symptoms. Many of these parents provided written guidelines to child care providers about managing their children's behavior, including instructions not to hit or spank them. They often note that had they known about SBS, their instructions would have included "Do not shake my child for any reason."

CONCLUSION

While there is some controversy about the preventability of SBS cases, data collected nationally from those receiving information about the dangers of shaking babies clearly indicates that the message increases knowledge, is valued, and should be more widely disseminated. The best approach to prevention is to start with children at an early age and implement a system of redundancy in the message to never shake a baby or child, how to manage anger, and ways to approach child behaviors that cause frustration. The responsibility to disseminate the message that it is never okay to shake a baby or child belongs to each of us, both in our professional venues and our personal lives.

REFERENCES

Alexander, R., Crabbe, L., Sato, Y., Smith, W., & Bennett, T. (1990). Serial abuse in children who are shaken. *American Journal of Diseases of Childhood, 144,* 58-60.

American Academy of Pediatrics Committee on Child Abuse and Neglect. (1993). *Pediatrics, 92,* 872-875.

Becker, J.C., Liersch, R., Tautz, C., Schlyeter, B., & Andler, W. (1998). Shaken baby syndrome: Report on four pairs of twins. *Child Abuse & Neglect, 22,* 931-937.

Bruce, D.A., & Zimmerman, R.A. (1989). Shaken impact syndrome. *Pediatric Annals, 18,* 482-494.

Caffey, J. (1972). On the theory and practice of shaking infants. *American Journal of Diseases of Childhood, 124,* 161-169.

Caffey, J. (1974). Whiplash shaken infant syndrome: Manual shaking by the extremities with whiplash-induced intracranial and intraocular bleedings, linked with residual permanent brain damage and mental retardation. *Pediatrics, 54*, 396-403.

California Medical Association. (1990). Shaken infant syndrome. *Healthtips, April 1990*, Index 366.

Chadwick, D. (1988). Commentary: Stop shaking for apnea. *AAP News*, 6.

Chiocca, E.M. (1995). Shaken baby syndrome: A nursing perspective. *Pediatric Nursing, 21*, 33-38.

Coody, D., Brown, M., Montgomery, D., Flynn, A., & Yetman, R. (1994). Shaken baby syndrome: Identification and prevention for nurse practitioners. *Journal of Pediatric Health Care, 8*, 50-56.

Couser, S. (1993). Shaken baby syndrome. *Journal of Pediatric Health Care, 7*, 238-239.

Curran, M. (1984). Shaken infant syndrome `secret' form of abuse. *Pediatric News, 19*, 1 & 46.

Dykes, L.J. (1986). The whiplash shaken baby syndrome: What has been learned? *Child Abuse & Neglect, 10*, 211-221.

Eagan, B.A., Whelan-Williams, S., & Brooks, W.G. (1985). The abuse of infants by manual shaking: Medical, social and legal issues. *Journal of the Florida Medical Association, 72*, 503-507.

Frank, Y., Zimmerman, R., & Leeds, N. (1985). Neurological manifestations in abused children who have been shaken. *Developmental Medicine & Child Neurology, 27*, 312-316.

Gessner, R.R., & Runyon, D.K. (1995). The shaken infant: A military connection? *Archives of Pediatric Adolescent Medicine, 149*, 467-469.

Krugman, R.D. (1985). Fatal child abuse: Analysis of 24 cases. *Pediatrician, 12*, 68-72.

Ludwig, S., & Warman, M. (1984). Shaken baby syndrome: A review of 20 cases. *Annals of Emergency Medicine, 13*, 104-107.

Showers, J. (1989). Behaviour management cards as a method of anticipatory guidance for parents. *Child: Health, Care and Development, 15*, 401-415.

Showers, J. (1991). Child behavior management cards: Prevention tools for teens. *Child Abuse & Neglect, 15*, 313-316.

Showers, J. (1992a). "Don't shake the baby": Effectiveness of a prevention program. *Child Abuse & Neglect, 16*, 11-18.

Showers, J. (1992b). Shaken baby syndrome: The problem and a model for prevention. *Children Today, 21*, 34-37.

Showers, J. (1993). Assessing and remedying parenting knowledge among women inmates. *Journal of Offender Rehabilitation, 20*, 35-46.

Showers, J. (1994). Shaken baby syndrome: What have we learned about victims and perpetrators? *"Don't Shake the Baby" Campaign News, 3*, 1-2.

Showers, J. (1996). *Executive summary, "Don't Shake The Baby: Replication of a Successful Model."* Final report to the National Center on Child Abuse and Neglect (NCCAN Grant #90-CA-1523).

Showers, J. (1997). *The National Conference on Shaken Baby Syndrome: Executive summary.* Alexandria, Virginia: National Association of Children's Hospitals and Related Institutions.

Showers, J. (1998). *Victims and alleged perpetrators in 1,145 cases of shaken baby syndrome.* Unpublished manuscript.

Showers, J., & Apolo, J. (1986). Criminal disposition of persons involved in 72 cases of fatal child abuse. *Medicine, Science, & the Law, 26,* 243-247.

Showers, J., Apolo, J., Thomas, J., & Beavers, S. (1985). Fatal child abuse: A two-decade review. *Pediatric Emergency Care, 1,* 66-70.

Showers, J., & Johnson, C.F. (1984). Students' knowledge of child health and development: Effects on approaches to discipline. *Journal of School Health, 54,* 122-125.

Showers J., & Johnson, C.F. (1985). Child development, child health and child rearing knowledge among urban adolescents: Are they adequately prepared for the challenges of parenthood? *Health Education, 16,* 37-41.

Spaide, R.F., Swengel, R.M., Schane, D.W., & Mein, C.E. (1990). Shaken baby syndrome. *American Family Physician, 41,* 1145-1152.

Starling, S.P., Holden, J.R., & Jenny, C. (1995). Abusive head trauma: The relationship of perpetrators to their victims. *Pediatrics, 95,* 259-262.

Thayer, J.T. (1996). Shaken baby syndrome: Symptoms and diagnosis. *BNA Criminal Practice Manual, 10,* 131-136.

Chapter Eighteen

Controversies in Shaken Baby/ Shaken Impact Syndrome

Robert M. Reece

SUMMARY. Controversies invariably exist when hypotheses about biological phenomena cannot be studied directly (in clinical settings where information is readily available) or indirectly (with the creation of biological models approximating the organism in question). This creates missing links in the chain of logic and results in incomplete faith in some conclusions about these phenomena. Such is the case in shaken baby / shaken impact syndrome. Because abusive head trauma occurs without witnesses other than the perpetrator in most cases, we need to infer certain information to fill the gaps of validated facts. This leaves room for scientific and legal challenge. But there is increasing clinical and research data elucidating this condition. Although SBS cannot be studied in the bench laboratory tradition or even in the tradition of the hospital-based research scientist, there is a generation of new knowledge that is providing answers. These answers are being found in studies done by a wide range of scientists who have contact with abusive head trauma cases at some point in the process of care. Emergency department clinicians, intensive care specialists, hospital attending clinicians, forensic pediatricians, pediatric ophthalmolo-

[Haworth co-indexing entry note]: "Controversies in Shaken Baby/Shaken Impact Syndrome." Reece, Robert M. Co-published simultaneously in *Journal of Aggression, Maltreatment & Trauma* (The Haworth Maltreatment & Trauma Press, an imprint of The Haworth Press, Inc.) Vol. 5, No. 1(#9), 2001, pp. 367-388; and: *The Shaken Baby Syndrome: A Multidisciplinary Approach* (ed: Stephen Lazoritz, and Vincent J. Palusci) The Haworth Maltreatment & Trauma Press, an imprint of The Haworth Press, Inc., 2001, pp. 367-388. Single or multiple copies of this article are available for a fee from The Haworth Document Delivery Service [1-800-342-9678, 9:00 a.m. - 5:00 p.m. (EST). E-mail address: getinfo@haworthpressinc.com].

gists, neurosurgeons, radiologists, forensic and neuro-pathologists all have contributed to this literature. *[Article copies available for a fee from The Haworth Document Delivery Service: 1-800-342-9678. E-mail address: <getinfo@haworthpressinc.com> Website: <http://www.HaworthPress.com> © 2001 by The Haworth Press, Inc. All rights reserved.]*

KEYWORDS. Syndrome, bleed-rebleed, second impact, modeling, shaking plus impact, lucid interval

INTRODUCTION

The term *syndrome* has come into general usage in medicine and is defined as "a number of symptoms occurring together and characterizing a specific disease or condition" by Webster (1988) and "the sum of signs of any morbid state; a symptom complex" in Dorland's Medical Dictionary (1994) which contains 21 pages of various medical syndromes in usage. When modified by *shaken baby* or *shaken impact,* it is used to describe the condition characterized by a combination of historical information, clinical presentation, physical examination, and imaging findings in an infant or young child. The history of the injury may be one of a confessed or witnessed act of shaking and/or throwing the victim against a hard or soft surface, an accidental fall from a low height, or there may be no history of any kind of injury. The clinical signs are variable, with a combination of alteration of one or more vital signs (respiration, cardiac rate, temperature, blood pressure), and one or more neurological signs (poor feeding, vomiting, signs of increased intracranial pressure, lethargy, irritability, seizures, posturing, apnea, unresponsiveness, coma or death) being seen. There may or may not be external signs of traumatic injury to the head or body. Retinal hemorrhages are present in the vast majority of cases; retinal folds and vitreous hemorrhages have been described in some. Head computerized tomograms (CT) and/or magnetic resonance imaging (MRI) show subdural or subarachnoid bleeding (or both) and may be combined with parenchymal alterations as well.

Shaken baby/shaken impact syndrome (SBS/SIS) represents a spectrum of injury, the severity of which seems to be dependent on the duration and severity of the forces of injury. Because it covers this wide range of presentations, clinical findings and imaging abnormalities, together with the imprecision (and often the fabrication) of the history, the diagnosis rests on the synthesis of these elements. There is no single specific physical finding or laboratory test that absolutely confirms the diagnosis and it cannot be subjected to a litmus test for authentication. The diagnosis must be inferred (derived from reasoning).

The characteristic of being an inferred diagnosis places SBS/SIS in familiar company with most conditions seen in clinical medicine. For example, a patient with a productive cough and fever suggests the possibility of pneumonia. A chest radiograph showing an infiltrate in one of the lobes of the lung strengthens the inference that this is pneumonia. A blood count may or may not reflect an infectious response. Culturing of the sputum may or may not grow a pathogen. Treatment with an antibiotic and subsequent improvement infers that bacterial pneumonia was present. But certainty is not at hand, since if the pathogen had been viral (or even bacterial), clinical improvement could be spontaneous and not due to the treatment. If clinical improvement did not occur, one would infer that the organism responsible for the infiltrate was not susceptible to the chosen antibiotic or that the disease could be due to some other process (tuberculosis, or a clinically resistant bacterium, a virus, a fungus, an immunocompromised host, or a wide variety of other diseases). But the thought process engaged in diagnosis is one of *reasoning*, bringing together as many elements as possible to arrive at a diagnosis and a plan for management of the patient. This reasoning process is also employed by pathologists who piece together the puzzle of the cause and manner of death by examining the diseased or injured tissue and then inferring the diagnosis.

This is the context within which differences of opinion are bound to occur. Controversies and debate are the crucible for the emergence of fresh ideas, new concepts and ultimately new truths. Historically, the medical literature is rife with controversy and progress in medical science over the last several decades and is testament to the value of such controversy. We build our knowledge on accumulated evidence and hypotheses are accepted as fact when the evidence is sufficient and convincing. The balance of this chapter will address those areas of controversy within the evolving science as it applies to SBS/SIS.

CONTROVERSIES ARISING IN THE MEDICAL COMMUNITY

The Biomechanics of Head Injury–Shaking versus Impact

Weston (1968) reported on three infants who had been the victims of severe shaking and who had sustained subdural hematomas. Guthkelch (1971) published an account of two babies with subdural hematomas with no other injuries and linked these findings to whiplash injuries acquired during shaking admitted by the perpetrators. Caffey (1972) wrote about "the theory and practice of shaking infants" and two years later coined the term "whiplash shaken infant syndrome" to characterize this condition (Caffey, 1974). The concept of shaken baby syndrome producing these lesions was generally accepted by the majority of the medical community but in 1987 Duhaime et al. published a report based on a retrospective review of 48 cases of SBS in which 2/3 had external evidence of head trauma. They tested the hypothesis that infants sustain these injuries from shaking alone by constructing models of infants implanted with accelerometers to measure the results of shaking or impact. Three types of models were used since the mechanical properties of the infant neck had not been studied. Both a fixed center or rotation with zero resistance (hinged) and moving centers of rotation with low and moderate resistance (rubber neck) models were used. Care was taken to insure the heads were as close as possible in size and weight to a human infant's head. The accelerometer was attached to the vertex in a coronal plane through the center of the neck. Each model was subjected to repetitive violent shaking and impact. They found the mean peak tangential acceleration for 69 shaking episodes was 9.29 G; mean peak tangential acceleration for 60 impacts was 428.18 G, nearly 50 times that of shaking. The mean time interval for shakes was 106 msec and for impacts 21 msec. Both differences are statistically significant. It was their conclusion, based on this review and experimental data, that shaken baby syndrome, at least in its most severe form, is not usually caused by shaking alone.

The information about forces and head injury derives from earlier work done by Ommaya, Faas, and Yarnell (1968) in the mid 1960s. They used rhesus monkeys secured in a contoured fiberglass chair mounted on a carriage for experiments. This apparatus could move freely on wheels over a 20-foot long track. Impacts were delivered to the carriage by an air compression-driven piston and movies were taken to allow measurement of the rotational or angular displacement of the monkeys' heads. Based on these experiments, they concluded that subdural hematomas can be produced by rotational displacement of the head on the neck alone, without significant direct head impact. Gennarelli and Thibault (1982) reported producing experimental subdural hematomas by delivering a single acceleration-deceleration pulse to the helmeted heads of experimental rhesus monkeys. This rotated the head through a 60 degree arc in times varying from 5 to 25 milliseconds. They recorded the acceleration-time history by a device mounted in the helmets and concluded from these experiments that acute subdural hematoma (ASDH) occurs because of head acceleration associated with rapid rates of acceleration onset (high strain rate). They state that

> It is apparent that nothing need strike the head in order for ASDH to occur. It is sufficient that the head undergo the appropriate acceleration

strain-rate conditions, since in this animal model nothing strikes the head. Thus those mechanical events that result from an object contacting the head are not necessary for ASDH. Although impact to the head is certainly the most common cause of clinical ASDH, it is the acceleration induced by the impact and not the head contact per se that causes ASDH. (Gennarelli & Thibault, 1982, p. 246)

The authors go on to discuss why athletes can sustain ASDH in the absence of impact to the skull owing to the diffusion of focal loading by helmets but who can still sustain ASDH because of the head acceleration.

Since Duhaime et al.'s (1987) article, there has been a lively discussion in the literature as to the relative merits of shaking versus shaking plus impact as the origin of these lesions. Alexander, Sato, Smith and Bennett (1990) reported that 50% of 24 infants diagnosed as SBS had no evidence of impact. Reece (unpublished data) reported on 27 SBS infants, 48% of whom had no evidence of impact to the head. Others (Gilliland & Folberg, 1996; Kirschner, 1998a; Zepp, Bruhl, Zimmer, & Schumacher, 1992) have reported similar findings. Kirschner (1998b) concluded "that shaking, in and of itself, is sufficient" based on his experience in the Cook County Medical Examiner's office where he did autopsies on "many shaken babies who showed no evidence of trauma to the head and elicited caretakers' confessions that described shaking alone." Budenz, Farber, Mirchandani, Park, and Rorke (1994) and others (Elner, Elner, Arnall, & Albert, 1990; Frank, Zimmerman, & Leeds, 1985; Gianciocomo, Khan, Levine, & Thompson, 1988; Riffenburgh & Sathyavagiswaran, 1991; Wilkinson, Han, Rappley, & Owings, 1989; Zimmerman, Bilaniuk, & Bruce, 1979) report their observations suggesting that pure shaking injury may lead to fatal intracranial injury. Gilliland and Folberg (1996) reviewed the literature and demonstrated that cases of fatal intracranial injury can have shaking as the sole apparent mechanism. In their own prospective, postmortem study of 80 children they defined evidence of shaking to include at least two of the following: (1) finger marks and/or rib fractures, (2) subdural and/or subarachnoid bleeding, or (3) a history of vigourous shaking. Three groups were identified: (1) shake with two or more criteria without scalp or skull injuries; (2) combined (direct scalp or skull injuries and two shaking criteria) and (3) blunt (impact injuries without sufficient shaking criteria). Victims of head trauma were thus divided into shake group (11.3%); combined (37.5%); and blunt deaths (51.3%). High frequencies of peripheral retinal hemorrhages were seen in the shake and combined group but in only 19 of 47 in the blunt group. They concluded that "shaking alone is a lethal mechanism of injury in some infants in this study" (p. 116).

Kleinman (1998) states that

> All of these studies, in conjunction with extensive anecdotal experience, both clinical and pathologic, in the past 30 years indicates that impact is not necessary to produce significant intracranial injury in shaken babies. Furthermore, the presence of an impact site in cases of SBS does not preclude the possibility that the shaking and not the impact is responsible for the intracranial injuries. . . . The infant brain is incompletely myelinated and has a higher water content than that of the older child. The infant brain is surrounded by a larger volume of CSF and is more free to move about within a cranial cavity that is not as rigidly constricted because of the open fontanels and sutures. Furthermore, it is reasonable to conclude that the repetitive angular accelerations that occur with violent infant shaking may generate sufficient cumulative biomechanical forces to produce intracranial injury.

Lazoritz, Baldwin, and Kini (1997) compared the explanation of injuries and the skeletal injuries seen in Caffey's (1972, 1974) original reports and their own series of 71 children and concluded that Caffey's syndrome has been broadened to include all forms of abusive head injury. They argue against using the term "shaken impact syndrome" and suggest that the term "shaken infant syndrome" should be applied only to severe head injury to infants caused by either shaking alone or shaking plus impact.

Pounder (1997) reported on an adult whose interrogation during captivity included repetitive shaking by his captors and subsequent death. The postmortem exam revealed few external injuries other than bruises of the shoulders and anterior chest. There was no evidence of trauma to the neck, face or head. Subdural hematoma, subarachnoid bleeding, cerebral edema with herniation, diffuse axonal injury, and retinal hemorrhages were present.

> There is no reason to doubt the account of the circumstances surrounding the death, which indicates that the victim was repeatedly shaken but not struck about the head or face. This accords with the view that the same pathological changes seen in Shaken Baby Syndrome can be produced by rotational acceleration alone without any direct impact to the head. (p. 323)

Since the center of the controversy revolves around the issue of forces necessary to produce the observed damage in abusive head trauma, a return to examination of the biomedical mechanics was prompted. Hymel, Bandak, Partington, and Winston (1998) summarized the extant knowledge about the biomechanical forces associated with pediatric head trauma and suggested a new paradigm for the analysis of such injuries. Beginning with a review of

Newton's laws of motion and several engineering concepts (load, kinetic energy, strain, translational and angular acceleration), they apply these principles to the forces involved in head trauma. They define contact injuries as deformations occurring from cranial impact if the head is not moving, and non-contact injuries as those resulting from cranial acceleration (deceleration). Severe or fatal head injuries are most often the result of primary acceleration strains by movement of the brain within the skull leading to rupture of the bridging veins and by producing strains within the brain itself. Because cranial impact may induce severe cranial acceleration, patients frequently demonstrate combined contact and acceleration injuries. Secondary hypoxia and/or ischemia, altered autoregulation of cerebral blood flow, venous vasospasm, intracranial hemorrhage, acquired coagulopathy, brain swelling and generation of free radicals and calcium influx into cells also contribute to brain damage. The authors then link specific cranial injuries to their biomechanical origins. Focal forces lead to one or more of the following: skull fracture, cortical contusions, subdural, epidural and parenchymal hematomas. Diffuse forces lead to concussion and diffuse axonal injury. They propose five questions, the answers to which can be used for a biomechanical analysis of pediatric head trauma:

1. What are the specific head injuries?
2. How can these be classified (focal or diffuse)?
3. Was cranial contact or acceleration required to produce each injury?
4. What biomechanical circumstances of cranial impact were necessary for the injuries?
5. Are these specific required biomechanical circumstances evident in the history provided?

In this manner, the authors believe the clinician will be better equipped to separate inflicted from accidental head injury.

The major problem in the "shaking alone" versus "shaking plus impact" controversy is that no one has been able to devise a model that even closely approximates the head and neck of the human infant. There are so many properties of the scalp, skull, meninges, brain, blood vessels and neck musculature that are unknown and variable from infant to infant that an attempt to determine the amount of force required to produce particular injuries in tissues of such unknown properties is meaningless. Biomechanical engineers cite mathematical models which purportedly "prove" certain forces are necessary to produce certain results. But with so many critical elements of the equation unknown, definitive answers based on a biomechanical formula are elusive. The infant brain, composed of 25% more water than that of the adult, is quite soft and said by some to have a gel-like consistency. How do we know what forces are required to cause damage to such a delicate structure? The skulls of infants are generally thin and the dimensions vary depending upon what portion of the head they occupy. The thickness of the occiput is greater than the frontal bone which in turn is thicker than the tempero-parietal plate. The skull is a growing organ and so a one-month-old skull is different than a 12 month-old skull, which is different still from a 20-month-old skull where the fontanels have closed. The forces required to produce a fracture depend on these and many other variables. The bridging veins are variable and depend upon location, age and the tissue characteristics of the individual child. Different models capturing all of these variables of age, tissue properties and individual differences would be necessary for testing to arrive at any degree of certainty about what forces cause particular injuries. Furthermore, the different variations in the forces involved in shaking are too numerous to count and to reproduce them taxes the imagination.

We are therefore currently left with the dilemma of believing the few studies done on monkeys, derived mathematical equations about the forces measured in these experiments, and the clinical and pathological studies presented in the literature about pediatric head injuries. There are some descriptions of the act of inflicting the head injuries by confessed perpetrators, but the reliability of these is open to question. We should not "let the measurable crowd out the important" when, clinically, the production of the head lesion in this age group is based more on the findings than on the reliability of the history. The literature and clinical experience instruct that the classic triad of SDH, RH and cerebral edema in this age group should be considered SBS/SIS as the first consideration, and that investigation for other possible causes should be done in the best medical tradition of thoroughness as well as for social and legal reasons.

THE BIOMECHANICS OF RETINAL HEMORRHAGES

According to Levin (1990), the term "retinal hemorrhage" is non-specific, analogous to the generality of the term "fracture." The defining characteristics of the lesions, i.e., the number, distribution, proximity to retinal vessels, association with papilledema, and presence of retinoschisis, have much to do with their significance in relating them to SBS/SIS and should always be specified when considering the etiology. The incidence of retinal hemorrhages in SBS/SIS is reported to be from 50% to 100% (Billmire & Myers, 1985, Duhaime et al., 1987; Ludwig & Warman, 1984; Zimmerman et al., 1979). Retinal hemorrhages in SBS/SIS usually involve the posterior pole in the nerve fiber and ganglion cell layers, but may involve any retinal layer. They are usually flame-shaped rather than dot/blot/boat-shaped hemorrhages typical of intraretinal or preretinal hemorrhages (Annable, 1994). They may be unilateral or bilateral but are much more commonly bilateral, occurring in up to 100% of cases of SBS/SIS (Annable, 1994; Han & Wilkinson, 1990; Levin, 1990;). In a morphometric analysis of retinal hemorrhages in the shaken baby syndrome (Betz, Puschel, Miltner, Lignitz, & Eisenmenger, 1996) retinal hemorrhages were seen covering 11.8% to 73.2% of the entire retina in seven cases involving SBS as contrasted to 1.18% and 3.33% of the retina in two cases of retinal hemorrhages seen in accident victims, both adults suffering massive cranial injury. The time of resolution of retinal hemorrhages is variable, ranging from 10 days to several months (Levin, 1990). In infants and children under the age of two years, retinal hemorrhages are overwhelmingly more common as the result of abusive head trauma than any other cause (Billmire & Myers, 1985; Buys et al., 1992; Duhaime et al., 1992; Eisenbrey, 1979; Johnson, Braun, & Friendly, 1993; Levin, 1990).

The pathogenesis of retinal hemorrhages is the subject of controversy. Three major etiologic theories are advanced by those studying the phenomenon. The first suggests that they are due to increased pressure arising from transmission of cardiothoracic pressure. The second purports that they are due to increased intracranial pressure causing obstruction of the return of blood through the central optic vein. The third is that the forces generated from shaking produce traction on the layers of the retina causing movement within the layers and resultant tearing of the rich capillary beds within the layers leading to rupture and extravasation of blood.

RETINAL HEMORRHAGES DUE TO INCREASED CARDIOTHORACIC PRESSURE (PURTSCHER'S RETINOPATHY)

This condition is a hemorrhagic retinal angiopathy characterized by preretinal and retinal hemorrhages, retinal exudates and decreased visual acuity. It has been described in adults following a sudden compression of the thoracic cage and is postulated to be the result of the transmission of an acute increase in intravascular pressure to the head and eyes giving rise to retinal hemorrhages.(Marr & Marr, 1962; Purtscher, 1910). There was only one pediatric case of Purtscher retinopathy reported in the literature (Morgan, 1945) prior to the 1975 report of Tomsai and Rosman (1975) who described retinal hemorrhages they called Purtscher's retinopathy in two battered children with clinical signs of traumatic brain injury. These cases were seen and treated before CT head scans came into common usage and were probably SBS/SIS. The retinal hemorrhages as described in the paper are not classic Purtscher's retinopathy which is associated with cotton-wool exudates and superficial hemorrhages. The retinal hemorrhages of SBS/SIS are multiple, multilayered and are not associated with exudates.

The theory of increased cardiothoracic pressure causing transmitted intravascular pressure to the head and resultant retinal hemorrhages led clinicians to consider the possibility of cardiopulmonary resuscitation causing such a chain of events. Goetting and Sowa (1990) reported on twenty children who had received cardiopulmonary resuscitation, two of whom had retinal hemorrhages. One of these children, a 2 year-old, was immersed in water, resuscitated by emergency medical personnel en route to the hospital, and remained in a coma for four days until her death. Autopsy showed no preceding traumatic events. No information was given as to the brain findings on autopsy but one can assume there was cerebral edema, giving rise to raised intracranial pressure before death. The second, an infant of 1.5 months, died of SIDS in the hospital and had a single, fresh hemorrhage in one fundus. Kanter (1986) reported on 54 children, 45 of whom had had a traumatic event prior to resuscitation. Six had retinal hemorrhages, five of whom were victims of abusive head trauma. The one child with retinal hemorrhages after CPR with no preceding traumatic event had had a seizure at home, arterial hypertension in the hospital, and subsequently died. There was no description, however, of the type and extent of the retinal hemorrhages. His conclusion was that retinal hemorrhages should not be attributed to CPR. Recently, much larger studies of this problem have been conducted. Gilliland and Luckenbach (1993) performed postmortem examinations of the eyes of 169 children. One hundred-thirty-one had resuscitation for 30 minutes or more. No retinal hemorrhages were found in 99 children, 70 of whom had been resuscitated. Retinal hemorrhages were found in 70 children, 61 of whom had been resuscitated. Of these 61, 56 had craniocerebral trauma, both intentional and accidental, three had central nervous system causes of death (tumor, infection) and one had sepsis—all conditions known to be associated with retinal hemorrhages. One died of undetermined causes. The authors concluded that no case in this study was found to support the hypothesis that retinal hemorrhages are caused by resuscitation. Odum, Christ, and Kerr (1997) examined the retinas of 43 hospitalized children who had received at least one minute of CPR. One patient with a coagulation defect had small punctate retinal hemorrhages, which were morphologically different from the RH found in SBS/SIS. Fackler, Berkowitz, and Green (1992) produced cardiac arrest in six newborn piglets, followed by controlled mechanical cardiopulmonary resuscitation for 50 minutes. After sacrificing the animals, postmortem examinations of the eyes revealed no retinal hemorrhages.

The overwhelming conclusion from all of these studies is that cardiopulmonary resuscitation is rarely, if ever, associated with the production of the retinal hemorrhages seen in SBS/SIS and that classic Purtscher's retinopathy is distinctly different from the retinopathy of SBS/SIS.

RETINAL HEMORRHAGES DUE TO INCREASED INTRACRANIAL PRESSURE

A second theory about the etiology of retinal hemorrhages purports that they are the result of increased intracranial pressure. Khan and Frenkel (1975) attribute retinal hemorrhages to acute intracranial hypertension following cerebral injury, resulting in retinal venous hypertension. In a presentation of one case and a review of the extant literature, Lambert, Johnson, and Hoyt (1986) state that "while retinal hemorrhages may arise from multiple causes in the shaken baby syndrome, it seems likely that a sudden rise in intracranial pressure significantly contributed to their occurrence in our patient." Older accounts in the adult literature claim intracranial hypertension to be responsible for intraocular hemorrhages (McRae, Teasell, & Canny, 1994; Muller & Deck, 1974). Munger, Peiffer, Bouldin, Kylstra, and Thompson (1993) examined the eyes of 12 infants with retinal hemorrhages who had died subsequent to suspected violent shaking. Ten had subdural hemorrhage and cerebral edema; nine had subarachnoid hemorrhage. Retinal detachment with the formation of retinal folds were found in five. Hemorrhage around the retro-bulbar optic nerve was seen in nine. Although accepting the possibility of the more superficial hemorrhages being due to retinoschisis from vitreous traction during shaking, they found it difficult to attribute the choroidal and intrascleral hemorrhages to vitreous traction and were inclined more to accept the concept of increased intracranial pressure as the pathogenic mechanism.

RETINAL HEMORRHAGES DUE TO TRAUMATIC RETINOSCHISIS

Greenwald, Weiss, Oesterle, and Friendly (1986) describe five infant victims of abusive head trauma with severe bilateral retinal hemorrhages. Vitreous hemorrhage developed after a delay of several days in three cases. In several eyes, intraretinal blood-filled cavities were seen acutely in the macular region and elsewhere. Subdural hemorrhages were seen in four cases. They proposed that the forces of shaking are responsible for the traumatic retinoschisis in battered babies. One of the effects of shaking would be to make the lens move forward and back within the ocular fluids.

In infancy, firm attachments exist between the lens, the vitreous gel, and the retina, especially in the macular region. Transmission of force through these connections could result momentarily in significant traction on the retina, particularly in the posterior pole. This abrupt tugging on the retina could create a separation along some plane within the tissue, possibly more than one. Elner et al. (1990) reported the findings in 10 children dying of blunt abusive head trauma. Retinal, vitreous and subdural optic nerve hemorrhages were present in seven. In four cases there was traumatic retinoschisis or tractional retinal folds. Intracranial hemorrhage was present in all cases with ocular findings. They believed that the full thickness hemorrhagic retinal necrosis in five and retinoschisis and perimacular folds in four suggested that severe anteroposterior acceleration-deceleration forces directly produce retinal injuries in abused children who die of blunt head injury and further that blunt head trauma may be necessary to produce significant vitreoretinal traction resulting in the constellation of severe retinal injuries seen in such children.

They further stated that

> subdural optic nerve hemorrhages . . . are not thought to be extensions of intracranial, subdural or subarachnoid hemorrhages, or to result from transmission of increased intracranial venous pressure. Rather, they are caused by local rupture of dural-pial bridging vessels. . . Subdural hemorrhages may result from severe intracranial hypertension which is transmitted to the optic nerve subarachnoid space and causes increased pressure within, and subsequent hydrostatic rupture of optic nerve dural-pial vessels. (p. 1099)

Gaynon, Koh, Marmor, and Frankel (1988) reported about two children with SBS in which they saw extensive retinal hemorrhages and bilateral symmetric white ring-shaped retinal folds encircling the macula outside the vascular arcades. They suggested that these retinal folds may be a hallmark of shaking injuries in child abuse victims. Smith has said that these are pathognomonic of shaking injury (Smith, L. personal communication).

If retinal hemorrhages are caused solely by increased intracranial pressure, one would expect to see them in accidental head trauma to the same extent as in inflicted head injury. Johnson et al. (1993) reported on 140 children (median age 4.5 years, range 3.5 months to 19.5 years) whose head injuries were thought to be accidental and in whom an ophthalmologic examination was performed. Motor vehicle accidents and falls accounted for 90% of these head injuries. Retinal hemorrhages were found in only two patients, both of whom were in the back seat of a motor vehicle impacted from the side. These data are borne out in numerous other studies (Betz et al., 1996; Duhaime et al., 1987;

Duhaime et al., 1992; Elder, 1991; Gilliland, Luckenback, & Chenier, 1994). Clinical experience to date has instructed that most children with head injuries with increased intracranial pressure admitted to pediatric intensive care units do not have retinal hemorrhages.

DATING OF RETINAL HEMORRHAGES

Ophthalmologists, when describing retinal hemorrhages in acutely inflicted head injured children, usually describe the retinal hemorrhages as "fresh," meaning of recent origin. Clinically, it is difficult to be more precise. The characteristics of "fresh" retinal hemorrhages are similar to the findings of blood elsewhere in the body, (i.e., if it is bright red blood it is considered to be secondary to new bleeding). This has been proven to be of clinical value in other disease states and probably represents reasonably accurate determination of age.

In deceased babies with retinal hemorrhages, Perl's iron stain has been used to demonstrate iron-laden (hemosiderin) macrophages. The significance of this finding is debated (Elner, Elner, Albert, & Arnall, 1991; Lambert et al., 1986; Rao, Smith, Choi, Xiaohu, & Kornblum, 1988) since these macrophages may be detected within 48-72 hours after injury. Budenz et al. (1994) found these macrophages in four of 13 abused children with an average survival time 5.5 days. Gilliland, Luchenback, Massicote, and Folberg (1991) state that

> one source (claims that) hemosiderin . . . may be identified as early as one day after injury, although other authors are fairly circumspect and suggest that an interval of several days must pass before hemosiderin is deposited; macrophages that assemble ferritin into hemosiderin are identified at injury sites within 48-72 hours. (p. 321)

These investigators "have detected hemosiderin in the optic nerves or retina in eight of 28 children who survived for at least three days on a respirator before dying" (Gilliland et al., 1991, p. 322). Elner et al. (1991) state that "although hemosiderin first appears three days after injury, (it) does not become obvious on histochemical staining for five to seven days after trauma" (p. 1100).

CONTROVERSIES ARISING IN THE LEGAL SYSTEM

Alternative Explanations for Head Injuries

Accidental falls are the most common explanation for the head injuries seen as being likely due to abuse. The child who falls from a high chair, off a bed, couch or changing table, falls down stairs, strikes a coffee table or other objects while falling from an adult's arms, or a fall from a walker are common histories seen in cases found later to have been due to SBS/SIS. The reasons these histories are known to be incorrect derive from a combination of numerous clinical studies on falls in childhood and from study of the biomechanical forces needed to produce head injuries of SBS/SIS.

Clinical studies on falls in childhood date back to 1977 when Helfer, Slovis, and Black (1977) reported on 176 incidents of falls at home and 85 in the hospital. In both of these populations there were no life-threatening injuries, particularly, no significant head injuries. Others (Chiavello, Cristoph, & Bond, 1994; Joffe & Ludwig, 1988; Lyons & Oates, 1993; Nimityongskul & Anderson, 1987) have studied falls from beds, down stairs and in baby walkers and have come to the same conclusion, namely, that children do not sustain serious or life-threatening injuries from short falls. There is one important exception to this: epidural hemorrhage resulting from short falls and produced by focal impact to the skull, causing an arterial tear in the epidural space. In this situation, one that is unlikely to be confused with abusive head trauma, a short fall can cause serious head injury.

Conversely, when studies of childhood falls, from heights greater than 10 feet are considered, the numbers of serious head injuries increase. Musemeche, Barthal, Cosentino, and Reynolds (1991) found in a study of 70 children falling a mean of two stories that there were no fatalities but two had subdural hematomas and three had epidural hematomas. In 106 witnessed falls, Williams (1991) found 14 intracranial injuries in falls ranging from five to 40 feet. Chadwick, Chin, Salerno, Landsverk, and Kitchen (1991) examined seven fatal cases of 100 children who had fallen less than four feet by history. However, after case fatality review, the histories were thought to have been falsified. The conclusion from all of these studies is that short falls do not cause life-threatening serious injuries of the kind seen in SBS/SIS and it is necessary to fall at least the equivalent of two stories to generate the required forces.

UNIQUE THEORIES OF CAUSATION

Retinal Hemorrhages Resulting from Seizures

Seizures are a common manifestation of traumatic brain injury and so are frequently claimed as the reason for retinal hemorrhages. That seizures do not cause retinal hemorrhages has been recognized empirically for many years (Levin, 1998). A recent study by Sandramouli, Robinson, Tsaloumas, and

Willshaw (1997) in which prospective eye examinations were performed within 48 hours of motor seizures in 33 children found no retinal hemorrhages.

Second Impact Syndrome

This phenomenon is described primarily in the sports medicine literature and refers to a situation in which an individual receives a blow to the head causing concussion with residual cerebral symptoms. This is followed later by another episode of head trauma leading to massive cerebral edema and collapse and death in some cases. It has been reported in athletes engaging in hockey, football and boxing and involves high impact blows to the head (similar to the experimental models of Gennarelli and Ommaya), followed at variable times later with another blow to the head. Cantu (1998) reports on five boxers, aged 17-24 years of age, who suffered such injuries and later died. It is hard to evaluate these cases because of insufficient information about the neurological evaluation and absence of CT scans after the initial episodes. Was there subdural bleeding? Was there evidence of cerebral edema? Were they symptomatic prior to reinjury? Were these second injuries truly minor? These cases are in adults whose skulls are rigid structures with no capability for expansion as is the case in the infant skull with open fontanels and sutures. A second traumatic episode conceivably could have produced space-occupying intracranial bleeding which led to a rapid rise in the intracranial pressure and brain herniation or there may have been autoregulatory phenomena leading to irreversible cerebral edema after multiple blows. This is dissimilar to the situation in SBS/SIS *where the lesion is cerebral trauma and edema, not subdural bleeding.*

The "Bleed-Rebleed" Theory

The concept of the triggering of bleeding of an older organizing subdural hematoma through trivial secondary trauma leading to sudden collapse and death has been advanced in a number of recent court cases involving allegations of SBS/SIS. This unique theory of causation hypothesizes that an injury, several days to weeks old, produces a subdural hematoma in an infant, unrecognized by the caretakers and presumably causing insufficient symptoms to seek medical attention. Then, a new, trivial injury occurs, provoking rebleeding in this older subdural hematoma. This new bleeding allegedly then produces a rapid rise in intracranial pressure leading to the onset of symptoms and signs of neurological impairment, coma and death. There is a flaw in this line of thinking. The blood in subdural bleeding is venous in origin and consequently under low pressure. In most circumstances of venous bleeding in restricted spaces (pericardium, within muscular tissue, within the skull), tamponade occurs early in the course of the bleeding. There is no reason to believe that venous bleeding within the tight space of an old subdural clot within the cranial vault would be not be subject to the tamponade effect.

This theory also presumes a "lucid interval" between the older injury and the new injury. A "lucid interval" refers to that period of time between a significant head injury and the onset of symptoms and signs commensurate with the seriousness of the head injury. It has been described only in adults, who, having sustained a major head injury "walk and talk and die" over a period of hours or even days. A postmortem examination demonstrates the presence of intracranial bleeding and brain damage. The delay in the onset of signs and symptoms is thought to be due to the gradual development of increased intracranial pressure.

This same phenomenon has not been described in infants and children. In fact, when evidence for a lucid interval has been sought, it has not been found. Willman, Bank, Senac, and Chadwick (1997) reviewed the case histories of 95 fatally head injured children 16 years of age and younger. The head injuries were all accidental and involved blunt, non-penetrating head injuries. All cases had been witnessed and the time of injury ascertained. Survival time was calculated from the first documented time post-injury to death. All cases were reviewed for the occurrence of a lucid interval, defined as a time when the child had a Glasgow Coma Scale of 14-15, or when the terms "lucid interval" or "conscious" were used to describe the patient's clinical status. In all but two cases the mechanism of injury was a motor vehicle accident. Cerebral injuries included SAH (76%), SDH (53%), EDH (15%), cerebral, cerebellar or brainstem contusion (55%), skull fracture (55%) and cerebral edema (48%). Thirty cases had head CT scans. The shortest interval between injury and CT scans demonstrating severe brain swelling was 1 hour 17 minutes. Among those with head CT scan performed less than three hours post-injury, six (26%) had severe brain swelling, 10 (44%) had moderate swelling and six (26%) had mild swelling. In only one case of a CT scan being done under three hours was there no brain swelling. CT scans done later than three hours after injury demonstrated various degrees of brain swelling. In only one case was there a "lucid interval": an 11-year-old boy with an epidural hemorrhage who died of a surgical complication.

The proponents of the "bleed-rebleed" theory point, in some cases, to the presence of "subdural neomembranes" at the time of autopsy, as the scientific basis for their theory. Subdural neomembranes have been classified by Leestma (1988). The ages of neomembranes according to the modified criteria are: 0-2 days–intact red blood cells with few or no fibroblasts (possibly autopsy artifact); 3-5 days–proliferation of fibroblasts aligned parallel to dura, and macrophages; breakdown of red blood cells and hemosiderin; 6-10 days–layered fibroblasts of several cells thickness and hemosiderophages; 11-21 days–fibroblastic layering and neovascularization 12 or more cells thick; many hemosiderophages; 3-6 weeks–giant capillaries and early collagen deposition; > 6 weeks–hyalinization of dense collagen, regressing neovascularization. Rogers, Itabashi, Tomiyasu, and Heuser (1998) examined the cranial dura of 36 consecutive infants dying of Sudden Infant Death Syndrome and 16 control infants dying from other causes for the presence of neomembranes. These were present in 19 of the 36 SIDS cases (53%) and in three of 16 (19%) of control cases. When very recent (0-2 days) cases, which could have been due to artifact, were excluded, neomembranes were seen in 11/36, or 31% and 2/16 (13%) of controls. The overall prevalence of neomembranes, excluding very recent ones, was 25%. The authors state that it is not clear why the subdural neomembranes occurred. Kirschner (1998a) comments that the "authors fail to consider the possibility that these 'microscopic neomembranes' are not pathological processes at all but might represent normal developmental findings which need to be distinguished from traumatic lesions." Because subdural neomembranes have been described in SIDS and in infants dying of other non-traumatic causes, and because there is some question as whether these are a consequence of normal development within the infant dura-pia-arachnoid complex, it is unclear as to their significance.

The critical element in SBS/SIS is *traumatic brain injury*. It is this phenomenon, not the presence of blood in either the subdural or subarachnoid space, that produces the signs, symptoms and clinical course of this condition. Subdural hematoma, subarachnoid hemorrhage and even retinal hemorrhages are *markers of injury*, but in and of themselves are not responsible for the clinical picture of SBS/SIS. The combination of traumatic destruction of brain tissue, resultant cerebral edema, hypoxia from apnea during shaking and consequent to ischemia, release of free radicals, and calcium influx into the cells, all lead to an enormous increase in intracranial pressure and its neurological consequences. This cascade of events occurs rapidly, usually within 1-4 hours, and nearly always within 24 hours. The concept of rebleeding within an old subdural hematoma causing this intraparenchymal chaos is untenable from a logical standpoint. Moreover, there is nothing in the medical literature or in clinical experience to support the concept that an infant can sustain the degree of injury to the head required to cause subdural bleeding, be asymptomatic for a period of days or weeks, and then have new bleeding and suddenly collapse and die.'

Controversies do exist within the scientific community about shaken baby/shaken impact syndrome. But there is a body of knowledge supported by the scientific evidence published over the past 50 years, in more than 260 peer-reviewed articles, and clinical experience that is accepted by knowledge-able physicians with professional familiarity with abusive head injury. There is general consensus on the following:

1. SBS/SIS is seen more commonly in the young infant before the first birthday, but has also been reported in older children, and even in an adult under unique and well-documented circumstances.
2. SBS/SIS is diagnosed by the presence of diffuse brain swelling, subdural hemorrhage and retinal hemorrhages in the absence of docu-mented extraordinary blunt force such as an automobile accident (Kirschner, 1998a). Subarachnoid hemorrhage, diffuse axonal injury and progression toward CT images of "black brain" are seen in some cases, in addition to the classic triad above.
3. Cerebral edema and resultant neurological symptoms commence within a short time after shaking, usually within 24 hours and often much sooner, in the range of 1-4 hours, especially in fatal cases.
4. The injuries to the brain, not the bleeding in the subdural or subarachnoid space, cause the signs and symptoms and determine the course of SBS/SIS.
5. Retinal hemorrhages occur in the vast majority but not all cases of SBS/SIS. They are numerous, can be unilateral or bilateral, and occupy multiple layers of the retina extending to the periphery.
6. Signs of external trauma to the head and body may or may not be pres-ent.
7. Classic metaphyseal lesions of the long bones and posterior rib frac-tures, two types of fractures highly specific for inflicted injury, may be seen in some cases and when present add re-inforcing evidence of the inflicted nature of the head injury.
8. Injuries to the neck muscles or cervical vertebrae are distinctly uncom-mon in SBS/SIS.
9. The injuries in SBS/SIS are caused by violent assault on the infant by the perpetrator and are not the result of rough play or short falls.
10. Esoteric disease states, such as osteogenesis imperfecta and glutaric acidemia, can be distinguished from inflicted injury by careful clinical evaluation augmented by laboratory studies.
11. SBS/SIS can be a single event in a child's life or it can be a series of events.
12. Based on limited information on outcome, 15-30 percent of SBS/SIS victims die, while the survivors are normal in less than 10% of the cases.

The epidemic of child abuse is a major public health problem, comparable to cancer, heart disease, stroke and AIDS. Abusive head injuries are the single most important cause for death due to physical abuse. The medical community, and the general public, have unanswered questions about shaken baby syndrome. More research on SBS/SIS is needed to answer these questions. These answers can be provided with prospective, multi-institutional efforts, adequately funded by public and private sources.

REFERENCES

Alexander, R., Sato, Y., Smith, W., & Bennett, T. (1990). Incidence of impact trauma with cranial injuries ascribed to shaking. *Amer J Dis Child, 144*, 724-726.

Annable, W.L. (1994). Ocular manifestations of child abuse. In R.M. Reece (Ed.), *Child abuse: Medical diagnosis and management* (pp.143-146). Malvern, PA: Lea and Febiger.

Betz, P., Puschel, K., Miltner, E., Lignitz, E., & Eisenmenger, W. (1996). Morphometric analysis of retinal hemorrhages in the shaken baby syndrome. *Forens Sci Int, 78*, 71-80.

Billmire, M.E., & Myers, P.A. (1985). Serious head injury in infants: Accident or abuse? *Pediatrics, 75*, 340-342.

Budenz, D.L., Farber, M.G., Mirchandani, H.G., Park, H., & Rorke, L.B. (1994). Ocular and optic nerve hemorrhages in abused infants with intracranial injuries. *Ophthalmology, 101*, 559-565.

Buys, Y.M., Levin, A.V., Enzenauer, R.W., Elder, J.E., Letourneau, M.A., Humphreys, R.P., Mian, Morin, J.D. (1992). Retinal findings after head trauma in infants and young children. *Ophthalmology, 99*, 1718-1723.

Caffey, J. (1972). On the theory and practice of shaking infants. Its potential residual effects of permanent brain damage and mental retardation. *Amer J Dis Child, 124*, 161-169.

Caffey, J. (1974). The whiplash shaken infant syndrome: Manual shaking by the extremities with whiplash-induced intracranial and intraocular bleedings, linked with residual permanent brain damage and mental retardation. *Pediatrics, 54*, 396-403.

Cantu, R.C. (1998). Second-impact syndrome. *Clin Sports Med, 17*, 37-44.

Chadwick, D.L., Chin, S., Salerno, C., Landsverk, J., & Kitchen, L. (1991). Deaths from falls: How far is fatal? *J Trauma, 31*, 1353-1355.

Chiavello, C.T., Cristoph, R.A., & Bond, G.R. (1994). Infant walker-related injuries: A prospective study of severity and incidence. *Pediatrics, 93*, 974-976.

Dorland's illustrated medical dictionary (28th ed.). (1994). Philadelphia, PA. WB Saunders Co.

Duhaime, A.C., Alario, A.J., Lewander, M.D., Schut, L., Sutton, L.N., Seidl, T.S., Nudelman, S., Budenz, D., Hertle, R., & Tsiaras, W. (1992). Head injury in very young children: Mechanisms, injury types, and ophthalmologic findings in 100 hospitalized patients younger than two years of age. *Pediatrics, 90*, 179-185.

Duhaime, A.C., Gennarelli, T.A., Thibault, L.E., Bruce, D.A., Margulies, S.S., & Wiser, R. (1987). The shaken baby syndrome. A clinical, pathological and biomechanical study. *The Journal of Neurosurgery, 66*, 409-415.

Eisenbrey, A.B. (1979). Retinal hemorrhage in the battered child. *Child's Brain, 5*, 40-44.

Elder, J.E. et al. (1991). Retinal haemorrhage in accidental head trauma in childhood. *J Paediatr Child Health, 27,* 286-289.

Elner, S.G., Elner, V.M., Albert, D.A.M., & Arnall, M. (1991). In reply, Letter. *Arch Ophthalmol, 109,* 322.

Elner, S.G., Elner, V.M., Arnall, M., & Albert, D.M. (1990). Ocular and associated systemic findings in suspected child abuse. A necropsy study. *Arch Ophthalmol, 108,* 1094-1001.

Fackler, J.C., Berkowitz, I.D., & Green, R. (1992). Retinal hemorrhages in newborn piglets following cardiopulmonary resuscitation. *Amer J Dis Child, 146,* 1294-1296.

Frank, Y., Zimmerman, R., & Leeds, N.M.D. (1985). Neurological manifestations in abused children who have been shaken. *Dev Med Child Neurol, 27,* 312-316.

Gaynon, M.W., Koh, K., Marmor, M.F., & Frankel, L.R. (1988). Retinal folds in the shaken baby syndrome. *Amer J Ophthalmol, 106,* 423-425.

Gennarelli, T.A., & Thibault, L.E. (1982). Biomechanics of acute subdural hematoma. *J Trauma, 22,* 680-686.

Gianciacomo, J., Khan, J.A., Levine, C., & Thompson, V.M. (1988). Sequential cranial computed tomography in infants with retinal hemorrhages. *Ophthalmology, 95,* 295-299.

Gilliland, M.G.F., & Folberg, R. (1996). Shaken babies-some have no impact injuries. *J Forens Sci, 41,* 114-116.

Gilliland, M.G.F., & Luckenbach, M.W. (1993). Are retinal hemorrhages found after resuscitation events? A study of the eyes of 169 children. *Amer J Forens Med Pathol, 14,* 187-192.

Gilliland, M.G.F., Luckenbach, M.W., & Chenier, T.C. (1994). Systemic and ocular findings in 169 prospectively studied child deaths: Retinal hemorrhages usually mean child abuse. *Forensic Sci Int, 68,* 117-132.

Gilliland, M.G.F., Luchenbach, M.W., Massicote, S.J., & Folberg, R. (1991). The medicolegal implications of detecting hemosiderin in the eyes of children who are suspected of being abused. *Arch Ophthalmol, 109,* 321-322.

Goetting, M.G., & Sowa, B. (1990). Retinal hemorrhage after cardiopulmonary resuscitation: An etiologic re-evaluation. *Pediatrics, 85,* 585-588.

Greenwald, M.J., Weiss, A., Oesterle, C.S., & Friendly, D.S. (1986). Traumatic retinoschisis in battered babies. *Ophthalmology, 93,* 618-625.

Guthkelch, A.N. (1971). Infantile subdural haematoma and its relationship to whiplash injuries. *Br Med J, 2,* 430-431.

Han, D.P., & Wilkinson, W.S. (1990). Late ophthalmic manifestations of the shaken baby syndrome. *J Pediatr Ophthalmol Strab, 27,* 299-303.

Helfer, R.E., Slovis, T.L., & Black, M. (1977). Injuries resulting when small children fall out of bed. *Pediatrics, 60,* 533-535.

Hymel, K.P., Bandak, F.A., Partington, M.D., & Winston, K.R. (1998). Abusive head trauma? A biomechanical approach. *Child Maltreatment, 3,* 116-128.

Joffe, M., & Ludwig, S. (1988). Stairway injuries in children . *Pediatrics, 82,* 457-461.

Johnson, D.L., Braun, D., & Friendly, D. (1993). Head trauma and retinal hemorrhages: Accidental head trauma and retinal hemorrhage. *Neurosurgery, 33,* 231-235.

Kanter, R.K. (1986). Retinal hemorrhage after cardiopulmonary resuscitation. *Journal of Pediatrics, 108,* 430-432.

Khan, S.G., & Frenkel, M. (1975). Intravitreal hemorrhage associated with rapid increase in intracranial pressure (Terson's syndrome). *American Journal of Ophthalmology, 80,* 37-43.

Kirschner, R.H. (1998a). The pathology of child abuse. In M.E. Helfer (Ed.). *The battered child* (5th ed.), (p. 273). Chicago: University of Chicago Press.

Kirschner, R.H. (1998b). Contributing editor's note. *The Quarterly Child Abuse Medical Update, 3,* 00.

Kleinman, P.K. (1998). *Diagnostic imaging of child abuse.* St. Louis: CV Mosby.

Lambert, S.R., Johnson, T.I., & Hoyt, C.S. (1986). Optic nerve sheath and retinal hemorrhgaes associated with the shaken baby syndrome. *Archives of Ophthalmology, 104,* 1509-1515.

Lazoritz, S., Baldwin, S., & Kini, N. (1997). The whiplash shaken infant syndrome: Has Caffey's syndrome changed or have we changed his syndrome? *Child Abuse and Neglect, 21,* 1009-1014.

Leestma, J.E. (1988). *Forensic neuropathology.* New York: Raven Press.

Levin, A.V. (1990). Ocular manifestations of child abuse. *Ophthalmology Clin N Amer, 3,* 249-264.

Levin, A.V. (1998). Contributing editor's note. *The Quarterly Child Abuse Medical Update, 3,* 11.

Ludwig, S., & Warman, M. (1984). Shaken baby syndrome: A review of 20 cases. *Annals of Emergency Medicine, 13,* 104-107.

Lyons, T.J., & Oates, R.K. (1993). Falling out of bed: A relatively benign occurrence. *Pediatrics, 92,* 125-127.

Marr, W.G., & Marr, E.G. (1962). Some observations on Purtscher's disease: Traumatic retinal angiopathy. *American Journal of Ophthalmology, 54,* 693-705.

McRae, M., Teasell, R.W., & Canny, C. (1994). Bilateral retinal detachments associated with Terson's syndrome. *Retina, 14,* 467-469.

Morgan, O.G. (1945). A case of crush injury to the chest associated with ocular complication. *Trans Ophthmol Soc UK, 65,* 366-369.

Muller, P.J., & Deck, J.H.N. (1974). Intraocular and optic nerve sheath hemorrhage in cases of sudden intracranial hypertension. *Journal of Neurosurgery, 41,* 160-166.

Munger, C.E., Peiffer, R.L., Bouldin, T.W., Kylstra, J.A., & Thompson, R.L. (1993). Shaken baby syndrome and retinal hemorrhages: Ocular and associated neuropathologic observations in suspected whiplash shaken infant syndrome. *Am J Forens Med Pathol, 14,* 193-200.

Musemeche, C.A., Barthal, M., Cosentino, C., & Reynolds, M. (1991). Pediatric falls from heights. *Journal of Trauma, 31,* 1347-1349.

Nimityongskul, P., & Anderson, L.D. (1987). The likelihood of injuries when children fall out of bed. *J Pediatr Orthoped, 7,* 184-186.

Odum, A., Christ, E., Kerr, N. (1997). Prevalence of retinal hemorrhages in pediatric patients after in-hospital cardiopulmonary resuscitation: A prospective study. Electronic article. *Pediatrics, 99,* e3.

Ommaya, A.K., Faas, F., & Yarnell, P. (1968). Whiplash injury and brain damage: An experimental study. *Journal of the American Medical Association, 204,* 285-289.

Pounder, D.J. (1997). Shaken adult syndrome. *Amer J Forens Med, 18,* 321-324.

Purtscher, O. (1910). Moch unbekannte Befun nach Schaeltrauma. *Ber Dtsch Ophthalmol Ges, 36,* 294.

Rao, N., Smith, R.E., Choi, J.H., Xiaohu, X., & Kornblum, R.N. (1988). Autopsy findings in the eyes of fourteen fatally abused children. *Forensic Sci Int, 39,* 293-299.

Reece RM. Unpublished data.

Riffenburgh, R.S., & Sathyavagiswaran, L. (1991). Ocular findings at autopsy of child abuse victims. *Ophthalmology, 98,* 1519-1524.

Rogers, C.B., Itabashi, H.H., Tomiyasu, U., & Heuser, E.T. (1998). Subdural neomembranes and sudden infant death syndrome. *Journal of Forensic Science, 43,* 375-376.

Sandramouli, S., Robinson, R., Tsaloumas, M., & Willshaw, H.E. (1997). Retinal hemorrhages and convulsions. *Arch Dis Child, 76,* 449-451.

Tomsai, L.G., & Rosman, N.P. (1975). Purtscher retinopathy in the battered child syndrome. *Amer J Dis Child, 129,* 1335-1337.

Third Webster's new world dictionary college edition. (1988). New York: Simon and Schuster.

Weston, J.T. (1968). The pathology of child abuse. In C.H. Kempe, & R.E. Helfer (Eds.), *The battered child* (3rd ed.) (pp 77-100). Chicago: University of Chicago Press.

Wilkinson, W.S., Han, D.P., Rappley, M.D., & Owings, C.L. (1989). Retinal hemorrhage predicts neurologic injury in the shaken baby syndrome. *Archives of Ophthalmology, 107,* 1472-1474.

Williams, R.A. (1991). Injuries in infants and small children resulting from witnessed and corroborated free falls. *Journal of Trauma, 31,* 1350-1352.

Willman, K.Y., Bank, D.E., Senac, M., & Chadwick, D.L. (1997). Restricting the time of injury in fatal inflicted injuries. *Child Abuse and Neglect, 21,* 929-940.

Zepp, F., Bruhl, K., Zimmer, B., & Schumacher, R. (1992). Battered child syndrome: Cerebral ultrasound and CT findings after vigorous shaking. *Neuropediatrics, 23,* 188-191.

Zimmerman, R.A., Bilaniuk, L.T., Bruce, D. (1979). Computed tomography of craniocerbral injury in the abused child. *Radiology, 130,* 687-690.

Index

389